ISLAMIC SOCIETY AND THE WEST

The Royal Institute of International Affairs is an unofficial and non-political body, founded in 1920 to encourage and facilitate the scientific study of international questions.

The Institute, as such, is precluded by its Royal Charter from expressing an opinion on any aspect of international affairs. Any opinions expressed in this publication are not, therefore, those of the Institute.

ISLAMIC SOCIETY AND THE WEST

A Study of the Impact of Western Civilization on Moslem Culture in the Near East

BY

H. A. R. GIBB AND HAROLD BOWEN

Volume One

ISLAMIC SOCIETY IN THE EIGHTEENTH CENTURY

PART II

Issued under the auspices of the Royal Institute of International Affairs

OXFORD UNIVERSITY PRESS
LONDON NEW YORK TORONTO

Oxford University Press, Amen House, London E.C.4

GLASGOW NEW YORK TORONTO MELBOURNE WELLINGTON
BOMBAY CALCUTTA MADRAS KARACHI LAHORE DACCA
CAPE TOWN SALISBURY NAIROBI IBADAN ACCRA
KUALA LUMPUR HONG KONG

First edition 1957
Reprinted 1962 *and* 1965

PRINTED IN GREAT BRITAIN

AUTHORS' NOTE

IN issuing the second part of our study on the eighteenth century, we are conscious that in several sectors our expositions, in this as in the preceding volume, are being or likely to be quickly overtaken by current research. The opening of the Ottoman archives has in recent years enabled both Turkish scholars and those from other countries to investigate the institutions of the Empire on the basis of exact documentary materials; and it is evident that these newer studies will modify or correct in detail, and possibly even in principle, many of the conclusions which we have reached on the basis of the available secondary materials. However rapidly this work of revision may proceed, it will be many years before the enormous mass of documents in the Turkish archives can be critically examined and published. The corrections which we have gratefully received from reviewers of the first part of this study have seldom gone, as yet, beyond points of detail. We are encouraged by this to hope that the second part also may serve a useful purpose as a general survey of the field until such time as our successors will be able to rewrite it on the basis of a thorough monographic exploitation of the Ottoman and other relevant documents.

H. A. R. G.

H. B.

1957

CONTENTS

AUTHORS' NOTE v

PART II

VII. TAXATION AND FINANCE
- i. The Fiscal System 1
- ii. The Arab Provinces 37
- iii. Currency 49
- iv. Egypt and Syria in the Eighteenth Century 59

VIII. THE RELIGIOUS INSTITUTION 70

IX. THE *'ULEMÂ* 81

X. THE ADMINISTRATION OF LAW
- i. The Nature of Islamic Law 114
- ii. The *Ḳâḍîs* 121
- iii. The *Muftîs* 133

XI. EDUCATION 139

XII. RELIGIOUS ENDOWMENTS (*AWḲÂF*) 165

XIII. THE *DERVÎŞES* 179

XIV. THE *ḎIMMÎS* 207

BIBLIOGRAPHY OF WORKS CITED 263

INDEX OF ARABIC AND TURKISH TERMS 273

INDEX OF PERSONAL NAMES 278

INDEX OF PLACE-NAMES 280

GENERAL INDEX 283

CHAPTER VII

TAXATION AND FINANCE

I. THE FISCAL SYSTEM

THE Ottoman fiscal system comprised two main elements, which it eventually proved impossible to maintain in satisfactory equilibrium. The feudal system, combined with that of the *Awḳâf*, could perhaps, if it had been all-embracing, have provided for the livelihood of every person who filled a public office, including the monarch himself. But the Ottoman economy was never in fact organized on a purely feudal basis. Even while the first Sultans were asserting their power as independent rulers, they were always able to draw on some revenues beyond those accruing from the domains they allotted to their own use; and it was their possession of these extra resources that enabled them to form and maintain the slave Household, paid in cash, on which they soon came to depend for the exercise of their authority.

The expense of the powerful military and administrative organization into which the slave Household developed was eventually, it is true, met in part from feudal revenues. As we have noted, it was not only military offices that were originally provided for by fiefs, but a number also of offices partly or wholly administrative. When in time these came to be filled by the Sultans' slaves, the *Ḳapî Ḳullarî*, it was still by the revenues these fiefs provided that those slaves, like their free predecessors, were remunerated. On the other hand, the various military corps that sprang from the Household, headed by the 'standing' cavalry and the Janissaries, on which the Sultans' power in the state ultimately depended, continued, with most of the Household proper, to be paid in coin; and the fiscal problem with which the central government was faced, and which it succeeded, except occasionally, in solving satisfactorily down to the last quarter of the sixteenth century, was to provide cash enough for the support of the paid servants of the state without damaging the sources from which the feudatories derived their means of life.

We have already enumerated the tithes and dues exacted by *ḳânûn* from peasants and nomads for the benefit of their 'landowners'.[1] Nearly all these revenues, except those collected from the Imperial Domains, were spent by the landowners (feudal or *waḳf*) who received them, and yielded nothing to the Treasury wherewith to defray expenditure on the Household or the standing army.

[1] See Part I, pp. 240 sq.

Apart from those of the Imperial Domains the only revenues originally accruing to the Sultans were the following: the poll-tax on non-Moslems (and in certain fiefs even this was collected and spent by the holders);[1] one-fifth of all war spoils; tribute from dependent Christian states; the yield of the customs; and the produce of mines, salt-works, and rice-fields.[2] We shall consider these contributions in detail later. Here it is enough to remark that all these revenues (like the tithes and dues paid to the feudal and *wakf* landowners) were regarded as *şer'î*: i.e. having the sanction of the Sacred Law. This in Ottoman eyes was an important consideration. Ottoman writers on fiscal matters dwell at length on the distinction between the taxes so sanctioned and those levied in case of need by virtue of the Sultan's *'urfî*, or monarchical, authority,[3] about the legitimacy of which they display certain misgivings.[4] They would have been happier if the Sultans could have made do with only *şer'î* revenues. But in practice this proved impossible. It is true that as the Empire was enlarged the yield of the *şer'î* revenues we have listed increased more or less in proportion; and for some time, apparently, the Treasury contrived to make ends meet with them alone. But at some point, probably towards the end of the fifteenth century, they began, at times, to prove inadequate; and then, regrettably, the monarchs' *'urfî* authority had to be invoked for the imposition of further contributions on all their subjects resident in the provinces then composing their dominions.

The Sultan's *'urfî* authority was invoked for the benefit of the Treasury in various ways: to allow, firstly, the imposition of general supplementary taxes; secondly, the exaction of certain services free in exchange for an exemption from the payment of those taxes (or, later, of a money payment in lieu of such services); and, thirdly, the exaction of certain dues, or fees, designed to cover expenditure on particular objects from individuals whose interests were served by the transactions in question.

The general taxes so levied were in later times, if not to begin with, termed *'avâriḍi dîvânîye*, '*Dîvân* levies', because they were imposed, with the Sultan's consent, by decision of the *Dîvân*.

[1] In *ocaklıks*, see below, p. 16.

[2] Seyyid Muṣṭafâ, in listing the sources of revenue originally accruing to the Treasury at i. 19, omits the mines and rice-fields. He adds the mines at i. 65, however, and no doubt reckoned the revenues from rice-fields among those of the Imperial Domains, to which in fact they for the most part appertained—see below, p. 19.

[3] For the Sultan's *'urfî* authority see Part I, p. 23.

[4] The substitution for (or addition to) the *şer'î* dues of other forms of taxation had always been regarded by the '*Ulemâ* as illegal. But for many centuries prior to the Ottomans their protests had proved unavailing, since all medieval Moslem dynasties drew the greater part of the revenues of their Central Treasuries from 'illegal taxes'.

They were apparently resorted to at first only occasionally, in times of financial stress, when the Sultan's *'urfî* authority could be justifiably exercised in the interests of the community. But even so some equitable method had to be invented for their collection, because their incidence differed from that of all existing taxes, which were either paid or collected only by certain categories of the Sultan's subjects; and the method chosen was typically Ottoman. In all those parts of the Empire where it was applied the authorities divided the *ḳaḍâs* (districts in the jurisdiction of a *Ḳâḍî*) into what were termed *'avârıḍ-ḫânes*, 'levy-houses', each of which was liable for the payment of an equal proportion of the whole levy. In drawing up lists of these 'levy-houses' the authorities gave careful consideration to the character of each *ḳaḍâ*, of its inhabitants and their resources, and then declared each to comprise one or more houses or fractions of a house. These contributions were exacted of course only from non-*'Askerîs*; the individual inhabitants paid according to their means—in the usual three classes: rich, middling, and poor; and collection was effected through the *Ḳâḍîs*. Nor was the arrangement inflexible. If some district declined in prosperity—through becoming a battlefield for instance, as frontier districts were apt to do—the 'houses' were duly adjusted.[1] Whenever this system was first put into operation, by the middle of the seventeenth century (as we can see from an extant finance summary of the time)[2] various levies collected in this way had become a regular annual source of revenue to the Central Treasury; and so they continued down to the era of reform.[3]

It was the imposition of *'avârıḍ* and the institution of *'avârıḍ-ḫânes* that enabled the Ottoman authorities to profit by the use of the Sultan's *'urfî* authority in the second way we have mentioned. For it allowed them to secure the performance of certain services

[1] For a previous reference to *'avârıḍ* see Part I, p. 135. This needs correction: these exactions were not, as there stated, restricted to townsmen; see the article 'Avarîz' by Ö. L. Barkan in the *Islâm Ansiklopedisi*, from which most of the information here supplied is taken. For the numbers of *'avârıḍ-ḫânes* in two areas, one on the early sixteenth and the other in the early nineteenth century, see Ö. L. Barkan, *XV ve XVI inci asîrlarda Osmanlî Imparatorluğunda Ziraî Ekonominin Hukukî ve Mâlî Esaslarî* (hereafter referred to as *Z.E.E.*), i. 21; *Ḳânûn* of 1517 for the Livâ of Biğa; and Aḥmed Refîḳ, *Türk Idâresinde Bulğaristan*, 75 (Doc. No. 96): a *fermân* of 1832 relating to the *Ḳaḍâ* of Ṭoyran in Rumelia. Luṭfî Paşa (*Aṣafnâme*, ed. Tschudi, text, 42), writing in the reign of Süleymân I, states that *'avârıḍ* were levied once in the reign of Selîm I, and thereafter every four or five years at the rate of 20 *aḳçes* a head. But the *'avârıḍ-ḫâne* system was certainly in existence at least as early as the reign of Bâyezîd II: see Barkan, *Z.E.E.* i. 18—*Ḳânûn* of 1487 for Ḫüdevendigâr.

[2] That of Ṭarḫuncu Aḥmed Paşa, presented to Meḥmed IV in 1655, published in 'Abd al-Raḥmân Vefîḳ, *Tekâlîf Ḳavâ'idi*, i. 327 sq., and Aḥmed Râsim, ii. 214 sq., notes. A note at the end of the text states that the summary was drawn up in 1064 (1654); but this appears to be an error, since revenues for the year 1065 are mentioned earlier.

[3] See D'Ohsson, *Tableau générale, de l'Empire ottoman*, vii. 239.

and the supply of certain commodities free (so to speak) by the simple device of exempting those peasants or townsmen who could furnish such assistance from the payment of these taxes. The authorities apparently did this by exempting a whole 'house' at a time; upon which its constituent members seem to have lost their subject status and to have become, as it were, *'Askerîs* of a humble type. This at least would seem to follow from the curious fact that by the seventeenth century in many cases the members of such exempted 'houses' had ceased to furnish the supplies, or to perform the services, in return for which their predecessors had been accorded this immunity, but that, instead of their reverting to ordinary 'subject' status and paying *'avâriḍ* like their compeers, they were instead charged with the payment of special contributions in lieu of fulfilling the duties in question.[1] Exempted *'avâriḍ-ḫânes* were in fact approximated to *ocaḳs* and in some cases are even referred to as such.[2]

The payments made to the Treasury by the exempted 'levy-houses' in lieu of the services or supplies their members were supposed to render or furnish were known as *bedelât*, 'substitutes'.[3] But far from being confined to them this term—*bedel*—was applied to money payments of all kinds made in place of contractual or obligatory contributions for which the Treasury agreed to compound by this means. For instance the Hospodars made annual fixed remittances to the Treasury in lieu of the poll-tax which, if the Principalities had been incorporated in the Empire as ordinary *eyâlets*, would have been exacted from their *ḏimmî* inhabitants; and these payments were called *bedeli cizye*, 'Poll-tax Substitutes'.[4] So widely, indeed, was the practice of com-

[1] See 'A. Vefîḳ, i. 109 sq., for a reference to the inhabitants of certain districts who were charged with supplying saltpetre, coal, timber, and flax to the Admiralty and certain government workshops at Istanbul, and to others who were excused payment of *'avâriḍ* in return for maintaining certain roads. All these in the end paid special dues instead of furnishing the supplies or performing the services in question. See, e.g., a *fermân* of the late sixteenth century (Doc. No. 36 in Aḥmed Refîḳ, 26), in which we find the sheep-raisers and sheep-drovers of Filibe (Philippopolis) being obliged by the Porte to pay a *bedel*—a cash payment in lieu (see below)—because they have fallen short in their supplies of sheep to the capital.

It is possible, on the other hand, that *'avâriḍ* were *originally* not cash contributions at all, but the obligatory performances of services or the furnishing of supplies. In this case *'avâriḍ* cash contributions—known as *'avâriḍ aḳçesi*—will themselves from the first have had the character of a *bedel*. It was in any case a principle followed as long as the system remained in force that contributors *either* performed services (or furnished supplies) *or* paid money in lieu, or discharged their obligations partly by one method, partly by the other; cf. Barkan in the article 'Avarîz' already cited.

[2] In the summary of Ṭarḫuncu Aḥmed Paşa there is an actual reference to the *'avâriḍ-ḫânes* of the oarsmen (*kürekçis*) as constituting their *ocaḳs*.

[3] Arabic *badal*, 'something exchanged for something else'.

[4] Aḥmed Râsim, i. 380, note.

pounding for revenue by the acceptance of such substitute payments applied by the Treasury authorities, that in the seventeenth-century finance summary we have mentioned more than half the items of revenue listed are substitutes of one kind or another.[1] The growth of this practice was due to, and is again evidence of, the ever-increasing need of the government for cash receipts. It is true that when accepting 'substitutes' in lieu of some service or supply the Treasury had, at any rate in theory, to get the work done by some other agent or the material furnished from some other source, and was accordingly obliged to spend money to those ends. But for some reason, whether because in fact it neglected to do so, or because the 'substitute' payments exceeded any disbursements to which it was forced, its acceptance of them became more and more general.

The third way in which the Treasury benefited by invoking the Sultan's *'urfî* authority was more indirect. It was by the leave given to officials of various types to exact fees from individuals for whom they performed services. These fees were not paid into any fund from which the officials in question were remunerated, but were pocketed by them direct. The Treasury benefited because this practice enabled it to avoid increasing the salaries it paid officials in some cases, and even paying them any salaries at all in others. An early instance of the authorization of fees is that accorded to *Ḳâḍîs* as far back as the end of the fourteenth century. Their salaries were then found to be insufficient for their needs; but instead of increasing them the government authorized the *Ḳâḍîs* to exact fees from persons whom they supplied with legal documents.[2] A similar permission was granted at one time or another to many officials of the central and provincial administrations. Although the occupants of such posts in these organizations as had been created in early times subsisted—or were meant to subsist—on the fiefs allotted to each such post, officials holding appointments of later creation were not so provided for. Some, it is true, were given salaries, but comparatively few.[3] Moreover, as we have seen, some offices had come into being and risen to

[1] If we count the money paid in lieu of the *'adedi ağnâm* (see below, p. 34), though this was not actually called a *bedel*.

[2] See Seyyid Muṣṭafâ, i. 20, and Hammer, *Staatsverfassung*, i. 59, 206.

[3] In the *Ḳânûn-nâme* of Meḥmed II (*T.O.E.M.*, Nos. 13 sq.), though salaries are frequently mentioned, they are nearly all those allotted to *'Ulemâ* of various ranks, members of the Household and the armed forces, retired officials, or the children of officials, officers, and *'Ulemâ*. In fact the only officials of the administration proper referred to as sometimes receiving salaries are *Vezîrs* and *Defterdârs*, who might be so remunerated instead of receiving fiefs (pp. 28–29). That the remuneration of officials by means of salaries continued to be rare is shown also by a list of officers, officials, and servants receiving salaries in the reign of Murâd III, where only 267 recipients belonging neither to the armed forces nor to the Household are listed, namely:

importance without any formal recognition.[1] In so far, therefore, as these offices of later creation carried no state-paid salaries, some other means had to be found of remunerating their holders. Hence the authorization of large numbers of fees payable to officials of various ranks in return for services of all kinds. These fees were often shared in fixed proportions by seniors and juniors in a department. Nor were those who benefited only officials who received no salaries. Many fees were payable to salaried officials and even to those, from the Grand *Vezîr* downwards, whose offices entitled them to the revenues of fiefs.[2] This system naturally relieved the Treasury of a heavy burden. But it bore an unmistakable likeness to legalized bribery. Indeed it seems possible, and even probable, that some at least of these fees were in origin bribes. For we know of more than one instance in which actual bribes *were* legalized: as, for example, when a Grand *Vezîr* of the mid-seventeenth century, at his wit's end for revenue, declared that the presents then regularly accepted by him and his colleagues from recipients of office should thenceforward be reckoned as Treasury income.[3] Later in this chapter we shall have occasion to note some of the consequences of these practices.

It was also by exercise of the Sultan's *'urfî* authority that dues or tolls were exacted in certain places where special expenditure was necessary from persons benefiting from the facilities thereby provided—as, for instance, a number of dues levied on travellers through mountain passes where guards had to be posted and the roads, bridges, and water conduits maintained,[4] or the due im-

The Hospodars' *Ḳapî Kâhyalarî* (and, presumably, their subordinates)	13
Dîvân secretaries	24
Treasury secretaries	16
Treasury clerks (*ṣâgirds*)	133
Secretaries of the *Defterdâr*'s Court	20
Unspecified recipients of *monthly* pay (the pay of the other persons on this list being calculated on a daily basis)	25
Water-carriers of the *Dîvân*	36

[1] e.g. the *Kâḥya Bey*—see Part I, p. 120.

[2] See, for instance, the list of dues, nine in all, payable *by* officials on receipt of authorizations of various kinds in 'A. Vefîḳ, i. 100. These were evidently payable to other officials whose duty it was to utter the orders in question. How the system worked is shown in a section of the *Ḳânûn-nâme* of Meḥmed II, which fixes the 'signature fee' (*ḥaḳḳi imḍâ*) to be taken by the *Defterdâr* for authorizing *Mültezims* and *Emîns* to collect the taxes in *ḫâṣṣ* fiefs—namely, 1 per cent. of the sum involved; authorizes him to take as 'weighing commission' (*kesri mîzân*) 22 out of every 1,000 *aḳçes* paid into the Treasury; and lays it down that he shall receive food supplies from the tithes of the Imperial fiefs. The same section also authorizes the *Defterdâr*'s clerks to exact a *ḥaḳḳi kitâbet* or 'secretarial due' (*T.O.E.M.*, No. 19, p. 29).

[3] 'A. Vefîḳ, i. 323; Seyyid Muṣṭafâ, ii. 98. The Grand *Vezîr* in question was Melek Aḥmed Paşa. Cf. p. 48 below.

[4] See the list of *'urfî* dues in 'A. Vefîḳ, 91 sq., twelve of which were levied for these purposes under such names as *derbend resmi* ('pass due') and *ṣu yolcu maṣrefi* ('conduitmen's expenses').

posed on merchant ships sailing from the Straits.[1] These, however, bore a strong resemblance to other dues or tolls recognized as having the sanction of the Sacred Law; and the fact that the former were regarded as *'urfî* was perhaps due only to historical accident.[2]

This does not entirely exhaust the list of *'urfî* contributions levied on the Sultan's subjects. We shall have to mention some others when considering the revenues of the Central Treasury derived from both *şer'î* and *'urfî* taxation. Before we return to these central revenues, however, all of which in early times were, as we have indicated, *şer'î* in character, in order to balance our general review of *'urfî* taxation we may briefly consider the *şer'î* imposts (other than those, already described, of a feudal character) which were for the most part collected and spent in the provinces.

These imposts were all related in one way or another to trade. Hence, apart from a special toll levied at certain passes on flocks of sheep driven through them, they were all exacted in towns or country markets and were collected by the local *Muḥtesib* and his assistants. As we have noted,[3] the guildsmen of the towns paid the *Muḥtesib* a due for the right to conduct their businesses. This was called *yevmîyei dükâkîn*, 'daily shop due'.[4] But the *Muḥtesib* also collected others, the most important of which was the *bâcî pâzâr* or 'market due'.[5] This was payable on the sale of any living creature and almost any commodity brought into a market from the surrounding district. Hay, clover, and other products grown within the limits of the town, were exempt: only those imported from outside them were so taxed.[6] Nor could any 'imports' be subjected to the *bâc* if they were sold elsewhere than in the market; but such transactions were frowned on, and the authorities were

[1] Called *Iẕni sefîne* ('ship's permission'). This was exacted in return for leave to sail. See 'A. Vefîḳ, i. 104 sq. Cf. a *fermân* of 1726 printed by 'Oṡmân Nûrî, 370.

[2] There would seem, for instance, to be little difference in principle between the tolls (*'urfî*) levied at passes on travellers and those (*şer'î*) levied also at passes and elsewhere on flocks of sheep. 'A. Vefîḳ, i. 26, 31, lists three of the latter: the *selâmet akçesi* ('safety money'), the *geçit resmi* ('pass due'), and the *ṭopraḳ baştî parasî* (literally 'it trod the ground money'); and it may be noted that one of the *'urfî* tolls bore a name almost identical with the first of these: *selâmetlik resmi*. Another, moreover, is said to have been called *bâc*, though tolls termed *bâc* (which were of various types—see below), were usually regarded as *şer'i*—ibid. i. 103. Cf. Aḥmed Râsim, iii. 1157, 1160, 1219, 1221, notes.

[3] See Part I, p. 288. [4] From Arabic *yawm* ('day') and *dukkân* ('shop').

[5] M. F. Köprülü points out in his article 'Bac' in the *Islâm Ansiklopedisi* that the word (Persian) is of vague significance denoting any, and not a special, tax or due. It is in fact more or less the equivalent of the Arabic *rasm* (Turkish *resim*). The *bâcî pâzâr* is said to have been adopted by 'Oṡmân I in imitation of Selcuḳid practice (see 'Oṡmân Nûrî, 364–5). The following details of the market dues exacted are taken from the *Ḳânûn-nâme* of Süleymân the Magnificent published in the *T.O.E.M.*, No. 16, pp. 21 sq.

[6] Cf. Hammer, *Staatsverfassung*, i. 153.

instructed to prevent them. The amount levied by way of *bâc* varied according to the nature of what was sold, being regulated by elaborate tariffs. No *bâc* was exacted, however, on the sale of 'real estate'—houses, mills, gardens, &c., or on jewels and precious metals. Nor, if a purchaser resold what he had bought in the same market, was the due exacted a second time, except in the case of slaves and live animals. But the rule for these latter was in any case special. For whereas *bâc* was exacted only from the vendor in other transactions, purchasers of slaves and animals had to pay an equal amount as well.[1] The purchaser as well as the vendor had likewise to pay the due exacted for anything weighed in the public warehouses called *ḳapan*,[2] where certain commodities were stored. This weighing due was also, at least in early times, collected by the *Muḥtesib* and his men,[3] and seems, together with the *bâc*, the stamp due, and fines from shopkeepers who neglected the *nerḫ*,[4] to have accounted for most of the revenues that accrued to him. The stamp due[5] was a kind of excise, complementary to the *bâc*, since it fell only on goods produced in the centre concerned. Thus weavers had to submit each roll and piece of stuff they made to the *Muḥtesib* and pay this due to him before they could sell. So had blacksmiths to submit horseshoes and metal-workers their vessels of gold, silver, and copper. The object here was to ensure

[1] The *Ḳânûn* seems somewhat contradictory on this point. Thus whereas it lays down on the one hand, apparently in general, that the purchaser as well as the vendor shall pay dues on the sale of slaves, horses, mules, camels, and oxen, on the other it also shows particular dues payable only by the vendor on horses (*bargir*), oxen, and pigs, imported into Istanbul (?) from the *sancaḳ* of Semendre (then on the frontier). The oxen and pigs may of course have been sold only after slaughter.

[2] 'Oṣmân Nûrî, 370. For *ḳapan* see Part I, p. 324, n. 3. The word is also used in Arabic in the form *ḳabbân*, but does not seem to be of Arabic origin. As well as *ḳapan* and *çardaḳ*, these warehouses were sometimes termed *mîzân* (another Arabic word for 'scales') and *mangane* (from the Greek *makhinê*) meaning 'a press'.

[3] 'A. Vefîḳ, i. 43 (cited by Aḥmed Râsim, iii. 1225, note, and 'Oṣmân Nûrî, 362) states that among the dues collected by the *Muḥtesib* were those called *mîzân*, *evzân*, and *ekyâl*. *Mîzân*, as we have observed, is the equivalent of *ḳapan*. In Arabic *evzân* (plural of *wazn*, Turkish *vezin*) means 'weights' and *kayl* (*kile* in Turkish usage), of which *ekyâl* is likewise the plural, denotes a particular measure used chiefly for grain. These were clearly all weighing dues, as was also one called *ḳanṭar* (*ḳinṭâr* in Arabic denoting another particular weight) or *ḳanṭar ücreti* ('*ḳanṭar* hire') or *ḳanṭarîye*. In the same way the *ekyâl resmi* was sometimes called *kiyâliye*.

[4] See the *Ḳânûn-nâme* of Süleymân (*T.O.E.M.*, No. 19, p. 66. This section deals with the abolition of noxious or superfluous innovations (*bid'at*—for further reference to which see below, p. 34). One whose abolition it orders is the levying of 1 *aḳçe* per shop in the *bezistan* (see Part I, p. 291) of Ḳonya by way of '*assasîye* (for '*assâs* see Part I, p. 324), since a special watchman has been appointed, and another the exaction of a weekly due from shopkeepers concerned with baking implements, of 2 *aḳçes* from bakers on baking days. The levying of '*assâsîye* at Mardîn, Diyârbekir, and Erḍerûm is also recorded by Hammer, i. 247 and 250. For the *nerḫ* see Part I, p. 283.

[5] *damğa resmi*.

that the metal used was up to standard; and the *Muḥtesib* had likewise to ensure the accuracy, and exact the stamp duty from the makers, of scales, weights, and measures, before they could be sold to shopkeepers.[1]

These, it would seem, were the three chief regular dues collected everywhere by the *Muḥtesibs*; but taxation in the *ḳaḍâs*, far from being uniform, differed widely both in character and nomenclature from place to place owing to differences in local products and traditions. In the Arab provinces added to the Empire by Selîm I an immense body of customary dues had been established under their previous Mamlûk governors, on a variety of pretexts and to the increasing distress of the population. All these dues had been investigated after the conquest and a large number of the more vexatious abolished,[2] though some of them, it may be presumed, were not long in reappearing. It is not always easy to judge from the documents whether a given named due is in fact an impost separate from or included in one of those numbered above, or indeed a *ḳaḍâ* due at all.[3] Again, in some documents we find mention of a transit due on goods passing through a town, called *bâci̊ 'ubûr*; but whether this was ever payable to the *Muḥtesib* is not clear. It seems at any rate to have been distinct from the customs duties that we shall shortly describe.[4]

As for the revenues of the Central Treasury, some of these accrued to one, some to the other, of the two sections into which it was divided. These were, as we have mentioned, the 'Public' or 'State' Treasury—which was synonymous with the Finance Office and was commonly called the *Mîrî*[5]—and the 'Private'[6] or 'Inner'[7] Treasury, also called 'Treasury of the Inside'.[8] These

[1] See 'A. Vefîḳ, i. 49 (cited by Aḥmed Râsim, loc. cit., and 'Oṣmân Nûrî, 364), and cf. Süleymân Sûdî, iii. 159, who, however, omits any reference to scales, weights, and measures; states that silver vessels other than those made by the Jewellers' guild were passed for standard at the Mint; and gives no information about gold ones. For the stamping of weights and measures see too a *fermân* of 978 (1570–1) addressed to the *Ḳâḍî* of Filibe (Aḥmed Refîḳ, 16) and another of 1800 addressed to the Istanbul Ḳâḍisi ('Oṣman Nûrî, 373–4), and Hammer, i. 215, 250, 254.

[2] See for Egypt, *Ḳânûn-nâma*, ap. Digeon, ii. 199, 233, 234, 236; and for Syria, Hammer, i. 228, 230.

[3] e.g. the numerous dues listed in the *Ḳânûn-nâme* of Süleymân under the heading of 'Ḳânûn of the vilâyet of Semendre', and the dues payable on the slaughter of animals and preparation of parts of their carcasses for food; see Süleymân Sûdî, ii. 123, and the list in 'A. Vefîḳ, i. 26 sq.

[4] e.g. in an eighteenth-century document on the customs at Trebizond (referred to later) mention is made of a *bâci̊ 'ubûr* exacted there on tobacco. It is contrasted here with the customs dues, the text reading: *gümrükten başka bâc taḥṣîl olunup*, 'the *bâc* having been collected apart from the customs'. Süleymân Sûdî, iii. 41, mentions a due called *murûrîye*. As *murûr* (Arabic) also means 'passage' or 'transit', this may have been another name for the *bâci̊ 'ubûr*.

[5] *Ḥazînei 'Âmire*, see Part I, 128, n. 5, and 133, n. 4.

[6] *Ḥazînei Ḥâṣṣa*.

[7] *İç Ḥazîne*.

[8] *Ḥazînei Enderûn*, cf. Part I, p. 78, n. 2.

two sections were not independent institutions: they formed a single whole, the 'Inner' Treasury being the section in which were conserved, not only accumulated funds, but valuables of all kinds, and the 'State' Treasury that in which all such revenues were received as might be drawn on for current expenditure. It seems possible that originally the Central Treasury was not so divided, but that all the revenues accruing to the Sultan were paid into a single office-cum-depository, from which his ministers withdrew such funds as were required for the remuneration of all those of his servants, including the 'standing' forces, who were paid in coin, and for the maintenance of the whole Ruling Institution, in so far as this was not provided for feudally. Nor, even after the division, if this was not primitive, were the two sections organized as it were on parallel lines. Thus, though certain revenues were payable direct into the Inner Treasury, all were apparently collected by the *Mîrî*; and though some of the 'running' expenditure of the *Ḥarem* and the Inside Service was presumably met direct from the Inner Treasury, it seems to have been the *Mîrî* that paid the salaries of the rest of the Imperial Household and furnished the supplies necessary for its well-being.[1] The *Mîrî*, moreover, was not entitled to accumulate any funds of its own. It was obliged to pay any annual surplus of revenue over expenditure into the Inner Treasury. Similarly it might, when faced with a deficit in any year, provided the Sultan were willing, draw on the Inner Treasury to balance its accounts.[2] The Inner Treasury was thus primarily no more than a hoard of accumulated wealth, whereas the *Mîrî* was the 'operational' section of the Treasury institution as a whole. In later times the Inner Treasury came to be regarded as in a special sense the Sultan's property. But this was probably a development dating from the sixteenth century, when, as we shall relate, annual deficits became usual. For it was with great reluctance that the Sultans agreed to deplete the Inner Treasury for the benefit of the *Mîrî*. And this naturally created something of an opposition between the two Treasuries, in which the *Mîrî* came to be thought of as appertaining to the Central Administration as distinct from the Palace.[3]

[1] See the items of expenditure in both the summary of Ṭarḫuncu Aḥmed Paşa and that of the so-called *Eyyûbî Ḳânûn-nâmesi*, a statement of revenue and expenditure for the year A.H. 1071 (A.D. 1660–1)—printed in Aḥmed Râsim, ii. 225 seq., notes. These between them include not only the salaries of most of the Household, but also expenditure on the Imperial kitchens, on clothing-materials for the *Enderûn*, on the wages of the *ḫuddâm* (generally eunuchs, but perhaps here merely 'servants') of the various Imperial palaces (paid through the *Şehir Emîni*, see Part I, p. 84), and other palace expenses.

[2] See D'Ohsson, vii. 260; Hammer, ii. 168; Aḥmed Râsim, ii. 379–80, notes.

[3] The *Eyyûbî Ḳânûn-nâmesi* contains a curious passage which suggests that all the revenues collected by the Central Treasury were regarded as the Sultan's 'pocket-money' (*ceybḫarcliği*). It is not altogether clear, however, what revenues

Advances from the Inner Treasury to the *Mîrî* were made against acknowledgements of indebtedness authorized by the two *Ḳâḍî-ʿaskers* and signed by the Grand *Vezîr* and the *Defterdâr*.[1] They were in fact loans, not subject to interest, and exhibiting a marked unreality. For though in theory the Sultan could call in such loans at any moment, there was in practice no source, apart from *waḳf* funds (from which, it is true, the *Mîrî* also borrowed in later times), on which the *Defterdârs* could draw but the Inner Treasury itself; and since any surplus he might achieve was payable to that institution in any case, such recalls would have been senseless. No doubt, when the Inner Treasury was first obliged to succour the *Mîrî* with such a payment, it did so on condition that taxation for the following year should be increased enough to allow the *Mîrî* to pay in, not only the surplus it should receive in any case, but the amount lent to it as well. But this was to assume a deficit exceptional; whereas before long expenditure came to be nearly always in excess of revenue. The fact that such withdrawals from the Inner Treasury were not automatic, however, but were conventionally loans requiring authorizations of great formality, as well as some effort to provide for their repayment, no doubt restrained the more improvident Grand *Vezîrs* and *Defterdârs* from involving the finances in even greater disorders than those which pervaded them as it was.

Although, according to the rules of the *Şerîʿa*, the various taxes it authorized had to be applied to specific objects,[2] it would seem, from extant Ottoman finance summaries, that all the revenues at the *Mîrî*'s disposal—excluding, that is to say, those payable direct into the Inner Treasury—were applied indifferently to general expenditure. Most of the objects to which the *Şerîʿa* directs that the taxes it authorizes shall be devoted are, however, charitable; and under the Ottoman régime they were provided for out of the yield of *Awḳâf*. The attribution of all agricultural land to the state, moreover, virtually did away with some of the most productive *şerʿî* taxes; while the *cizye*, for instance, might in any case be

are here referred to. The passage occurs at the beginning of the section devoted to expenditure, and the revenues in question are reckoned in gold, whereas the items in the previous section, on sources of income, are reckoned in silver. At the same time it seems unlikely that the 6 million gold pieces here mentioned were revenues accruing to the Sultan *apart* from those collected by the *Mîrî*. The latter are shown as amounting to 581 million *aḳçes*. At the period of this *Ḳânûn-nâme* about 120 *aḳçes* went to the gold piece. 581 million *aḳçes* would therefore represent rather less than 5 million gold pieces; and, seeing that certain revenues appear in the expenditure section as accruing direct to the Sultan, it seems probable that the 6 million described as his 'pocket-money' constituted the entire income accruing to the Central Treasury as a whole.

[1] D'Ohsson, loc. cit.

[2] For the *Şerîʿa* 'budget' see, e.g., Süleymân Sûdî, i. 61 sq. Cf. ʿA. Vefîḳ, i. 9 sq.

devoted to expenditure on the armed forces and officials. The amalgamation annually in one fund by the *Mîrî* of all the revenues it might spend was not, therefore, in flagrant contradiction of the *Şerî'a* regulations; and the government in practice ran no risk of misusing them, since expenditure on objects to which they might be correctly applied was invariably much higher than their yield.

We have come across no single document that shows clearly which revenues were payable direct into the Inner Treasury. It appears, however, that among them were the 'tribute' from Dubrovnik,[1] the property left by deceased *Ḳapî Ḳullari*, fines paid in lieu of the death penalty by criminals, profits from the operations of the Mint,[2] and the yield of the taxes called 'Travel Substitute' and 'Imperial Army Substitute'[3]—the two latter items, if not the others, constituting a war reserve fund.[4] The contents of the Inner Treasury were also, of course, perpetually increased by the gifts presented to the Sultans by the wealthy among their subjects and by foreign potentates, and by choice items of war booty. To Grand *Vezîrs* and *Defterdârs* the distinction between the revenues expendable by the *Mîrî* and those that must be paid into the Inner Treasury was of the greatest moment, since applications for aid from the Sultan were received with slight enthusiasm. But in view of the interchanges that took place between the two Treasuries, our picture of the Ottoman finances is not, perhaps, very seriously blurred by our uncertainty on this point; and rather than speculate on it further we will attempt (for, as will be seen, the accounts do not furnish a complete picture here either) to determine which of all the revenues collected accrued to the Central Treasury as a whole; and may begin with the customs dues, since most of these were closely related to, and on occasion even collected with, the above-mentioned *bâc* dues, levied by the *Muḥtesibs*.

The customs dues, called *gümrük*,[5] were levied not only on foreign, but also on internal, trade. As regards the latter they differed from the *Muḥtesib*'s *bâc* in that, whereas the *bâc* fell primarily on products originating within the *Muḥtesib*'s own *ḳaḍâ*, the *gümrük* was imposed on commodities imported from other areas into any centre, by sea or land, whether for sale there or for further transmission, and on commodities exported from it. The basis of the system was in fact rather regional than imperial. For there was no difference in principle between these internal cus-

[1] This appears from the *Eyyûbî Ḳânûn-nâmesi*. It was payable to the 'Imperial Stirrup', whereas the '*Cizye* Substitute' from the Principalities (see below, p. 17) is shown in the same summary as being collected for the *Mîrî*.

[2] D'Ohsson, vii. 251.

[3] See below, pp. 31–32.

[4] See the summary of Ṭarḫuncu Aḥmed Paşa.

[5] Said to come from the Latin *commercium* through Greek *koumerkê*.

toms and those imposed on commodities imported from places outside the Empire, or exported to them.[1] On the other hand, the charges imposed differed from place to place according to long-established usage and the kind of trade characteristic of each;[2] and distinctions were often, but not always, made according to the status of the merchant concerned: whether he was a Moslem, a *Dimmî*, or a '*Ḥarbî*'—that is, an inhabitant of the Domain of War.[3] The dues were reckoned sometimes on a percentage basis by the local selling price of the goods, sometimes by their weight or size, or by the load or bale.[4] Moreover, as well as the customs proper the merchant would have to pay what seem to have originated as registration fees. Of these one, called *der âmed* or *âmedîye*,[5] was payable on imports, and another, apparently of somewhat later creation, called *reftîye*,[6] on exports; while from the beginning of the seventeenth century yet a third was exacted, called *maṣderîye*, imposed on commodities imported from abroad into an Ottoman centre and there sold.[7] The customs imposed on goods transported for trade purposes within the Empire from one town to another by land were appropriately called *ḳara gümrükleri*;[8] and

[1] Süleymân Sûdî, iii. 23. [2] Ibid. 29.

[3] See, for instance, the *Ḳânûn* of 1650 for Rhodes and Cos, in Barkan, *Z.E.E.* i. 338–9, which lays it down that Moslem importers are to pay 2 per cent., whereas *Ḥarbîs* are to pay 4 per cent. customs duty (having previously paid 3 per cent.); the *Ḳânûn* for Mitylene of 1709 (ibid. 335), which requires Moslems to pay 2 per cent., *Dimmîs* 4 per cent., and *Ḥarbîs* 5 per cent. (except on imports from Venice and the 'lands of the Franks', on which 5 per cent. is chargeable in all cases); the regulations for Trebizond (also of 1709), which require Moslems and *Dimmîs* alike to pay 3 per cent. on goods imported by land for local consumption, and 4 per cent. on those re-exported, *Ḥarbîs* having to pay 5 per cent. (Süleymân Sûdî, iii. 30); and the *Ḳânûn* for the Morea of 1716 (on its recovery by the Porte), which exacts 5 per cent. customs duty on silk from *Ḥarbîs* and only 4 per cent. from others (Barkan, i. 329). The much earlier *Ḳânûn* for Şâm (1548)—ibid. 221—shows 'Frankish' exporters as having to pay *gümrük* and other dues from which Ottoman subjects were exempt.

[4] See, for instance, Süleymân Sûdî, iii. 32–33, for the difference between the methods employed in the two centres he chooses as examples, Trebizond and Toḳat (*Ḳânûns* of 1709 and 1710 respectively), and Barkan, i. 211 (*Ḳânûn* of 1571 for Tripoli of Syria).

[5] From the Persian *där âmäd*, 'it came in'. Cf. Part I, p. 122, for the *Âmedci*.

[6] From the Persian *räft*, 'it went'.

[7] Or *mastarîye*. Süleymân Sûdî, iii. 25, explains this term as meaning 'additional due', and states that it was of later origin than the *âmedîye* and the *reftîye*. Cf. A. C. Wood, *A History of the Levant Company*, 213, for the imposition of the '*misteria*' on Frankish merchants under Aḥmed I. 'A. Vefîḳ, i. 55, records that the *maṣderiye* was levied on foreign imports only.

Both 'A. Vefîḳ and Süleymân Sûdî write of the *âmedîye*, *reftîye*, and *maṣderiye* as if between them they formed the actual customs dues. But the *Ḳânûn* of 1571 for Tripoli (see note 4, above) shows the *der âmed* as an alternative name for the *ḳalem resmi* or 'bureau due', separate from the *gümrük*; in the celebrated French Capitulations of 1740 (see G. Pélissié du Rausas, *Le Régime des Capitulations*, i. 175) mention is made of the *maṣderiye* in contrast to the '*droit de douane*' and the '*droit de bon voyage*' (the *reftîye*?); and D'Ohsson, vii. 238, writes of the '*Amed*' and the '*Mastariya*' as exactions additional to the customs proper.

[8] *Ḳara* meaning 'land' (as opposed to sea).

it appears that, although by the eighteenth century they, like the customs collected at ports and at frontier posts,[1] had come to be farmed for the Central Treasury, earlier their yield had sometimes been spent locally, and in some cases had even been collected for their own benefit by certain classes of fief-holders.[2] Where this was not so, all the customs were at first no doubt collected by salaried officials, *Emîns*;[3] whereas under the later system they were of course collected by the contractors. The latter's farms, however, never covered the customs of the whole Empire. Each would apply to those of a single town or region, and include, sometimes, other imposts due in it too.[4]

In fixing the rates of the customs dues the Porte seems to have aimed at encouraging the consumption of commodities within the area of their production and at discouraging the re-export from any centre of foreign commodities imported into it.[5] Such must have been the effect, for instance, at Trebizond in the early eighteenth century of the relative rates of the local *reftîye* and *maṣderîye* dues, at 4 per cent. and 3 per cent. respectively.[6] Moreover, the export from the Empire as a whole of certain commodities was entirely prohibited. Among them were weapons and war materials, grain, olive oil, tallow, wax, silk, cotton thread, fleeces, various types of leather, timber, pitch, sulphur, and lead. From 1669, however, the Porte would sometimes waive this rule in response to requests by foreign merchants or their governments. In such cases special *fermâns* would be issued; and the exceptions thereby introduced into the customs regulations for the larger ports, which they chiefly affected, added to the general lack of uniformity in their imposition.[7] Another concern of the Porte was to promote the importation of goods into the larger centres of population, and Istanbul in particular; and to do so it excused importers the payment of *gümrük* elsewhere than at the centre in question. On goods imported, for instance, by land from Europe no exactions would be made at the frontier or at any other town through which they passed *en route*.[8]

In large ports and towns the business involved in the collection of customs became so extensive that responsibility would be

[1] Called respectively 'coastal' and 'frontier' customs—*sevâḥil ve ḥudûd gümrükleri*.

[2] Seyyid Muṣṭafâ, ii. 125; Süleymân Sûdî, ii. 58–59. Cf. Barkan, i. 236, for the collection of *gümrük* at Gallipoli by the *Sancaḳ Beyi* (*Ḳânûn* of 1519).

[3] As at Tripoli (cf. Barkan, loc. cit., at p. 13 note 4 above).

[4] As at Trebizond (Süleymân Sûdî, iii. 30 sq.).

[5] Ibid. 38.

[6] Ibid. 32. Even greater variations are attested in the Arab provinces. See, for Egypt, the detailed statement by Estève, 338–44; for 'Irâḳ, Olivier, ii. 450–1; for Damascus, Hammer, *Staatsverfassung*, i. 221. The duties exacted at these entrepôts were, of course, additional to those paid on entry at the ports.

[7] Süleymân Sûdî, iii. 33–34.

[8] Ibid. 37.

divided between two local bureaux (*ḳalems*), one for imports and the other for exports;[1] and at Istanbul, for instance, the storage and weighing of goods on which dues were payable led to the creation of a much larger and more complicated organization still.[2] In smaller centres, on the other hand, the collection of customs was generally amalgamated with that of other taxes and dues, particularly the *bâc*, which was imposed in addition to the customs dues on certain goods in some places.[3] In later times, indeed, except in Istanbul itself, the customs and *Iḥtisâb* contributions—that is, the dues payable to the *Muḥtesib*—were generally administered together.[4] Whereas merchants might be required to pay no more than 5 per cent. of the value of the merchandise they imported or exported by way of customs proper, accordingly, by the time they had met all the demands made on them by the customs and allied functionaries, they might well find this percentage increased to as much as 9.[5]

Concessions regarding the customs duties payable by foreign merchants were, of course, one of the chief features of the Capitulations granted by the Sultans to European sovereigns. *Ḥarbîs* were originally obliged as a rule to pay at higher rates than the Sultan's own subjects.[6] But for political reasons Murâd III was moved to reduce what was then apparently the usual rate of 5 per cent. of the value of both imports and exports to 3 per cent. for English merchants only, a privilege later embodied in the Capitulations granted in 1599 by Meḥmed III to Elizabeth I;[7] and it was perhaps to offset this reduction indeed that the *Maṣderîye* was introduced shortly afterwards under Aḥmed I. In 1673, after prolonged negotiations, the French first obtained a similar concession;[8] and in the course of the eighteenth century so did all the other European powers whose subjects traded in the Ottoman Empire.[9]

[1] Ibid.

[2] Ibid. 38.

[3] Ibid. 39: whereas wheat and barley, if eligible for *gümrük*, did not pay local dues, articles of adornment, such as silk, and of enjoyment, such as coffee, tobacco, and snuff, were subject, not only to *gümrük*, but also to *mîzân* and dues called *ruḥṣatîye* and *iʿmâliye*.

Merchants, on payment of *gümrük* on commodities on which local dues were not also payable, received a *tezkere* or certificate, intended to protect them from further exactions. Cf. the *fermân* to the *Ḳâḍî* of Filibe dated 1698–9 in Aḥmed Refîḳ, 46 (Doc. 69): 'Those who trade safely and securely in My well-guarded dominions, once they have paid *gümrük* according to the *Ḳânûn* and have received their certificates, are not again to be pestered with demands for *gümrük*, *bâc*, and other imposts on the same goods.'

[4] Süleymân Sûdî, iii. 39, states that they were always so administered. But he also shows (ibid. 33) that at Toḳat the due on imports—*Âmedîyei gümrüğü Toḳat*—was farmed separately.

[5] Ibid. 41.

[6] See above, p. 13, note 3.

[7] Wood, 14, 27–28.

[8] du Rausas, i. 63 sq.

[9] Thus D'Ohsson, vii. 235, states that the rates were 3 per cent. for Europeans, 4 per cent. for Moslems, and 5 per cent. for *Ḍimmîs*. Hammer, i. 215, mentions only two rates, 3 per cent. for foreigners and 5 per cent. for

Of the other four sources of *şer'î* revenue accruing from early times to the Central Treasury the poll-tax on non-Moslems was the most important.[1] But as we are to describe its incidence and collection fully when treating of the *Dimmîs* in the Ottoman Empire, we need say little more of it here except to touch on two particular points. In the first place it appears that though the bulk of its yield was collected (in later times by tax-farm) on behalf of, and spent by, the Treasury, in fiefs of the kind called *ocaklık*[2] the local *cizye*, like the local customs, was treated as an item in the revenues of the fief.[3] Secondly, the Chevalier D'Ohsson adds to his account of the *cizye* proper as a source of revenue a paragraph on the tribute paid by the Gypsies of the Empire, and implies that it was a kind of *cizye*, exacted not only from those who were Christians but also, improperly, from those of them who professed Islâm because they were regarded as schismatic.[4] A recent study, however, has explained this apparent anomaly. What D'Ohsson took to be a form of the *cizye* levied on Moslem Gypsies was in fact a *bedel*.[5] In the sixteenth century the Gypsies of Rumelia had been formed into *Müsellem ocaks* enjoying the usual privileges of *'Askerî* status; but when, later, they ceased to perform military duties, instead of being reduced to *ra'îyet* status they were subjected to special taxation, which was farmed from 1622 onwards. The Christian Gypsies paid more than the Moslem, as D'Ohsson states; but the only part of these contributions that can be regarded as *cizye* is the difference between the amounts paid by the two classes.[6]

natives. Cf. also Estève, loc. cit., who makes it clear that these were the basic rates, and that special classes of luxury goods such as tobacco, coffee, porcelain, and Indian textiles paid higher rates (in Egypt at least) of from 8½ to 10 per cent. European traders escaped most of the additional duties, but were exposed in return to payment of considerable sums in gifts and 'donatives'; see, e.g., Charles-Roux, *Les Échelles de Syrie*, 50 sqq.

[1] We retain for this tax the technical term *cizya/cizye*, although in Ottoman Turkish usage it is frequently replaced by *harâc*. In so doing, the Turkish jurists and writers were in reality reverting to the original significance of *harâc*, as applying to every form of tribute-tax paid by non-Moslems (in distinction from tithes); but in medieval Moslem usage it was confined to land-tax, the poll-tax upon non-Moslems being distinguished as *cizya* or *cawâlî*, and the latter term continuing to be officially employed in Egypt down to the end of our period.

[2] See Part I, p. 48.

[3] Seyyid Muṣṭafâ, ii. 125. Süleymân Sûdî, ii. 58–59, goes farther, stating that even ordinary fief-holders collected both the local *cizye* and the local *gümrük* for their own benefit.

[4] vii. 237. There was never, so far as we know, any discrimination made between orthodox and heterodox Moslems in the field of taxation.

[5] See above, p. 4.

[6] See the article 'Çingeneler' by M. T. Gökbilgin in the *Islâm Ansiklopedisi*, based, as far as the Gypsies of the Ottoman Empire are concerned, on recently examined archives. It is curious that although D'Ohsson refers to the Gypsies as if they were to be found only in the Asiatic provinces, these documents show

The 'tribute from neighbouring Christian states', which we may list next among the items of revenue we are considering, was also a kind of *cizye*. It was imposed, however, not individually on Christians and other 'people of scripture' as direct subjects of the Moslem conqueror, but collectively on whole populations whose rulers, by contracting to pay it, thereby attached their possessions as vassal dependencies to the conqueror's empire. The three states that paid tribute to the Porte at the time of our survey were, as we have noted, Wallachia, Moldavia, and Ragusa;[1] and the nature of this tribute was indicated by the name for it to which we have alluded: 'Poll-tax Substitute'.[2] It was first paid regularly by Wallachia in 1417, by Ragusa in 1459, and by Moldavia in 1511; and from 1541 to 1699 tribute was also forthcoming from the kingdom of Transylvania.

From early in the sixteenth century, moreover, the Treasury could also depend on the fixed contributions it began receiving, after the conquests of Selîm I, from the 'Arab' provinces.[3] These, called *irsâlîyât* ('remittances'), were from an accountancy standpoint very similar to the tribute paid by the dependent European states. We may therefore place them next the 'Poll-tax Substitutes' on our list. They were, however, of quite a different nature, being in principle merely substitute payments for what the Treasury might have collected from the provinces concerned as the proceeds of general taxation, if they had been governed direct.

It appears that in later times at any rate the Treasury sometimes arranged for fixed payments[4] to be made also by provinces usually administered in the ordinary way. It did so, for instance, in 1142 (1729–30), when fixed remittances were exacted from the recently acquired provinces of Tiflîs and Hamadân, whose finances were at first managed (or rather mismanaged) by local *Defterdârs*;[5] and in the mid-seventeenth-century finance summary which we have mentioned similar fixed contributions are shown as due from the *Defterdâr* of Bosnia and the *Sancaḳ Beyi* of Herzegovina. When,

that there were Gypsy communities all over the Balkans from the sixteenth century and apparently make no mention of any elsewhere, except near Izmid and Bursa. For a reference to the *Çingene müsellems* of the *sancaḳ* of Çirmen see the *fermân* of 975/1568 published in Aḥmed Refîḳ, 14.

[1] See Part I, p. 24.

[2] *bedeli cizye*, see p. 4 above.

[3] For these and the varying computations of their amounts see below, pp. 41, 45. The Egyptian tribute, originally fixed at 150,000 gold pieces a year, was distinguished from that of the Asiatic provinces by being specifically assigned to the Sultans' private Treasury (*Pâdişâhi 'âlempenâhe bi 'z-zât ceyb ḫarcliği olmaḳ için*; Luṭfî Paşa, *Aṣafnâme*, text, 39; but cf. p. 10, n. 3 above); see also Combe, *L'Égypte ottomane*, 73.

[4] The word we translate by 'fixed' is *maḳṭû'* (Arabic), which is used in relation to payments or prices as signifying 'settled in advance'.

[5] See the interesting article 'Events of the year 1142' by 'Arif in the *T.O.E.M.*, No. 2.

as was so by this time, nearly every item of revenue was collected by tax-farm—so that in any case the Treasury received nearly all its funds in the shape of sums fixed in advance by contract—it can have made little difference to those responsible for the state finances by whom these sums were furnished: whether by tax-farmers or by provincial governors. But by the end of the seventeenth century the evil effects of short-term tax-farming had become all too apparent; and it seems probable that what amounted to *irsâlîyât* from such *eyâlets* as Bosnia and Tiflîs was resorted to in an attempt to counteract them. How similar in the eyes of the Treasury such fixed contributions were to the 'Poll-tax Substitutes' from the dependent states is shown, if the text as printed is correct, by this same item in the summary, which places the tribute from the Hospodar of Moldavia together with the contributions from Bosnia and Herzegovina.[1]

There is little we need remark about the two remaining 'original' sources of *şer'î* revenue. In early times war booty was of course one of the richest, the Sultans being entitled by Moslem tradition to one-fifth. Booty included prisoners; and it was from the Sultan's share—one man in five—that the *Ḳapî Ḳullarî* were recruited before the institution of the *devşirme*, while the price of those sold on government account was, in the fourteenth century if not later, devoted to the upkeep of mosques and the maintenance of learned men.[2] As for mines, salt-works, and rice-fields, these were, for the most part, apparently, regarded as appertaining to the Imperial Domains from early times; and any profits resulting from their exploitation accrued to the Central Treasury. In the eighteenth century, according to D'Ohsson, the contractors who exploited the gold and silver mines were supposed to deliver their entire output to the Mint at a price 30 per cent. below its market

[1] The text as printed by 'A. Vefîḳ, i. 328, may well, however, be incorrect. The item reads: '115 purses—money agreed on for the payment of the troops from the *Beylerbeyi* of Moldavia, the *Defterdâr* of Bosnia, and the *Bey* of Herzegovina.' But the reference to a *Beylerbeyi* of Moldavia is surprising. The Hospodar was not usually so designated. Should we perhaps read Bağdâd for Boğdân (the Turkish name for Moldavia)? This would involve a change of only one letter in the Arabic script. It is odd, moreover, that if by the Moldavian contribution the 'Poll-tax Substitute' is meant, it should be described as earmarked for a special purpose, and that the summary should contain no mention of tribute from Wallachia and Ragusa. The summary, however, is evidently defective, since the sums shown in the several items do not account for the total revenue mentioned separately. A final puzzle is this: that financial contributions should be forthcoming both from Herzegovina and from Bosnia, since the former was a *sancaḳ* of the *eyâlet* of Bosnia. One would therefore have expected the *Defterdâr* of Bosnia to include revenue forthcoming from Herzegovina in the contribution he made from the whole *eyâlet* to the Porte.

[2] See Hammer, i. 56, 59, 213; Seyyid Muṣṭafâ, i. 19, 65. As the latter author observes, booty also enriched the feudal officers. Neither for them nor for the Sultans, however, was it a very constant source of revenue, depending as it did on the fortune of campaigns.

value, but in fact, with the tacit connivance of the Treasury, obtained a reasonable profit by appropriating and selling part of it for their own benefit. Those who exploited the copper mines, on the other hand, were obliged to deliver only a definite quantity of their produce and could dispose as they pleased of any surplus they might extract—with the result that these mines were better run. D'Ohsson also refers to the use of forced labour in the mines, remarking that the local inhabitants feared their exploitation on this account.[1] But if this implies that the contractors were empowered to impress labour for this purpose—and not that some *'avâriḍ-ḫâne* arrangement was used whereby the men who were enrolled were excused the payment of *'urfî* dues in return—the government in authorizing such a measure was overstepping the recognized limits of the Sultan's *'urfî* powers.[2] Rice-fields were called *çeltik*; and both rice-growers (*çeltikçis*) and salt-workers (*tuzcus*)[3] enjoyed a privileged status which, at least in some areas, exempted them from payment of *'avâriḍ*.[4] Not all *çeltiks*, however, appertained to the Imperial Domains. Some appertained to ordinary fiefs and the *ḫâṣṣ* fiefs of *Sancaḳ Beyis* and *Subaşîs*.[5] The general rule appears to have been that the rice crop should be divided in equal shares between the 'landowner' and the grower, since the former supplied the seed and ensured the water-supply, while the latter performed the necessary labour on the land.[6] Thus on *çeltiks* appertaining to the Imperial Domains, the Sultan, through the Domain administrators, took half the crop. On *çeltiks* appertaining to other fiefs, moreover, he received an *'uşr* of the crop grown.[7] As for salt, it would seem that the sale of this, at least generally, was a government monopoly, and that the government salt stores[8] were supplied by the *tuzcus* free, as a service for which, as mentioned above, they were excused payment

[1] vii. 252–3.

[2] Süleymân Sûdî, i. 25, classifies forced labour (*angarya*) as a state exaction of the unlawful type called *şâḳḳe*. *'Urfî* exactions, he states, were of two types: *'âdîye* or *mu'tâde* (meaning 'customary') and *şâḳḳe* (meaning 'difficult' or grievous').

[3] *Tuz* meaning 'salt' in Turkish.

[4] For the exemption of *çeltikçis* see the *Ḳânûn* for Iç Il (1584) (cf. Hammer, i. 267), the *Ḳânûn* for Sis (1519), and the *Ḳânûn* for Özer (temp. Meḥmed III) in Barkan, *Z.E.E.* i. 54, 202, 228, and for that of *tuzcus* see the *Ḳânûn* for Silistre (temp. Süleymân I), ibid. 275.

[5] See, e.g., the *Ḳânûn* of 1528 for Aydîn (ibid. 7).

[6] See the *Ḳânûn* for Iç Il cited above and the *Ḳânûns* of 1528 for Kütâhya and Malaṭya, ibid. 28, 111.

[7] This at least would appear from the *Ḳânûn* for Aydîn cited above, which states that in such *çeltiks* '*'uşr* is to be taken both from the cultivator's share and from the fief-holder's share'; and this *Ḳânûn* was framed to bring local practice in the matter of *çeltiks* into line with that of the other *vilâyets* (*sâyir vilâyetlerden olan ḳânûn üzere* . . .).

[8] *Beylik anbarlarî*.

of *'avâriḍ*. *Re'âyâ* living in the neighbourhood of salt deposits were, however, permitted in at least one *sancaḳ* to collect salt for their own consumption without payment of *bâc*;[1] and though *bâc* was usually payable on loads of salt imported into a centre,[2] in another *sancaḳ* no such due was imposed on the ground that the vendor was the government itself.[3] In later times it appears that the *tuzcus* sometimes engaged labourers to produce the salt for them and that the government paid them for what they supplied. In that case they presumably forfeited their exemption from *'avâriḍ*, though not their right to effect supplies, and merely profited by the difference between what they received in payment from the government and what they themselves paid the labourers.[4]

Such, apparently, were the revenues with which the Treasury contrived to meet its commitments up to the last quarter of the sixteenth century. There were indeed crises when disbursements exceeded income in one or two earlier reigns, notably that of Bâyezîd II, when special taxation had to be imposed for a time;[5] and even during the reign of the great Süleymân there was a deficit in more than one year.[6] It was not, however, until half-way through that of his grandson, Murâd III, that, as we have remarked, the finances began to get seriously out of hand. Habits of luxury acquired during the heyday of Süleymân had bred corruption. Certain Grand *Vezîrs* had even then begun surreptitiously taking bribes for appointments;[7] and though the able *Vezîr* Ṣoḳollu[8] managed affairs with skill and probity during the reign of Selîm II and the first years of Murâd, after his death there began an orgy of expenditure which the Treasury was in no posture to meet. The reign of Murâd was one of constant campaigning in both Europe and Asia, which may have caused the vast expansion of the standing army that then took place to appear less wanton than it was. But this expansion was in fact fatal in the long run not only to the standing army itself, since the admission to its ranks of unsuitable and untrained men rapidly compromised its efficiency,[9] but also to the feudal forces, since one of the chief measures adopted by the Treasury to cover the great increase in expenditure entailed by the expansion was, as we have mentioned,[10] the seizure of such large

[1] See the undated *Ḳânûn* for Divriki in Barkan, i. 119.

[2] e.g. at Bolu, Diyârbekir, Urfa, Mardîn, Harput, Gence, Çirmen, Serim, and Bosna—see the *Ḳânûns*, of various dates, for these places in Barkan.

[3] See *Ḳânûn* for Biğa cited above.

[4] See the *Ḳânûn* for Rhodes and Cos of 1650 (Barkan, i. 340).

[5] Seyyid Muṣṭafâ, i. 65.

[6] Ibid. 147–8. Cf. Aḥmed Râsim, ii. 177 (citing the *Destûrü 'l-'Amel*, see below, p. 25, note), and Luṭfî Paşa, *Aṣafnâme*, text, 35. In 1566 it proved necessary to melt down some of the Sultan's plate for coin.

[7] Cf. Part I, p. 178.

[8] See Part I, p. 110.

[9] Cf. Part I, p. 180.

[10] Part I, p. 189.

and productive fiefs as fell vacant and their addition to the Imperial Domains. The acquisition by this means of considerable extra revenues was the salvation, for the time being, of the central finances. But thenceforward those revenues were no longer available for the maintenance of the important feudal officers whose *dirliks* these fiefs had constituted. The imposition of *'avâriḍ* must already have militated, if only slightly, against the feudal economy, in that it weighed on the contributors by whom that economy was sustained. But it was in this perversion of fiefs from their intended purpose that the antagonism of the two elements—the feudal and the non-feudal—in the Ottoman fiscal system was first brought glaringly to light.

The reign of Murâd III also saw a notable extension of the tax-farming system, to which we have already made numerous references. This system was not essentially pernicious: regarded indeed from the fiscal standpoint it had much affinity with the feudal system in that it endowed the contractors with powers similar to those of the *Sipâhîs*, but unless carefully controlled it invited abuse. When it was first resorted to under the Ottoman Sultans is not clear. It may have been used as early as the reign of the Conqueror. A *Ḳânûn-nâme* of that monarch at any rate contains a reference to it. But it is possible that the published text of this document, reproducing a copy made over a hundred years later, in 1620, contains interpolations;[1] and by the accounts of most authorities[2] it was not before the reign of Süleymân the Magnificent that the system was regularly used, and then only for the collection of revenue from the Imperial Domains. This, which had originally been effected by salaried officials, was then leased yearly to officers who had distinguished themselves in war. They contracted to pay the Treasury a fixed sum, determined in relation to the normal yield of the lands concerned, in

[1] See the introductory note to the *Ḳânûn-nâmei Âli 'Os̱mân* published in *T.O.E.M.*, Nos. 13 and 14. The reference to tax-farming is at p. 29 (No. 14) and runs: 'It is the perquisite of my *Defterdârs* to take as signature fee 1,000 *aḳçes* a *yük* (that is, a sum of 100,000 *aḳçes*) on however many *yüks* are forthcoming from those of my Imperial *ḫâṣṣes* that are given to *Emîns* both by *iltizâm* and by *imânet*.' From this it would appear that the *Emîns* to whom the collection of revenue from the Imperial Domains was confided could either deliver all the proceeds to the Treasury while drawing a salary for their trouble, or could buy the right to pocket the proceeds themselves by paying the Treasury an agreed sum in advance. It was the latter system that was known as *iltizâm*; and originally the distinction between this and the other term used for a tax-farm, *muḳâṭa'a*, seems to have been that the first was used, as here, for the collection of revenues from the Imperial Domains, whereas the second was applied to the collection by contract of other revenues—see 'A. Vefîḳ, i. 62. In the case of *iltizâms* the contractor was called *mültezim* (Arabic *multazim*); in that of a *muḳâṭa'a* he was called *muḳâṭa'aci*.

[2] e.g. Seyyid Muṣṭafâ, i. 124; Tischendorf, *Das Lehnswesen*, 50; Isma'îl Ḫüsrev, 170. On the other hand, D'Ohsson, vii. 242–3, also ascribes the introduction of tax-farming to the Conqueror.

return for the right to collect, for their own benefit, all the tithes and taxes legally due from the inhabitants to the 'landowner' (who was in this case the Sultan). The lessees thereby relieved the Treasury not only of the trouble and expense involved in this collection, but of any uncertainty over the income flowing to it from this source. They were not empowered to exact more than the amounts authorized by *ḳânûn* from the inhabitants of the Imperial Domains; but their contracts allowed them a sufficiently wide margin of profit, supposing the normal yield was forthcoming, to render the assumption of these *ḫidmets*,[1] as they were called, a much sought-after privilege.

As long as the system was restricted to the original Imperial Domains, it appears to have worked satisfactorily. But when the Treasury added the military fiefs it seized to those Domains, and very naturally also farmed out the new revenues it thus acquired, the difficulties of control must have been much enhanced. Moreover, the advantages to the Treasury of tax-farming were so evident, and its attractiveness for the lessees was so great, that the system was soon extended to other items of the central revenues, until nearly all appear to have been collected by this means. These contracts came to be known collectively as *Muḳâṭaʿâtî Mîrîye*, 'Treasury Leases'; and in the financial summary we have mentioned represent by far the largest single item of revenue. But the results of this development, on the peasantry as well as on the armed forces, were, as we have shown, disastrous.[2] The introduction, at the end of the seventeenth century, of *mâlikâne* leases,[3] by giving the contractor a life interest in the yield of whatever revenue source he was empowered to tap, did much, it is true, to improve the taxpayers' position. But this innovation had a grave drawback from the standpoint of the Porte, always over-jealous of its authority, in that *mâlikâne* lessees, whom the government was powerless to displace, tended to acquire a power over and a prestige among the taxpayers they dealt with, to what was often a highly unwelcome degree.[4] Moreover, owing to a general rise in prices at this period, the life lessees made inordinate profits, whereas the Treasury, though its expenditure was forced up in proportion, having once sold a lease on the understanding that

[1] Cf. Part I, p. 328, n. 6.

[2] Part I, pp. 189, 255 sq.

[3] *mâlikâne* means 'as if in ownership'.

[4] Cf. the article 'Ayan' by I. H. Uzunçarşılî in the *Islâm Ansiklopedisi*. The author attributes the rise to influence of the *Aʿyâns* (for whom see Part I, pp. 198–9 and 256–7) in the latter half of the eighteenth century largely to the adoption of the *mâlikâne* system, which, since it was the *Aʿyâns* alone who were rich enough in the first place to take up these leases, eventually gave them so firm a control of local affairs that the Porte became powerless to assert its authority against them.

the lessee would pay it the same sum every year until he died, was unable to alter this arrangement and could profit only when his death allowed it to put the lease up to auction afresh. Perhaps on this account yet another expedient for raising funds was tried under the careful Muṣṭafâ III, in the middle of the eighteenth century. The Treasury then uttered shares, bearing interest at 5 per cent., on the yield of certain revenues such as the customs for a term of eight or ten years. The yield in question was presumably obtained from existing contracts, *mâlikâne* or other. But the conditions on which these shares were taken up were such that they more than covered the interest payable, while one year's interest was in addition forgone by the purchaser by way of fee for the conclusion of the transaction.[1] This experiment seems, indeed, to have proved one of the happier measures introduced by the ever-indigent Treasury; and the share system, as well as that of the *mâlikâne* and ordinary tax-farms, was still in force at the time of our survey.

In arranging tax-farms of every kind the Treasury did not deal direct with the farmers. Farms were put up to auction by the Chief Treasury Crier;[2] but before the highest bidder could clinch the bargain, however rich and reliable he might be, he had to appoint a banker or money-changer[3] to guarantee the payment on his behalf to the Treasury of the sums due to it, under the contract, at stated periods. Only bankers whose names were registered with the Treasury could assume this responsibility. An ordinary banker, wishing to do so, submitted his name to the authorities of the 'Inner' Treasury, who examined his qualifications and if they were found to be satisfactory sought the approval of the Porte for his registration. If the Porte in turn agreed, the banker was then furnished with an official licence, called *ḳuyruḳlu berât*,[4] and was thenceforth entitled to deal with the Treasury over tax-farm and other official business. Treasury bankerships were even hereditary (supposing a son desired to succeed his father in the profession), and any suits brought by or against their holders were heard in the Treasury courts. These bankers therefore formed a privileged corporation, entry into which was much coveted and had to be bought with the payment of a considerable fee to the authorities before a licence was granted. The bankers, once licensed, when underwriting a tax-farm, had also to pay fees proportionate to the sums due to the Treasury under the terms of the contract, both when it was signed and when the obligations it

[1] Seyyid Muṣṭafâ, iii. 99; Aḥmed Râsim, iii. 1147, note.

[2] *Mîrî Dellâl Başî*—D'Ohsson, vii. 245.

[3] *ṣarrâf*—from Arabic *ṣarrafa*, 'he changed money'.

[4] *ḳuyruḳlu* means 'having a tail (*ḳuyruḳ*)'. For *berât* see Part I, p. 122. These licences were so called because they were signed with a tail-like flourish.

involved were finally discharged.[1] At what period the employment of licensed bankers as sureties for tax-farmers was adopted does not appear. In early times, when few of the revenues were farmed, there seems to have existed a special class of functionaries, called 'overseers',[2] who collected taxes on behalf of the Treasury, but whether they were bankers also is not stated. One curious feature of the system was a division of the profits to be derived from tax-farming between Moslems and *Dimmîs*. For whereas only Moslems were eligible to take up farms, the bankers were invariably Christians or Jews, since True Believers were debarred from lending money at interest, and the whole advantage accruing to the bankers from these transactions lay in the high interest they were able to charge the contractors on the money they advanced to meet the latter's obligations.[3]

These bankers also profited by the chronic embarrassment of the Treasury in later times. The *Defterdârs* appear to have made no attempt at any period to estimate in advance what expenditure they would have to meet in any year. If enough revenue was coming to cover outgoings, well and good: in the heyday of Ottoman rule revenue was usually in such excess of expenditure that the funds of the Inside Treasury could be regularly augmented from the surplus. If, on the other hand, as was all too often so from the end of the sixteenth century, revenue fell short of what the Treasury required, the *Defterdârs*' practice was to borrow what was immediately needed and to cover both the deficit and the interest payable on these loans from the revenues of the following year which they would increase by means of special imposts. This practice brought further high profits to the bankers. But how these special imposts, which, though reckoned as *'urfî* in character, the *Defterdârs* were careful to have authorized in a *Ḳâḍî*'s court, were levied—whether by a general increase of *'avâriḍ* or otherwise—is unhappily not made clear.[4]

How far the embarrassment of the Treasury in the last quarter of the sixteenth century was due to the increase in the number of persons receiving salaries from the state may be seen from a pas-

[1] The fee payable by the *ṣarrâf* for his final discharge was called *reddiyei temessük* ('return of document due'). Other similar fees payable by *mültezims* and *ṣarrâfs* were those called *ḫarci reddîye* ('return fee due') and *ta'ahhud temessükâti* ('contract documents'). See 'A. Vefîḳ, i. 102–3. This account of the functions of *ṣarrâfs* in relation to *muḳâṭa'as* is taken from Süleymân Sûdî, ii. 26–27.

[2] *mubâşir*. See note to the *Ḳânûn-nâme* of the Conqueror at *O.T.E.M.*, No. 13, p. 19.

[3] So D'Ohsson, vii. 248–9.

[4] See Süleymân Sûdî, i. 85, and 'A. Vefîḳ, i. 108. The latter work lists four imposts levied to cover these deficits and interest payments, called *ṣarrâfîye* ('bankers' due), *aḳçe başî* ('premium'), *güzeşte* ('interest'), and *senelik nemâ* ('usury for the year').

sage in the *Destûrü 'l-'Amel.*[1] Whereas in 1562–3 (four years before the death of Süleymân) these numbered only 41,000, by 1609 (six years after the accession of Aḥmed I) they numbered 91,000. So, whereas there was already a deficit of 6 million *akçes* in the last year of the reign of Süleymân,[2] in 1597 the deficit is reported to have reached as much as 600 million.[3] Although the tapping of fresh sources of revenue seems to have improved the situation somewhat during the reigns of Meḥmed III and Aḥmed I, between 1606 and 1611 the Treasury was again faced with an acute crisis.[4] Moreover, between 1617, when Aḥmed died, and 1622, when Murâd IV came to the throne, there were no less than four accessions, and for each the now traditional largesse, which amounted to more than the average annual revenue of the period, had to be disbursed to the standing troops. Vast sums, also, were spent with little effect by the mother of Muṣṭafâ I in attempts to secure their support for her crazy son.[5] Funds for the accession largesse of Murâd IV had in consequence to be borrowed from private bankers and eked out by the coining of melted plate.[6] Nor was it till 1632, when Murâd was twenty, that he was able to take affairs into his own hands and, by ruthlessly reducing the numbers of the paid soldiery at whose mercy the government had lain since his accession, to put the finances once again on a satisfactory footing. So they continued into the reign of Murâd's unbalanced brother and successor Ibrahîm. But after the execution in 1642 of the Grand *Vezîr* Kemânkeş Ḳara Muṣṭafâ Paşa, they again fell into disorder. The number of paid troops, and their pay, were wildly increased; and it was not until Köprülü Meḥmed Paşa, the first of his remarkable family to hold the office, was

[1] Of Ḥâccî Ḫalîfe the Kâtib Çelebi (text in Aḥmed Râsim, ii. 177 sq., notes, and translation by Behrnauer in *Z.D.M.G.* xi. 125 sq.).

[2] According to Seyyid Muṣṭafâ, citing Na'îmâ and 'Aynî 'Alî. Ḥâccî Ḫalîfe states that two years earlier there was also a deficit of over 6 million. It may be noted that all the figures given by Behrnauer in his translation are ten times too high, owing to his confusion of a *yük* (100,000) with a million.

[3] So Ḥâccî Ḫalîfe, citing the historian 'Âlî. This figure seems almost incredibly high. But if Ḥâccî Ḫalîfe is correct in stating that even under Murâd IV, when the finances were restored to fairly good order, the annual expenditure was still as high as 600 million, the figure of 900 million for 1597 (against revenue of only 300 million) may well have been reached. As we remark below, however, it is doubtful how far Ḥâccî Ḫalîfe's figures may be relied on.

[4] See Belin, 'Essais sur l'Histoire économique', in *J.A.*, Série VI, tom. 4, 292, citing Nâ'îmâ. According to Seyyid Muṣṭafâ, on the other hand, the financial situation was quite satisfactory down to the death of Aḥmed.

[5] Muṣṭafâ, deposed as being insane after a few months' reign in 1618, was restored for a year on the murder of 'Young' 'Osmân II in 1622.

[6] 'A. Vefîḳ, i. 322; Seyyid Muṣṭafâ, ii. 97–98. This author states that almost 300 million *akçes* were distributed at each accession. These donatives were called *cülûs bahşişi* ('accession gratuity'). The last previous figure we possess for revenue is that of 1597, when it was also 300 million, and the next supplied by Ḥâccî Ḫalîfe is 361 million for the year 1648.

raised by Meḥmed IV to the Grand *Vezîrate* in 1656 that state expenditure was again reduced to a level at which the revenues were sufficient to meet it.[1] After this, up to the time of our survey, there was only one other period during which the Ottoman government was again seriously embarrassed for funds, namely, during the seventeen years of continuous campaigning which elapsed between that notable turning-point in the fortunes of the Empire, the defeat of the Sultan's forces before Vienna in 1682, and the conclusion of the Peace of Carlovitz in 1699. During the eighteenth century, though in its first decades the Porte engaged in several further wars both European and Asiatic, these were of short duration and put no intolerable strain on the Ottoman revenues; and in the course of the thirty years of peace in Europe which preceded the terminal date of our survey, the *Defterdârs* continued regularly to collect so much more revenue than was needed to cover their commitments that they were able, with the eager co-operation of Muṣṭafâ III (at the very end of our period), once more to accumulate considerable reserves in the Sultan's private treasury.[2]

Of the sources of revenue additional to those originally accruing to the Central Treasury which the latter tapped as its obligations increased, the earliest, apart from the revenues of the vacant military fiefs that it added to the Imperial Domains, seem to have been a tax on intoxicants and the confiscated property of officials and other persons, whether on their death or during their lifetime.

The attitude of the Ottoman authorities to the production and

[1] 'A. Vefîḳ, i. 324; so Seyyid Muṣṭafâ, ii. 98–99. He is not, however, borne out by Ḥâccî Ḫalîfe. The latter jumps from 1597 to the reign of Murâd IV (1623–40), when, as we have noted above, he states that the yearly expenditure amounted to over 600 million, after which it was reduced in 1643 (the year after the execution of Kemânkeş) to about 550 million and still stood at that figure in 1648. According to his figures as shown in the text printed by Aḥmed Râsim, in the latter year the deficit was 229 million, in 1650 it was 154 million, and in 1653 160 million. Behrnauer's translation, however, shows two of the figures for 1648 differently, viz. 500 million (5,005 million according to his mistaken reckoning—cf. above, p 25, n. 2) instead of 550 million for expenditure, and 361 million instead of 321 million for revenue. Moreover, the 'summary' of Ṭarḫuncu Aḥmed Paşa (dated 1066–1655—cf. note 2 at p. 3 above) shows expenditure in that year as standing at 656 million *aḳçes* and revenue as producing 580, the deficit therefore amounting to only 76 million (1,897—or roughly 2,000—purses). From these calculations, accordingly, it would appear that the financial position improved, if anything, in the interval between the death of Murâd IV and the appointment of Köprülü. But as we know that the reign of Ibrahîm was one of wild extravagance, this is incredible. We can only conclude that Ḥâccî Ḫalîfe's figures, as they have come down to us, are unreliable. On the other hand, the figures given in the *Eyyûbî Ḳânûn-nâmesi* for the year 1071 (1660–1), four years after the appointment of Köprülü, do show a remarkable improvement on those of the Ṭarḫuncu 'summary'. For whereas expenditure then amounted to 592 million *aḳçes*, the revenues produced as much as 581, so that the deficit was only 12 million.

[2] Seyyid Muṣṭafâ, ii. 98–99, iii. 97–98; 'A. Vefîḳ, i. 335–6.

consumption of wine was naturally conditioned by that of previous Moslem governments. This was somewhat equivocal: although the prohibitions of the *Ḳur'ân* and the *Sunna* were of course explicit, they had been weakened to no small extent by the antinomian doctrines and practice of the *Ṣûfîs*. In so far as the Ottoman Sultans abandoned and grew hostile to the *ṣûfî* movement that had established the power of their ancestors, they tended to adopt a puritan attitude to such indulgences as wine-drinking. At the same time no previous Moslem dynasts had ruled so many wine-drinking *d̲immî* subjects as they. Hence from halfway through the sixteenth century, if not earlier, it seems in general to have been their policy, on the one hand, to prevent their Moslem subjects from being corrupted in this respect by their *d̲immî* neighbours, and, on the other, to profit financially from the latter's addiction to the manufacture and drinking of wine. Thus Süleymân himself, towards the close of his life, was overtaken by an access of piety, which caused him not only to abandon the use of silk clothing but also to abolish the post of Wine Commissioner and to close all the wine-shops in the capital;[1] and though Selîm his son earned himself the sobriquet of 'the Sot', there are extant a number of decrees uttered by their successors, enjoining the *Ḳâḍîs* of various districts to see that *D̲immîs* should not sell wine to Moslems; that *d̲immî* revellers should not disturb the devotions of the faithful; and once again—at Adrianople in 1695–6—that the maintenance of wine-shops should no longer be countenanced.[2] In the meantime, however, when faced with the need, during the reign of Murâd III, to broach new sources of revenue, the government had embarked on what was really a contradictory policy in the imposition of an Intoxicants Due,[3] since this gave the Treasury an interest, which it should have repudiated on religious grounds, in the prosperity and development of the wine-trade. As levied at first this due was highly distasteful to the *D̲immîs* on whom it, of course, exclusively fell. No doubt, though this is not stated, it was levied according to the quantities of wine and spirit made and sold by them. Presumably in the hope of escaping with a lighter burden they therefore petitioned the Porte for the new due to be converted into a fixed annual payment additional to their poll-tax payments. This request was granted; and thenceforward the *D̲immîs* who made or sold wine, whether

[1] Aḥmed Râsim, i. 265–6, note (from the *History* of Ṣolaḳzâde). We have come across no other reference to a *Ḫamr Emîni* or Wine Commissioner.

[2] See Aḥmed Refîḳ, *Türk Idâresinde Bulğaristan*, 17, 31, 41 (Docs. Nos. 20, 43, and 65). A passage from the text of the last exhibits the usual tone: 'Since it is definitely against my Imperial consent that wine-shops should do business and that wine, spirit, and other intoxicants (being a source of misdemeanours) should be bought and sold, secretly or openly, in my well-guarded dominions....'

[3] *müskirât resmi*.

rich, middling, or poor, paid half as much by way of intoxicants due as they paid by way of poll-tax. The yield of this additional imposition accrued, like that of the poll-tax itself, to the Central Treasury and was duly farmed as one of the 'Treasury Leases'.[1]

The confiscation to the Treasury of the property of deceased officials and other persons—the practice of *muṣâdara*, as it is called—was by no means new; it had been applied not only to deceased, but also to dismissed, officials under the Caliphate and all the succession states, both East and West.[2] It appears to have roused little opposition; it was sanctioned by long custom; and the jurists could obviously justify it in so far as it involved the resumption of property acquired illegally and to the detriment of public welfare; while public opinion welcomed it as a just, if belated and often vicarious, retribution for the abusive exercise of authority. To these already strong pretexts the Ottoman Sultans added another and still stronger one. In dealing with the organization of the *Ḳapı̊ Ḳulları̊* we have already seen that all the principal offices of the Ruling Institution were held by actual slaves of the Sultan, or by persons assimilated to the status of slaves.[3] Since in Islamic, as in Roman, law the master of a slave is his sole heir, the Treasury had an incontestable claim to inherit the property of all persons of slave status; and it appears that when casting about for additional sources of revenue, the Treasury of Murâd's time then first began regularly seizing certain types of property left by eminent officers and officials on their demise.[4] This practice was even authorized by *ḳânûn*.[5] It was laid down that the property of deceased state employees,[6] whether they left heirs or not, was to pass to the Porte,[7] since normally in the case of free-born *re'âyâ*,

[1] Seyyid Muṣṭafâ, i. 148. Cf. Ahmed Râsim, ii. 361, note.

[2] See D. Santillana, *Istituzioni di Diritto Musulmano Malichita*, i. 284–5; and for the *Dîwân al-Muṣâdarîn* at Bağdâd, H. Bowen, *'Alí ibn 'Ísà*, 259; R. Levy, *The Sociology of Islam*, i. 329–30. The jurists were even able to cite an instance in which the Caliph 'Umar had confiscated half the possessions of a deposed governor.

[3] See Part I, pp. 43–45.

[4] Seyyid Muṣṭafâ, i. 148. These estates appear in the lists of sources of revenue as *muḫallefât*—'things left behind (at death)'.

[5] See *T.O.E.M.*, No. 19, p. 70. Certain ordinances, of which this is one, appear in a section of the *Ḳânûn-nâme* of Süleymân that the editor shows to be a later addition. It is probably later indeed than the reign of Murâd III, but perhaps based on a *Ḳânûn* of his time.

[6] *menṣab ve ciheti olanlar*—'those holding an office or receiving a salary (or pension)'.

[7] *Beytü 'l-Mâl cihetle veya 'aṣavîyet cihetle*—'whether by way of *Beytü 'l-Mâl* or by way of residuary inheritance'. In Ottoman parlance *Beytü 'l-Mâl*, originally signifying merely the public Treasury, although sometimes still so used, generally meant the property of a deceased person without heirs, because all such property had originally accrued to that Treasury. *'Aṣavîyet* (properly *'aṣabîyet*), on the other hand, means the status of *'aṣaba*, heirs other than those for whom the *Şerî'a* prescribes specific shares in two-thirds of what a deceased

and presumably up to this time in that of the *Ḳapî Ḳullarî* also, it was only when a man had no heirs that the state—and not always even then[1]—was entitled to the property he left. At the same time it appears that, even after this date, the Treasury did not as a rule seize *all* the property of a deceased *Ḳapî Ḳulu*. In practice a distinction seems to have been drawn between two types of property so left. Most of the more successful *Ḳapî Ḳullarî* contrived to amass considerable fortunes, as with the large revenues allotted to them they might often do without resorting to nefarious transactions; and if with this wealth they bought land and houses, these were allowed to pass to their heirs as if they had been legally free men. All that the Treasury seized was any coin, valuables, and military equipment,[2] found among their effects at death; and so anxious were the Sultans (or perhaps the other *Ḳapî Ḳullarî* who managed their affairs and foresaw what might ensue when they died themselves) not to leave the relatives of their grandees unduly hard up, that when one of them died possessed of no property of the kind that, under this rule, his relatives could inherit, the latter were provided for with pensions from the state.

When hard pressed for funds, or under the direction of some conscienceless *Defterdâr*, nevertheless, the Treasury did on occasion appropriate everything left by a rich *Ḳapî Ḳulu*. Nor was it rare for a *Ḳapî Ḳulu*'s property to be seized in his lifetime; it is indeed to seizures of this type that the term *muṣâdara* is strictly appropriate. They too were, of course, a source of revenue to the Treasury, though even more irregular. But it appears that they were made as a rule only when the officers and officials affected had acquired the riches in question by improper means or were otherwise deserving of punishment.[3]

As regards free-born Moslems and other *re'âyâ* the Treasury had no title to inherit their property at all unless they died heirless. But since certain estates were legally liable, on this ground, to sequestration, it maintained in each province a *Beytü 'l-Mâl Emîni*,[4] whose duty it was to impound them.[5] It is clear from the

Moslem leaves, plus as much of the remaining third as has not been exhausted in the payment of funeral expenses, debts, and legacies. In this passage it would appear merely to be contrasted with the *Beytü 'l-Mâl*, the 'way of *'aṣavîyet*' here meaning that of property for which heirs existed. In either case it was to pass to the central Treasury (as all *Beytü 'l-Mâl* property did not—see the next following note). *Ḳapîma müteveccih ola*, says the *Ḳânûn*: 'let it be remitted to my Porte'.

[1] See, for instance, the *Ḳânûn* of 1522 for the *Livâ* of Ankara in Barkan, *Z.E.E.* i. 34, where it is laid down that *Beytü 'l-Mâl* property shall go to the *Sancaḳ Beyi*, or that of 1517 for the *Livâ* of Biğa (ibid. 19), which directs that it shall accrue to the administrators of *waḳfs*.

[2] Such as weapons, animals, and tents.

[3] Seyyid Muṣṭafâ, ii. 102 sq.

[4] Or *Emîn* (or *Ḍâbiṭ*) *Beyti 'l-Mâl*.

[5] The duties of the *Beytü 'l-Mâl Emîni* for Egypt are defined in the *Ḳânûn*-

sources that the interpretation put upon the phrase 'liable to sequestration' was exceedingly wide, and that the estates not only of *Paşas* and *Ağas*,[1] but also of men of all ranks and classes, including even *Şeyẖs* of moderate fortune, were placed under seal.[2] To what extent this action was purely arbitrary it is difficult to say, since it has already been shown that there existed numerous wealthy families, not only of merchants, but also of government servants;[3] and it appears to have been open to the latter to have their accounts audited on retirement,[4] presumably as a precautionary measure against eventual sequestration.

During the seventeenth century, when at various periods the Porte suffered more than at any others from lack of funds, the Treasury sought desperately for new sources of revenue; and some of the taxes, the yield of which it thus secured for its own purposes, continued to accrue to it permanently, whereas others were abolished by the various Grand *Vezîrs* who succeeded for the time being in restoring the central finances to order. One of the former —those that came to stay—had a name that we may perhaps best translate as 'Travel Substitute',[5] and seems to have been added to the exactions imposed on the 'levy-houses' we have described above, so that in at least one document these are referred to as 'Travel and Levy Houses'.[6] The services or supplies instead of

nâme (Digeon, 251–3), which also lays down that all cases relative to the succession of the *Beytü 'l-Mâl* (as, for example, when the Treasury claims the estate of a subject who has died intestate and without direct heirs) are to be judged by the Chief *Ḳâḍî* in the presence of the *Paşa*.

[1] e.g. Murâdî, ii. 62, iii. 286, iv. 8, 14; Ğazzî, iii. 300. On occasions a *ḳapîcî* was sent from Istanbul for the purpose: Murâdî, iii. 16.

[2] Murâdî, iii. 230. Sequestration of the property of a *Şâh-bandar* of Cairo: Carbartî, iv. 6, viii. 14.

[3] As'ad Paşa of Damascus bribed the Sultan to allow him to execute a prominent Treasury official and to seize his property; see Part I, p. 220, n. 2.

[4] Murâdî, iv. 38.

[5] *bedeli nüzül*, or *bedeli nüzûl*. *Nuzl* (Arabic) means 'what is prepared for the entertainment of a guest', *nuzûl* 'descent or arrival at a place'. In Turkish usage, according to Redhouse, both were used to mean 'a halting station where travellers bivouac' or 'provisions, especially for a march or journey'. If so, this would bear out D'Ohsson's explanation noted in the text below. For a previous reference to the *bedeli nüzûl* see Part I, p. 135. This, like that to *'avâriḍ*, needs correction. The tax was not levied only on town-dwellers, as D'Ohsson states.

[6] *nüzûl ve 'avâriḍ-ẖânesi*—Aḥmed Refîḳ, 75 (Doc. No. 96). The transliterated text has *nezil*, but *nüzül*, as stated above, appears to be the correct form. Seyyid Muṣṭafâ, ii. 101, also links the *'avâriḍ* and *bedeli nüzûl* together, in a context indicating that they were first imposed on Ottoman taxpayers and their yield first appropriated by the Treasury in the late sixteenth or some time in the seventeenth century. But we have many references in documents dating from earlier in the sixteenth century to *'avâriḍ*; and though we are told that in some cases the proceeds of *'avâriḍ* imposed on peasants were divided between their *Sipâhîs* and their *Sancaḳ Beyis* (see Belin, 'La Propriété foncière', *J.A.*, Série VI, tom. 19, 259), it seems certain that the Treasury had received at least part of the yield from the first. Seyyid Muṣṭafâ's actual words in this passage are: 'Moreover, although a tax was imposed on the inhabitants of the well-guarded dominions under the name of *'avâriḍ* and *bedeli nüzûl* . . . .'

which this 'substitute' was paid had apparently been rendered and furnished originally by the local inhabitants to officers and officials travelling from place to place. If we are to believe D'Ohsson, whose account of this contribution is certainly incorrect in one particular,[1] when the 'Travel Substitute' was first exacted the proceeds went in part to the governors of provinces and in part to the travelling functionaries who had earlier received the services and supplies it replaced. We know, however, that by the beginning of the reign of Meḥmed IV (succeeded 1648) its proceeds—or at least some of them—were being paid into the Central Treasury, since 1,200 purses figure as its annual yield in the 'summary' of Ṭarḫuncu Aḥmed Paşa to which we have several times alluded. In the course of his comments on the summary the Grand *Vezîr* remarks, further, that the yield of the 'Travel Substitute' and that of the 'Imperial Army Substitute',[2] with which he links it, are not available to meet current expenditure, since they constitute a war reserve fund—by which we may perhaps suppose him to mean that they were payable to the 'Inside' Treasury.[3] The 'Imperial Army Substitute', no other reference to which we have come across, was perhaps synonymous with another impost called 'War-time Assistance',[4] which appears to have been a particular variety of *'avâriḍ*, at first levied only when extra funds were needed to defray expenditure on a campaign. It was in due course, however, converted like most *'avâriḍ* into a permanent contribution, the authorities, ingeniously enough, exacting it under the alternative names of 'War-time' and 'Peace-time Assistance'[5] as was appropriate. Some support for our guess that the 'Imperial Army Substitute' was yet another name for this same tax may perhaps be found in a speculation of Seyyid Muṣṭafâ,[6] who, writing of the *'avâriḍ* and the 'Travel Substitute', suggests that they and one or other of the two varieties of 'Assistance' were taxes all exacted together, but that the yield of the Assistance was spent in the provinces on local needs such as the maintenance of roads, bridges,

[1] He states that the Treasury first appropriated the proceeds of the *bedeli nüzûl* only in the reign of Aḥmed III (1703–30), which we know was not so.

[2] *bedeli orduyu hümâyûn.*

[3] See text in 'A. Vefîḳ, i. 332, and Aḥmed Râsim, ii. 214, 222, notes.

[4] *imdâdîyei seferîye.*

[5] *imdâdîyei ḥaḍarîye.*

[6] Loc. cit. His argument is that the yield of the *'avâriḍ* and *bedeli nüzûl* was so small in comparison with what similar taxes yielded in his own day (allowing for an appropriate decline in the value of money) that the taxpayers must in practice have paid much more, and that they did so by way of the *seferîye* or *ḥaḍarîye* taxes, which were spent on local works.

These *imdâdîyes* figure also among the ninety-seven *'urfî* imposts listed in the *Tekâlîf Ḳavâ'idi*, which confirms that their proceeds were not always sent to the capital (see i. 94–97 and Aḥmed Râsim, iii. 1156, 1158, notes). Aḥmed Râsim also states elsewhere (iii. 1146, note) that the *seferîye* was the earliest *'urfî* tax to be imposed under Ottoman rule.

and post-horses. It would, of course, have been very much in accordance with Ottoman practice for the Treasury to appropriate for itself revenues that had originally been imposed for spending in the provinces; it actually did this, as we have indicated, in the case of the 'Travel Substitute'; and the fact that the 'Imperial Army Substitute' was so called may show in itself that this tax was the replacement of another.

Among the other measures adopted by the Treasury during the seventeenth century to increase the revenues at its disposal was one that struck another blow at the efficiency of the feudal forces. This was the exaction of a payment in cash from all fief-holders, who were thus deprived of as much as half their revenues. The payment in question was called 'Fief Substitute'.[1] It was first levied in 1650,[2] but whether it thereafter became a permanent exaction is not clear. It appears as a revenue item in the 'summary' of Ṭarḫuncu Aḥmed Paşa five years later, when it yielded 6 million *aḳçes*,[3] but may have been one of the imposts abolished by Köprülü Meḥmed Paşa, whose sound policy it was to forgo revenues whose payment was calculated to diminish future returns or was otherwise harmful to the state. It seems probable that the exaction of contributions from fief-holders, once it had thus been proved practicable, was a measure resorted to subsequently by the Treasury in periods of special embarrassment; and it may be that the contribution referred to by D'Ohsson as the 'Armed-Retainer Substitute',[4] which he describes as a special war-time levy, was the 'Fief Substitute' revived under another name.[5]

A particularly desperate measure resorted to after the restoration of Muṣṭafâ I in 1622 was the seizure by the Treasury of the

[1] *bedeli timar.*

[2] By Melek Aḥmed Paşa—Belin, 'Du Régime des fiefs militaires', in *J.A.*, Série VI, tom. 15, 289.

[3] 150 purses (each purse containing 40,000 *aḳçes* at this period).

[4] *bedeli cebeli* (*'bedel djebelu'*).

[5] D'Ohsson, vii. 258. Reference to the payment of an 'Armed-Retainer Substitute' by fief-holders is made also in the *Naṣâ'iḥü'l-Vüzerâ* of Sarî Meḥmed Paşa—see Wright, *Ottoman Statecraft*, text, 117, trans., 145. This, in the reign of Aḥmed III, was clearly paid by fief-holders who could not, or failed to, furnish the *cebelis* they were obliged to by *ḳânûn* (see Part I, p. 50). It may be (if the *bedeli timar* is the same payment under another name) that they had ceased furnishing *cebelis* because of this exaction, or, alternatively, that the payment was first enacted because they had not furnished the *cebelis*. The references to the *bedeli timar* suggest, it is true, that it was a general levy on fief-holders made without regard to the fulfilment of their obligations. But a yield of only 6 million *aḳçes*, if in fact as much as half the revenue of the fiefs affected was exacted, would account for only a very small number of fiefs. The revenues of *timars* and *zi'âmets* ranged, as we have noted, from 2,000 to 99,999 *aḳçes* a year; so that even if we take 5,000 *aḳçes* as an average yield (since holders of fiefs yielding less than 4,000 *aḳçes* a year were not under an obligation to furnish a *cebeli*), 6 million would account for half the revenues of only just over 2,000 fiefs.

surplus yield of the *Awḳâf*.[1] But this, like the imposition ten years later by a Grand *Vezîr* of special contributions called 'Boot, Fowl, and Barley Money',[2] appears to have been only temporary. A number of unspecified new taxes were again imposed after the defeat of the Ottoman forces before Vienna in 1683, but were abolished by Köprülü Muṣṭafâ Paşa, during his one year's tenure of the Grand *Vezîrate*, only to be revived for a while by his successor.[3] Owing to the steep decline in the value of money since the sixteenth century, on the other hand, Köprülü Muṣṭafâ quite justifiably raised the rates of the poll-tax contributions.[4] Under his régime, moreover, the tax on tobacco, apparently imposed earlier, was first farmed as a 'Treasury Lease'[5] and if not by him, at least under Süleymân II, the Sultan he served as Grand *Vezîr*, a tax, called 'Innovation Due',[6] of 8 *aḳçes* for Moslems and 10 for others, was imposed on every *oḳḳa* of coffee imported into Istanbul.[7] The Greek community had taken to drinking coffee as early as the reign of Süleymân the Magnificent, when, in an engaging couplet, a poet linked this new fashion with that monarch's suppression of the wine-shops to which we have referred;[8] but it does not seem to have been generally adopted by Moslems till near the end of the sixteenth century, at about which time the smoking of tobacco in *nargiles* also became common. The *'Ulemâ* were much exercised at the spread of these indulgences. The Sacred Law naturally contained no doctrine on the subject; and, the Gate of Interpretation having been shut, they were at a loss. This did not prevent them from expressing their views with much vehemence, however; and several Sultans—notably Murâd IV who,

[1] Belin, 'Essais sur l'histoire économique', in *J.A.*, Série VI, tom. 14, 296. A chronogram was devised to mark the inauspicious date: *yuḫrabu'l-awḳâf* ('The *waḳfs* are plundered')—10+600+200+2+1+30+1+6+100+1+80=1031 (1621–2).

[2] *çizme paha, ṭavuḳ paha, arpa paha*—Belin, 306. Presumably this *çizme paha* is not to be identified with the fee of the same name to which the administrators of *awḳâf* were entitled—see below, p. 171, n. 1.

[3] Seyyid Muṣṭafâ, iii. 97. Muṣṭafâ was the second son of Köprülü Meḥmed Paşa. He was killed in battle after only eleven months in office. Both he and his elder brother Aḥmed (Grand *Vezîr* in succession to their father from 1661 to 1676) were honoured with the epithet *fâḍil*, 'Excellent'.

[4] Ibid. 100. He brought the rates into a true relation with those laid down in the works of traditional Moslem jurisprudence, by which rich *Ḏimmîs* paid 48, middling 24, and poor 12 *dirhems* of silver apiece per annum. At the date of this decree the *şerîfî* gold piece (see below, p. 50) was worth 12 *dirhems*. By the new scale, accordingly, 4 *şerîfîs* were exacted from the rich, 2 from the middling, and 1 from the poor. See further Ch. XV, pp. 253–4, below.

[5] See *Encyclopaedia of Islam*, art. 'Köprülü'.

[6] *bid'at resmi.*

[7] Aḥmed Râsim, ii. 65, note.

[8] *Ḫumlar şikeste, câm tehi: yoḳ vücud mey!*
Ḳîldîn esîr, ḳahve, bizi! hey, zemâne, hey! (metre: *muḍâri'*)
'The casks are smashed, the cup is empty: wine exists no more!
You, coffee, have enslaved us! Behold, fortune, behold!'
Aḥmed Râsim, i. 266, note.

being himself addicted to wine, closed all the coffee-houses and forbade the smoking of tobacco—uttered decrees of prohibition. These proved of no lasting effect, however, and, as in the case of wine, the government eventually decided to profit from such sad aberrations by taxing both products as we have indicated.[1] The 'Innovation Due' on coffee figures as a separate item in D'Ohsson's list of revenues.[2] The tax on tobacco, on the other hand, is no doubt included by him in the yield of the *bâc*.[3]

During the eighteenth century the yield of the market and weighing dues, which, as we have shown, originally accrued everywhere to the *Iḥtisâb* authorities, also came in many places to be collected by tax-farm for the Central Treasury.[4] Presumably the local needs these taxes had been instituted to meet were still met from these funds, and only the surplus was expendable centrally, the tax-farmers' contracts allowing for such local disbursements and guaranteeing the Treasury a fixed annual contribution—though this is nowhere made clear. But, apart from certain items in the summary of Ṭarḫuncu Aḥmed Paşa, of whose nature we have no further information,[5] and a special 'Innovation' mentioned by D'Ohsson as being levied in his time at Smyrna on raw and spun cotton and on wax,[6] these and the foregoing seem to be all the sources of revenue on which the Central Treasury was ever able to draw—except for a contribution of apparently rather a special type, called the 'Sheep Number',[7] about which we possess considerably more information.

The 'Sheep Number' is not to be confused with the 'Sheep Custom',[8] as from the similarity of their names in Arabic they easily may be. Whereas the 'Sheep Custom' was a feudal tax, collected and spent everywhere by the 'landowners', the 'Sheep Number' was levied only in Rumelia and had as its object the supply of mutton to the Palace and the Army. The sheep in question were originally raised by *ocaḳs* of registered shepherds.[9] These are men-

[1] Hammer, *Staatsverfassung*, i. 75; Cevdet, *Ta'rîḫ*, i. 48–50.

[2] D'Ohsson, vii. 238. He calls it 'le *Bid'at* de café'.

[3] Cf. p. 7 above.

[4] Seyyid Muṣṭafâ, iii. 98. Cf. D'Ohsson, vii. 238, where they are called *Mîzân* (see above, p. 8, nn. 2, 3).

[5] There are three such items in the 'summary' of Ṭarḫuncu Aḥmed Paşa, namely, the *bedeli ṭopu hümâyûn*', 'Imperial Canon Substitute', the *bedeli mu'âvenet* 'Assistance Substitute', and the *bedeli şâyi'*. All three were presumably payments in lieu of some services for the performance of which certain individuals, or *ocaḳs*, were exempted from some taxation. In the first case the service was clearly for the artillery, perhaps the furnishing of supplies to the foundry; but what 'assistance' was denoted by the second we cannot guess; and as for the third, *şâyi'* in Arabic can mean either 'what is bruited abroad' or 'common to those who have rights in an inheritance not yet divided'.

[6] He calls it '*Le Bid'at de Smyrne*'—vii. 238.

[7] *'adedi ağnâm.*

[8] *'âdeti ağnâm*—see Part I, p. 240.

[9] Called *celeb-keşan*, 'drovers' (from Arabic *calab*, 'an animal or article

tioned in various sixteenth-century documents,[1] from which it appears that, on the one hand, this sheep-raising was an attractive calling, which *'Askerîs* other than those enrolled in the *ocaḳs* had to be restrained from adopting, and, on the other, the numbers of both the shepherds and their flocks were apt to sink below the established total. As in many other fields, the original arrangements were altered as time went on, so that, instead of actually supplying sheep, the shepherds made the Treasury annual money payments in lieu. In order to raise the necessary cash the shepherds presumably sold their flocks to local butchers, while the Treasury, we know, had by the middle of the seventeenth century taken to using the money thus placed at its disposal for supplying the government butchers with funds wherewith themselves to buy the sheep required for the Palace and Janissary kitchens. Hence it is that in both Ṭarḫuncu Aḥmed Paṣa's statement and that of the *Eyyûbî Ḳânûn-nâmesi* we find as an item of revenue the yield of the tax-farm by which this contribution was then collected.[2] Although differently designated in the two documents,[3] it is evidently this tax-farm that is referred to in both, since it produced almost exactly the same amount in the two years in question.[4] The sums paid to the butchers, however, were far less than the yield of this farm—only just over two-thirds according to the first document,[5] and less than half according to the second.[6] The surplus was apparently applied to general expenditure—which no doubt explains why this 'substitute' payment was instituted, and also, if it was typical, why the whole substitute system was so welcome to the Treasury. As late as D'Ohsson's time the 'Sheep Number' still figured in the list of items composing the central revenues. But it had by then apparently developed into a general tax on sheep from which only *'Ulemâ*, Janissaries, and *Emîrs* possessing fewer than 150 were exempt. By this time also the name originally applied to members of the Rumelian *ocaḳs* responsible for supplying the animals required by the government had been transferred to the 'farmers' who undertook contracts for the collection of the substitute tax.[7]

brought to a market for sale', and Persian *käşîdän*, meaning (here) 'to drive')—or *celeb* for short.

[1] See Aḥmed Refîḳ, 8–10, 13, 23, 25.

[2] 'A. Vefîḳ, i. 328; Aḥmed Râsim, ii. 215 and 226, notes.

[3] By Ṭarḫuncu the item is called *celebkeşan ağnâmî mâli*, 'Drovers' Sheep Money', and in the *Eyyûbî Ḳânûn-nâmesi muḳâṭa'ayî ağnâm ḳalemi*, 'Sheep Farm Department'—all the items in the latter being shown according to the departments of the Finance Office to which the payments in question were made.

[4] 297 'purses' (see below, p. 58) in the earlier and 295 in the later.

[5] 188 purses—ibid. 222, note.

[6] 130 purses—ibid. 236, note.

[7] See D'Ohsson, vii. 239.

Special arrangements for the supply of other foodstuffs to the Court, the army, and the people of Istanbul were also in force. Thus, the peasantry of certain districts[1] were bound to send fixed quantities of wheat and barley yearly to the capital. These were bought by agents[2] appointed by the Barley Commissioner[3] at a very low fixed price; and in later times, when the discrepancy between this price and that obtainable for grain in the market became very great, if not from the first, when for any reason the total supply registered as being due from any district was not in fact exacted, the inhabitants were bound to pay these agents the difference in cash between the two prices on such grain (within the government 'quota') as they sold locally.[4] This practice is characterized by a modern Turkish writer who describes it[5] as 'pure tyranny'. It seems probable, however, that originally it differed but slightly from the system we have described, whereby 'levy-houses' of various types furnished supplies and services free in return for an exemption from some taxation—the difference in this case being that a fixed price was paid for the supplies; and that if the farmers in question suffered intolerably from the rapacity of the agents, as in the eighteenth century they undoubtedly did, this was due less to any intrinsic injustice in the system than to its unbridled abuse.[6]

In the eighteenth century, if not earlier, the government came to experience considerable difficulty in maintaining supplies of foodstuffs adequate to their consumption in Istanbul. For there was then a continual influx into the capital of desperate peasants who had been so plagued by the illegal exactions of local functionaries, and disheartened by the anarchy into which most of the provinces had by then declined, as to abandon their holdings and

[1] Mostly coastal, on the shores of the Black and Aegean Seas.

[2] Called *mubâya'acî*, 'wholesale purchasers', from Arabic *mubâya'a*, 'a contract of sale'.

[3] The *Arpa Emîni*—see Part I, p. 85.

[4] Seyyid Muṣṭafâ, iii. 104.

[5] 'Os̱mân Nûrî, 771.

[6] It is true that no mention is made of the exemption from any taxation of the farmers who grew the crops concerned; and it may be that they were not on an *'avâriḍ-ḫane* footing, but had originally been offered a fair price, which was not adjusted as prices rose. But the fact of their being obliged to hand over to the state whatever profits they might make on crops sold in the open market above the fixed price instead of to the agents suggests that they were registered as *'askerîs* bound to perform a regular service in exchange for some privilege, and were consequently entitled only to a fixed return on the crops they grew for state consumption, though they were presumably at liberty to pocket the whole price of such crops as they might grow above the government 'quota'. In the terminology of the *Dîvân* these 'quota' supplies were named *muḳâyese daḫâ'iri*, 'Comparison Provisions'—perhaps because the quantities forthcoming from each district were checked against the registers. That the system had given rise to an intolerable oppression was at length acknowledged after the terminal date of our survey, when in 1776 it was abolished by decree (see 'Os̱mân Nûrî, loc. cit.).

seek their fortunes as porters, boatmen, or artisans, in the great city. Repeated attempts were made to prevent this migration, which not only upset the good order of the guilds at the capital, but also itself reduced the growing of crops and the preparation of other supplies in the provinces. This reduction in turn, apart from enhancing local prices (to as much as five times those offered by the government agents), resulted in a deflexion of supplies from Istanbul to areas where they were short; so that, for example, a *fermân* to the *Ḳâḍîs* of various ports at which corn for Istanbul was loaded, promulgated in 1730, threatens the direst penalties for the future dispatch of 'one grain' to Anatolia or other *eyâlets* instead of to 'my Threshold of Felicity'.[1] On the other hand, we have come across no record of the use by the Central Treasury for general purposes of 'substitute' payments made by peasants bound to supply corn at the fixed price, when instead of so doing they sold locally and paid the agents the difference between the fixed price and whatever they were able to obtain. It may be that the funds forthcoming from this source were spent by the Barley Commissioner on supplies from other sources direct.

II. THE ARAB PROVINCES

Having thus described, as far as we are able, the taxes and dues exacted from the Sultan's subjects, and the methods by which they were collected for the benefit of the Central Treasury and the other agencies of government, we may now supplement this description by examining the working of the system, as seen from the standpoint of the Arab provinces.

The organization set up by the Ottoman Sultans in these provinces departed more in detail than in principle from the traditional system of their predecessors. Each *eyâlet* formed a separate and self-contained unit; out of its revenues were paid its own administrative and military expenses; and a fixed annual sum was laid down as the share of the Imperial Treasury. In special circumstances (as, for example, local military operations) a proportion of the amount due to the Porte might, with permission, be deducted to meet extraordinary expenses, but no instance appears to be recorded when the Porte made a contribution to the expenses of a provincial government from its other revenues. In addition to the tribute payable in money certain provinces were required also to furnish products in kind for specific purposes. The system was thus, in essentials, one of exploitation of the provinces for the benefit of the Imperial Court, Treasury, and army, offset in part

[1] Ibid. 769 sq. Cf. Cevdet, i. 106.

by the obligations of external defence and maintenance of the Islamic religion. The maintenance of internal security, on the other hand, was the business of the provincial administration.

The study of the *ḳânûns*, and particularly of the *ḳânûn-nâme* or 'Regulation' of Egypt,[1] shows that while the Ottoman legislator was concerned to protect the peasantry from oppression and injustice, his solicitude was inspired not by any spirit of liberalism, but solely by the desire to defend the Treasury from possible loss of revenue. On the one hand, the *Paşa* is ordered to furnish each village with a statement showing clearly the dues payable under each head, in order to prevent extortions by the *multazims*,[2] and it is laid down that the accounts drawn up by the village *ṣâhids* in concert with the collectors shall be regarded as valid evidence of payment of taxes;[3] on the other hand, it is strictly ordained that 'the peasants may not allow any land capable of cultivation to lie fallow',[4] and that the *multazims* amd *kâşifs* must supply on loan any seed required, on pain of severe penalties, and in the last resort cultivate the land at their own charges.[5] The *fellâḥ* who runs away from his village is to be forced to return, and if he runs away when his taxes fall due, he is to be put to death. Deserted villages are to be repopulated and exempt from taxation for the first year.[6] The lengthy instructions given to *kâşifs* and Arab *şeyḫs* are in the same vein.

'If a *kâşif* neglects to have inundated lands sown, ruins a village by his exactions, is guilty of malversation in the levying of impositions, or —which would be still more criminal[7]—by failing to repair broken-down dykes in order to facilitate the irrigation of the lands, allows them to remain dry, he shall not only be condemned to reimburse all the losses suffered by the cultivators and others, but shall be put to death by order of the *Paşa*, and ignominiously executed.'[8]

[1] 'Canoun-Namé ou Édits de Sultan Soliman, Concernant la police de l'Égypte', appended to Digeon, *Nouveaux contes turcs et arabes*, tom. ii (Paris 1781), 195–278. Hammer's version in *Staatsverfassung*, i. 101–43, is translated from this French version, which is, however, justly criticized by de Sacy, *Recherches, etc.*, i. 55–58. The Turkish text itself is now available in Barkan, *Z.E.E.*, i. 355–87.

[2] On *multazims* see Part I, p. 260, and p. 21 above, and for *kâşifs*, Part I, p. 260, n. 5.

[3] Digeon, 213; Barkan, 367, § 23 (not in de Sacy). The object of this provision was to prevent the *kâşifs* from demanding the taxes twice over, by taking advantage of the rule that in Moslem courts oral evidence alone is accepted.

[4] The ordinance proceeds: 'Their negligence in this matter shall be severely punished, and the same taxes shall be levied on the uncultivated lands as would have been levied if they were cultivated.'

[5] Digeon, 242–4; Barkan, 376–7.

[6] Digeon, 243–5; Barkan, 376–7.

[7] The expression in the text is 'God forbid!' (*'iyâẕan billâh*).

[8] Digeon, 197–8; de Sacy, i. 94; Barkan, 360, § 9. Similarly a *Şeyḫ el-Beled* (see Part I, p. 262) who fails to maintain proper irrigation is to indemnify the villagers and to be put to death: Digeon, 239; Barkan, 375, § 30.

If the harvest dues are not paid in full at the appointed time, the inspectors and *multazims* are to be held jointly responsible,[1] and the *multazim* who fails to dispatch the required quantities of grain in kind is to be replaced by another 'more zealous for the fertilization of our lands or who offers a larger contribution'.[2]

The same preoccupation is seen in the regulations for the Imperial granaries (*ṣûna*) and the customs. The rules for the prevention of fraud include, *inter alia*, the order that the weigher guilty of using false measures is to be hanged at the gate of the *ṣûna*.[3] The quantities of wheat and barley which the controller may dispose of locally in a good year are exactly defined, with the proviso that this concession is rarely to be used to the full extent.[4] The controller of customs is enjoined, in estimating the value of merchandise, neither to favour the merchants at the expense of the Treasury nor to injure them by making unjust claims.[5] Sub-farmers of customs revenues guilty of imposing supplementary duties are to be arrested, made to restore the sums exacted, and to receive rigorous punishment.[6] The supervision of all operations at the customs is entrusted to the local *Ḳâḍî*, who is ordered 'to take note of the number and cargoes of vessels, of the valuation of their merchandise, of the levying of the duties, of the legitimate means to augment these duties, and of everything that may relate to this portion of our revenues'. At the same time the *Paşa* is instructed to watch over the conduct of the *Ḳâḍîs* and 'to prevent any prevarication on their part'.[7] Such regulations, together with the warning reiterated in almost every paragraph, against neglect to 'hasten the payment in full of sums due to the Treasury', can have left no doubt in the minds of all administrative officials that the first and principal object of government was the levying and collection of taxes.

Detailed figures of the original distribution of taxation are available at present for Egypt alone of the Arab provinces.[8] The total

[1] Digeon, 211; Barkan, 366, § 21: a slightly different version in de Sacy, i. 105–6.

[2] Digeon, 222–3: this sentence is missing in Barkan (p. 369).

[3] Digeon, 216; Barkan, 368, § 25.

[4] Digeon, 220; Barkan, 369.

[5] Digeon, 223; Barkan, 370, § 26.

[6] Digeon, 229; Barkan, 371 foot.

[7] Digeon, 225; Barkan, 370 foot (the last sentence is missing).

[8] The following statement is based on the reports of Lancret and Estève in the *Description de l'Égypte* (see Part I, p. 15). It will be observed that the Egyptian figures are quoted in *paras*, although, as is noted later (p. 53, n. 1), the *para* became a regular minted coin only in the seventeenth century. The Egyptian *ḳânûn* (see p. 40, n. 6 below) itself uses the term *akçe* for the coins minted in Egypt, but adds that from every hundred *dirhems* of silver 250 *pâre* ('pieces') are to be struck. These 'pieces' were locally called, not *akçe*, but *mu'ayyidî*, colloquially pronounced *mîdî* and by the Europeans *medin*; and it appears that the Ottomans currently called them by the name of *pâra* ('money') (see art. 'Para' in Mehmet Zeki Pakalin, *Osmanli Tarih Deyimleri ve Terimleri Sözlüğü*).

revenues were made up of dues on lands, of assessments on holders of official positions out of the proceeds of their offices, and of customs, poll-tax, and other dues. A cadastral survey of the land was made in 1526 and revised in 1550,[1] and each parcel was assessed at a moderate and henceforth invariable rate.

The *mîrî* on land was fixed by Süleymân at 70,898,598 *paras* and augmented by subsequent Sultans to 78,311,491 *paras*.[2] The *multazims* were authorized to collect in addition certain fixed sums payable to the provincial governors and listed under the heads of specific services and for the upkeep of the provincial troops.[3] These, known under the name of *kuṣûfîya*, totalled 17,564,914 *paras*. Further, the *multazims* were authorized to collect a sum appropriated to their own use, theoretically variable according to the state of irrigation, and hence called *fâ'iḍ* or 'surplus'. The latter was calculated on a basis of 180,158,507 *paras* in a full year, or little less than double the combined total of *mîrî* and *kuṣûfîya*. The total of all these imposts was known as *mâl el-ḥurr*.[4] The *mîrî* was originally collected by the officers of the *Ça'uṣîya ocaḳ*, but subsequently by the *multazims* or their agents and paid in by them to the appropriate treasuries.[5] Since the *ḳânûn* itself fixed the ratio of 1,000 *paras* to 336 *dirhems*' weight of silver,[6] the total sum thus exacted from the produce of the land was 93 million *dirhems*' worth of silver, equivalent in the contemporary currency to 12 million Hungarian dollars,[7] or approximately 4 dollars per head

[1] De Sacy, i. 143–7.

[2] This augmentation was due to the increasing cost of the Mecca caravan (Estève, 385). Two small additional charges were also made: (i) 632,891 *paras* on account of *kürekçi* ('shoveller'), to pay for the removal of rubbish from Cairo to the sea; (ii) 1,073,508 *paras* as supplement of pay for the *Ça'uṣîya ocaḳ*, in return for their collection of the *mîrî*. When the *multazims* collected the taxes themselves, this amount was added to the *mîrî* and paid out by the Treasury at Cairo to the officers of the *ocaḳ*. The total *mîrî* on land thus amounted to 80,017,890 *paras*, and continued to be repartitioned in the eighteenth century exactly as it had been in the sixteenth, with the result that the rates of taxation per *feddân* varied enormously from village to village.

[3] The *Kâṣifs* or provincial governors were in theory required to send the balance of these taxes to the Central Treasury at Cairo, after deducting their *sâliyâne* or annual allowance: de Sacy, i. 95, 122.

[4] Meaning apparently 'lawful money', from *ḥurr* (Ar.), 'free', hence 'honourable'.

[5] The charge for collection was called *ḥaḳḳ el-ṭarîḳ* and was added to the sums due from the taxpayers (see n. 2 above). This procedure was sanctioned by Ḥanefî law, though rejected by the Şâfi'îs (Aghnides, *Mohammedan Theories of Finance*, 396). The *ḥaḳḳ el-ṭarîḳ* may perhaps be the Arabic equivalent for the *bedeli nüzül* referred to on p. 30 above.

[6] Digeon, 274; Barkan, p. 386, § 47 (in precise terms, 250 *paras* to be coined from 100 *dirhems* of silver 84 per cent. fine). The Turkish *dirhem* weight of 16 *ḳîrâṭs* was equivalent to 50 grains (3·2 grammes); the Egyptian *para* was therefore roughly the equivalent of the original Ottoman *aḳçe* (see p. 51 below). Owing to the depreciation of the *aḳçe*, the *para* at this time should have been worth 1⅜ *aḳçes*, and its exchange value about 24 to the Hungarian silver dollar.

[7] The Hungarian silver dollar of 1550 weighed 23·35 grammes (we owe this

of the population. The majority of *fellâḥs* in Lower and Middle Egypt paid these taxes in money; in Upper Egypt, however, certain taxes were payable in kind and the grain thus collected was transported by boat to the government grain-stores at Old Cairo.

In addition to the land-tax a variety of natural products was also included in the Egyptian tribute, such as rice, sugar, and vegetables for the *Serây*, and twine, tow, nitre, saltpetre, linseed oil, and cloth for the naval arsenal.[1] These do not appear to have been collected by taxation in kind, but were bought by the officers who had the duty of dispatching them from the coastal ports.

Neither artisans nor merchants were assessed directly for *mîrî*. Their contributions were made indirectly by the imposition of a fixed *mîrî* of 19,445,486 *paras* on the customs duties, and by assessments for *mîrî* totalling 10,870,773 *paras* upon the holders of official posts.[2] These were given leave to recoup themselves from certain recognized dues,[3] many of which were borne by merchants, traders, and artisans.[4] In addition, a large number of 'privileges' were accorded, for the most part to specified *ocaḳs*, on which *mîrî* was exacted. Such 'privileges' included the right of levying dues on all boats navigating Egyptian waters, monopolies or farms of the sale or manufacture of various products (cassia, senna, mutton, sal-ammoniac, &c.), the right of hall-marking silver,[5] and other levies on trades, merchants, and *wekâlas*.[6]

Of the total sum (116,651,727 *paras*) levied as state-tax in Egypt, only about a quarter (30,883,876 *paras*) fell to be sent to Istanbul, as the contribution of the province to the Private Treasury.[7] The remainder was accounted for by local charges under

information to the courtesy of the staff of the coin room at the Ashmolean Museum), and 93 million *dirhems* is the equivalent of 302 million grammes (4,650 million grains).

[1] See further Combe, 73.

[2] e.g. the *Paşa* was assessed at 1,625,000 *paras*; the eleven provincial governors together at 5,821,119 (net); the head of the public granaries at 294,332. As we have noted above (p. 9) the term *mîrî* strictly applied to the Treasury itself, but in current use it was applied primarily to the land-tax due to the Treasury, and subsequently to other dues as well.

[3] Called *rusûm 'urfîya*, i.e. dues authorized by the Sultans' *ḳânûns*; p. 2 above.

[4] The corporation of linen-weavers in the Fayyûm, for example, paid dues of 20,000 *paras* per annum (Girard, 598). But the profits of the *Paşaliḳ* were derived mainly from the customary exaction of three years' revenue in advance (*ḥulwân*) on succession to landed *iltizâms*, from profits on the grant of tax-farms, &c.; those of the mint from the margin between the price of silver and gold and the standard content of the coinage.

[5] Which included the right to levy or duty on the corporation of goldsmiths.

[6] List in Estève, 360 sqq. The total of *mîrî* due from these amounted to 3,172,846 *paras*. The farmer of the 'spice-dues' (*Emîn el-Buhâr*), i.e. of the duties exacted on imports from Arabia and India, remitted a quantity of spices, perfumes, drugs, &c., to Istanbul, in lieu of *mîrî*. On the *ḥurda* assigned to the *'Azeb ocaḳ*, see Part I, p. 277, n. 1.

[7] See p. 17, n. 3, above. Luṭfî Paşa's figure of 150,000 gold pieces is,

various heads, which in the original establishment were reasonably just and even generous. The principal heads of expenditure were for military pay and munitions (29,872,657 *paras*);[1] pensions to *'Ulemâ*, widows and orphans (8,438,994 *paras*); religious services (13,892,139 *paras*);[2] and expenses in connexion with the Mecca caravan (originally 11,320,543 *paras*, but subsequently increased, together with a portion of the *mîrî* in kind collected in Upper Egypt). The remainder was allocated to divers expenses, such as personal allowance to the *Paşa* and other officers, upkeep of the Nilometer, canals, and bridges,[3] and supplies for the Porte. All these charges were met by assignations (*câmikîya*) on the public Treasury, which were paid regularly every three months.[4]

In contrast to these very precise figures, for which we are indebted to the accident of the assumption by French experts of the administration of Egypt (and extracted even by them only with the greatest difficulty),[5] the figures for the Asiatic provinces are rough and unreliable. In the majority of these, as we have noted, a considerable proportion of the cultivated lands had been

however, inexplicable. At the original rate of 36 *paras* to the *şerîfî* or *sulṭânî* gold piece or Venetian ducat, the figure quoted in the text would correspond to approximately 850,000 gold pieces. Combe (p. 73) states that the tribute was originally fixed at 800,000 ducats, but that the normal figure fluctuated in the course of the sixteenth century between 800,000 and 600,000, and subsequently fell to 400,000. The figure of 600,000 is substantiated in a *fermân* addressed to Meḥmed Paşa (1553–5), quoted by J. J. Marcel (*L'Égypte depuis la conquête des Arabes*, 1848, 198): 'Qu'il te soit notoire que tu dois envoyer tous les ans aux pieds de notre étrier impérial la somme de 600.000 piastres [?] pour le *Khazneh* annuel de ton pachalyk; s'il t'est difficile de trouver des espèces d'or, nous condescendons à ce que tu soldes une partie en piastres et même en parats. Cinq cents hommes de nos Odjâqs seront employés à l'escorte dudit trésor.' The later decline to 400,000 is explained by the depreciation of the *para* to half its former value after 1584; see p. 51 below, and the table of exchange rates officially issued in A.H. 1102 (A.D. 1690–1), quoted by Ismâ'îl Ğâlib, *Meskûkât*, 238, which lists the value of the *para* at one-eightieth of the *şerîfî* gold piece. D'Ohsson (vii. 241) also gives the round figure of 1,200 Egyptian purses (each of 25,000 *paras*), i.e. 30 million *paras*.

[1] Exclusive of the expenditure for upkeep of provincial troops borne by the governors out of the *kuşûfîya* revenues and amounting to 20,335,518 *paras*.

[2] Of this sum 13,109,358 *paras* were allocated to upkeep of mosques, *dervîş* convents, and hospitals, and the remainder to tombs, festivals, 'turbans for converts to Islam', supplies to certain sanctuaries in Palestine, and various minor items.

[3] e.g. 16,000 *paras* were allotted to the *Bey* of Buḥayra (Beḥera), for the upkeep of the canal to Alexandria and supply of fresh water to the city (Estève, 373; Olivier, ii. 35, represents this sum as 23,750 piastres).

[4] Cf. Cabartî, iii. 212/trans. vii. 97.

[5] 'Au mois de juillet 1800 [Estève] rassembla chez lui, sous prétexte d'une communication officielle, les agens cophtes les plus entendus en matière de perception: puis, ayant fait entourer sa maison, il déclara à ces indigènes que leur liberté était au prix de la déclaration franche et sincère de leurs procédés de perception. On les retint alors en prison au nombre de cent environ, pendant l'espace de trois mois, au bout desquels ils avaient livré leurs documents': *Hist. scientifique et militaire de l'expédition française en Égypte* (Paris, 1830–6), tom. viii. 71.

assigned in the sixteenth century as *zi'âmets* and *timars*, whose possessors enjoyed the whole of the revenue derived from the land-tax on their holdings and from certain other dues.[1] But large areas were still retained as state domains and farmed out to tax-collectors or *multazims*, who were responsible for payment to the Treasury of the stipulated *mîrî* in full. With the partial resumption of fiefs by the central government at a later date and the establishment of *mâlikânes* we have dealt above.[2]

Apart from the differences in administration arising from the existence of *timars* and the enjoyment by the *Paşas* of a large *ḫâṣṣ* or apanage, there were also many points of detail on which the Syrian and 'Irâḳî systems diverged from Egyptian usage. The main heads of revenue were, as before, *mîrî*, *ḫarâc* (or *cizya*), import and export duties, passage dues on flocks and herds of nomad tribes during their annual migrations, and a certain number of privileges, monopolies, and market dues. The *mîrî* on land consisted usually either of a fixed sum[3] or of a tax calculated according to established rates on fruit and other trees;[4] in certain districts of inner Syria it was replaced by a cultivation tax of so much per *feddân*.[5] The imposition and rates of tax varied as between Moslem and non-Moslem cultivators, the latter being more heavily taxed than the former.[6] There seems, indeed, to have been little uniformity in land administration and taxation, the Ottomans having simply preserved established usages in all their variety.

In regard to market dues, warehouse dues, and the like, the *ḳânûns* confirm for the most part the regulations of the Mamlûk Sultan Ḳa'it-Bey (1468–96), only abolishing certain of the more arbitrary and oppressive taxes. In Syria the market dues consisted mainly of a small tax per load on goods and a percentage duty

[1] See Part I, pp. 202, 240.

[2] pp. 20–21, 22 above.

[3] Known in Syria as *deymûs* or *dîmûs* (δημόσιον), the system, as well as the name, being quite possibly inherited from the Roman provincial administration.

[4] Known as *ḳism* or *ḳasm*. See on these taxes generally the Syrian *ḳânûns* translated by Hammer, *Staatsverfassung*, i. 219–21 (Damascus), 224–6 (Jerusalem and Ṣafed), 228 (Tripoli), 239–40 (Aleppo), and for the *ḳasm* and other dues in Galilee, B. Lewis, *Notes and Documents from the Turkish Archives* (Jerusalem, 1952), 15–20. The distinction between *dîmûs* and *ḳism* lands was probably a matter of usage. The *ḳânûns* prohibit strictly the levying of taxes on fruit-trees in addition to *dîmûs* (Hammer 221). In most *timars* a large proportion of the taxation was paid in kind (ibid. 225, 229; Olivier, ii. 281).

[5] e.g. at Ḥomṣ: 40 aspers (*aḳçes*) per *feddân*; Hammer, i. 229; *çift* dues at Aleppo: ibid. 239.

[6] Hammer, i. 225–6, 229–30, &c.; Lewis, 19 and n. 38. Olivier (ii. 281) gives an account of the land-taxes in the region of Lâḏiḳîya (drawing a distinction between *timars* and state lands, farmed out annually; on the former the *fellâḥs* held long leases, on the latter they were annual tenants and the rates of taxation were lower). List of land-taxes in Nâblus quoted by Kurd 'Alî, *Ḫiṭaṭ el-Şâm*, v. 85 (cf. Hammer, i. 226).

on sales;[1] in Bağdâd tradesmen paid a monthly shop-tax, apparently in lieu of the latter.[2] Government privileges and monopolies embraced salt[3] and tobacco,[4] and (at Bağdâd) stamp duty on fine textiles.[5] It is remarkable that no general regulation is laid down for the taxation of the principal industries, such as weaving;[6] presumably it is understood that the existing corporation taxes should continue to be levied, unless direct orders were issued to the contrary.[7]

The collection of the *mîrî* was as a rule farmed out by the *Paşas* and *Sancaḳ Beyis* to third parties, who again farmed out the individual villages to sub-farmers. Once a year the *Paşa* himself,[8] accompanied by a military force, made the circuit of his *eyâlet* for the purpose of collecting the amounts due from each farmer-in-chief and *Sancâk Beyi*, and, if necessary, exacting payment in full by coercive measures.[9]

No accurate summaries appear to be available at present of the revenues and expenditure of the Syrian and 'Irâḳî *eyâlets* from the sixteenth to the eighteenth century, and the various estimates are

[1] Hammer, i. 222 sqq. The duties at Damascus were 1 asper per sack of vegetables, 2 to 4 per load of fruit, and an average of 5 aspers per load deposited in the *wekâlas*. Sales were taxed as follows: per horse, 6 aspers; per camel or buffalo, 8; per ass, 4; per sheep, 2½; per slave, 30; silk, per roll, 4; and 5 per cent. on market sales generally.

[2] Grocers, 3 aspers per month for a large shop and 2 for a small; bakers and cooks, 300 aspers per month; greengrocers and butchers, 200; silk merchants, 144; confectioners, 36; potters, 5: Hammer, i. 235. It should, however, be borne in mind that these were the rates established by *ḳânûn* in the sixteenth century, and that while the principles of taxation remained the same in the eighteenth, the actual rates were probably different and much higher.

[3] Salt monopoly at Tripoli: Hammer, i. 227–8; at Aleppo, Volney, ii. 41.

[4] The tobacco monopoly at Lâḏiḳîya was held by an officer directly subordinate to the farmer-general of tobacco at Istanbul (see p. 33 above). The yield at the end of the eighteenth century was estimated at from 500,000 to 700,000 piastres, the duty per *ḳanṭâr* being 22 piastres: Olivier, ii. 281.

[5] Hammer, i. 237; for stamp duty, see p. 8 above. At Bağdâd also gate tolls were levied (1 asper per horseman and 4 aspers per woman entering or leaving the city) and bridge tolls: ibid. 235–7. For bridge tolls and ferry tolls in Syria cf. Lewis, 21–22; Olivier, ii. 293, 328.

[6] Exceptionally, the annual tax (50,000 aspers) levied on the soap-boilers at Tripoli is mentioned: Hammer, i. 228. At Damascus they were taxed indirectly as well, by regulations for the supply of alkali: ibid. 223. The tax on water-mills at Ḥomṣ was 60 aspers per annum: ibid. 229; Lewis, 20 (with other industrial taxes).

[7] e.g. that no tax was to be levied on fabrics woven in private houses: Hammer, i. 231 (relating to Ḥomṣ). The same principle applied to other existing dues; thus it appears from a passage in Murâdî, ii. 195, that a house tax or family tax established by the Mamlûk Sultans was still levied in Syria in the eighteenth century. But in addition to the dues abolished by Süleymân, there are numerous examples of the abolition of customary dues at the instance of later *Paşas*; cf. Kurd 'Alî, v. 83–84; Murâdî, iv. 101.

[8] Except at Aleppo, where there was a special 'collector' (*Muḥaṣṣil*); see Part I, p. 201, n. 1, and Murâdî, iii. 151–2.

[9] Cf. Volney, ii. 13, 239; farming of taxes at Nâblus, ibid. 177. In 'Irâḳ the tax-farmers were known as *ḍâbiṭs* (*ẓâbiṭs*): cf. Rousseau, 65–66.

confusing and irreconcilable. In view of the large areas set apart for *timars* and crown fiefs in most districts, it is evident that the amounts handled by the provincial governments were very much smaller than was the case in Egypt. The following are given as the official figures relating to the *eyâlets*, as drawn up in the sixteenth century:[1]

	Ḫâṣṣ *of* Paşas *and* Begs (akçes)	*Revenue of* timars, *&c.* (akçes)	*Total revenue from taxation*	
			(akçes)	(*piastres*)
Moṣul .	1,513,284	2,240,000	1,660,346	41,508
Şehrizôr .	..	..	1,110,000	..
Bağdâd .	4,286,771*	..	7,349,887	183,747
Diyârbekir .	7,625,291	11,400,000	..	..
Raḳḳa .	1,797,388	..	..	..
Aleppo .	3,676,083	7,713,121	10,022,819	250,570
Şâm . .	2,934,403	6,558,660	6,337,588	158,439
Tripoli .	2,086,335	5,608,400	6,418,856	160,471

* For seven out of eighteen *sancaḳs* only.

But (to anticipate for a moment) these figures in no way represent the revenues and expenditure of the same provinces in the eighteenth century. In the absence of official figures, the summary given by Volney may be taken as a basis, though with all reserve. He estimates the total revenue of Aleppo at between 6 and 6½ million piastres, of which 800 purses (i.e. 400,000 piastres)[2] were sent to Istanbul for the 'farm' of the *Paşalıḳ*.[3] The *Paşas* of Tripoli and Ṣaydâ[4] were each under obligation to send 750 purses in tribute to the Porte and to furnish provisions for the Pilgrimage to the same value.[5] Damascus, according to his statement, sent only a nominal tribute of 45 purses to the Porte, the remainder of the surplus being affected to the expenses of the Pilgrimage and the payment of safe-conducts for the pilgrims to the Arab tribes on

[1] The figures for *ḫâṣṣ* and *timars* are from 'Aynî 'Alî Mu'addin-zâde (Tischendorff, *Das Lehnswesen*, 73–84), those of total revenue from Hammer, *Staatsverfassung*, ii. 265–70. N. Jouplain, *La Question du Liban* (Paris 1908), 83–84, gives the annual tribute figures as: Damascus (Şâm), 110,537 piastres; Tripoli, 98,154; Aleppo, 142,365; but does not state the source from which these are derived. The figures quoted from Turkish sources in Kurd 'Alî, v. 83, are also confused.

[2] The Turkish and Syrian 'purse' (*kîs*) at this time was of 500 piastres, or 20,000 *paras*, whereas the Egyptian purse was of 25,000 *paras*.

[3] Volney, ii. 41. His figures are usually given in francs or livres, which have been converted into piastres at the rate he mentions (i. 189, ii. 275) of 2½ livres to the piastre.

[4] It has been mentioned (Part I, p. 222) that the *Paşalıḳ* of Ṣaydâ was formed out of the coastal districts of the *eyâlet* of Şâm in 1660; its revenues included the produce of the sub-farms of the Druses, Maronites, and Arabs of northern Palestine.

[5] Volney, ii. 63–64, 74.

the road between Damascus and Mecca.[1] The Palestinian plain was not included in the revenue district of any *Paşalik*, but was divided into three *mâlikânes* (Ludd, Jaffa, and Gaza) assigned to fief-holders at Istanbul, and farmed out for 35, 120, and 185 purses respectively.[2]

The revenues of the *Paşalik* of Bağdâd were estimated by Rousseau at 7½ million piastres, derived from customs, ordinary taxes, produce of the farmed taxes, annual contributions of the governors and other officials, and the tribute due from the Arab tribes.[3] Başra and Moşul, on the other hand, enjoyed very modest revenues, and those of Başra were usually absorbed by the cost of defence, including subsidies to the neighbouring tribes.[4]

The ultimate responsibility for the collection and distribution of the revenues, and dispatch of the stipulated tribute to Istanbul, rested with the *Paşa*, assisted by the provincial *Defterdâr*.[5] But the levying of the *mîrî*, accountancy, and payment of sums due from the public Treasury was carried out by a special branch of the administration. In Egypt (and on much the same lines in the other provinces) the finance department consisted of an Administrator-general (*Rûznâmecî*),[6] nominated for life by the Sultan, and a board of *Efendis*,[7] who held their posts by virtue of heredity.[8] Each *Efendi* was responsible for a specific branch of

[1] Ibid. 135. But the figures which he supplies under these heads, viz. 6,000 and 1,800 purses respectively (i.e. 3,900,000 piastres), are barely credible.

[2] Ibid. 199–200 (cf. with the latter figures Cezzâr Paşa's farms of Cubeyl, &c., below (pp. 67–68). Several of the inland districts of Syria were also constituted as crown fiefs, including Ba'albek, Ḥomş, and Ḥamâ. The two latter were held in the eighteenth century by the *Paşas* of Damascus and farmed out by them. From a narrative in Murâdî (i. 69) it appears that the revenues of Ba'albek included silk manufactures.

[3] Rousseau, 30; the Kurds were exempted from fixed contributions in consideration of their frequent military service. But it would seem that Rousseau's figure includes the revenues of the *eyâlets* of Mârdîn and Şehrizôr, then attached to Bağdâd; otherwise a sum of 15,000 purses (equivalent to 300 million *paras*) is incredible in the conditions of 'Irâḳ in the eighteenth century. Olivier (ii. 397) gives an estimate of 4,000 purses, of which less than 500 were sent as tribute to Istanbul. The official figure for the contribution due from Bağdâd was 275,000 piastres (550 purses): D'Ohsson, vii. 241.

[4] Rousseau, 31, 43, 90. Olivier (ii. 357) estimates the net revenue of Moşul at 100 purses.

[5] On the *Defterdârs* see Part I, pp. 128, 201. It may be noted here that the dispatch of the *mîrî* to Istanbul was utilized by merchants as a means of negotiating bills of exchange on the capital; i.e. the local officials paid cash out of the *mîrî* to the European merchant, who gave in return a bill to be cashed at Istanbul: De Tott, ii. 327.

[6] On the *Rûznâmecî* see Part I, pp. 127, 136; for the *Rûznâmecî* in Syria, J. Deny, *Sommaire des Archives turques du Caire* (Cairo, 1930), 133. After reviewing the evidence, Deny suggests that it was one of the chief functions of the *Rûznâmecî* in all provinces to keep the registers of *timars* (ibid. 567).

[7] Officially called *Muḳâṭa'acis*, i.e. accountants of *muḳâṭa'as*: see Part I, p. 132. Murâdî also mentions accountants and 'secretaries of the *ocaḳs*' whose posts passed by heredity: i. 256; ii. 135, 220–1; iii. 206.

[8] See generally Lancret, 252–55, and Estève, 368–9; cf. Cabartî, iv. 91/viii.

accountancy (including one for each *ocak*) and had four subordinate *Efendis* as assistants, together with book-keepers, money-changers, and other minor officials,[1] most of whom were paid out of the *mîrî* revenues.[2] Their account was kept in a special script known as *ḳirma*,[3] which was the standard vehicle of the Ottoman financial administration, and it appears from a passage from the historian el-Cabartî[4] that it was checked against a duplicate account kept in Hebrew by Jewish clerks. These accounts were presented by the *Rûznâmecî* to the *Paşa* or his *Defterdâr*, and after approval sent to Istanbul. Upon occasions they were audited locally by an *Ağa* dispatched from the capital for that purpose.

It appears to have been the custom that a deposed or recalled *Paşa* had, before leaving Egypt, to reside in a private house assigned to him until his accounts were audited and he either paid in full or gave guarantees for the amounts which he owed. Similarly, a Mamlûk *Emîr*, on being sentenced to exile, was not permitted to leave the country until all his accounts were cleared—by the sale of his property and personal effects, if necessary.[5] The mutual claims of *Paşas*, *multazims*, and others were frequently settled by balancing entries against one another, without any actual passing of money.[6]

It would be idle to pretend that the system established by the Ottoman Sultans, for all its correctitude, protected the cultivator, artisan, or merchant from extortion and oppression. Almost from the first, abuses crept in; and we may be sure that for every abuse which is recorded by the chroniclers (and they are many) a hundred went unrecorded. The fault lay not in the regulations themselves, but in the defective and unscrupulous working of the regulations by officials and tax-farmers of every degree. The all too common placing of private interest above the interests of the community, and the tolerance which the administration displayed towards abuses, provided they were not too glaring, loaded the dice heavily against the administered.

201, and Deny, 131–43. The *Efendîs* were Moslems, not Copts, and the *Rûznâmecî* was generally selected from amongst their number. Their posts might be sold, on condition that the buyer was possessed of the necessary education and approved by the *Rûznâmecî*.

[1] The money-changers and some of the minor officials were Jews.

[2] And, like other officials, assessed for *mîrî* on their takings, the *Rûznâmecî* at 27,291 *paras*, and the *Efendîs* collectively at 515,831 (Estève).

[3] i.e. 'broken', *ḳirma* being the Turkish equivalent of the Persian *şikäste* (Deny, 142, n. 3); cf. also *J.A.* 2. i (1829), 379–91; Murâdî, iv. 185, 12; Ibrahim el-Mouelhy, 'Le Qirmeh en Égypte', in *Bulletin de l'Institut d'Égypte*, xxix (1946–7), 51–82. The language used in these documents was half Persian, half Turkish.

[4] Cabartî, iv. 170/ix. 7. In Damascus also the registers of the *mîrî* were kept by Jewish *şarrâfs*: Mich. Dam. 47.

[5] Cabartî, i. 255/ii. 226.

[6] Ibid. ii. 176 (omitted in the translation).

Still more fatal to any hope of clean government was the practice, established in the reign of Süleymân the Lawgiver himself, of assigning the offices of state and administrative posts of all kinds against the payment of a sum to the distributors of patronage. This was in turn erected into a system, in which every post had its price, payable annually on a given date.[1] In a Venetian consular report early in the eighteenth century it is affirmed that each of the Syrian *Paşalîks* cost from 80,000 to 100,000 ducats, the office of *Defterdâr* half that amount, and the office of chief *Ḳâḍî* a little less,[2] and lesser officials and tax-farmers were assigned estates and other privileges at proportionate rates.[3] Such a system amounted in practice to giving the official or tax-farmer the right to recoup himself by exactions from those placed under his charge, and more especially since (it would seem) he was liable to be removed from his post at any moment in favour of a higher bidder.[4]

Yet because it was erected into a system with more or less regular tariffs, it would seem that the purchase of offices, however much it lowered the moral tone of the administration, did not in itself endanger the social and economic stability of the provinces by organizing a régime of arbitrary extortion. With the usual capacity of Islamic society to adapt new circumstances to old processes, the consequent abuses were often, if not always, regularized by their transformation into fixed additional taxes and dues. Thus it became a regular practice for a new governor, on arrival in his *Paşalîk*, to demand a 'present' of money from the towns and villages of his government,[5] and we shall have occasion to note other examples in a later section of this chapter.[6] The chief vic-

[1] See Part I, p. 196.

[2] Quoted by Lammens, *La Syrie*, ii. 61. Volney asserts that the *muḥaṣṣil* of Aleppo paid eighty to a hundred thousand francs as 'prix de babouche' to the *Vezîr*: ii. 41.

[3] Cf. Muradi, i. 274; Cabartî, iii. 194/vii. 50 (translation inaccurate).

[4] Cf. *Ḳânûn-nâme* for Egypt (Digeon, 254; Barkan, 380, § 36). 'Si après la concession d'un Barat qui autorise le propriétaire à exercer en Égypte les fonctions d'Inspecteur ou Commis de droits de notre domaine, il se présente au Divan du Caire un enchérisseur qui offre d'en payer la finance à un plus haut prix, et que le bien public se trouve réuni à cet égard avec celui de notre service, l'on acceptera les propositions de l'enchérisseur, lequel entrera dès ce moment en exercice avec la puissance de toutes les attributions attachées à la place d'Inspecteur ou Commis; on séquestrera le Barat; on interdira toutes fonctions à celui qui en est le propriétaire, et l'on informera notre sublime Porte de ce changement.'

[5] At Damascus, e.g., the *Defterdârs* established a due called *ḳalamîya*, exacted from the holders of *mâlikânes* and tax-farmers: Murâdî, iii. 211.

[6] Mich. Dam. 30–31. There are two interesting features about this tax: firstly, that it is mentioned by the historian only in reference to an instance of complaint that a certain new governor exacted *too much*; secondly, this was one of the dues explicitly abolished (together with 'festival dues') by the *ḳânûns* of Süleymân: Hammer, *Staatsverfassung*, i. 228, 230.

tims of such practices were wealthy merchants and officials, who were frequently exposed to *avanias* or demands for loans, from which even the Frankish merchants did not escape. The point at which these illegal exactions threatened to ruin the entire economy of the provinces was not reached until the later decades of the eighteenth century, when, together with the weakening control of the central government and the growing appetites of insubordinate governors, sharpened by the costs of their military establishments, there set in a rapid depreciation and debasement of the currency throughout the empire. Before outlining the former development, therefore, we must turn our attention to the Ottoman coinage.

III. CURRENCY

While it is no part of our purpose to investigate the history of the Ottoman coinage at length (a topic which calls for special qualifications beyond our competence), the importance of the subject in relation to our study requires us to attempt a survey of its general development in some detail.[1]

From the establishment of the Ottoman dynasty up to the period of our survey certain foreign coins were in general use, and were recognized as legal tender, throughout the Empire, side by side with those minted by the Sultans themselves. Indeed, although the *akçe*—or, to give it its full name, the *akçei ʿoşmânî*: 'Ottoman little silver piece'[2]—was struck under Sultan Orḫân,[3] it was not until after the conquest of Constantinople that gold coins were first issued by an Ottoman mint. As the numerous references we have made to the *akçe* will have indicated, this was the coin used invariably up to the end of the seventeenth century for official calculations. Since the *akçe* was so much debased in the course of time, however, and its debasement plays such an important part in Turkish economic history, we had best begin our account of this by mentioning certain other coins, gold and silver, of more stable value, in order to measure the *akçe*'s decline.

[1] The standard works which we have consulted include S. Lane-Poole, *The Coins of the Turks in the British Museum* (London, 1883); Ismâʿîl Ğâlib, *Takvîm-i Meskûkât-i ʿOşmânîye* (Constantinople, 1307 H./1889); the works of Seyyid Muṣṭafâ (see Part I, p. 15) and Aḥmed Râsim; also the relevant articles in the Turkish *Islâm Ansiklopedisi*, and the still useful, though somewhat antiquated, work of Belin, 'Essai sur l'Histoire économique', in *J.A.*, Série VI, tom. iii.

[2] Or 'little white', *ak* being a word for white in Turkish, and *çe* a Persian diminutive. Early European authors usually refer on this account to the *akçe* as an 'aspre' from the equivalent Greek word for white. According to the *Islâm Ansiklopedisi* and Belin (p. 422), the term *akçe* was already in use under the Great Selcukids and the Ilḫânids.

[3] Aḥmed Râsim, i. 113, note.

We may take first two foreign coins, also silver, called by the Turks *ḳuruş*.[1] The word *ḳuruş* is a corruption, at second hand, of the Latin adjective *grossus*, applied to various types of *denarius* first coined by certain European rulers in the thirteenth century.[2] In early Ottoman times the type of *grossus* most in favour was one of Dutch or Flemish origin which, since it bore the effigy of a lion, was known as the *esedî* or *arslanî*.[3] In the fifteenth century, however, the *esedî* was gradually supplanted, though not entirely, by an Austrian *grossus*, known as the *riyal*[4] or *ḳara ḳuruş*,[5] whose weight was one-eighteenth greater.[6] Next, side by side with these foreign silver coins, were two foreign gold coins which enjoyed more or less exclusive favour in early times: the Venetian ducat or sequin, called by the Turks *filuri*[7] or *yaldiz altini*,[8] and the Austrian ducat, called by them *macar altini*.[9] It was in imitation of one of these that Meḥmed the Conqueror struck the first Ottoman gold coins.[10] The latter were at first also called by the names applied to their foreign models.[11] After the conquest of Egypt by Selîm I, however, they were given a name of their own—*ṣerîfî*[12]—by which they continued to be known as long as they were minted, i.e. for the best part of the next 200 years, with but slight varia-

[1] Spelt *ğuruş* in the Arabic, but always written with a *k* in the new Latin script.

[2] *Grossus* is represented in various European languages by the coin-names 'groat', 'gros', 'grosso', 'groschen'. It is presumably from the last that the Turkish *ḳuruş* is immediately derived.

[3] *asad* being Arabic and *arslan* or *aslan* Turkish for 'lion'. Belin, 438.

[4] Or *iryâl*—apparently from the Spanish '*real*' or 'piece of eight'.

[5] *ḳara*, 'black', here used in contrast to *ḳizil*, 'red', of coins that did not turn brown with use, to mean 'of good standard'.

[6] Belin, 439–40, who, however, states that it was only in 1642 that the names *riyâl* and *ḳara ḳuruş* were first used. Seyyid Muṣṭafâ's references to these names seem somewhat confused. Thus in one passage (iii. 106) he writes of 'the *direkli* and *ḳuşlu riyâls* known as the *esedî ḳuruş* and *ḳara ḳuruş*', as if *direkli* ('having a column or mast') were an alternative name for *esedî*, and *ḳuşlu* ('having a bird') an alternative name for *ḳara ḳuruş*. Elsewhere, however (i. 148–9), he writes of 'the *ḳara ḳuruş* or *direkli riyâl*', thus, apparently, attaching *direkli* to the Austrian rather than the Dutch coin, and refers again at ii. 98 to '*direkli riyâls*'. We have come across no coins to which the epithets *direkli* and *ḳuşlu* seem appropriate, other than the Spanish pillared dollar called in Egypt *abū midfa'*.

[7] i.e. 'florin'. Gold pieces, bearing a flower on the reverse (whence—from *fiorino*—the name) were minted at Florence in 1252. Venice followed suit with a gold coin of the same weight in 1284. This, at first known as a 'ducat' (i.e. ducal or doge's coin), was subsequently called a *zecchino* or sequin (apparently from the Arabic *sikka*, 'a coin').

[8] *yaldiz* means 'gilding' and *altin* 'gold' (both Turkish). The name was a tribute to the high standard of these coins: Aḥmed Râsim, i. 444, note.

[9] i.e. 'Magyar gold'.

[10] According to Seyyid Muṣṭafâ, i. 66, the Austrian ducat was taken as a model; according to Belin, 428, and Ismâ'îl Ğâlib, 53, the Venetian.

[11] Seyyid Muṣṭafâ, iii. 106.

[12] Or *eṣrefî*, apparently after the title adopted by the last three Mamlûk Sultans, *el-aṣraf* (the Most Noble); Belin, 429–30. By European merchants, however, they were more frequently designated by the name of *Sulṭânî*.

tions during the whole of this period in their standard weight of 53 grains[1] or fineness. Even after their introduction the foreign gold—and indeed silver—circulating in the Empire was certified to be legal currency by being stamped with the word *ṣaḥḥa* ('it is sound').[2]

From the reign of Orḫan, when it was first minted, down to the conquest of Constantinople, the original weight and standard of the *aḳçe*—or *'oṣmânî*, as it was then generally called[3]—seem to have been pretty well maintained at just over a third of a *dirhem*-weight of silver 90 per cent. fine. Between that event and the reign of Selîm I (1512–20), however, the *aḳçe* suffered a fall, in stages, to not much more than half its original value. From the reign of Selîm I down to the beginning of the reign of Murâd III (1574–95) its value again remained stable at this new level.[4] All sources are in agreement in presenting the rates of exchange in the middle of the sixteenth century as being roughly 40 *aḳçes* to the *ḳara ḳuruş* (foreign silver), 50 to the Austrian ducat (gold), and 60 to the Venetian ducat and Ottoman *şerîfî*.[5]

It was during the reign of Murâd III that the financial crisis provoked in the western half of the Mediterranean area from 1560 onwards by the influx of American silver[6] spread to the Ottoman territories also. Accelerated and intensified by this Sultan's imprudent expansion of the standing army, and (it would appear) by a simultaneous 50 per cent. devaluation of the Persian currency, the silver content of the *aḳçe* and of the Egyptian *para* were in 1584 reduced at one stroke by about half; and their value, in terms of the foreign coinage and of the *şerîfî* (which was not affected), fell in proportion.[7] This debasement was the second main measure adopted by the Treasury in order to meet its unprecedented liabilities (the other being the seizure of vacant military fiefs). But the advantages of debasement were, of course, all too transitory, and its drawbacks soon became disastrously clear. The cost

[1] In Turkish usage, 1 *dirhem*+1 *ḳîrâṭ*+a fraction, the *dirhem* (of 16 *ḳîrâṭs*) being equivalent to 50 grains or 3·2 grammes.

[2] Belin, 428.

[3] Ibid. 422.

[4] Though there appears to be as yet no general agreement on the details of this decline, the early history of the *aḳçe* may be summarized as follows on the basis of the *aḳçes* preserved in the British Museum. From Orḫân to Murâd II it weighed on an average about 18 English grains; under Meḥmed the Conqueror it weighed 14 grains, or about $\frac{2}{7}$ of a *dirhem*; and from the time of Selîm I to early in the reign of Murâd III it weighed about 10 grains, or roughly $\frac{1}{5}$ of a *dirhem*. See also the table appended to Ismâ'îl Ğâlib, 506–7, and Seyyid Muṣṭafâ, i. 148.

[5] Aḥmed Râsim, ii. 257, note; cf. F. Braudel, *La Méditerranée . . . à l'époque de Philippe II* (1949), 418.

[6] Braudel, 398 sqq.

[7] See n. 4 above; Braudel, 419 sq., 1043 sq., the *ḳara ḳuruş* rose to 80, and the *şerîfî* to 120 *aḳçes*, while in Egypt the *para* or *medin* fell to 85 to the *şerîfî*.

of living went up and the troops acquired a habit of rioting which kept the government intermittently at their mercy for the next fifty years and more, led to the first murder of a Sultan ('Young' 'Osmân II), and fatally dislocated the whole structure of the state.

Nor did the *akçe* ever recover from this decline. The Ottoman Treasury lacked the means by which the parallel difficulties were palliated in the Western countries, and the most that later competent *Vezîrs* ever succeeded in achieving was its restoration to this level from still lower depths.[1] To add to their troubles, a second scourge, spreading from the West in the reign of Meḥmed III (1595–1603) and his successors, alternately distracted and tempted the Treasury. This was the plague of false and adulterated money, which reduced the *akçe* to a rate of 220 to the *şerîfî*.[2] Some of the *akçes* issued early in the reign of Meḥmed IV (1648–87), when the confusion in public affairs was probably at its worst, were so obviously composed mainly of alloy that they were derisively called 'gypsy', 'wine-shop', 'red', and other uncomplimentary names;[3] while the Treasury's attempts to satisfy the troops and others with such worthless coin were naturally quite ineffective and the cause of further discontent and disturbance. As we have noted, by the reign of Süleymân II (1687–91), when for an all too brief term of office Köprülü Fâḍil Muṣṭafâ Paşa took over the management of affairs, the *akçe*, which had weighed some 10 grains in the reign of Selîm II, weighed no more than 2½.[4] This meant that the *kara kuruş* was then worth about 160 *akçes* and the Ottoman *şerîfî* about 240, in nominal value—i.e. that the *akçe* had fallen to about one-seventh of its original value, and, because of its adulteration, was worth in fact even less.[5]

The *akçe* certainly deserved the diminutive form of its name. It was a very small coin indeed, no larger than a silver twopenny piece.[6] Though seldom perfectly regular in shape, it was always intended (unless some square silver pieces occasionally minted in the African Regencies were regarded as *akçes*) to be round. Meanwhile, the more it lost value, the more inconvenient it became as a medium of exchange. Some larger denomination was needed in the interests of commerce, and in response to this demand two new silver coins were introduced early in the seventeenth century: the *para*, worth at first 4 and subsequently 3 *akçes*, and a 10-*akçe*

[1] Thus it was restored in 1600–1 to this level by Yemişçi Ḥasan Paşa after falling to 165 to the gold piece, and again in 1641 by Kemânkeş Ḳara Muṣṭafâ Paşa, after the disorders referred to below: 'A. Vefîḳ, i. 325.

[2] Braudel, 416 sq., 419, 1044.

[3] *çingene, meyḫâne, ḳizil*: 'A. Vefîḳ, i. 324.

[4] See p. 33, n. 3, above.

[5] A table officially issued in 1102/1691 lists the rate as 360 to the *şerîfî*: Ismâ'îl Ğâlib, 238.

[6] The Maundy twopence, half an inch across.

piece.[1] It is true that in some of the Asiatic and African provinces silver coins much heavier than the *akçe* had been struck at least from the reign of Süleymân I.[2] But it is not clear what relation these bore to it, and in any case they were not, presumably, in general currency. However that may be, it was seen, towards the end of the seventeenth century, that more radical measures than any yet taken were needed to supply the public need for a sound and convenient native coinage; and these were duly adopted under Süleymân II, when for the first time an Ottoman mint issued a native *kuruş*.[3] This comparatively bulky coin, though modelled on the foreign coins that had circulated in the Empire for so long under the same name, was considerably lighter than they, weighing no more than two-thirds of the *kara kuruş*.[4] Later, under Aḥmed III, another larger *kuruş* was minted, weigh-

[1] It seems to be uncertain when the *para* was first minted—cf. *Encyclopaedia of Islam*, s.v. Seyyid Muṣṭafâ, iii. 106, links it with the issue of the 10-*akçe* piece, which we know was introduced under 'Osmân II (see Belin, 414); and if, as is said, it originally weighed 16 grains and was worth 4 *akçes*, this date may well be right, since from the time of Meḥmed III until it made a slight temporary recovery under Murâd IV, the *akçe* was more than once reduced to no more than 4 grains, and the reign of 'Osmân II was one of special penury. Later, the *para* seems to have been debased even more than the *akçe*, so that the ratio between them changed to 1 to 3; and at this it remained for purposes of computation after the minting of *akçes* was finally discontinued in the eighteenth century.

[2] See Lane-Poole, p. xviii, note, and for the Egyptian *para* or *medin* p. 39, n. 8 above. Silver pieces of Süleymân minted at Âmid and Tyre, for instance, weighed as much as 61 and 40 grains respectively (the *akçe* then weighing 10), while as late as Meḥmed IV others minted at Aleppo and Bağdâd weighed 39 and 45.

Judging by the specimens in Lane-Poole and the data in Ismâ'îl Ğâlib's *Meskûkât*, the facts seem to be that between the reigns of Meḥmed III and Meḥmed IV, whereas the mint at Istanbul confined itself, as regards the silver currency, to the coinage of *akçes*, *paras*, and 10-*akçe* pieces, many provincial mints produced issues that cannot be regarded as *akçes*, or, necessarily, multiples of the *akçe*, being for the most part only of much heavier pieces, of almost any weight between 15 and 46 grains each, though there occur also a few coins of smaller or, so to speak, medium weight. It is notable that none of the heavier pieces weigh anything like a *kuruş*—some 300 grains at least. In this connexion see the next note.

[3] This is the usual view: that the first Ottoman *kuruş* was struck in 1099 (1688)—see, e.g., A. Râsim, i. 443, note; Lane-Poole, xxiv. There are, however, puzzling references to debased *kuruşes* at an earlier period. Thus a *kuruş* current in 1654 is said to have contained as much copper as silver (see Belin, 331, citing Hammer, *History*; and cf. A. Râsim, ii. 259, note); and referring to events of the following year Na'îmâ mentions 'clipped and low-standard (*makṣûṣ ve kem-'ayâr*) *kuruşes*' (Belin, 334). It may be that these were Ottoman imitations of foreign coins, and that the innovation of 1688 was only the issue of a *kuruş* Ottoman in design as well as in origin.

[4] It weighed 6 *dirhems* (about 300 grains), whereas the *esedî* (Dutch) weighed 8½ (about 425 grains) and the *kara kuruş* (Austrian) weighed 9 (about 450 grains). The table of exchanges quoted on p. 52, n. 5, above lists its value at 160 *akçes*. It was perhaps modelled on a smaller Austrian coin—a dollar of some 300 grains' weight. Dollars of this type were at any rate counterstruck a few years later, under Muṣṭafâ II, presumably to supplement the Ottoman issue proper (Lane-Poole, xxiv, note, and plate vi, No. 418).

ing one-third as much again as its predecessor and consequently almost as much as the *esedî*. But subsequent issues of this '*ṭuğralî*' *ḳuruş*, as it was called, became progressively lighter, till by the terminal date of our survey those in circulation were no heavier than the first Ottoman *ḳuruş* of Süleymân II.[1] In the meantime the relationship between the three types of silver coin had been fixed at 3 *aḳçes* to the *para* and 40 *paras* to the *ḳuruş*.[2] This left out of account yet another silver piece first minted also under Süleymân II and called, misleadingly enough,[3] *zolota*. But the *zolota*, though distinguished by a particular name, was in fact, or at least came to be, no more than a multiple of the *para*, representing 30 *paras* or three-quarters of a *ḳuruş*.[4] Other multiples of the *para*, and both fractions and multiples of the *ḳuruş*, were also coined in the eighteenth century, so that a considerable range of native silver was then available. No Ottoman coin earlier than the nineteenth century bears any indication of its denomination, however; and all Ottoman minting down to the time of our survey was somewhat haphazard and irregular. It is not always certain, therefore, precisely what any individual coin of those still extant was intended to be. All that can be done is to judge by their weights and what we know from documents to have characterized the various types and issues.[5]

The gold coinage also was reformed at the end of the seventeenth century. Under Muṣṭafâ II it was found that debased *şerîfîs* uttered in Egypt and the African Regencies were driving those minted in Istanbul out of circulation; and in 1696–7 the former were called in and a new gold piece was struck.[6] This piece exactly resembles in style, and was evidently the pattern for, the *ḳuruş* that was to be introduced under Aḥmed III; that is to say, it bears on the upper half of the reverse the names of the Sultan

[1] Lane-Poole suggests that this heavier *ḳuruş*—it weighed about 400 grains—may have been modelled on a Dutch dollar weighing 415 grains, of which an example, like the Austrian dollar mentioned above, was also counterstruck under Muṣṭafâ II. Aḥmed III's *ḳuruş* was called *ṭuğralî* because, like its predecessor, it bore the Sultan's *ṭuğra* on the upper part of its reverse. The *ṭuğras* used on coins from this time forward were of the true design (see below, p. 55, n. 1).

[2] Aḥmed Râsim, ii. 256, 260, 262, notes.

[3] Misleading, that is to say, if, as is presumably so, the word is derived from the Slav root meaning 'gold'. Perhaps the Turks adopted the word as meaning merely 'money' or because their *zolota* was similar, in silver, to some Slav coin so called.

[4] Cf. Seyyid Muṣṭafâ, iii. 106, who, however, states, what cannot have been the case, that the original *zolota*, though worth 90 *aḳçes*, weighed 7 *dirhems*. It obviously cannot have weighed more than 4½ (or, approximately, 225 grains).

[5] Lane-Poole, xxiii–xxiii.

[6] Belin, 355; but Lane-Poole questions this explanation. According to Ismâ'îl Gâlib, the gold coins struck at Istanbul under Süleymân II and Aḥmed II, and known by the name of *fîndiḳ altînî* ('hazel-nut gold') were lighter than the old *şerîfî* by 0·05 grammes (¾ grain), and it was this deficiency that was remedied in the new *ṭuğralî* issue of Muṣṭafâ II.

and his father in a true *ṭuğra*,[1] with the mint and accession year below it. This use of the *ṭuğra* on gold pieces being an innovation, the coin too was known as *ṭuğralî*. Down to this issue the names of the reigning monarch and his father had always been inscribed in ordinary writing on the reverse of all gold pieces, while the obverse had been adorned down to the reign of Murâd III with the formula 'Striker of that which glitters, Lord of Greatness and Victory on Land and Sea'.[2] The new formula, which had been first introduced in Egypt under Murâd and gradually ousted the other, ran 'Sultan of the Two Continents and Emperor of the Two Seas, the Sultan son of the Sultan'.[3] The 'new gold pieces' or *ṭuğralîs* of Muṣṭafâ II weighed about 53 grains, like the old *şerîfîs*, and were worth 300 *akçes*.

Fifteen years later, however, in 1711 under Aḥmed III, the gold currency was again reformed. Alongside the *ṭuğralî*, but of fine gold and slightly greater weight, the old *şerîfî* or *sulṭânî* was revived.;[4] it was distinguished from the former by the transference of the *ṭuğra* to the obverse, and only the mint and the Sultan's accession date (1115) appeared on the reverse. This coin, at first called 'Islâmbûl gold',[5] but more popularly the 'chainy' (*zencîrli*), seems to have been given in Egypt the name of *funduḳî*,[6] and this (in Turkish *fîndîḳlî*) seems to have become its usual denomination. In addition, an entirely new and lighter coin was struck, of the same pattern as the *ṭuğralî*, but weighing only 40 grains (2·5–2·6 grammes); this was called the 'favourite' (*zer-i maḥbûb*).[7] Under Aḥmed's immediate successors, 'chainies' (or *fîndîklîs*) and 'favourites', together with their multiples and fractions, continued to be issued from the capital,[8] and *ṭuğralîs* were apparently minted only at Cairo.

The gold pieces minted at Cairo, however, of which many were current at the capital, soon came, it appears, to be somewhat debased.[9] In 1725, at any rate, when Dâmâd Ibrâhîm Paşa promul-

[1] The emblems used on coins from the reign of Murâd III to that of Aḥmed III were not true *ṭuğras*, but only monograms in *ṭuğra* form; see Lane-Poole, pls. iii and iv.

[2] *ḍâribu'l-naḍri ṣâḥibu'l-'izzi wal-naṣri fi'l-barri wal-baḥri.*

[3] *sulṭânu'l-barreyni wa ḫaḳânu'l-baḥreyni al-sulṭânu 'bnu 'l-sulṭân.*

[4] Aḥmed III issued also pieces of 5 and of 2 *şerîfîs*.

[5] Because the legend on the reverse read 'Struck at Islâmbûl' in place of the hitherto universal 'Struck at Ḳusṭanṭînîya'; see Part I, p. 218, n. 1.

[6] Because the nodules which formed its borders showed up strikingly against the plain field of the *ṭuğra* and suggested either the links of a chain or tiny nuts. The Egyptian issue is, however, often called 'Egyptian chainy' (*mıṣır zencîrlisi*). See Lane-Poole, xviii–xx; Belin, 375–6; Aḥmed Râsim, i. 443, note; Seyyid Muṣṭafâ, iii. 106; Ismâ'îl Ğâlib, 272–4. Cabartî always calls them *funduḳlîs*.

[7] From Persian *zär* ('gold') and Arabic *maḥbûb* ('beloved').

[8] Maḥmûd I also issued a gold piece larger than the *fîndîklî*, called after him *Maḥmûdîye* and weighing 1½ *dirhems*, but this was in less common use.

[9] The Cairo mint was controlled by a Turkish superintendent (*emîn ḍarbḫâna*),

gated a schedule of the rates, in *akçes* or *paras*, for the various gold coins in circulation, we find that whereas the 'new Istanbul gold' (presumably the 'chainy') was rated at 400 *akçes*, the Egyptian 'chainy' was rated at 330 (or 110 *paras*), and the Egyptian *tuğralî* at 315, while the *yaldîz altînî* stood at 375 and the *macar altînî* at 360.[1] In 1733 the coining of *fîndîklîs* in Egypt ceased by imperial order, and only *zer-i mahbûbs* were struck there.[2] At the same time, the steady debasement of the silver currency is seen from the valuation under Ahmed's successor Mahmûd I of the Istanbul 53-grain piece at 450 *akçes* and the 'favourite' at 330.[3] So far did this go in Egypt that in 1762 a commissioner was sent from Istanbul to inspect the currency, and the *para* or *medin* was revalued at a fraction over one-third of its original weight in debased metal.[4]

Such were the various coins minted by or under the control of the Sultans.[5] Before leaving this topic, we must, however, pursue a little further the history of the Egyptian currency under its Mamlûk Beys. The commerce of Egypt had long been hampered by the absence of an intermediate coin between the *medin* and the gold piece, a state of affairs which necessitated the import of European coins for large operations. Accordingly, 'Alî Bey, on taking control of the mint at Cairo, struck half-piastres and piastres of 20 and 40 *medins*, the latter of 4½ *dirhems* weight, i.e. half a *dirhem* short of the value established only eight years earlier.[6] On the restoration of nominal Ottoman control the control of the Mint was assigned to the *Paşa* on payment of *mîrî*, and the *Paşa* regu-

whose duties were defined in the *kânûn* (Digeon, 274–6; Barkan, 386–7, §§ 47–49). He was required to maintain the coinage at the same standard as that of Istanbul, and paid 582,447 *paras* in *mîrî* to the Porte, in addition to a present of fifteen purses to the *Paşa* (Estève, 334), presumably out of the profits on the mint (for which see Samuel-Bernard, 406–7; also Cabartî, iv. 140–1/viii. 318–19). The Egyptian currency is investigated in the *Description* by Samuel-Bernard, 'Mémoires sur les Monnoies d'Égypte' (ii. 1, 321–468), and there are references also in Cabartî (iii. 352–4, iv. 313/vii. 420–4 (abridged), ix. 320), which agree in general with, but occasionally diverge in detail from, the statements made by Samuel-Bernard. The gold employed at Cairo was supplied from the Sudan, through Jewish brokers (cf. Part I, p. 299).

[1] Belin, 388; Lane-Poole, p. xxxv; Ismâ'îl Ğâlib, 281 (where the Egyptian *tuğralî* is listed at 319); and cf. Cabartî, i. 104/i. 241. There is no mention in this schedule of the *zer-i mahbûb*.

[2] Cabartî, i. 146/ii. 9–10. Samuel-Bernard is in error in stating that the weight of the 'sequin' was reduced about 1757 to 2·6 grammes.

[3] Belin, 483; Ismâ'îl Ğâlib, 302.

[4] 1,000 *paras* (*medins*) to 125 *dirhems*' weight (385 grammes) of silver of 58 per cent. fine: Samuel-Bernard, 383, 388.

[5] For our purposes, we may neglect the copper coin called *mangîr*, the name of which is derived (according to a note in Ahmed Râsim, i. 445) from a Mongol word *mûnkûn*, meaning 'money'.

[6] Cabartî, i. 334/iii. 51; Samuel-Bernard, 333, 384. 'Alî Bey also introduced punching machines into Egypt (the weight being still adjusted by filing the edge of the coins), but they were destroyed after his death (Samuel-Bernard, 333, 345). His coins also were withdrawn from circulation (Cabartî, i. 371/iii. 132), probably because he had surreptitiously struck his own monogram on them.

larly sold his privilege to the Mamlûk *Şeyẖ el-Beled*,[1] with the result that the debasement of the currency proceeded apace. The standard of gold in the coins minted at Cairo fell from 99·6 to as low as 71, but the government insisted on their acceptance at the old value, to the indignation of the merchants, who declared them to be made of silver-gilt.[2] When, about 1789, the proportion of gold in the Constantinople sequin was reduced, the coins struck at Cairo were still further debased, in spite of imperial *fermâns*.[3] Simultaneously the value of the *medin* declined; by 1789 the weight per thousand had sunk to 100 *dirhems*, and the Porte, on issuing orders to re-establish the old value, was persuaded instead to authorize a further depreciation, so that by 1799 it had been reduced by successive steps to 73 *dirhems*, a percentage diminution of 41⅔ in the space of thirty-seven years.[4] In the same time the standard of silver had been reduced to 34·8 per cent., equal to a depreciation of almost 40 per cent.[5] Nevertheless, the exchange value of the *medin* remained much greater than its actual worth, since it was the principal coin employed in both wholesale and retail transactions in internal trade and overseas commerce, and the quantities minted were insufficient for these commercial needs.[6]

Our information for Syria and 'Irâḳ during the same period, though fragmentary, shows the same rapid depreciation. In Jerusalem Egyptian money was current; but Damascus, Aleppo, and Bağdâd struck their own coinage.[7] The process of debasement, already far advanced, was carried farther by Cezzâr Paşa in 1791, although the exchange rates remained a little higher than those at Cairo.[8] Rousseau notes the decline in the commerce of Bağdâd owing to depreciation of the currency, but gives no details.[9]

After this discussion of the actual coinage, we have still to men-

[1] Estève, 334; cf. Cabartî, ii. 59/iv. 81 (relating to 1781). For the *Şeyẖ el-Beled* see Part I, p. 227.

[2] Samuel-Bernard, 387.

[3] Cabartî (ii. 179/v. 69) reports an Imperial order of this year fixing the standard of the Egyptian gold coins at 19 *ḳîrâṭs* (i.e. 79, on the 24-*ḳîrâṭ* scale) and reducing the exchange rates as follows: 120 *paras* to the Egyptian gold piece, 140 to the *Islâmbûlî* (i.e. *zer-i maḥbûb*), 200 to the *fındıḳlı*, 95 to the *abû midfa'* or Spanish dollar, and 210 to the Venetian sequin. (Cf. Volney, ii. 275–6, for the slightly higher rates previously current.) It would appear that the standard of Egyptian gold actually rose slightly at the end of the eighteenth century; it was as low as 15$\frac{15}{32}$ carats in the eighties, and 16$\frac{24}{32}$ in the nineties. The French authorities maintained it at the latter figure.

[4] Samuel-Bernard, 383.

[5] Ibid. 388.

[6] In 1798 the official rates were 340 to the Venetian sequin, 300 to the *fındıḳlı*, 200 to the *zer-i maḥbûb* of Istanbul, 180 to the *zer-i maḥbûb* of Cairo, 150 to the thaler, and 142 to the French 5-franc piece (Samuel-Bernard, 393; Chabrol, 299–301, gives figures which represent the rates of some twenty years earlier).

[7] See Ismâ'îl Ğâlib, *passim*. In the seventeenth century the coinage of Bağdâd was regarded as the next highest in standard to that of Istanbul: *Travels of Evliya Efendi*, trans. Hammer, ii. 166.

[8] Ḥaidar, i. 165; and cf. Mich. Dam. 6.

[9] Rousseau, 118.

tion one peculiarity of the system of accountancy employed in the Central Treasury, namely, that both the *aḳçe* and the gold piece were reckoned by purses of varying content.[1] These were actual purses: the coin was weighed and sealed up in them and so deposited in the Treasury, from which the purses were in due course distributed to those whom the *Defterdâr* must pay. Thus in the 'budgets' of finance summaries we have mentioned the various items are generally reckoned in purses or half-purses of *aḳçes*, except as regards sums amounting to less than half a purse, when the actual number of *aḳçes* is shown. The content of a purse varied from age to age. Under the Conqueror and Bâyezîd II, 30,000 *aḳçes* made up a purse of silver and 10,000 *filûrîs* (then equivalent to 40 *aḳçes* each) a purse of gold. Under Süleymân the Magnificent purses of 20,000 *aḳçes* were the rule, whereas from the middle to the end of the seventeenth century this figure was raised to 40,000 and thereafter to 50,000. Accountancy was further complicated, at least in later times, by the coexistence of various types of purse, namely, the Istanbul, the *dîvânî*, the Greek, and the Egyptian, each containing a different quantity of silver,[2] while in the African Regencies yet another type was in use, containing only 1,000 gold pieces.[3] Quite apart from purses, moreover, *aḳçes* were also reckoned in 'loads',[4] which often enough were not whole multiples of purses, since these varied as we have indicated, whereas a load represented 100,000 *aḳçes*. In a single financial statement some items will be shown in purses, others in loads, and yet others again in *aḳçes*.[5] No doubt the clerks of the old *ḳalems* found these variants as easy to manipulate as we our pounds and guineas, florins and half-crowns. But when it is considered that their special notation[6] has not yet yielded up all its secrets, it will be seen that a finance account of the *ancien régime* is often more than a modern student can wholly unravel,[7] and in any case requires the reduction of purses and loads to *aḳçes* before even the figures take on an intelligible appearance.

[1] *kîse*, from Arabic *kîs* (cf. Part I, p. 122, n. 5) was the usual word; but *ṣurra* (also Arabic) is said to have been used in early times for purses of gold coins (see Aḥmed Râsim, i. 113, note). Hence the designation of the official placed in charge of the presents sent annually by the Sultans to the *Şerîfs* of Mecca: *Şurra Emîni*, 'Purse Commissioner'.

[2] D'Ohsson gives particulars of the last three. The purse most used in his day was the Greek (*kîsei Rûmî*) containing 500 *ḳuruşes* (equivalent to 60,000 *aḳçes*). The *dîvânî* contained 416⅔ *ḳuruşes* (equivalent to 50,000 *aḳçes* or half a *yük*—see below). The Egyptian (*kîsei Mişrî*), used only in that country, contained 620 *ḳuruşes* (equivalent to 25,000 *paras*: see above, p. 45, n. 2).

[3] Aḥmed Râsim, loc. cit.

[4] *yük* (Turkish).

[5] e.g. the 'summary' of the *Eyyûbî Ḳânûn-nâmesi* in Aḥmed Râsim, ii. 225 sq., notes.

[6] *ḳirma*; see p. 47 above.

[7] Cf. the remarks even of Seyyid Muṣṭafâ (ii. 100) on the obscurity of Ṭarḫûncu Aḥmed Paşa's summary.

Thus there remain some dark gaps in our knowledge of both the fiscal and the finance systems of the Ottoman state. From the information we possess, however, it is clear that the fiscal system was well shaped for the task it was originally created to fulfil. Although, like the whole Ottoman polity, it was mainly derivative, the rulers who first adopted it modified it intelligently to suit such features of the Ottoman state as were unlike those of its Moslem models. The system broke down chiefly owing to the coincidence of the depreciation of silver at the end of the sixteenth century with the growing corruption of Ottoman institutions, and was indeed exaggerated by the frantic efforts made by Grand *Vezîrs* and *Defterdârs* to adapt it piecemeal to circumstances unforeseen when it was framed. For the most part, no doubt, these functionaries, and the Sultans they advised, were quite incapable of foreseeing any but the most obvious consequences of such new measures as they might put into operation. It was probably fortunate for them that the prestige of traditional practice was strong enough to circumscribe their innovations within narrow limits. Uninstructed in economic principles as they were, they could only modify the rules of thumb they worked by in ways that promised immediate advantage. But if, in their ignorance, they had strayed farther from the traditional path, it seems probable that they would have fared even worse than they did.

It is extraordinary, however, that the central government seems to have made no attempt to revise the schedules of taxation except in the minor features that we have already noted.[1] Whether this is to be ascribed to respect for the established *ḳânûns*, or to the advantages accruing to the officers of the administration from the practice of tax-farming while the schedules remained at their old rates, it by no means follows that the dues and taxes actually levied upon the subjects remained stationary. The omissions of the Treasury were duly 'rectified' by the provincial authorities. Since the fullest information we possess as yet on this subject again relates to Egypt and Syria, we shall proceed to describe the actual situation in these provinces as it developed in the course of the eighteenth century.

IV. EGYPT AND SYRIA IN THE EIGHTEENTH CENTURY

In Egypt, from about 1700 or perhaps somewhat earlier,[2] the *multazims* had made a practice of exacting additional sums from

[1] See pp. 26 sqq. above, and cf. Muṣṭafâ Akdağ in *Belleten* of the Türk Tarih Kurumu, vol. xiii, pt. 51, p. 540.

[2] Lancret, 237, states that the practice 'is not well attested before 1700'; Estève, 310, that 'it goes back to a very distant date'.

their cultivators, ostensibly to meet various charges or to stabilize the customary 'presents'. These, collectively termed *muḍâf* ('supplementary') and afterwards 'old *barrânî*', become in course of time a regular charge. But during the later decades of the eighteenth century the growing needs of the *multazims* led to the multiplication of further charges, collectively termed 'new *barrânî*'.[1] Similarly, the provincial governors, especially in the time of 'Alî Bey, began to augment arbitrarily the *kuşûfîya* dues. These additions were consolidated about 1775 as a new tax, hopefully termed 'removal of wrongful dues' (*raf' el-maẓâlim*), but only a few years later a second tax was instituted, the provincial taxes being nearly tripled in consequence.[2] The Ottoman *Ḳaptan Paşa* Ḥasan attempted in 1786 to abolish the additional taxes but was unable to do so, with the result, as the historian Cabartî remarks, that these taxes, hitherto surreptitious, now acquired a kind of legality.[3] A parallel increase in taxation is recorded in Syria, where in the course of the century new taxes were devised to meet financial deficits and the cost of buying farms.[4]

This augmentation of the taxes is certainly explained, to a large extent, by the steady devaluation of the coinage. The dollar in the middle of the century was worth, in Egypt, 85 *paras*; by 1798 it was worth 150. Rapid as the increase in taxation was, it could not keep pace with this fall in money values, and Estève calculates that the total sums due by taxation in 1798, although almost double the amount established in 1526, fell short of the real value of the latter by about 25 per cent.[5] The fault thus lay not in the raising of the taxation in itself, but in the failure of the Ottoman administration to regularize the increase, so leaving it to the individual action of the governors and *multazims*.

In so far as these taxes were regularly levied, however, they were less destructive in their effects than the abuses of the second order: the arbitrary impositions to which the cultivators were exposed.

'Since [the register] does not include the so-called incidental and

[1] Even at the end of the century, however, it was still the practice to show on the registers of taxation the ostensible purpose of the various charges, such as purchase of camels and other livestock, presents to *multazims*, &c. The total figures for the additional imposts of the *multazims* are given by Estève, 309, as: old *barrânî*, 47,350,673 *paras*; new *barrânî*, 48,718,849.

[2] Estève, 308: cf. Cabartî, ii. 83/iv. 127–8 (translation inexact). The *raf' el-maẓâlim* amounted to 16,274,839 *paras*, and the second tax (*farḍat el-taḥrîr*, 'due for exemption', i.e. from *avanias*) to 7,096,194 *paras*, plus a charge for collection amounting to 8,944,547 *paras*. It should be remembered that each *Bey* held the government of the same province for one year only (Lancret, 248).

[3] Cabartî, ii. 141, 146/iv. 274, 288.

[4] Kurd 'Alî, *Ḫiṭaṭ el-Şâm*, ii. 292. He notes also the frequency with which landowners failed to pay their dues at this period, with the consequence that the government had to employ military force.

[5] Estève, 320–1.

customary expenses, nor those which, being levied by the military, were not even inserted on the assessment-sheet drawn up for each village, and since almost every year the tyranny of the bey, the greed of the *multazim*, the needs of the government and the rapine of the Arabs raised these to an amount as large as that constituted by the sum of the regular taxes, it is easy to reconcile what we have said on the moderation of the written impositions with the oppression and misery which in fact overwhelm the cultivator of the most fertile soil in the world.'[1]

The *Kâşifs*, or lieutenants of the Beys, were constantly on tour of their provinces with their Mamlûk attendants; and many villages were under the direct supervision of resident *Ḳâ'im-maḳâms*, who were theoretically paid by the Bey but forced the peasantry to furnish most of their requirements.[2] Moreover, from the time of 'Alî Bey onwards, few years passed without the levying of extraordinary contributions from the villages to meet the expenses of the military armaments and constant warfare between the Beys.[3]

While the peasantry doubtless suffered more severely from these exactions, the artisans and merchants of the cities were by no means exempt from similar abuses. It is probable that down to the time of 'Alî Bey in Egypt, and of Cezzâr Paşa in Syria, the close association of the artisans with the *ocaḳs* gave them a certain measure of protection. But with the change in the composition of the military forces[4] this guarantee ceased to be effective, and the chronicle of the last thirty years of Mamlûk rule is filled with accounts of the seizure of goods, animals, and money from merchants and artisans of all classes, with or without pretext. It is unnecessary to insist on the opening which the complicated system of recognized dues afforded for all kinds of unauthorized exactions, especially as these 'privileges', like most other sources of revenue, came in course of time to be concentrated in the hands of the rich and powerful Mamlûks. The continual increase of monopolies and duties is attested also by the fact that a large number of these did not carry a liability to payment of *mîrî* on the proceeds, and were, therefore, presumably established arbitrarily after the regulation of 1526;

[1] Estève, 321. He notes, however (p. 323), that the peasantry of Upper Egypt were far less affected by these abuses than those of Middle and Lower Egypt.

[2] Lancret, 249; cf. Chabrol, 317, and for the exactions of the collectors Cabartî, ii. 179/v. 70–71 and *passim*. The same in Syria: Volney, ii. 262–4. See also in *Recueil de Firmans Impériaux Ottomans, Sommaires* (Cairo, 1934), a *fermân* (No. 10) dated 1191 (1777) ordering a judicial process against the *Kâşif* of Ġarbîya for exactions from the peasantry.

[3] e.g. in 1771, Cabartî, i. 374/iii. 93; 1777, ii. 15/iii. 261; 1782, ii. 72/iv. 100 (inaccurate); 1787, ii. 154/v. 11; 1788, ii. 173/v. 56, &c. A special tax levied for the marriage of Ibrâhîm Bey's daughter: ii. 227/v. 158. Cf. Volney, ii. 117: the religious of Terra-Santa, who farmed the taxes of Nazareth, were forced to pay a present of 1,000 piastres each time Ẓâhir al-'Omar married a wife, 'et il avait soin de se marier presque toutes les semaines'. Cf. also B. Lewis, *Notes and Documents*, 20.

[4] See Part I, pp. 224, 229.

of these the most important was the salt monopoly, with which was united 'an infinite number' of duties on edibles, animals, &c., at village markets.[1]

'It would be impossible [writes Estève] to cite a single branch of industry or of consumption which was exempt from similar and analogous duties. . . . The *multazims*, the Beys, the *Serdârs* and *Ağas* holding local military commands, and the tax-farmers, all multiplied them in the districts under their authority as often as they could find occasion to do so. From this arises that confused complication which leaves so few means of distinguishing the charges imposed on the Egyptians by one or other of these parties. . . . In general the merchant and the cultivator were halted at every step by burdensome fees.'[2]

Our sources even allow us to trace in outline the successive stages by which an original *avania*, or at times even the simple payment of a gratuity, became established as a new regular imposition by the sheer force of precedent.[3]

Leaving aside for the moment the growth of monopolies, it would appear that the extortions and forced loans from the merchants[4] would not have proved so ruinous in themselves had they not been accompanied by an ignorant and grasping policy in regard to customs duties. Shortly after the middle of the century the administration of this department became markedly more oppressive. The farms of the customs in Egypt (and probably also in Syria) had hitherto been held by Jews, who paid the appropriate *mîrî* on their offices. 'Alî Bey broke with this usage by granting the farm of the Egyptian customs to a Syrian Christian, Ḥannâ Faḫr,[5] and it was henceforth held by Syrians[6] until the last eight

[1] Estève, 363–4. The *multazims* also imposed a duty known as *ḥamla* on the articles consumed in their villages (ibid.). These duties were, at least at the end of the eighteenth century, farmed out annually by auction (Cabartî, iii. 79/vi. 152), which in 1801 realized a sum of 18,000 purses (45,000,000 *paras*): Cabartî, iii. 191, 192/vii. 40, 45. At Medînet el-Fayyûm the market dues were farmed for 140,000 *paras* and the farmer netted 170,000 *paras* by a regular tariff on all goods exposed for sale (e.g. ten *paras* per *ardebb* on wheat) except spun cotton and fabrics, the dues paid by the corporation of weavers (see p. 41) apparently exempting them from further taxation (Girard, 626).

[2] Estève, 364; cf. Volney, ii. 42 (*avanias* on the corporations at Aleppo). On the 'privileges' of the *Ağas* at Alexandria see Olivier, ii. 10–11.

[3] Savary (Eng. tr. 2), i. 119, 189: exaction of a new tax from European visitors to the Pyramids, in return for protection against beduin tribesmen; Cabartî, ii. 179–80/v. 71: establishment of an imposition on river-borne traffic; Olivier, ii. 224: imposition of road tolls and entry dues on Frank merchants in the coast towns of Syria.

[4] See on these, e.g. Cabartî, i. 309; ii. 59, 73, 122, 123; iii. 15; iv. 82, 103, 250, 254.

[5] See Part I, p. 311.

[6] Estève, 350; cf. Volney, i. 190. In 1785 the amount paid by the Syrian farmer of the customs was 1,000 purses (ibid. 189), and in 1784 Cezzâr Paşa farmed the customs of his province for the same sum (ibid. ii. 278).

or so years of Mamlûk rule, when Murâd Bey took over the customs administration himself and ran it by means of agents at the ports.[1] The duties and export charges at once began to rise, and although the stimulation of commerce during the short reign of 'Alî Bey temporarily offset this,[2] during the twenty-five years that followed the merchants of Egypt were gradually stripped of both profits and capital, and sea-borne trade inevitably declined.[3] In the interior, moreover, caravans found themselves exposed to a succession of unauthorized and vexatious tolls,[4] apart from the 'presents' exacted by Beduin chiefs.

These abuses affected the European merchants scarcely less than Ottoman subjects. In Egypt the French consuls had until 1730 enjoyed (at a price) the support of the Janissary *ocaḳ*, but under the later Mamlûk Beys the *avanias* to which they were subjected increased steadily in number and magnitude.[5] The English merchants withdrew altogether from Egypt in the last third of the century.[6] Moreover, their Levantine competitors in the European trade gained a strong advantage through the control of the customs by their fellow countrymen and by the influence which they were able to use with the Beys.[7] The government of Murâd Bey brought matters to a head. The French merchants were practically assimilated in status to Ottoman subjects and exposed to such extortions that within a few years their trade was brought to the verge of ruin.[8] In Syria conditions were no better. The European trade

[1] His agent at Alexandria was Seyyid Muḥammad Kureym, who had begun his career as a public weigher; he 'increased the customs duties and confiscated the property of merchants, expecially of the Franks' (Cabartî, iii. 62–63/vi. 124).

[2] Between 1768 and 1774 French trade with Egypt (although 'Alî Bey treated the French merchants with great harshness) amounted to between 3½ and 4½ millions of livres, as compared with from 2½ to 3 millions before and after (Masson, ii. 596).

[3] e.g. coffee paid a duty at Suez of 59 piastres per bale (costing at Mokha about 95 piastres) prior to 1783; in that year the duty was increased by about 14 piastres, and in the time of Murâd and Ibrâhîm Beys the Suez coffee trade was completely ruined: Volney, i. 187; Estève, 350. Additional charge levied at Rosetta and octrois on goods entering and leaving the town: Estève, 352–8; Cabartî, iii. 169/vi. 317; decline of population in Rosetta from 25,000 to 12,000 since 1783: Olivier, ii. 51.

[4] Unauthorized duties imposed on caravans entering Egypt from the south: Estève, 348.

[5] Masson, ii. 302–3. The main *avanias* to which the European merchants were exposed consisted of forced loans and failure to pay for goods supplied: Girard, 678. See also generally F. Charles-Roux, *Autour d'une route*, 193–4, 334.

[6] Wood, *Levant Company*, 165–6. In 1773 a Greek was appointed to act as English agent at Alexandria.

[7] Masson, ii. 304: the jealousy of the 'Copts and Greeks' encouraged the Beys in their policy towards the Franks. But there is no evidence of Copt merchants engaging in the European trade, and it is probably the Syrians that are meant; see Part I, p. 310.

[8] Olivier, ii. 144 sqq.; Masson, ii. 312. It is well known that this supplied the pretext for Bonaparte's invasion of Egypt.

at Aleppo, which formerly maintained some twenty-five merchant houses, had by the end of the century so declined that Olivier found only nine French and two Italian houses still active.[1] Ẓâhir al-ʿOmar had endeavoured to attract European merchants to ʿAkkâ, but there were constant troubles and disputes.[2] Even the *Paşas* of Damascus joined in the movement, and in 1769 the Venetian agent at Jaffa was beaten by the agents of ʿOṯmân Paşa el-ʿAẓm until he paid 60,000 livres.[3] It must, however, be admitted that the European merchants, by their mutual jealousies, their misconduct, and their evasions and even contraventions of orders, often played into the hands of the local authorities.[4]

The conduct of the accountancy department was equally affected by the rapid worsening of the economic organization. It is true that in Egypt the accounts were presented in a form very little changed from that established by Süleymân, but they had become a grotesque misrepresentation of the actual state of affairs. The *kuşûfîya* dues, in spite of their increase, were rarely applied to their ostensible purposes, but were appropriated by the Beys, with the result that the provincial troops were reduced to skeleton cadres and the irrigation canals were allowed to fall into disrepair. The assignations on the Treasury, which had long been treated as a form of currency, being sold in the markets and regarded as bills payable to the bearer, began to depreciate at an alarming rate[5] and were bought up by the Mamlûks, who alone had the power to force the Treasury to honour them. The entries in the register of accounts consequently bore little or no relation to the actual destination of the money. Of the 30 million *paras* for military pay, the 8½ millions for pensions to *Şeyḫs*, widows, and orphans, and the 14 millions for religious services,[6] by far the greatest portion went into the pockets of the Beys and their attendants. The principal changes occur under the heads of the tribute to the Sultan's Treasury and the appropriation for the annual pilgrim caravan to Mecca, the former having sunk to 16,783,451 *paras*, and the latter expanded to 42 million *paras*, an increase largely explained by the fact that in the frequent Mamlûk duumvirates of

[1] Olivier, ii. 307–8. The English factory was closed down altogether in 1791, but some merchants stayed on in Aleppo for a few years: Wood, 162–3.

[2] Volney, ii. 8; Masson, ii. 289.

[3] Volney, ii. 16–17.

[4] Estève, 349; Charles-Roux, *Échelles, passim*; cf. Masson, i. 471–2 and ii. 280: 'D'ailleurs elles [les avanies] étaient encore trop souvent provoquées par l'inconduite ou par les imprudences des Francs: banqueroutes frauduleuses, exploits de corsaires, entreprises galantes, excès de zèle des religieux, sans-gêne des résidents.'

[5] Cf. Cabartî, iii. 212/vii. 97. Until the middle of the eighteenth century they were sold at a high premium, and frequently constituted as charitable or religious endowments (see Ch. XII below); but cf. below, p. 65, n. 4.

[6] See above, p. 42.

this period one of the two Beys always held the office of *Emîr* of the Pilgrim Caravan, either permanently or alternatively with that of *Şeyẖ el-Beled*.

Even the tribute figures, however, were largely illusory. ʿAlî Bey had refused to send any sums to Istanbul, and his successors, although they restored payment, gradually whittled down the amount on various grounds and pretexts. Thus by 1791 some 12½ million *paras* had been deducted by successive augmentations on account of the Mecca Caravan, until the personal allowance of the Commander stood at 20 millions.[1] During the last decade of the century the annual surplus was never allowed to exceed 7½ millions, various deductions being made from it for imaginary purposes.[2] Moreover, whereas Süleymân had laid down exact instructions and appropriations for the transport of the tribute to Istanbul by the *Paşas* of Egypt, by this time the Porte had to ask for the tribute and to send a special officer to fetch it.[3] A still more illuminating commentary on the times is furnished by the item 'Cash pensions payable at Mecca and Medîna', which in the original register stood at 5¼ million *paras*, and had now reached 16 millions. Of this sum nearly 8 millions were payable at Cairo to influential *Şeyẖs* and other persons, who had obtained the transfer to this head of the revenues hitherto secured on worthless paper assignations.[4]

That the *Efendis* were involved in the general corruption of these last decades seems to be an unavoidable conclusion from the facts already stated, since without their connivance such extensive misappropriations of state funds could hardly have been carried

[1] Estève, 381–9. This allowance was ostensibly for the purpose of hiring the military escort and paying subventions to the beduin tribes. As the Ottoman power declined the depredations of the Arabs increased, and the entire caravan was plundered in 1786 and again in 1792.

[2] e.g. 3 million *paras* for repairing the fortifications of Cairo, and 1½ millions for other fortified places; or again 2,783,451 'for expenses ordered by the *Şeyẖ el-Beled*'. The dispatch of the cereals and other furnishings in kind also was suspended or in arrears: see in *Firmans Impériaux Ottomans* (Cairo, 1934), 6, a *fermân* (No. 19) dated 1211/1796, complaining that the rice and lentil tribute had not been sent regularly 'for a long time past', and ordering their immediate dispatch.

[3] The last occasion when the *ẖazne* was sent to Istanbul according to the old usage was in 1180/1767: Cabartî, iii. 218/vii. 103; but already in 1173/1760 the Porte had sent a special mission to Egypt 'to collect the arrears of *mîrî*': Murâdî, iv. 249. Cf. also Lancret, 256, and Cabartî, ii. 191/v. 90.

[4] But not to much effect, apparently, for Estève (p. 384) notes that the 7,925,044 *paras* transferred under this head 'were no longer paid under the rule of Murâd and Ibrâhîm', i.e. were seized by the Mamlûks and their agents. The augmentation of the pension list by 10¾ millions of *paras* (including these transfers) is dated by Estève in 1138/1725, which would appear to indicate that the assignations were beginning to depreciate in value in the first quarter of the century. Cabartî (ii. 200/v. 111—translation inexact) apparently refers to this as 'the Sanctuaries and Sundries account' (*defter el-ḥarameyn wal-sâyira*). Murâdî, iii. 132, also refers to the transfer of a *wakf* to the *ḥarameyn* account.

through.[1] A specific instance is afforded by the misappropriation of the sums assigned for *kürekçi*, which it was the special business of one *Efendi* to administer. This contribution was intended to pay for the transport of rubbish from Cairo to the Rosetta and Damietta mouths, but for a very long time past this sanitary service had been totally neglected.[2] It is significant also that in the last years of Mamlûk rule the office of *Rûznâmecî* was put up for sale and frequently changed hands.[3]

Over and above the conversion of the greater part of the existing sources of revenue to their own use, the Beys had already towards the end of the Mamlûk period taken the first tentative steps towards a more revolutionary exploitation of the resources of the country. It began with the practice, followed with increasing frequency, of evicting the *multazims* and seizing their estates, which were then managed by agents.[4] About the same time the number of monopolies was increased, and forcible means were employed to effect the disposal of their products.[5] A still more serious derangement of the economic system was just beginning to arise before the French expedition, when Murâd Bey, who had already (as has been noted) monopolized the customs,[6] began to purchase a great part of the wheat crop at low rates or on credit and to sell it for cash at an excessive price.[7] It is very probable that the inspiration in this case came from Syria, where Cezzâr Paşa was engaging in a comprehensive monopolization of the entire marketable produce in his *eyâlet*. The Mamlûk system, in which the ruling Bey (like the earlier Mamlûk Sultans) held but a precarious authority over the other Beys, his peers in status and potentially his rivals, would seem to place very great obstacles in the way of such a diversion of public and private property to the profit of one man. Yet the student of history cannot help drawing a suggestive parallel between the oppressive and monopolistic régime which preceded the extinction of the Mamlûk Sultanate at the beginning of the

[1] Lancret, 258, however, states that they enjoyed a good reputation for 'honesty, character and education', and Cabartî gives a very good character to the last of Murâd's *rûznâmecîs* (iii. 291/vii. 296; cf. however, iv. 81/viii. 177).

[2] Estève, 307, who adds: 'La cessation de la dépense à laquelle il devoit pourvoir, a produit, dans les environs du Kaire, des collines factices d'où s'élèvent continuellement des exhalaisons et une poussière désagréables et malsaines'; cf. Cabartî, i. 383/iii. 162. Similar negligence was shown by the *efendi* who had the duty of accounting for the expenses charged to the Sultan for the upkeep of the main canals, bridges, and forts: Lancret, 253.

[3] Cabartî, ii. 156/v. 16.

[4] Cabartî (i. 309/iii. 16) accuses 'Alî Bey of setting the example; and cf. Ḥaidar, i. 76.

[5] As early as 1750 an 'appalto' of senna was created and foreign merchants were forced to purchase quantities of senna, to their grievous loss: Masson, ii. 303–4.

[6] See p. 63 above.

[7] Olivier, ii. 162, note.

sixteenth century,[1] and the economic situation of Egypt in the years immediately preceding the second and final destruction of Mamlûk rule. The same impoverishment of agriculture, industry, and commerce, the same fiscal exactions and monopolization of commercial products in an endeavour to screw more money out of the country and its people to pay for a swollen military budget, the same official venality, the same interference with the traditional social usages, all gave warning that a new crisis was approaching in the affairs of Egypt.

The classic instance of monopolization in the eighteenth century is, however, supplied by the rapacious government of Aḥmed Paşa Cezzâr in the *eyâlet* of Ṣaydâ. The example had already been set by Ẓâhir al-ʿOmar, or rather by his Minister, the Syrian Greek Ibrâhîm el-Ṣabbâğ, who 'seized all the objects of commerce; he alone sold the wheat, cotton, and other goods; he alone bought the woollens, indigo, sugar, and other imported merchandise'.[2] Cezzâr Paşa continued and improved on this programme. He took possession of the agricultural lands and had them cultivated for his own profit, associated himself with the artisans and merchants, constituted himself their banker and money-lender, fixed arbitrary prices for their goods, and farmed out the customs at excessive rates.[3] The customs duties were raised in consequence, and the protests of the French merchants (who held a practical monopoly of the commerce of Ṣaydâ as against their European competitors) were cut short by their expulsion, maintained even in the teeth of imperial orders.[4] The historian of Damascus is less explicit, but the terms in which he writes of Cezzâr's administration leave no doubt that he practised the same exactions and monopolizations there as well, and that all protests were stifled by executions and probably also by evictions.[5]

In addition to the profits gained by these methods, Cezzâr screwed up the revenue from direct taxation by farming out the towns and districts of his province for almost incredible amounts. The Druse *Emîrs* of southern Lebanon had hitherto paid an annual tribute of 80 purses to the *Paşas* of Ṣaydâ.[6] By exploiting the rivalries of the leading Druse families, he raised the farm of the

[1] Cf. G. Wiet, in *Précis de l'histoire d'Égypte*, ii (Cairo, 1932), 260–3.

[2] Volney, ii. 29.

[3] Ibid. 75, 116; Olivier, ii. 262–3; Charles-Roux, *Les Échelles*, 140. Volney estimates his annual profit from these sources at between seven and eight thousand purses.

[4] Masson, ii. 293–7; Charles-Roux, 141. The European trade could still, however, be carried on via Leghorn and on coasting vessels by Syrian merchants, who were more amenable to his exactions.

[5] Mich. Dam. 6, 13; and cf. the passage quoted Part I, p. 224.

[6] Volney, i. 448, 454; the Maronite country (Kesrawân) was farmed by the *Emîr* Yûsuf in 1783 for an additional thirty purses (ibid. ii. 65).

Druse country in successive stages until at one time it reached 3,000 purses.[1] The 'Christians of Beyrût' were farmed out for 500 purses,[2] and even the smallest towns, with their surrounding agricultural lands, were made to produce large sums for his Treasury.[3] It is probable also that he was the originator of the system of requiring from each town and village a quantity of produce in kind in addition to the money taxes.[4] With such resources Cezzâr Paşa was little pressed to find the 1,500 purses which constituted the annual tribute of his *eyâlet*, and which he was careful to acquit regularly. He differed also from Ẓâhir al-'Omar in another respect: his intendants and treasurers were chosen from among his own mamlûks, although (a rather surprising fact after his savage treatment of the Jewish *ṣayârif* at Damascus) his principal *ṣarrâf* was a Jew, Ḥâyîm Farḥî.[5]

The direct effects of Cezzâr's measures were probably less momentous than their indirect effects. The Moslem populations of the southern Syrian coast, living in disjointed and economically backward communities, were too disconnected from the main body of Moslem society for their immediate misfortunes to produce any noticeable dislocation. The persecutions by which the *Muṭawâlî* organizations in the Cebel 'Âmila were completely and finally broken up need not evoke any excessive sympathy with the victims, since the *Metâwila* (as they were known) constituted an irreconcilable element of disorder both in the Lebanon and in northern Palestine.[6] The equally ruthless subjugation of the Lebanon, on the other hand, was destined to have important consequences; since both directly, by the imposition of Turkish control, and indirectly, by converting the Druse *Emîrs* into instruments of financial oppression on behalf of the Turkish authorities,[7] Cezzâr prepared the way for the collapse of the feudal system and for the Lebanese expansion which followed in the nineteenth century. Similarly, his interference with the economic organization of Damascus, relatively brief though his periods of governing the

[1] Cezzâr, after his first deposition of Yûsuf, offered to reinstate him on payment of an annual tribute of 1,200 purses, but Başîr finally obtained the post by offering 250 purses a month: Ḥaidar, i. 150, 159. This figure was not maintained, however, and by the end of his governorship Cezzâr was content with 80 purses a month from Başîr: ibid. ii. 407.

[2] Ibid. i. 160.

[3] Cubeyl farmed to a Maronite for 120 or 150 purses: ibid. 172; Ḥâsbeyyâ farmed to a Druse *Emîr* for 60 purses: Volney, ii. 119. Cezzâr's exactions from the religious at Nazareth provoked a *fermân* from the Porte ordering restitution, but his only reply was the assassination of their dragoman: Olivier, ii. 263.

[4] It will be seen later that this system was in force in the *eyâlet* of Şaydâ in the time of his second successor, 'Abdallâh Paşa (1818–32).

[5] Ḥaidar, ii. 408, 436, &c.; Miḫa'îl Muşâḳa, 52–53.

[6] See Volney, i. 474.

[7] e.g. rack-renting of the Biḳâ' by the Druse *Emîrs*: Mich. Dam. 25.

eyâlet of Şâm had been, must without doubt be taken as the starting-point in the process of economic disintegration which can be traced through the nineteenth century in Syria. For the example which he set found other imitators besides the Mamlûk Beys in Egypt.[1] The all but universal shout of joy which went up at the report of his death in 1804[2] proved to be premature. Not only did his successors in the Mamlûk 'dynasty' of Ṣaydâ and ʿAkkâ maintain (with varying severity, according to their temperaments) his organization in that *eyâlet*; several of the *Paşas* of Damascus also, in the early decades of the nineteenth century, steadily pursued a policy of monopolization.[3] But it was left to his most illustrious pupil, Meḥmed ʿAlî, to carry this policy to its farthest limits both in Syria and in Egypt.

[1] Already during his lifetime the *Ağa* who farmed the revenues of Gaza attempted to monopolize the alkali used for soap manufacture there, but succeeded only in destroying the industry, since the beduins would not bring it for the price he paid, nor the citizens buy it at the price he demanded: Volney, ii. 109.

[2] Mich. Dam. 14; cf. Ḥaidar, ii. 408–9 ('God gave men rest from the tyranny of Cezzâr and cast him to eternal punishment'); also *Le Moniteur*, report from Constantinople dated 30 May (1804): 'La mort de Dgézar-Pacha paraît avoir fait ici une sensation assez agréable' (quoted in preface to Olivier, ii).

[3] Especially Yûsuf Paşa (1807–10) and Süleymân Paşa of ʿAkkâ (1810–12): Mich. Dam. 20–28.

CHAPTER VIII

THE RELIGIOUS INSTITUTION

THE term 'Islamic Society' applied to the social organization which we are analysing implies that its distinguishing features are related in some way or another to the religion of Islâm. Yet in those groups and activities which have been considered up to this point there is little which can be regarded as specifically Islamic; on the contrary, the organization of village and industrial life belongs rather to a stage of social evolution which finds close parallels in many non-Islamic regions of Europe and Asia; and that of the Court and the army, though of a more peculiar type, is based upon principles to which such Islamic elements as they display appear to be purely incidental. Before we go on, then, to examine the various functions which were specifically allotted to the religious institution, it is desirable to ask ourselves in what manner the religion of Islâm, apart from its ecclesiastical and legal side, stamped its peculiar imprint on the society as a whole, in order that the place and contribution of each religious function may be adequately understood and appreciated.

A partial reply to this question has already been given in the first chapter of this book, in discussing the place of the *Şerîʿa* in the Empire. Substance and detail can now be added in the light of the subsequent chapters, although a full appreciation of the social function of Islâm must wait until our survey is completed.

Here again it is only in the light of the historical process that the situation can be grasped. From the very first, Islâm stood in the minds of its adherents not for a body of religious beliefs only, but for a community which was animated by those beliefs and had the duty laid upon it of actively promoting them. The earliest political pronouncement of the Prophet Muḥammad was 'Ye are one Community over against Mankind'. Henceforth the Religion and the Community were inseparable in theory. No distinction was made at first between the secular and the religious offices of government; the Imâm was omnicompetent, and even in later times sovereignty carried with it an authority which was more than purely secular. But in practice the religion had to create the larger community. The task, already difficult in the limited area of Arabia, became infinitely more so when, as a result of the conquests of the first century, the religion was spread from Central Asia to the Atlantic. Wide variations in language, in culture, in prior religious tenets, and in customs and institutions precluded any prospect of early unification. The imposing Empire of the early Caliphs, so far from forming a unity of any kind, consisted of an ill-assorted group of provinces held together by the military forces and moral prestige of the central government. The Community was represented by a relatively small body, chiefly of Arabs, who formed a governing caste in the midst of vast populations which had submitted to their rule. This fact was destined to have two consequences of the utmost importance. It associated Islâm, in the minds of Arabs and subjects alike, with Arabdom, and it gave to the form of Islâm patronized by the governing classes (for already sectarian differences had begun to appear amongst the Arabs) the character of a state Church or 'established' religion. The result of the first of these consequences was to place Arabicization before Islamization in the process of moulding the constituent elements of the Empire into a unity. The result of the second was to cause those who accepted Islâm but who were hostile to the governing classes to lean towards the sectarian rather than the 'established' interpretation of the religious creed. This is most clearly seen among the Persian converts; the nobles and the official class generally adopted the *Sunnî* creed of the Arab aristocracy, while the population of the great cities and some parts of the country-side showed a preference for the extremer forms of Şî'ism, or even, in some provinces, for the *Ḫâricî* or literalist doctrine.[1]

The gradual spread of Islâm among the subject peoples did not, therefore, imply that a corresponding degree of religious unity had been attained. On the contrary, whereas the disputes amongst the Arabs themselves had been political rather than doctrinal in essence, the infiltrations from without widened and deepened the cleavage. Thus, by an apparent paradox, the stronger Islâm grew in numbers, the weaker became its power to promote a genuine religious unification and the more persistently was the established church (already rent internally by disputing parties) challenged by the *Şî'î*—and more pacifically by the *Şûfî*—sectaries. Yet such divisions were almost inevitable in a church which was itself rapidly expanding in an age of expanding material culture. They were, indeed, a sign of vigour and religious zeal—however much the latter, from the orthodox point of view, might appear to be misplaced.

By the end of the ninth century A.D. the contrast between the *Sunnî* or established church, and the *Şî'î* or opposition sects, appears in its most intense form in the open revolutionary movement led by the *Ḳarmaṭîs* or 'Carmathians'. To the former belong the Court, aristocracy, and army, the bureaucracy, the *'Ulemâ* or

[1] The inheritance of pre-Islamic religious beliefs also played a part in this, which may, however, be neglected here.

representatives of the orthodox religious institution, and all who were associated with these groups. To the latter belong large sections of the lower classes in the towns and country-side and of the nomadic Arabs on their frontiers. With such a distribution of forces the consequences of open revolt might be foreseen, but forcible suppression of the rebels could not in itself furnish a solution of the underlying problem.

The real strength of the orthodox party lay, however, as we can now see, not in its stronger military force but in its more practical idealism. Whereas Ṣî'ism never ceased to be conscious of its character as a sectarian and opposition movement, the orthodox '*Ulemâ* held unswervingly to the conviction that they represented the Universal Church,[1] and that the task before them was to realize in fact the theory of the Religious Community. We have already seen the consequences in political theory of this steady effort to maintain the doctrine of the 'Community in being',[2] and the same spirit of tolerance and realism with which they patiently laboured to accommodate unwelcome actualities in this field was shown in the wider field also. Their attitude and conduct may be labelled as unheroic, but it saved them from falling into the irreparable error of persecuting their opponents, save in a few isolated and untypical instances, and it is impossible not to admire the conciliatory and yet tenacious way in which they pursued their object.

It is of the essence of *Sunnî* mentality—and implied in the very term—that what has been established by sound tradition as good and true must not be departed from. But this conservative (or, as some would put it, reactionary) element in the intellectual outlook of the '*Ulemâ* was, and has continued to be, counterbalanced amongst at least a proportion of them by a certain openness of mind as to what might be regarded as consistent with this postulate. This flexibility enabled the orthodox church to take in successive centuries a series of steps by which it incorporated one by one all but its irreducible opponents, even if at a price. It is outside the scope of this work to enter into this process in detail, but a glance at the manner in which it was accomplished is not without importance, both for an understanding of the religious situation in the eighteenth century and as in some sort a precedent and object-lesson for more recent developments.

The first task of the early *Sunnî* '*Ulemâ* was to close the breach in their own ranks caused by the intrusion of Greek philosophy and dialectic. The conservative majority, in reaction against the

[1] This is implied in the word *Sunnî*, which, though interpreted as 'adhering to the *Sunna* or Tradition of Muḥammad and the Elders', means in fact 'adhering to the *Sunna* of the Community'. On the other hand, the *Şî'î* writers speak of those who deserted Ṣî'ism for Sunnism as 'joining the majority'.

[2] See Part I, p. 27.

'advanced' and non-traditional theses of its admirers, refused at first to have anything to do with scholasticism. But when it was proved, after a century and more of controversy, that scholasticism might be used as a weapon in defence of tradition,[1] the battle was virtually won, though its echoes were to rumble on for a long time to come.

The problem of Şî'ism was more complex. But the *Sunnîs*, *'Ulemâ* and laymen alike, had from very early days shared the sympathy of the *Şî'a* for the house of 'Alî, though not their political or dogmatic tenets. This sympathy offered a bridge by which, in the fifth and sixth centuries of the Hegira era, when revolutionary Şî'ism had spent itself, the orthodox church (by means of the alliance with Ṣûfism which will be referred to immediately) was able to win over a large proportion of those who had been attracted to Şî'ism for social or political reasons. Henceforth Şî'ism seemed to be the creed of a dying sect, until Şâh Ismâ'îl the Ṣafavid in the sixteenth century A.D. fanned the embers into a blaze and made it the national or 'established' church in Persia. But within the Ottoman Empire, Şî'ism survived only as the religion of small and isolated groups of mountain-dwellers in parts of Anatolia, Syria, and Yemen, except for the strong *Şî'î* bloc in lower 'Irâḳ.

In both these advances the orthodox establishment had yielded little in comparison with what it had gained; it had not compromised its rigid adherence to the Tradition of the Community, though it had admitted, on the one hand, a vein of arid scholasticism and, on the other, a vein of sentimental attachment to the House of the Prophet. In the third, and most difficult, task which lay before it, the incorporation of the mystical doctrine of the *ṣufî* adepts, it was led into a path of compromise which in the long run threatened to submerge the orthodox teachings entirely. This danger, though implicit from the beginning, was not immediately obvious. Ṣûfism, in its theological aspect a compound of asceticism and gnosticism, represented in its social aspect a movement for social justice and equality by appealing to the conscience of individuals. Like Şî'ism, it spread mainly amongst the lower middle classes (and in these circles it retained down to the nineteenth century several traces of this early association); unlike Şî'ism, it relied on pacific methods and was relatively disorganized. But since they relied on religious conversion for the attainment of their ends, the *ṣûfî* leaders were strongly opposed to the worldliness of the orthodox *'Ulemâ*, and it was this opposition that formed the chief obstacle to more harmonious relations. On the other

[1] This was the movement associated with the names of el-Aş'arî in 'Iraḳ and el-Mâturîdî in Ḫorâsân, at the beginning of the fourth Islamic century (tenth century A.D.).

hand, there were many features in the life of orthodox circles in the fourth and fifth centuries that drove earnest religious teachers to seek in Ṣûfism a means of deepening religious conviction, and through their efforts a bridge was built. The orthodox, though with some hesitation, agreed to countenance the *ṣûfî* methods, on the understanding that the *Ṣûfîs* would observe the rites and subscribe to the official teaching of the established church.

It must not, of course, be imagined that any agreement was drawn up, or that an arrangement of this kind was ever formally sanctioned. The Islamic religious structure, true to its egalitarian principles and conscience, had never countenanced any form of external organization or any kind of hierarchy. Although it recognized *icmâ'*, the 'Consensus' of the doctors, as a valid source of doctrine, there was neither Council nor Curia to promulgate its decisions. The volitional element that runs through all the pre-Ottoman Islamic institutions, and that made their efficacy dependent on their appeal to the will rather than on careful regulation of duties and powers, was naturally at its strongest in this sphere. To 'broaden down from precedent to precedent' was characteristic of Islamic usage long before the birth of the British Constitution. Each forward step was secured by tacit assent on the part of those who were most qualified to express an opinion, and from whom the rank and file took their cue. No one was prevented from opposing and from trying to gain support for his opposition, but within a generation or two controversy on the point at issue would die out. So it was in this instance also, although the magnitude of the issues involved and the events which followed raised up a current of opposition, more especially on the part of the *Ḥanbalîs* (the most hostile to 'innovations' of the orthodox 'schools'), which lasted for some centuries.[1] But in the long run the *Ḥanbalîs* were routed, and their school sank to the position of a tiny remnant until the events of the nineteenth century brought fresh life to it.

At first, however, the compromise with *taṣawwuf* offered little ground for serious apprehension and much for congratulation. It seemed that the *'Ulemâ* would henceforth be in a position to exercise some control over the movement and restrain it from dangerous excesses, and they had gained in return valuable allies in their task of creating a united community. It was a moment of opportunity, and there were many indications that it was being put to good use. The first results, indeed, were all that could be hoped for. Within the ancient boundaries of Islâm the *ṣûfî* teachers took the lead in a new

[1] Note, however, that the founder of the Ḳâdirî order, 'Abdu 'l-Ḳâdir el-Gîlânî, was a *Ḥanbalî*, and the mother convent of the order at Bağdâd remains *Ḥanbalî* to this day.

campaign, which captured a large share of the former *ṣî'î* organizations, and for the first time brought the great mass of the population within the fold of the orthodox Community. Simultaneously, in the vast territories which were in process of annexation to the Domain of Islâm, notably in Anatolia, Central Asia, India, and Indonesia, they were the real missionaries of the conquering faith.

Yet for all this success, there were several elements in the movement that disturbed the confidence of the *'Ulemâ*. The leaders in this campaign were often men who, though of undoubted piety and purity of character, were rude and unlettered, and sometimes set little store by the rituals and dogmas of the orthodox. In many instances they were men who themselves sprang from the people amongst whom they laboured, and who shared in consequence their deep-seated religious traits and traditions; and these traits showed themselves in a tendency to relax the strict principles of orthodox Islâm, and to compromise with ideas and practices incompatible with them, although they had the merit of easing the path of conversion. All over the Islamic world there were to be found larger or smaller groups which acknowledged their adherence to the Community, but whose conceptions of orthodoxy were derived from the teachings of such preachers and their followers, who revered them as saints and ranked them above the official *'Ulemâ*. The legacies of animism, of paganism, of Christianity, of Hinduism, often remained almost intact under a thin veneer of Islâm.

Simultaneously, in the old-established lands of Islâm, the *ṣûfî* movement began to create an organization for itself, as noted teachers formed groups of disciples in convents and these in turn founded daughter-convents in other lands and cities. Thus, by an unpremeditated process, in both town and country, great 'brotherhoods' or *ṭarîḳas* were established with loose hierarchies of teachers and their own independent schools, rituals, and meeting-houses, each with a vast body of adherents who looked mainly or entirely to them for spiritual guidance. Ṣûfism became a profession, with a body of teachers rivalling the *'Ulemâ* and often enjoying a wide influence, especially amongst the artisans and lower classes. But the penalty had to be paid in a gradual hardening of the entire structure, as each order relapsed into a rigid traditionalism; and it was not long before the seeds of decay began to appear.

A third factor which contributed to give Ṣûfism the character of an organization rivalling the orthodox church was the elaboration of its theology along independent lines. This was the work of Ibnu 'l-'Arabî (d. 1240), a Spanish Moslem whose spiritual affiliation goes back to the pious but unlettered Berber revivalists of the preceding century, and whose tomb is still one of the principal sanctuaries of Damascus. His monist doctrines intensified the natural pantheistic bent of *ṣûfî* thought and supplied the philosophic basis for a vast literature in the next centuries.

The *'Ulemâ*, having opened the gates to 'orthodox' Ṣûfism, were but little prepared for the flood which poured through them. Nevertheless, they could not (and there is no evidence that they desired to) repudiate the alliance, and their only means of counteraction—since all hopes of controlling the *ṭarîḳas* were illusory—was to utilize the influence of the moderate *ṭarîḳas*, such as the *Ḳâdirî* brotherhood, and to strengthen their own instrument of education and propaganda, the *madrasas* or religious seminaries.[1] The enormous numbers of *madrasas* founded during the thirteenth, fourteenth, and fifteenth centuries in almost all the Islamic lands give evidence of the vigour with which this policy was carried out.

It was during this period that the Ottoman Empire came into existence, and we shall have occasion in a later chapter to discuss in greater detail its relations with the rival religious organizations.[2] For the time being, we may note that it bestowed its patronage on both alike, while the policy to which we shall refer in a moment led the *'Ulemâ* to place a greater value upon their association with the brotherhoods. The outcome was a kind of symbiosis of the two institutions, each contributing to the support of the other, though not without occasional friction. The outward sign of their closer co-operation was not so much the spread of the more 'orthodox' *ṭarîḳas—Ḳâdirîs, Naḳşbendîs, Ḫalwetîs*[3]—over the whole central area of the Empire, as the gradual inclusion of the whole body of the *'Ulemâ* in one or other (and sometimes more than one) of these brotherhoods, a process which reached its culmination during the eighteenth century. By this time, membership of the religious orders was practically synonymous with the profession of Islâm; there were so few who stood outside them that when it occurs the fact excites remark.[4] The more considerable *şeyḫly* families had their private *ṭarîḳas*, affiliated to one or other order, and even the *Ḥanbalîs* no longer remained unaffected.[5] In return, the orders taught their members the ritual and ethics of Sunnism, and to pay due respect to the *'Ulemâ*; and at the principal religious festivals and ceremonies *'Ulemâ* and *dervîşes* with their brotherhoods participated on an equal footing.

[1] The original purpose of the foundation of *madrasas* had been largely to combat the influence of Şî'ism.

[2] See Ch. XIII below.

[3] See pp. 197–9 below.

[4] Murâdî, iii. 148.

[5] e.g. Murâdî, ii. 305; iii. 192; iv. 85. Note also the large proportion of Ṣûfistic works in the lists of books written by *'Ulemâ* as given by Cabartî and Murâdî. The term *şeyḫly* here and below is applied to families which were hereditarily associated with the religious institution.

It was thus only within the Ottoman period that the ideal of unity was at length achieved within the *sunnî* Islamic fold, even if at a price and in a way which the fathers of the church could not have foreseen. With the effects of this compromise in dogmatics and religious ethics we are not at present concerned, except to note that in all circles the primitive teachings were to a greater or less extent overlaid by a superstructure of Ṣûfism, and that, as in all other religious systems, a wide gulf existed between the conceptions and principles of the doctors and the ideas and practices of the proletariat.[1] But the social effects were correspondingly great, since, almost for the first time, the religious institution embraced the whole fabric of Moslem society.

It has already been pointed out[2] that that society was composed of a vast number of small social groups, almost self-governing, with a wide gap interposed between the governing class of soldiers and officials and the governed class of merchants, artisans, and cultivators. The religious institution was thus charged with a double task: on the one hand, to fill the major gap, and, on the other, to knit the separate small groups together by supplying a common ideal and a common organization superimposed upon the group loyalties and if need be overriding them in a wider common loyalty. One other institution also embraced them all, that of administration, but its function, as we have seen, was negative and oppressive. The necessities of economic life linked individual groups together, more closely perhaps than religion did, but their range was narrowly limited. Even language was a dividing rather than uniting factor, since Turk and Arab were mutually unintelligible, and the dialects of each region stamped their speakers as foreigners to the men of the others. Religion alone offered that positive link which enabled the Turk, the 'Irâḳî, and the Egyptian to feel the warmth of a common possession, and brought the peasant into organic relation with the Sultan.

But it is not enough to regard the relationship as one solely of a common religious allegiance, important as that aspect may have been in creating a common ground and softening the asperities of official intercourse. Nor must the binding element of common obligation to the *Şerî'a* be over-emphasized; for, as we shall see, there were limits to the community of law, and the *Ḳâḍî*'s functions went beyond the simple administration of justice. The teachings of orthodox Islâm, by their pursuit of the egalitarian ideal and consequent emphasis on the dignity of the individual believer, might even be said to have had a dissociative effect so far as the ordinary urban and agricultural populations were concerned. When all were equal and co-ordinate the purely pan-

[1] See also pp. 203 sqq. below. [2] See Part I, Ch. IV.

Islamic appeal could produce only accumulation without cohesion. It could focus opinion, but it lacked the means of action. The great benefit which the alliance of orthodoxy with Ṣûfism had brought to the religious institution was that it supplied a concrete organization which spread over all ranks of society and found a place in it for every member. Each village, each craft, each group had its own *ṣûfî* 'lodge', affiliated to one of the great *ṭarîḳas*, and enrolled in its brotherhood. It was behind the banner of its *ṭarîḳa* that each took part in the religious festivals, and the ceremony both symbolized their conviction that all were indeed parts of a single continent, and expressed the means whereby that association was nourished and sustained. The connexion which existed between the craft-guilds and the orders has already been described,[1] and it was the existence of similar connexions throughout the social range which in reality constituted the cement of the whole system.[2]

It must be admitted, however, that even with this support, the religious institution fell short of creating a complete unity. For the orders themselves, though well organized internally, lacked an organization to knit them to one another, other than their common membership of the Community. Each was an autonomous unit, and, more serious still, there were marked lines of cleavage between them. As will be more fully shown in a later chapter, the moderate or orthodox orders were sharply opposed to the antinomian orders, with the grave consequence that the Janissaries, who belonged to the antinomian *Bektâşî* order, were dissociated from the main body of the religious institution to a considerable extent. Another significant line of cleavage was between the principal Turkish orders, the *Mevlevîs* and *Bektâşîs*, and those which had the widest following in the Arab provinces, the *Ḳâdirîs*, *Rifâʿîs*, *Şâḏilîs*, and various local orders. During the seventeenth and eighteenth centuries, it is true, an attempt was made to remedy this division by the *Ḫalwetî* and *Naḳşbendî* orders, but though they met with some success, especially amongst the *ʿUlemâ*, they did not materially affect the situation. Moreover, full co-operation between *ʿUlemâ* and *Ṣûfîs* was hindered by the contempt with which the former regarded the popular orders and their practices.

Yet when all due allowance is made for these elements of weakness, the fact remains that the religious institution was successful to a remarkable degree in creating a sense of corporate unity between the varied racial and social groups, hitherto often

[1] See Part I, p. 277.

[2] It is astonishing that this has been so consistently overlooked by Western observers. Even Lane, although he states that 'almost all the darwishes of Egypt are tradesmen or artisans or agriculturists' and refers to the fact that almost all the members of the *Ḳâdirî* order in Egypt were fishermen, nowhere explicitly brings out the importance of this relationship.

antagonistic, which came within the range of its influence. The measure of its success can be most fully gauged from the contrast offered by those who stood outside it. The Ottoman government, by leaving the task of social unification to the religious institution, condemned the non-Moslem and heterodox Moslem groups under its control to exclusion from effective incorporation in the Ottoman structure of society; and it was for this reason, and not from deliberate anti-Christian policy, that the *millet* system proved fatal to it in the end. The same considerations apply to the *Şî'îs* of 'Irâḳ and Syria, to the *Yezîdîs* of Mesopotamia, and to all other dissident Moslem groups, except that in these cases it was their own hostility to the *ṣûfî* orders rather than any regulation on the part of the government that condemned them to isolation. Since it had come about that only through membership—direct or indirect—of the *sunnî* community could the individual achieve his social orientation in the *Dawla*, the more successful the *sunnî* religious institution was in this office the more it emphasized the relegation of all others to the outer margins.

While it was true, however, that the Empire was officially the patron and protector of Islâm and the *Şerî'a*, the development we have just traced was not due to its initiative or even to its encouragement. For we must be careful to avoid confusing the religious institution in its social aspects with the political state. Church and state in Islâm were one only in the realms of theory. The religious institution, it is true, claimed not merely to control the state but to be itself the state; but long experience had compelled it to recognize the existence of a civil power which it did not in fact control. Hence it was another characteristic feature of the *sunnî* religious institution that from the early days of Islâm it was not only inclined to hold aloof from the state, but had shown more than a tinge of hostility towards it. Fear of anarchy, as we have seen,[1] had led the *'Ulemâ* to condone the steady encroachment of the military power and the usurpation of authority by military Sultans, but they pursued with all the more determination the task of building up their own institution on independent lines. Moreover, the feeling of hostility to the state was even more marked in *ṣûfî* circles, although they consistently preached a doctrine of quietism; and the alliance of orthodoxy with Ṣûfism tended in consequence to strengthen the current of opposition to state interference.

The effect of this was to create eventually a sharp line of demarcation between the state and the religious institution. Each had its own functions and rarely overstepped them. The state was concerned with military, administrative, and economic affairs; the

[1] Part I, p. 31.

religious institution with doctrine, law, education, intellectual life, and social relations. The universalism of the Church, with its converse of exclusivism, was therefore independent of and unaffected by the local political situation. While it taught submission to established authority—especially when, as in the Ottoman Empire, that authority endeavoured to govern in accordance with the *Şerî'a*—it was no part of its duty to organize the life of the community in relation to a particular political structure, least of all amongst those who stood outside its own borders. On the contrary, the fundamental task of the *'Ulemâ* was to ensure that, no matter what political changes might come about, the religious institution, with all that it stood for, should remain unshaken.

Moslem Sultans and governors, too, for their part, had learned to reckon with this situation, and had consequently adopted a peculiar two-sided attitude towards the religious leaders. On the one hand, they were careful to cultivate their goodwill by outward deference, by giving their support to religious activities, by creating endowments and building mosques and *madrasas*, and by avoiding as far as possible any violation of religious usages or of the persons of the *'Ulemâ*. On the other hand, they endeavoured to exercise some form of control over them through the officers to whom they 'delegated' their own religious functions. Of these officers the two most important were the *Ḳâḍî* and the *Muḥtasib*. Both were in principle religious functionaries—the one charged with administering the legal provisions of the *Şerî'a*, the other with maintaining public morality. In reality they had much more extensive duties. The *Ḳâḍî*, as we shall see, took but a small personal share in legal business, but was expected to maintain a close supervision over all administrative acts; and in particular, himself an *'Âlim*, he was the intermediary of the government in its dealings with the *'Ulemâ*. The *Muḥtasib* was a subordinate judicial officer whose function of preventing and punishing all sorts of fraudulent and dishonest dealings made him a valuable instrument of control over the guilds and lodges of the artisans and other classes of townsmen.

This dual policy was inherited by the Ottoman state amongst its other legacies from earlier Islamic states, and was developed with characteristic thoroughness by the Ottoman Sultans. The genuineness of their religious conviction and of their patronage of the religious life need not be called in question; but with that tendency towards centralized organization which is seen in all their administrative enactments, it is not to be wondered at that they attempted to apply it also to the religious institution. How far they were successful in controlling it will appear from the following chapters.

CHAPTER IX

THE 'ULEMÂ

IT was suggested in the preceding chapter that the office of the *'Ulemâ* was to maintain the Islamic Community as an integral institution united and homogeneous in its structure and principles, indifferent to distinctions of race, and independent of the political organizations which might from time to time claim to govern this or that portion of Moslem territory. In contrast to the ruling institution, whose power and authority derived from military force, the religious institution rested upon the voluntary submission of men and women to the ideals for which it stood. Its strength as an institution and the power which its members were able to wield was therefore dependent on the degree to which, firstly, these ideals continued to command general recognition, and, secondly, the *'Ulemâ* continued to enjoy general respect as their representatives and defenders.

The first essential function, then, of the religious institution was to indoctrinate all ranks of society (including the members of the ruling institution) with habits of thought and principles of action and judgement in conformity with its ideals. The second was to raise up and maintain a body of scholars and teachers who would by their learning safeguard the principles upon which the religious institution was founded, and by their manner of life win the respect and affection of the people. Both of these tasks called for the organization of education, in the narrower sense, and to this we shall devote a separate chapter.

The foundation of the religious institution was *'Ilm*, 'Knowledge' in the sense of Sacred Learning, and the acquisition of some portion of *'ilm* was the necessary condition for admission into the ranks of the *'Ulemâ*, 'Those who Know', i.e. the possessors of *'ilm*.[1] But although *'ilm* remained in principle one and indivisible, the growth and organization of the religious institution compelled some differentiation of functions and services. At a relatively early stage a broad distinction was created by the specialization of some scholars upon the theory and practice of the Sacred Law; this study was termed *Fiḳh*, and those who specialized in it were *Fuḳahâ* (sing. *Faḳîh*). Nevertheless, this did not form a sharp line of division, since every *'Âlim* studied at least the principles of *fiḳh*, and every *Faḳîh* had some knowledge of the disciplines which formed the staple of Moslem education. Among the *Fuḳahâ*, in

[1] *'Ilm* is the verbal noun or infinitive of the Arabic verb *'alima*, 'know', and *'âlim* (pl. *'ulamâ*) its active participle.

turn, there was a distinction between the scholastic students of the *Şerî'a* and those who, as *Ḳâḍîs*, or 'givers of decisions', administered it in the law courts under delegated authority from the Imâm or the secular ruler. The ceremonial conduct of public prayers and other devotional exercises brought about a similar specialization of duties among the *'Ulemâ* who were attached to the service of the mosques, as will be explained later. Still a third division appeared when the foundation and endowment of college-mosques (*madâris*, sing. *madrasa*, in Turkish *medrese*) and of professorial offices of various kinds encouraged the rise of a specialized body of teachers.

Although these distinctions and divisions were at no time rigid—so that even in the Ottoman Empire and down to the present day teachers, preachers, legists, and *Ḳâḍîs* moved from one office to another—the tendency towards specialization was further reinforced by economic and political causes. In the earliest centuries it had been a common opinion that learned duties, because of their connexion with religion, should not be performed for gain, and that *'Ulemâ* should, if not possessed of independent means, earn their livelihood by other occupations.

The first breach with this principle was the payment of *Ḳâḍîs* by the 'Abbâsid Caliphs; then, as time went on, the increasing profusion of endowments for mosque services and educational posts in the *madrasas* provided an assured source of income for the bulk of the *'Ulemâ* and considerable wealth for some. But this in turn carried with it a certain loss of independence. *Ḳâḍîs*, as government servants, were more especially liable to pressure on the part of the administration, which they must be singularly upright and resolute to resist; and among the strictly pious, in consequence, they enjoyed no very high esteem. In spite of the fact that the discharge of a judge's duties was, apart from this embarrassment, regarded as a meritorious service to the community, very many examples could be cited of the refusal by *'Ulemâ* who had acquired a high reputation for rectitude, beginning with Abû Ḥanîfa himself, to take office as judges in order to avoid the risks of contamination.

While these risks were less in the other learned professions, the provision of state pensions and salaries for certain mosque duties and the organization of the *'Ulemâ* in corporations, each headed by a local *Re'îs* with powers of admission and ejection, allowed governments to bring a measure of pressure upon them also. At certain times and in certain states, notably the Mamlûk Sultanate of Egypt, the intervention and control of the secular power had already gone a considerable way, tempered only by the characteristic fluidity of Islamic institutions, the *esprit de corps* of the

'*Ulemâ*, and the respect which they inspired by their generally high level of rectitude. But it was reserved for the Ottoman Sultans to attempt a thorough-going regulation of the religious institution.

During the first century of Ottoman rule the religious life of the expanding Empire was, as we have repeatedly observed, dominated by more or less heterodox influences, which had, indeed, affected the '*Ulemâ* themselves in some degree. Nevertheless, as guardians of the *Şerî'a*, they had always tended to reconcile them as far as possible with orthodox teaching. The '*Ulemâ*, whom the Ottoman Sultans were bound to employ, made it their aim, accordingly, to influence Ottoman government in the direction of orthodoxy,[1] but their progress seems to have been slow. The Sultans are said to have established *Ḳâḍîs* in towns as they acquired them,[2] and the third of the line, Murâd I, at the beginning of his reign already felt the need for a *Ḳâḍî*-in-chief, whom he entitled *Ḳâḍî 'l-'asker* or (in Turkish construction) *Ḳâḍî-'asker*, Judge of the Army, since this dignitary followed his headquarters about in the field, instead of remaining at the capital.[3] But even as late as the beginning of the fifteenth century learned men were scarce in the Empire, or at least insufficient to satisfy its growing needs. The Sultans accordingly imported them from neighbouring lands,[4] and by using them for the instruction of their born subjects, as well as for immediate governmental purposes, created by the end of the century a learned corps of sufficient size and capacity for their requirements.

Since the provision of *madrasas* was necessary for this purpose it was accordingly the Sultans' care to found and endow such centres of learning, particularly in their three successive capitals Bursa, Adrianople, and Istanbul. The *madrasas* of these three cities enjoyed a special eminence, while those of Istanbul were naturally the most honoured, as they were the most numerous of all. To obtain any government post of the type to which he might aspire, a learned man must not only have studied but also have taught in a *madrasa* and possess a certificate declaring him eligible for appointment. To obtain any of the more important of such posts he must have been trained in a *madrasa* of one of these royal cities, and to obtain those of the highest grade he must have been trained in a succession of *madrasas* in Istanbul itself. By the time

[1] Cf. P. Wittek, *The Rise of the Ottoman Empire* (London, 1938), 42–43.

[2] *Die altosmanische Chronik des 'Āšiḳpašazāde*, 20.

[3] The Mamlûk Sultans had already established the practice of appointing army judges in Egypt and Syria, but these were inferior to the *Ḳâḍîs*-in-chief; see Gaudefroy-Demombynes, *La Syrie à l'époque des Mamelouks* (Paris, 1923), pp. lxxvii, 161, 209, &c., and for the earlier history and organization of the institution, E. Tyan, *Histoire de l'organisation judiciaire en pays d'Islam*, ii (Beirut, 1943), 289–306.

[4] See 'Oṣmân Nûrî, i. 265.

of Süleymân, *'Ulemâ* aspiring to high office were required to pass successively first as students, and later as professors, through twelve of them in a fixed order.[1] This educative process might occupy as long as forty years.[2] Promotion from one grade to another was accorded, after a candidate's proficiency had been certified, by seniority. Consequently many candidates contented themselves with no more than part of the full course, and were then appointed to such subordinate posts as suited their attainments.

By this time a hierarchy of learned posts had been established and in a manner unprecedented in Islâm; indeed, it has been suggested that the Ottomans, in so organizing what came nearest in their polity to a state Church, were influenced by the example of the Greek Orthodox hierarchy under the Byzantines. Already before the conquest the *Ḳâḍî-'asker* had risen to a position of political power greater than had ever been enjoyed by chief *Ḳâḍîs* of the past, with the result that, during Meḥmed II's reign, a Grand *Vezîr*, jealous for his own, persuaded the Sultan to double the post and create a second *Ḳâḍî-'askerlik*, to be styled 'of Anatolia', whereas the original office should be styled 'of Rumelia'.[3] But the influence of the *'Ulemâ*, if this move in fact reduced it in comparison with that of the ruling institution, was restored under Süleymân the Magnificent by the official recognition of the *Muftî* of Istanbul as head of the learned corporation, under the title of *Şeyḫü 'l-Islâm*.[4]

[1] See Cevdet, i. 111, and p. 146 below for details of this scheme.

[2] So D'Ohsson, iv. 486 sq. Seyyid Muṣṭafâ (ii. 90) puts the usual time required for students in the seventeenth century at from fifteen to twenty years.

[3] The Grand *Vezîr* was Ḳaramanî Meḥmed Paşa and the change was made in 1480: *Encyclopaedia of Islam*, art. 'Ḳāẓi-'Asker'.

[4] For *Muftîs*, see below, Ch. X. III. That the *Şeyḫ* attained pre-eminence only in the reign of Süleymân seems to be generally accepted; see, e.g., *Encyc. of Islam*, arts. 'Ḳāẓī 'Asker' and 'Shaikh al-Islām'. Nevertheless, the *Şeyḫ* is referred to as already *Re'îs* or Chief of the *'Ulemâ* in the *Ḳânûn-nâme* of the Conqueror published in *T.O.E.M.*, No. 13, Appendix, p. 10. His relationship to the *Ḳâḍî-'askers* is not there specifically mentioned, though he and the Sultan's *Ḫoca* (see below, p. 90) are said to be in a higher category than all the *Vezîrs* and to take precedence of them, while the *Vezîrs* take precedence of the *Ḳâḍî-'askers*. Moreover, he and the *Ḫoca* are placed so nearly on a level with the Grand *Vezîr* that of the latter it is said that 'it is fitting for the Grand *Vezîr* to take the lead of them' (*üstüne almaḳ*) only 'out of propriety' (*re'âyeten*). Though there are evidences of later redaction in the text of the *Ḳânûn-nâme* (cf. introduction, 4), especially in the frequent, though not invariable, doubling of the *Ḳâḍî-'askers*, whereas the *Ḳâḍî-'askerlik* of Anatolia had not yet been created, it is hard to believe that the passage referred to above has been interpolated. Again, in the section devoted to the forms of address to be used to various dignitaries set forth in the same *Ḳânûn-nâme* the *Şeyḫ* (here called *Muftî*), the *Ḫoca*, and the *Ḳâḍî-'askers* (plural here) are placed together in this order, and the actual specimen form supplied is one for a *Şeyḫ* (p. 30).

It may also be remarked that the second *Muftî* of Istanbul, *Mollâ* Ḫusrev, became first *Ḳâḍî-'asker* (before the conquest), then *Ḳâḍî* of Istanbul, and finally, after a period of retirement, *Şeyḫ* (*Encyc. of Islam*, art. 'Khosrev Molla'). His successor, Şemsu 'l-Dîn Kurânî, likewise became *Şeyḫ* after being earlier

There seems to have been more than one reason for this development. It has been suggested, again, that the office of *Şeyh* was created to parallel that of the Oecumenical Patriarch. The elevation of a *Muftî* (i.e. a consultative jurist), rather than a *Ḳâḍî* (as Moslem precedent would have indicated), was certainly due to the activity displayed under the Sultans from the Conqueror to Süleymân in *Ḳânûn*-making. For *Ḳânûns*, as we have explained, were supposed to harmonize with the prescriptions of the Sacred Law; and when framing them the officials of the ruling institution naturally applied for decisions upon these prescriptions to the *Muftî* of the capital. That this was their practice may be seen from the form in which some (but not all) early *Ḳânûn-nâmes*, or collections of *Ḳânûns*, were cast. They are in fact collections of *fetwâs*: questions put to the *Muftî* by the authorities, together with his replies.

Another theory accounting for the peculiar position of the *Şeyhü'l-Islâm* sees in his office an imperfect imitation of the 'Abbâsid Caliphate under the Mamlûk dynasties of Cairo. For the fiction was maintained, down to the conquest of Egypt by Selîm I, that the Mamlûk Sultans derived their authority from these Caliphs. The Cairene 'Abbâsids owed their fictitious authority solely to their birth. Nevertheless, they were probably regarded as in some sense hallowing the rule of the Mamlûks, and it may well be that the mystical traditions on which the early Ottoman state was nourished survived the encroachments of Sunnism strongly enough to require that the Sultan's civil authority should be supported by a dignitary whose functions were exclusively religious, comparable in honour to the Grand *Vezîr*.

Regarded ideally, indeed, the office of *Şeyh* was in a sense superior to that of the Sultan himself, since he might issue a *fetwâ* declaring a Sultan's deposition to be required by the exigencies of the *Şerî'a*. Nor might war be declared, or policies, such as the slaughter of the Sultan's male relatives, be pursued without the *Şeyh*'s official sanction. But the Sultan's supremacy was in practice usually assured by his ability to dismiss a *Şeyh* who opposed his wishes, and appoint a more amenable successor. It was only in the seventeenth and eighteenth centuries, when the Sultans had lost their absolute control of affairs, that *Şeyhs* were

Ḳâḍî-'asker (ibid., art. 'Kurānī'). It therefore seems likely that the *Muftilik* was already in the fifteenth century regarded as a post superior to that of *Ḳâḍî-'asker*. Possibly the change introduced in the reign of Süleymân regarded the *Şeyh*'s authority over *Mollâs* and other learned officers rather than his rank (cf. Seyyid Muṣṭafâ, i. 114).

As for the term *Şeyhü 'l-Islâm*, it had long been one of the honorific titles applied to eminent *'Ulemâ* before it was adopted more or less exclusively for the *Muftî* of Istanbul under the Ottoman régime; see *Encyc. of Islam*, art. 'Shaikh al-Islām'.

sometimes able to command sufficient support in the ruling institution or among the inhabitants of the capital to oppose them with success, and even then they very often suffered subsequently for doing so.

From the time of Süleymân the *Şeyḫü 'l-Islâm* was ranked virtually equal with the Grand *Vezîr*.[1] Both were the only officials to receive their investiture at the Sultan's own hands. At ceremonies the two advanced together so that neither should take the lead of his fellow. When either paid a ceremonial visit to the other he was received with equal, and peculiar, honours. The *Vezîr* had, of course, the greater power. But the *Şeyḫ* enjoyed the greater esteem, and the fact that he stood outside the Sultan's service was marked by the necessity in which the latter was placed by custom of paying him periodical visits. The influence of the *Şeyḫ* was such indeed that only when he and the *Vezîr* could work in harmony was either secure in office; otherwise their mutual intrigues led soon to the fall of either one or the other. The Grand *Vezîr* was bound to keep in constant touch with the *Şeyḫ* on state affairs. He did this (since the *Şeyḫ* was not a member of the *Dîvân*) by paying him frequent calls, incognito, to obviate ceremony. When the *Şeyḫ* was required to issue a *fetwâ*, the official application was preceded by informal consultations between the ministers of the Porte, on the one hand, and not only the *Şeyḫ*, but also the other principal *'Ulemâ*, on the other. The *Şeyḫ* was, indeed, so much involved in political business that he was obliged to maintain a special assistant, called *Telḫîṣci*,[2] to act as his intermediary with the Porte, as well as a secretary-general to control his chancery. His household was managed, like that of a *Paşa*, by a *Kâḫya*, who also administered the pious foundations that were confided to his inspection; and the private, as opposed to the governmental, applications for *fetwâs* that were addressed to him were dealt with in a special department of his office, called *Fetvâ-ḫâne*, controlled by a commissioner known as the *Fetvâ Emîni*. All these offices were filled by *'Ulemâ* of a special grade.[3]

Immediately below the *Şeyḫü 'l-Islâm* in the hierarchy of the learned came the *Ḳâḍî-'askers* of Rumelia and Anatolia, and below them again a number of other *Ḳâḍîs*, who together with the two former and the *Şeyḫ* constituted the highest order of the *'Ulemâ*. The *Ḳâḍî-'askers* and these *Ḳâḍîs* were dignified by the title of *Mollâ*,[4] meaning lord; but as this title was commonly applied also

[1] See Seyyid Muṣṭafâ, i. 114.

[2] Cf. Part I, p. 364 and note.

[3] D'Ohsson, iv. 490, 501–6, 508–12, 514–15. The adjutancies of the *Şeyḫ* were given to *'Ulemâ* who had qualified to be *Mollâs* or *Muftîs* and were awaiting appointment.

[4] *Mollâ*, or more properly *Môlâ*, and *Menlâ* (an alternative often used in state documents) are both corruptions of the Arabic *Mawlâ*, 'lord, master', otherwise

to judges of the second order we propose to refer to those of the first as 'Great' *Mollâs* by way of distinction.

The *Ḳâḍî-'askers* enjoyed one distinction that the *Şeyḫ* did not: they had places in the Imperial *Dîvân*. They, on some occasions, and certain of their colleagues among the Great *Mollâs* on others, were the learned men that assisted the Grand *Vezîr* in his duties as a magistrate. Moreover, they conserved some of the special powers that they had enjoyed before the elevation of the *Şeyḫ*. When creating the second *Ḳâḍî-'askerlik* the Conqueror had divided the functions formerly discharged by the single *Ḳâḍî-'asker* more or less evenly between the two, though according a definite pre-eminence to the *Ḳâḍî-'asker* of Rumelia, which increased as time went on. Thus the *Ḳâḍî-'asker* of Rumelia was to accompany the army when it operated in Europe, and had the nomination of all European *Ḳâḍîs*, other than *Mollâs* (who were nominated by the *Şeyḫ*), and mosque ministers; whereas the *Ḳâḍî-'asker* of Anatolia discharged similar duties and enjoyed a similar authority in the Asiatic provinces. The *Ḳâḍî-'askers*, moreover, dealt in their respective areas of jurisdiction with all cases of inheritance, marriage, and the emancipation of slaves in which *'Askerîs* were concerned; whereas similar cases concerning *re'âyâ* were dealt with by local *Mollâs* or *Ḳâḍîs*.[1] Each *Ḳâḍî-'asker*, apart from such subordinate officials as were attached to all judges, had three principal assistants[2] to deal with the appointment, pay, and registration of the provincial *Ḳâḍîs* under his authority, another[3] to deal with the appointment and pay of mosque ministers, and a secretary-general[4] to control his correspondence with the inferior tribunals dependent upon his own.

During the seventeenth century, however, the *Ḳâḍî-'askerlik* of Anatolia was deprived of most of its authority. By that time in any case all matters of law and order had been removed by *ḳânûn* from the competence of *Ḳâḍîs*.[5] When cases to which their com-

corrupted, in North Africa, to *Mouley*. With other meanings the same word is pronounced in Turkish *mevla*, and the office of a *Mollâ* was called *mevlevîyet* (Arabic *mawlawîya*). The name of the Mevlevî *dervîş* order has the same derivation, from the term *Mawlânâ*, 'our lord', applied to its founder Celâlü'd-Dîn Rûmî (see below, p. 194). The spelling with double *l* has been adopted in the new Turkish Latin-character dictionaries.

[1] See the sixteenth-century *Ḳânûn-nâme* published in *T.O.E.M.*, No. 17, Appendix, p. 40, and the *Ḳânûn-nâme* of 'Abdu'r-Raḥmân Tevḳî'î, *M.T.M.* i. 540.

[2] Called *Teẕkereci* (cf. Part I, p. 119), *Maṭlabci* and *Taṭbîḳçi*. The first saw to the distribution of pay; the second kept the list of *Ḳâḍîs* and put forward the names of senior candidates for vacant posts; the third kept the seal-impressions, deposited with him, of all provincial *Ḳâḍîs* in order to verify the authenticity of documents received from them by the *Ḳâḍî-'askers*: D'Ohsson, iv. 539–40.

[3] Called *Rüznâmeci*; cf. Part I, p. 127.

[4] *Mektupçu*: D'Ohsson, loc. cit.

[5] See the *Ḳânûn-nâme* of 'Abdu'r-Raḥmân Tevḳî'î, *Ḳânûn* of the *Mollâs* and Town-*Ḳâḍîs*, *M.T.M.* i. 541.

petence did still extend arose in the Imperial *Dîvân*, they were now handed over exclusively to the *Ḳâḍî-'asker* of Rumelia. His colleague of Anatolia now took no more than a formal part in the proceedings unless the Grand *Vezîr* should charge him expressly with some particular business.[1] By the eighteenth century, again, owing to the then almost universal affiliation of merchants and artisans to the Janissary *ortas*, the term *'Askerî* had come to be virtually synonymous with 'Moslem'.[2] Consequently, and because of the loss of his former powers by the *Ḳâḍî-'asker* of Anatolia, all cases of inheritance in which Moslems were concerned were now heard by the *Ḳâḍî-'asker* of Rumelia; and, possibly on the same ground, that they were *'Askerî* affairs (i.e. affairs of the ruling institution), so were all cases in which the Treasury was a party. Formerly, like all judges, each *Ḳâḍî-'asker* had been assisted in inheritance cases by a *Ḳassâm* or divider,[3] and in general business by a deputy[4] and a recorder.[5] Now, however, only the *Ḳâḍî-'asker* of Rumelia was provided with these subordinates, to the number of whom was added another, the *Mîrî Kâtibi* or Clerk to the Treasury, who dealt in his name with all cases to do with state finance.[6] Finally, the *Ḳâḍî-'asker* of Rumelia acquired the right of bringing before his court all cases pending in the inferior tribunals of the capital, and of placing under seal all property of persons dying therein. The object of this procedure was to preserve such property intact for the heirs or, in the case of *Ḳapî Ḳullarî*, for the Treasury. It was pursued with zest, since in practice heirs to such property had to pay for its release.[7] The *Ḳâḍî-'asker* of Anatolia, on the other hand, though conserving the rest of his authority, practically ceased to function as a judge altogether.[8]

None of the other *Mollâs* had special duties or powers except the *Ḳâḍî* of Istanbul, who ranked next below the *Ḳâḍî-'askers*, and the *Ḳâḍîs* of Ğalaṭa, Üsküdar, and Eyyûb, who were all of a lower grade.[9] These four sat in the *Dîvân* once a week, on Wednesdays, taking the place of the *Ḳâḍî-'askers* as assistants of the Grand

[1] See op. cit., *Ḳânûn* of the *Ḳâḍî-'askers*, *M.T.M.* i. 540; and cf. D'Ohsson, iv. 535–6.

[2] See D'Ohsson, iv. 535.

[3] By *Ḳur'ânic* law property has to be divided between various relatives of a deceased person in definite proportions.

[4] *Nâ'ib* (see below, p. 124). The *Ḳâḍî-'asker*'s *Nâ'ib* was called *Şerî'atî*.

[5] *Vaḳâ'i' Kâtibi*, literally 'Secretary of Proceedings'. All *Ḳâḍîs* had such recorders.

[6] D'Ohsson, iv. 538, 541.

[7] Ibid. 537–8.

[8] His having no *Ḳassâm*, *Nâ'ib* or *Vaḳâ'i' Kâtibi* is enough to prove this.

[9] It is perhaps these four *Mollâs*, of Istanbul, Ğalaṭa, Üsküdar, and Eyyûb, resident at the capital, that are referred to in the *Ḳânûn-nâme* of the Conqueror as *Taḫt Ḳâḍîsis*, 'Ḳâḍîs of the Throne' (*T.O.E.M.*, No. 13, Appendix, p. 30). They are not to be confused with the *Taḫta Başîs* (see below, p. 122).

Vezîr in the administration of justice; and the *Ḳâḍî* of Istanbul was obliged, after this session, to accompany the Grand *Vezîr* on his rounds of inspection.[1] Otherwise the *Mollâs* were ordinary *Ḳâḍîs*; and the functions of an ordinary *Ḳâḍî* will be examined later.

In the second half of the seventeenth century there were in all forty-three *Mollâs*, the first eleven of whom held what were called *Pâye Menâṣib* (Posts of Rank), because they might obtain in turn promotion from the lowest to the highest. The remaining thirty-two were apparently grouped in two categories, the first twelve again forming one, the last twenty the other; and of these last twenty we are told that they stood 'on an equality'.[2] In the next century, however, the order of *Mollâs* was reorganized, probably during the reign of Aḥmed III.[3] The total number of *Mollâs* was then reduced to twenty-seven, but of these seventeen were now reckoned as 'great' and ten as 'lesser'. Moreover, these 'Great' *Mevleviyets* (i.e. Mollaships)[4] were at the same time grouped in six grades, from each one of which promotion might be obtained to the next higher. The posts of the two *Ḳâḍî-'askers* and that of the *Ḳâḍî* of Istanbul formed the first three grades. Then came the *Ḳâḍîs* of the two Holy Cities, in one grade, and those of the two former capitals (Bursa and Adrianople) and the two former seats of the Caliphate (Damascus and Cairo) in another. Finally, in one grade, came the *Ḳâḍîs* of the three suburbs of Istanbul already mentioned, together with those of Jerusalem, Smyrna, Aleppo, Salonika, and Yeni-şehir.[5] The rank of the *Ḳâḍîs* of this lowest of the 'great' categories was called *maḫrec*, 'going-out' or 'exit', because they obtained it after completing their long training as professors in the twelve *madrasas* of the capital. After securing one of the eight posts it comprised, any one of these *Ḳâḍîs* became eligible for promotion to a *ḳâḍîliḳ* of the next higher category, and so on until he rose to be *Şeyḫü 'l-Islâm*. Down to the end of the

[1] See *Ḳânûn-nâme* of 'Abdu 'r-Raḥmân Tevḳî'î, *Ḳânûn* of the Wednesday *Dîvân*, *M.T.M.* i. 503 sq.

[2] Ibid., *Ḳânûn* of the Ranks of Learned Posts, *M.T.M.* i. 538. No comment is made on the middle group of *Mollâs*. It is not clear, therefore, whether they were equal in rank or not. In reckoning eleven *Mollâs* of the highest category we have included the *Ḳâḍî* of Istanbul, who is omitted from the list in the *Ḳânûn-nâme*.

[3] D'Ohsson (iv. 542) states that it was in 1720 that Aḥmed III placed Medîna (which in the *Ḳânûn-nâme* comes eighth on the list, if we insert the rank of *Istanbul ḳâḍîsi*) on an equality with Mecca (which in the *Ḳânûn-nâme* comes fourth, as it continued to do).

[4] The term 'Great Mollaship' (*Büyük Mevleviyet*) is actually used in the *Ḳânûn-nâme* of 'Abdu 'r-Raḥmân Tevḳî'î, *M.T.M.* i. 539.

[5] A comparison of the two lists in D'Ohsson and 'Abdu 'r-Raḥmân Tevḳî'î shows that the first seventeen *Mevleviyets* (again allowing for the insertion of the *Istanbul Ḳâḍîsi* in the list of the *Ḳânûn-nâme*) are the same, with one exception: Filibe (Philippopolis in Bulgaria) appearing as fifteenth in the *Ḳânûn*, but as a 'Lesser' *Mevleviyet* in D'Ohsson's list.

seventeenth century Great *Mollâs* were appointed for life, that is to say they held each post in the hierarchy until a vacancy in the next higher grade permitted those of inferior rank to move up; they were not, except for some fault, dismissed.

As well as the *Şeyẖ* and these seventeen judges five other *'Ulemâ* were reckoned as belonging to the highest order. They were all officers of the Household, in describing which we no more than mentioned their collective existence.[1] The first was the *Mu'allim* or *Ḫoca*, i.e. Preceptor, of the Sultan, whom he instructed in the principles of religion. At the time of the Conqueror the *Ḫoca* was a personage of little less reverence than the *Şeyẖ* himself, being referred to in the *Ḳânûn-nâme* as *Serdâr* or Head of the *'Ulemâ*, whereas the *Şeyẖ* is there called *Re'îsü 'l-'ulemâ*.[2] The office retained its importance down to the beginning of the eighteenth century; but then the promotion to be *Şeyẖ* by Muṣṭafâ II of a man who before his accession had been his *Ḫoca* and whose influence was far-reaching and disastrous resulted in its reduction to comparative insignificance.[3] Thenceforward it was regarded as a promotion if the *Ḫoca*, exceptionally, were given a 'Great' Mollaship.

The next of these officers were the two Imperial Imâms, whose duty it was to lead prayers in the *Serây* 'chapel' and in whatever mosque the Sultan visited on Fridays. The other two were the Head Physician (*Ḥekîm Başî*) and the Head Astrologer (*Müneccim Başî*). The Head Physican had under him a number of assistants and surgeons all of whom were accounted *'Ulemâ*.[4] The Astrologer's chief duty was to prepare a calendar, showing propitious moments for various actions.[5] Astrology retained its prestige even at court up to beyond the date of our survey, such matters as the appointment of ministers by the Sultan being delayed till the hour was deemed favourable.[6]

The Great *Mollâs* enjoyed various privileges. Thus they were permitted to wear ermine cloaks like *Vezîrs* and were each provided with a number of pursuivants (*Muḥḍir*),[7] headed by a *Muḥḍir Başî*, who was usually appointed from among the door-

[1] In Part I, p. 82.

[2] *T.O.E.M.*, No. 13, Appendix, 13: *Ve şeyẖü'l-islâm 'ulemânîn re'îsidir ve mu'allimi sulṭân daẖi keẕâlik serdârî 'ulemâdîr. Mu'allim* means 'teacher' in Arabic. *Re'îs* (Arabic) and *serdâr* (Persian) are roughly equivalent. For *ẖoca*, properly *ẖwâcâ*, see Part I, p. 135, n. 7.

[3] The *Şeyẖ* in question was a certain Feyḍu'llah Efendi; see *Encyc. of Islam*, s.v. (*Faiẓullah*) and art. 'Muṣṭafâ II'—also below, p. 109, n. 9.

[4] D'Ohsson, iv. 548. Cf. Hammer, *Travels of Evliya Efendi*, ii. 116. For the Jewish physicians employed by the Sultans see below, pp. 217, 220.

[5] Cf. C. Niebuhr, *Description de l'Arabie* (1774), 104.

[6] D'Ohsson, iv. 551–5.

[7] Cf. Part I, p. 316, and *Evliya* (transl. Hammer), ii. 111, 116.

keepers (*Ḳapîcî*)[1] of the Palace. They were also admitted, together with the principal professors of the Istanbul *madrasas*, to the ceremony at which a new sovereign was accorded allegiance,[2] and to that at which this allegiance was twice yearly reasserted during each of the two feasts.[3] Until the middle of the seventeenth century, again, they and these professors were entitled to wait in a body on the Grand *Vezîr* every Friday after morning prayers, before the session of the *Dîvân*.[4] The two *Ḳâḍî-'askers* were further distinguished by being invested in their robes of office in the presence of the Grand *Vezîr*.[5] They were also permitted to hear the cases brought before them in their own mansions; whereas the other *Mollâs*, like ordinary *Ḳâḍîs*, discharged their duties in a court (*maḥkeme*). The *Şeyḫ* enjoyed a similar privilege, of performing his functions at his own residence.[6] No official headquarters was provided for him until the nineteenth century. Finally, the *Şeyḫ* and the two *Ḳâḍî-'askers* were allowed to drive in carriages and, on the declaration of war, were given *ṭuğs* to set up before their tents.[7]

In the seventeenth century, as we have indicated, there were two orders of *Mollâs* below those of the 'Posts of Rank'. After the reorganization there were still two orders of judges superior to ordinary *Ḳâḍîs*, only in neither case were they properly called *Mollâs*. Those of the higher order were indeed popularly designated by the term—no doubt because their predecessors in these posts had enjoyed the distinction—and we propose to refer to them as 'Lesser' *Mollâs*. The posts in question, however, were now, according to D'Ohsson, properly known as *Menâṣibi Devrîye*, 'Posts held in rotation',[8] because, as we shall explain when describing the corruption of the *'Ulemâ*, by the eighteenth century a curious system had come into being by which every appointment of this category (as indeed of others) was held yearly by several dignitaries in turn. They were the judgeships of ten important cities, four in Europe and six in Asia.[9]

[1] See Part I, p. 131. [2] *Bey'a* (Arabic).

[3] *Mu'âyada* (Arabic, meaning 'repetition'): D'Ohsson iv. 550, 551.

[4] See the *Ḳânûn-nâme* of 'Abdu'r-Raḥmân Tevḳî'î, *Ḳânûn* of the Attendance of Mollâs and Müderrises, *M.T.M.* i. 539–40.

[5] D'Ohsson, iv. 552.

[6] Ibid. 580–1.

[7] Ibid. 554–5. For *ṭuğs* see Part I, p. 139.

[8] Ibid. 578. Nevertheless D'Ohsson himself refers to these judges as *Mollâs* (pp. 566–7).

[9] Namely, Mer'aş, Bağdâd, Bosna (i.e. Serayevo), Ṣofya, Belgrade, 'Ayntâb, Kütâhya, Ḳonya, Filibe (Philippopolis), and Diyârbekir. In the *Ḳânûn-nâme* of 'Abdu'r-Raḥmân Tevḳî'î, of these ten posts Filibe, Bağdâd, Diyâr Bekir, Ṣofya, and Belgrad are shown, in this order, as 'second-class' *Mevlevîyets*; Bosna and Mer'aş as 'third-class' *Mevlevîyets*, and 'Ayntab, Kütâhya, and Konya are not shown among the *Mevlevîyets* at all. It seems strange that such important places as Ḳonya and Kütâhya should be so omitted. Surely they cannot have

The second order below that of the Great *Mollâs* in the eighteenth century was composed of five special judges called *Müfettiş*, 'Investigator',[1] whose sole business it was to deal with cases regarding Imperial *waḳfs*, i.e. pious foundations. Some of these foundations were under the control of the *Şeyḫü'l-Islâm*, some under that of the Grand *Vezîr*, and the rest—those of the Holy Cities—were under the control of the Chief Black Eunuch.[2] Of the five *Müfettişes* three were resident in the capital, each dealing with the business of one of these three classes of *waḳfs*. One of the other two resided at Adrianople and the other at Brusa, and both were dependent on the *Müfettiş* of the Holy Cities.[3] No reference to these judges occurs in the *Ḳânûn-nâme* of 'Abdu'r-Raḥmân Tevḳî'î, though their posts were presumably in existence before the reorganization.

The remaining two orders, those of the ordinary *Ḳâḍîs*[4] and their substitutes, called *Nâ'ibs*, are dealt with in Chapter X. II below.

Besides these regular posts, certain others of a temporary nature were open to *Ḳâḍîs* of various kinds. Thus the 'Great' *Mollâ* of Damascus was as a rule appointed yearly as *Maḥmal Ḳâḍîsi*, or Judge of the Litter,[5] to accompany the pilgrimage caravan from Syria to Mecca. Secondly, an ordinary *Ḳâḍî*, chosen by the Ḳaptan Paşa and appointed by the *Ḳâḍî-'asker* of Rumelia, sailed with the fleet on its yearly cruise to the archipelago.[6] Thirdly, when the Grand *Vezîr* commanded the army in war, an ex-*Mollâ* of the first grade was chosen to accompany him, since the *Ḳâḍî-'askers* left the capital only when the Sultan led his forces in person. Both these judges were known as *Ordu Ḳâḍîsi*, Judge of the Camp.[7]

Another important office which, from the end of the seventeenth

been mere *ḳâḍîliḳs*? It may be that the list in the *Ḳânûn* as published is incomplete. On the other hand, equally important centres, such as Erḍerum and Ḳayseri, both of which appear as 'third-class' *Mevlevîyets* in the *Ḳânûn* list, are not shown as even lesser *Mevlevîyets* by D'Ohsson (iv. 566–7). See also Hammer-Purgstall, *Hist. de l'Empire Ottoman*, trad. par Hellert, xvii. 5 sqq.

[1] From Arabic *fattaşa*, 'search with care, ferret out'.

[2] The *Ḳizlar Ağasi*—in the eighteenth century, that is to say. Down to near the end of the sixteenth they were controlled by the Chief White Eunuch, and during the seventeenth were shared between the two; see 'Aṭâ, i. 160, 265. The three chief Investigators were called *Şeyḫü 'l-Islâm Müfettişi*, *Vezîri A'ẓam Müfettişi*, and *Ḥarameyn Müfettişi*.

[3] D'Ohsson, iv. 568.

[4] In the *Ḳânûn-nâme* of 'Abdu'r-Raḥmân Tevḳî'î they are called *ḳuḍâtî ḳaṣabât*, *Ḳâḍîs* of towns, as opposed to *Mollâs*, who are there called *ḳuḍâtî mevlevîyet*, *Ḳâḍîs* of Mollaships: *M.T.M.* i. 541.

[5] *Maḥmal* here means 'litter'. The *Maḥmali şerîf* was the sacred litter in which the Sultan's gifts to the Holy Cities were conveyed.

[6] See *Ḳânûn* of the *Ḳaptan Paşa*, ap. 'Abdu'r-Raḥmân Tevḳî'î, *M.T.M.* i. 538.

[7] D'Ohsson. iv. 576–7.

century, was invariably filled either by one of the two *Ḳâḍî-ʿaskers* or by the *Ḳâḍî* of Istanbul was that of *Naḳîbu 'l-Aşrâf*, or Marshal of the *Şerîfs*. *Şerîf* (meaning 'noble') is one of the terms applied to descendants of the Prophet, and since this honourable status was generally reckoned as heritable through female as well as through male descent, the number of persons in the Empire claiming it—whether rightfully or not—was extremely large.[1] The *Aşrâf* (in Turkish spelling *Eşrâf*) or *Seyyids*, although by no means all professional men of religion, amongst their number being persons of all occupations and trades (many of them of quite humble social position),[2] enjoyed a special respect and formed a separate and privileged corporation of which the *Naḳîb* was the chief executive officer. They were distinguished from the generality in later times by the wearing of green turbans.[3] Like the *Ḳapi̊ Ḳullari̊*, moreover, they could be tried and punished for misdemeanours only by other members of their clan, and no *Şerîf* could be put to death without the *Naḳîb*'s consent.[4]

It was in order to exert the necessary control, and to prevent the arrogation of *şerîf*-hood to themselves by impostors, that the office of *Naḳîb* existed. It was first instituted, under the Ottomans, by Bâyezîd II, in imitation of ʿAbbâsid and Mamlûk usage;[5] and for the next two centuries the Sultan appointed any eminent *Şerîf* to fill it that he might choose. Thereafter it came to be a perquisite of the Great *Mollâs* in question. If, as was seldom the case, none of the three was by birth a *Şerîf*, the office was con-

[1] The term *Şerîf* (like the appellation of *Seyyid*, and occasionally that of *Emîr* or *Mîr*) was and is commonly applied to all descendants of the Prophet through his daughter Fâṭima and her husband, the Prophet's cousin, ʿAlî. But in strict usage—especially in Arabia—*Şerîf* was the term denoting descent from ʿAlî's eldest son Ḥasan, and *Seyyid* descent from his second son Ḥuseyn. Cf. Niebuhr, 10–12.

[2] One of the Keylânî family of *Şerîfs*, for example, was a saddle-maker in Aleppo: Murâdî, iii. 132.

[3] According to the *Encyc. of Islam*, s.v., this custom apparently dates only from the end of the sixteenth century, although green had from early times been considered the especial colour of the Prophet's family.

[4] Cf. Niebuhr, loc. cit.; Russell, 122; Chabrol, 201; Olivier, ii. 308–9. The latter remarks: 'Un pacha ou un officier public ne fait donner la bastonade à un parent du prophète qu'après lui avoir fait quitter son turban vert, et avoir baisé ce turban avec un respect apparent.' In Egypt there was a separate prison for *Şerîfs*.

[5] The classical exposition of the functions and privileges of the *Naḳîb* is given by the jurist el-Mâwardî (d. A.D. 1058) in the eighth chapter of his famous work on the Institutions of Government (*al-Aḥkâm al-Sulṭâniya*, trans. E. Fagnan (Algiers, 1915), 199–207). For the office of *Naḳîb* in earlier times and under the Mamlûks see E. Tyan, ii. 329–41, and Gaudefroy-Demombynes, pp. lxxviii and 163. According to D'Ohsson, during the interregnum that followed the defeat of Bâyezîd I by Timur, one of the Sultan's sons established a chief of the *Şerîfs* under the title of *Nâẓir* or inspector, but the office was later abolished by the Conqueror. According to Seyyid Muṣṭafâ the *Niḳâba* was instituted by Bâyezîd I himself, abolished later, and re-established by Süleymân the Magnificent.

ferred on a *Mollâ* of lower grade. In any case the holder continued to perform his judicial duties, and the appointment was for life. Only if he should rise to be *Şeyḫü 'l-Islâm* must the *Naḳîb* relinquish it. For it was feared that otherwise odious comparisons might be drawn between the honours due to the Sultan (with his unfortunate lack of Apostolic blood) and those that might be commanded by a doctor endued with this double authority. In eminence and the exercise of certain privileges, though not in precedence, the *Naḳîb* ranked second only to the *Şeyḫ* himself.[1] He had jurisdiction over all the provincial *Naḳîbs*, some of whom, as we shall show later, played a rather more influential part in provincial affairs than the *Naḳîb* himself played at the capital.

This complicated organization of the judicial service, into all the details of which we are far from having gone, was clearly elaborated gradually. As we have noted, it was reorganized early in the eighteenth century, and most of our description applies to its final form. It is clear from the *Ḳânûn-nâme* of the Conqueror, however, that its main lines had been laid down already in the fifteenth century. Thus that document refers to the gradually increasing salaries[2] received by the professors in the then existing *madrasas* of the capital,[3] and shows that they could be promoted to minor judgeships even from the lowest grade.[4] Again it mentions judges of four grades of pay,[5] and states that those of the two highest have the rank of *Mollâ*.[6] At this time it was evidently common also for *'Ulemâ* to serve in the ruling institution as *Ḥocas* of various ranks. Thus professors of the three foremost *madrasas* of the capital might become *Defterdârs* or *Nîşâncîs*, whereas *Mollâs* of the second rank might become provincial *Defterdârs*.[7] In later times the employment of *'Ulemâ* in such posts appears to have been unusual.

The second order of the *'Ulemâ*, counting that of the *Mollâs* and *Ḳâḍîs* as the first, was that of the *Muftîs*. These were organized, under the *Şeyḫü 'l-Islâm*, on a system roughly parallel with the

[1] D'Ohsson iv. 555–66; Seyyid Muṣṭafâ, i. 114.

[2] They rose from 20 to 50 *aḳçes* a day by increments of 5 (*T.O.E.M.* No. 13, Appendix, p. 20).

[3] The grades of *madrasas* mentioned are the *Ḫâric*, *Dâḫil*, and *Ṣaḥn* (see p. 146, n. 1 below), as well as the *madrasas* of Aya Ṣofya. There is also a general reference to the *madrasas* of Iç Il, meaning those not only in Istanbul but in or near Adrianople and Brusa as well. The *Ṣaḥn madrasas* were those built near his mosque by Meḥmed II. The date of this *Ḳânûn-nâme* has been partly determined by a reference in it to their building: *ḥâlâ binâ eylediğim medârisi 'alîyeye ṣaḥn diye ism ḳonulmuşdur*, 'The name *Ṣaḥn* [i.e. courtyard] has been given to the lofty [or perhaps, 'august'] colleges that I have recently constructed' (*T.O.E.M.*, No. 13, Appendix, p. 201).

[4] A professor of any college in the Iç Il receiving only 20 *aḳçes* a day might be appointed a *Ḳâḍî* at 45 *aḳçes* a day (ibid.).

[5] i.e. 45, 150, 300, and 500 *aḳçes* respectively (ibid.).

[6] Ibid. The professors of the principal *madrasas* of Istanbul were also held to rank as *Mollâs*.

[7] Ibid. 15, 20.

organization of *Ḳâḍîs*, but we shall reserve fuller details for the chapter to be devoted especially to them.

The next following order was that of mosque ministers. There were in later times five classes of such ministers, of greatly varying importance and functions. The term 'minister' is perhaps misleading, for these functionaries had nothing of the priest about them; they underwent no form of ordination, took no vows, were not necessarily celibate, and might retire when they chose from the service. The duties discharged by two of these types of minister, namely, the *Imâms* and *Ḫaṭîbs*, appertained in the earliest days of Islâm to the sovereign himself. For as *Imâm* he was leader not only of the forces of the Moslems, but also of their prayers, and in particular the Friday midday prayer, the chief Moslem weekly service. When, as the Caliphate grew, the sovereign appointed governors to represent him in provincial capitals, they again led these prayers on his behalf. But in time the Caliphs ceased to discharge this duty, except occasionally, in person; and so, in imitation, did their lieutenant-governors. The duty came instead to be delegated to learned men as a distinct occupation, and was extended to comprise a general supervision over the mosques in which they performed it. The term *Imâm*, though still used by political theorists of the sovereign, was then in ordinary parlance confined to designating these prayer-leaders of the *'Ulemâ* class.

This levelling-down of the term, however, was counterbalanced by a levelling-up in another direction. From the earliest times, custom and decorum, authenticated by sayings attributed to the Prophet, required that of any group of Moslems at prayer one should act as *Imâm* or leader. In this sense, therefore, any member of the community could be an *Imâm*, without needing any authorization beyond the assent of the other members of the group. But it was the usual practice of Believers to congregate for prayers in a particular place, called *mascid*;[1] and the principal *mascid* in a town or district, being that in which the whole community (at least in theory) assembled for the Friday midday prayers, was distinguished by the title of *câmi'*.[2] Professional *Imâms* were, in all probability, first appointed only to a *câmi'*; but eventually every mosque, of the first type as well as of the second, was placed in the care of an *Imâm*. Meanwhile, and at still an early date in Moslem history, a new subdivision of functions grew

[1] Meaning 'a place in which prostrations are made'. It is from this word that the English 'mosque' is derived, through It. *moschea*.

[2] Meaning 'that which collects', i.e. in this case the people in a congregation, without which, unlike ordinary prayers, the Friday prayer was not valid. Large cities had necessarily several *câmi's*, since only in these could the Friday midday prayers be lawfully held.

up within the *câmi'* in consequence of its monopoly of the Friday services; and although the *Imâm* (or chief *Imâm*, if there should be more than one) continued to lead the devotions, the chief office at the Friday service had come to be assumed by another minister, the *Ḫaṭîb*.

The *Ḫaṭîb* is so called because at the Friday prayers he pronounces two harangues, both termed *ḫuṭba*, in which God is praised, the people are exhorted, and blessings are called down on the Prophet, his family, and Companions, and on all Moslems, headed by the sovereign, who is mentioned by name.[1] The Prophet and the early Caliphs used often to pronounce the *ḫuṭba* themselves, but when the sovereign-*Imâms* ceased to lead the Friday prayers the pronouncement of the *ḫuṭba* devolved exclusively on the *Ḫaṭîb*; and since the mention of anyone's name as a ruler on whom blessings were invoked came, with other signs, to mark the official recognition of his authority, the *Ḫaṭîb* acquired political importance enough to elevate him above the (minister-) *Imâm* as a principal figure at the Friday service. Since prayers were said much more often than this, however, all mosques but the smallest were supplied with two or more *Imâms* to serve in rotation,[2] whereas no *câmi'* had more than one *Ḫaṭîb*.[3]

This development placed the *Imâms* not only below the *Ḫaṭîb* in importance, but also below yet a third type of minister, the *Wâ'iẓ* or preacher, though his office had no such august antecedents as either of the others. The *Wâ'iẓ*, or *Şeyḫ*, as he was popularly called, would deliver sermons after the Friday service, and at midday or in the afternoon on other days of the week, generally on points of doctrine and morals. Not only all *câmi's* but also most *mascids* were provided with these preachers and sometimes with several of them, according to the provisions of the pious foundation or foundations, on the funds provided from which the mosque itself was kept up and all the ministers were furnished with salaries.[4]

The other two classes of ministers were those of the *Mü'eẕẕins* or Callers to Prayer,[5] and the *Ḳayyims* or supervisors of mosque servants.[6] Neither were necessarily *'Ulemâ* in the sense of being doctors trained in *madrasas*. *Mü'eẕẕins* indeed were chosen pri-

[1] See Part I, pp. 31, 34.
[2] *Encyc. of Islam*, artt. 'Masdjid', 'Khaṭīb', 'Imām'; and cf. D'Ohsson, iv. 590–1.
[3] According to D'Ohsson. In earlier times some mosques seem to have had several *Ḫaṭîbs*—see *Encyc. of Islam*, locc. cit.
[4] D'Ohsson, i. 369; iv. 587–90; and see Ch. XII below.
[5] *Mü'eẕẕin* (Arabic *Mu'aḏḏin*) is derived from *Aḏân*, the usual term for the call to prayer.
[6] *Kayyim* (Arabic) = a person set in charge of someone or something.

marily for their voices.[1] They had been employed from the earliest times, even before minarets had become an essential feature of mosques, when they not only summoned the people to the five daily prayers, but compelled them to obey the summons. The Call to Prayer was gradually elaborated, till in Ottoman times it came to be intoned in a variety of modes.[2] Besides calling to prayer *Mü'ezzins* recited litanies and performed certain functions at the Friday prayers.[3]

The number of servants—door-keepers, water-carriers, sweepers, &c.—employed in any mosque depended on its size and wealth, as did the number of *Ḳayyims* that controlled them and, for the matter of that, the number of the *Mü'ezzins*, of whom in the larger *câmi's* there might be as many as a dozen.[4] In small *mascids*, on the other hand, there was sometimes no minister other than an *Imâm*, who acted as *Şeyḫ*, *Mü'ezzin*, and *Ḳayyim* as well.[5]

Mosque ministers were all nominated by the persons controlling the foundations from which their salaries were forthcoming. The only exceptions to this rule were the *Wâ'izes* of the Imperial *câmi's* of Istanbul, who were appointed by the *Şeyḫü 'l-Islâm*. These *Wâ'iẓes*, indeed, formed a corps apart, being gradually promoted from the most recently founded of these mosques to the oldest, namely, Aya Ṣofya, and on this account enjoyed precedence of the *Ḫaṭîbs* of these same mosques, whereas elsewhere the *Ḫaṭîb* was the superior of the *Wâ'iẓ*.[6] Once nominated, however, the other ministers had to receive confirmation in office from either the *Şeyḫü 'l-Islâm*, if they served mosques in the capital, or from one of the two *Ḳâḍî-'askers* according as the mosques they served were situated in Europe or Asia. Their actual diplomas were issued, on the recommendation of these dignitaries, from the Imperial chancery.[7] Only *Ḫaṭîbs*, as the Sultan's representatives at the Friday service, were appointed by rescripts signed by the

[1] See above (Part I, App. (B) 2, *ad fin.*) for the education as *Mü'ezzins* of palace pages possessed of fine voices.

[2] The *Mü'ezzins* being distinguished by terms indicating the modes they used: D'Ohsson, iv. 592.

[3] *Encyc. of Islam*, artt. 'Masdjid', 'Mu'adhdhin'; D'Ohsson i. 168, iv. 591–2.

[4] As in all the Imperial *câmi's* of the capital. Only that of Sultan Aḥmed (built at the beginning of the seventeenth century) had more—as many as thirty-six—because in later times it became the Imperial mosque *par excellence*. It also had thirty *Ḳayyims*. D'Ohsson, iv. 592.

[5] Ibid. 593; *Encyc. of Islam*, artt. 'Masdjid', 'Mosque Servants'.

[6] D'Ohsson, iv. 590, 593.

[7] From the *Ru'ûs* department (see Part I, p. 122). Having obtained these certificates the ministers had to present them at the department of the Treasury called *Ḫarameyn Muḥâsebesi*, if their posts were European, or at that called *Ḫarameyn Muḳâṭa'asi* if they were Asiatic, and again at the *Mâlîye Ḳalemi* where, apparently, they received brevets authorizing them to draw the salaries due to them. For these departments see Part I, pp. 132, 135.

monarch himself and called *Ḫaṭṭî Şerîf.*[1] Their diplomas of appointment were issued likewise from the chancery to all the other orders of the *ʿUlemâ*, whether, as in the case of *Mollâs*, *Müfettişes*, and *Muftîs*, they were nominated by the *Şeyḫü 'l-Islâm*, or, as in that of *Ḳâḍîs*, by the *Ḳâḍî-ʿaskers*. It is for this reason that the Grand *Vezîr* was said to appoint all post-holding *ʿUlemâ*.[2] This does not mean that the choice of persons to be so appointed rested with him, though the highest dignitaries were chosen only after consultation between the *Vezîr* and the *Şeyḫ* or the *Ḳâḍî-ʿaskers*. It means only that their actual diplomas were issued from the *Dîvân*.[3]

In comparison with the rigid and hierarchical organization of the *ʿUlemâ* at Istanbul and in the Turkish provinces, those of Egypt and the Arab lands still retained in some measure the traditional elasticity of their order and the characteristic Islamic aversion from formal external organization. The situation in all provinces was not alike, however; and the freedom of the local corps of *ʿUlemâ* was roughly proportional to their distance from Istanbul. At Aleppo the influence of Ottoman usage was very strong, and no doubt reinforced by the Turkish constituents in its population and the widespread use of the Turkish language. At Damascus it was plainly a rather artificial superstructure, maintained in part by a system of 'honorary' assimilation to Ottoman grades,[4] and by the fact that a certain number of religious offices was in Ottoman gift. In Egypt and the Holy Cities there is little trace of Ottomanization. Externally there was a measure of co-ordination; the principal religious dignitaries in each province were the Ottoman *Ḳâḍî*, appointed on annual tenure from Istanbul, the *Naḳîb el-Aṣrâf*, also appointed or reappointed annually by diploma from Istanbul,

[1] D'Ohsson, iv. 593–4. In Egypt, however, the *Ḫaṭîbs* received their diploma of appointment from the Chief *Ḳâḍî*: Muḥ. Tawfîḳ el-Bekrî, *Beyt el-Ṣiddîḳ* (Cairo, 1323), 61–62, quoting from the journal of Şeyḫ ʿAbdu'l-Ġanî el-Nâbulusî.

[2] See, for instance, in the *Ḳânûn-nâme* of ʿAbdu 'r-Raḥmân Tevḳîʿî, the *Ḳânûn* of the Grand *Vezîrs* (*Ḳânûnî Vüzerâyi ʿUẓâm*): '[The Grand *Vezîr*] is the Sultan's absolute representative for . . . conferring of . . . Ḫaṭîbships and Imâmships . . ., the appointment of *Mollâs* . . ., in short the conferment and withdrawal of all posts military and learned.'

[3] These diplomas had various names:

Those of	professors	were called	*Ru'ûs* (cf. Part I, p. 122).
,,	*Mollâs*	,,	*Tevcîh Fermânî*, 'Order to confer'.
,,	*Ḳâḍîs*	,,	either *Teẓkere* (above, Part I, p. 49) or *Menṣab Kâğidî*, 'Post paper'.
,,	*Muftîs*	,,	*Iẓn-nâme*, 'Permission document', i.e. permission to issue *fetwâs*.
,,	*Nâ'ibs*	,,	*Murâsele*, 'Communication'.
,,	Ministers	,,	*Berât* (cf. above, Part I, p. 49).

See D'Ohsson, iv. 597.

[4] Cf. Murâdî, ii. 217, &c.

the Chief Ḥanefî *Muftî*, and the head of the local *'Ulemâ*.[1] But while the principle of Ottoman supremacy was maintained by this system, the real test of the strength of Ottoman control may be found in the extent to which the authorities at Istanbul or in the provinces were able to present their own nominees to the three latter posts or were under the practical necessity of recognizing the choice made by the local *'Ulemâ*.

This relative independence was most marked in Egypt. The direct intervention and control of the civil authorities were limited to the judicial service; in all other branches of learned activity and organization neither the authorities at Istanbul nor the local officials, though preserving a direct or indirect right of confirmation, interfered with the traditional institutions or with their personnel and methods. The Ottoman legislator realized the necessity of conciliating the powerful religious interests established at Cairo,[2] and in addition to other marks of favour allowed them to retain, practically unimpaired, their autonomy under their native leaders.[3] The corporation of *'Ulemâ* in Egypt appears to have been less rigidly organized than those of the merchants and artisans. The *Şeyḫ* of el-Azhar, assisted by a council of leading *'Ulemâ*, maintained a general supervision over the *Şeyḫs*, expelling those who were guilty of heresy or immorality, and arbitrating in their disputes. But the financial reasons for close administrative organization were lacking, as the *'Ulemâ* paid no contributions to the state. On the other hand, the distribution of revenues and pensions[4] implies an organization of some sort, and there is evidence that the *'Ulemâ* of the larger provincial towns were grouped in separate

[1] For the *Naḳîb* and the *Muftîs*, see pp. 93–94 above. The Ḥanefî *Muftî* himself was often (e.g. at Damascus) the head of the local *'Ulemâ*, but in several other provinces and districts the latter belonged to a different group altogether, as, for example, the *Şeyḫ el-Azhar* in Cairo, and the *Şeyḫ* of the Sanctuary (*Şeyḫ el-ḥaram*) in each of the Holy Cities and in Jerusalem (cf. Murâdî, iii. 89).

[2] It should be remembered that until the fall of the Mamlûk Sultanate in 1517 Cairo was the chief religious centre in the Moslem world, not because of the artificially resuscitated Caliphate, but because, after the destruction of its former rivals in Persia and 'Irâḳ, education and learning tended to concentrate in Cairo.

[3] The tact with which the religious seminary of el-Azhar (see below, p. 154) was spared, not only from interference, but even from having to sustain a rivalry with Istanbul, is particularly noteworthy. Although the Ottoman hierarchy was recruited exclusively from the schools of Istanbul, even as late as the eighteenth century the Turks professed to regard Cairo as 'the spring of virtues and of scientific knowledge' (according to Cabartî, i. 187/ii. 111).

[4] See above, p. 42. There is no suggestion that the *'Ulemâ* paid any gratuity (*ma'lûm*) to the *Şeyḫ el-Azhar*. It is not clear who benefited from the sale and purchase of religious offices; Chabrol (199) states that the Imâms were under the control of the *Ḳâḍî*, and it seems probable that they and the other religious officials paid a due to the *Ḳâḍî* on appointment (see below, p. 124). The sole relevant narrative in Cabartî relates only that the office of *Ḫaṭîb* in a Cairo mosque was purchased on behalf of a certain *Şeyḫ* and afterwards resold—presumably by the holder (i. 378/ii. 149).

and subordinate corporations.[1] It speaks eloquently for the independence of the Egyptian *'Ulemâ* that, although the Ḥanefî rite was officially adopted by the Ottoman Sultans, no Ḥanefî *Şeyḫ* held the coveted post of *Şeyḫ el-Azhar* until the French occupation, and that it was monopolized during the greater part of the eighteenth century by the *Şâfi'îs*.[2]

In the Asiatic provinces the Ottoman authorities appear to have had much greater powers of interference and control, probably owing in large measure to the lack of any institution with the traditional prestige of el-Azhar, and the stronger influence enjoyed in consequence by the *Ḳâḍîs* and *Muftîs* appointed from Istanbul. It is even doubtful whether the *'Ulemâ* of a single city were united in a common corporation, as appears to have been generally the case in Egypt; the evidence suggests rather that they were divided between a number of professional corporations, each with its own *Şeyḫ* or *Ra'îs*.[3] The authorities at Istanbul not only made direct appointments to offices in the mosques and *madrasas*,[4] but not infrequently sold or conferred the right to make such appointments to third parties.[5] Such rights of appointment (*tawliya*, pl. *tawâlî*) appear frequently in the list of revenues enjoyed by notables, and their lucrative character may be gauged from the fact that the *tawliya* of the Umayyad Mosque at Damascus changed hands for 2,000 gold pieces.[6]

Much the same situation is revealed in our sources in regard to the office of *Naḳîb el-Aşrâf*.[7] The office was an annual one, its holder being appointed or reappointed by the *Naḳîb* at Istanbul, and like other high officers he paid a high premium for his investiture as well as sending an annual gift.[8] Nevertheless, the *niḳâba* at Cairo was generally held for life by members of different local

[1] Cabartî, ii. 184/v. 79.

[2] See the list in J. Heyworth-Dunne, *Introduction to the History of Education in Egypt*, 37, n. 4. In 1192/1778 a determined attempt was made by the Ḥanefî *Muftî* to obtain the post, with Syrian and Mağribî support, but although he was actually appointed by Ibrâhîm Bey, the Egyptian *Şeyḫs* finally forced Murâd Bey to invest the rival *Şâfi'î* candidate (Cabartî, ii. 53–54/iv. 67–70).

[3] *Ra'îs* of the *fuḳahâ* at Aleppo: Murâdî, i. 24; *Ra'îs* of the *ḫuṭabâ* at Jerusalem: ibid. iv. 94. Similarly at Medina there was a *Ra'îs* of the *Ḥanefî 'Ulemâ* (iv. 23) and a *Şeyḫ* of the *ḫuṭabâ* (iv. 17). The term *Şadr* is used in some passages (e.g. i. 62; iv. 18) as if it implied the headship of the *'Ulemâ* at Damascus, but in others it appears to be simply an epithet (e.g. i. 205).

[4] Murâdî, iv. 15, 118, 142.

[5] Ibid. iii. 135; iv. 40 (*tawliya* of a *madrasa* held by a military officer). But the religious offices in certain mosques, &c., seem to have been in the gift of specific families: ibid. iii. 127, 275.

[6] Ibid. iv. 235. For *tawliyas* of religious endowments see below, Ch. XIII.

[7] See above, p. 93.

[8] Chabrol (200–1) puts the price of his investiture at about 40,000 paras; cf. Cabartî, iv. 243/ix. 169. But Chabrol is in error in stating that the *Naḳîb* usually arrived in Egypt in company with the Ottoman Chief *Ḳâḍî*.

families and often passed by heredity.[1] On several occasions persons arrived from Istanbul with diplomas of appointment as *Naḳîb*, but usually without much success. One was murdered on his arrival, another was not allowed to enter on his functions but was granted a pension from the revenues of the office,[2] a third was turned down by the *Aşrâf* on his arrival, and though afterwards formally invested by the *Paşa*, was dismissed after a few weeks.[3] Apart from this practical right of veto by the *Aşrâf*, the powers of the *Naḳîb* at Cairo were to some extent counterbalanced by the existence of another important personage, the *Şeyḫ el-Sâdât* or '*Şeyḫ* of the *Seyyids*', the head of the *Wafâ'î* corporation of *Şerîfs*. Other towns which boasted a number of *Seyyids* in their population also had a local *Naḳîb el-Aşrâf*.[4]

Whereas in Egypt the *niḳâba* was a purely socio-religious office, in several of the cities of Syria it had also a military and political aspect. It will be recalled that the military forces of both Aleppo and Damascus included large bodies of professed *Seyyids*, who were at constant feud with the local Janissaries.[5] Even though the *Naḳîb* was usually a person of juridical education and attainments,[6] he was in consequence drawn into political rivalries. His office was too important to be left for long in the same hands; and it is evident that as a result of political changes it often passed from one candidate to another, although the same person might hold it several times.[7] In Syria, as in Egypt, the *Aşrâf* were known to show open hostility to strangers who arrived with diplomas from Istanbul,[8] and in 1685 the *Naḳîb* of Aleppo was set upon by the mob and stoned to death.[9] Even in the smaller towns the *Naḳîbs* sometimes played a political role. At Ḥamâh (as at Bağdâd) the

[1] Its monopolization by the Bekrî family began only in 1816; see Muḥ. Tawfîḳ el-Bekrî, 45.

[2] The revenues of the *Naḳîb* were derived from the possession of several villages: Chabrol, 200–1. Cf. the Report of Ḥuseyn Efendi, in *Bulletin of the Faculty of Arts of Fuad I University*, iv. 25.

[3] See for references to the *Naḳîb el-Aşrâf* at Cairo, Cabartî, i. 74, 160, 165, 231; ii. 72, 101, 252; iii. 203–4, 207, 208, 211; iv. 193 (trans. i. 179; ii. 42, 53, 180; iv. 102, 167–8; v. 201; vii. 75–77, 84, 86, 94; ix. 56). Also Murâdî, i. 169–70.

[4] *Naḳîb el-Aşrâf* at Rosetta: Cabartî, iv. 50/viii. 107; at Damanhûr: ibid. iv. 82/viii. 180; at Damietta: Carali, i. 2, p. 44. For the *Wafâ'î Şerîfs* see p. 197, n. 6.

[5] See above, Part I, pp. 218 sqq.. Olivier, ii. 308–9, estimates the *Şerîfs* of Aleppo at 3,000–4,000 families and remarks on their insolence.

[6] Very often the same person held the double office of *Ḥanefî Muftî* and *Naḳîb*: Murâdî, iii. 85; iv. 261 (both at Aleppo); the Ḥamza family at Damascus (i. 22–24; ii. 157; iii. 66–67), and the historian Murâdî himself.

[7] Murâdî, iii. 67, 207.

[8] Ibid. ii. 294–5. The victim in this instance was a member of the displaced Keylânî family of Ḥamâh. One of the rejected *Naḳîbs* in Egypt was also a Keylânî: Cabartî, ii. 101/iv. 167–8.

[9] He was accused of having taken bribes from the grain merchants and of poisoning the governor: Ğazzî, iii. 291. Another *Naḳîb* of Aleppo was removed in 1766 and exiled for tyranny and cupidity: ibid.

office was hereditary in the family of el-Gîlânî (or Keylânî), descendants of the founder of the widespread *Ḳâdirî ṭarîḳa*, who enjoyed in consequence an immense prestige in all parts of Western Asia.[1] About 1700 they obtained the government of Ḥamâh from the Porte, but their rule was so oppressive that in 1730 the population rose against them and drove them out, and the *niḳâba* was transferred to another family.[2] In 1706 the *Naḳîb* of Jerusalem revolted and drove out the Governor; a strong force was sent against him and he was captured and executed at Istanbul.[3]

Although, like other groups and corporations, the *şeyḫly* class was recruited chiefly by inheritance, it never formed a closed caste. The border line between *Şeyḫ*, merchant, and educated clerk or artisan was not always very clear, since the education of these latter classes also was mainly of a religious character.[4] There are numerous examples not only of sons of military officers and secretaries who gave up the service of the ruling institution and adopted the *şeyḫly* profession,[5] but also of *Şeyḫs* who began life as weavers, dyers, and other artisans.[6] Very often, too, professional *'Ulemâ* engaged in trade and industry, sometimes out of religious scruples, since they regarded it as unlawful to accept stipends out of revenues which were not sanctioned by the *Şerî'a*.[7]

For sons of *Şeyḫs* to take up other professions was apparently rare; it was considered a step down when a member of a *şeyḫly* family took up even the profession of secretary.[8] One very unusual case is recorded of a *Şeyḫ* who became *Kâḫyâ* to the *Paşa* of Ṣaydâ, much against his will, and was afterwards killed in fighting

[1] Murâdî, i. 219–20; iii. 46, 247–8; and other passages. Cf. also Pococke, ii. 144. For the *Ḳâdirî ṭarîḳa*, see below, p. 196.

[2] Murâdî, iii. 47, 260.

[3] Kurd 'Alî, *Ḫiṭaṭ el-Şâm*, ii. 287; cf. Râşid, *Ta'rîḫ* (ed. 1740), fols. 49ª, 56ª. A later *Naḳîb* of Jerusalem also came into conflict with the *Paşa* of Damascus and was deposed, the office passing to his son: Murâdî, iii. 126 (cf. Cabartî, i. 412/iii. 212). Murâdî mentions also *Naḳîbs* at Ṣaydâ (i. 278) and Nâblus (iii. 83; iv. 183).

[4] Cf. Cabartî iv. 25/viii. 54; Murâdî, ii. 20, 158, 219, 230–1, &c.

[5] e.g. Murâdî, i. 256; iii. 57–58, 176–8; iv. 16; and Cabartî, iv. 215/ix. 108. Whether entry into a religious corporation involved any formality of transfer (as in Turkey; cf. Thornton², i. 139) is not stated.

[6] e.g. Murâdî, i. 256–7; ii. 281; iv. 238–9. The *şeyḫly* house of Ṭabbâḫ at Aleppo was founded by the son of a cook who made his fortune by hiring out brass utensils (ibid. ii. 30–31). On the other hand, it seems to have been very rare for the son of a *fellâḥ* to become a *Şeyḫ*, and Murâdî records (iii. 276) some of the sarcasms directed at a prominent *Şeyḫ* in Damascus because of his village origin.

[7] Murâdî, i. 68, 132; iii. 59; iv. 13; Cabartî, ii. 181/v. 73. For the same reason it was customary to grant pensions to *Şeyḫs* from the revenues received under the head of poll-tax from non-Moslems; cf. Murâdî, ii. 33, and *Firmans Impériaux Ottomans*, Nos. 16, 18, 25–27, 31, 33–36, &c. (but sometimes also from customs revenues, ibid. Nos. 28–30, 39, &c.).

[8] Murâdî, iii. 108.

against the Persians at Baṣra.[1] On the other hand, there are several instances recorded of *Şeyḫs* who, by intermarriage with Turkish families, inherited military posts. Thus the father of the historian Cabartî inherited from his father-in-law the command of the forts at Suez, Ṭor, and Muwailiḥ, but subsequently resigned them.[2] A Syrian *Şeyḫ*, related by marriage to the 'Aẓm family, transferred to the military service and was appointed to the command of the castle of Telbîsa, between Ḥomṣ and Ḥamâh.[3] Cases are even recorded of *Şeyḫs* who, though remaining in their religious profession, possessed mamlûks.[4]

The *şeyḫ*ly class thus presents an almost infinitely graduated series from every point of view: in respect of learning, reputation and character, but above all in respect of wealth and position; and in spite of constant fluctuations these differences were accentuated by the common tendency towards hereditary transmission of offices.[5] Hence, to make any collective estimate of the activity and character of the *'Ulemâ* is impossible without doing injury to some of the parties. On the one hand, there are to be found *Şeyḫs* of pious and ascetic mind who lived in poverty and hardship,[6] who resigned their offices and revenues,[7] or who even refused to take office when it was offered to them.[8] Among the more wealthy families also many examples could be cited of pious and upright men.[9] But while these were presumably representative of the great majority of humble and forgotten *Şeyḫs*, *Imâms*, *Ḫaṭîbs*, and doctors, they naturally figure less prominently in the chronicles of

[1] ibid. iv. 15.

[2] Cabartî, i. 391/iii. 179. Other examples of intermarriage: Murâdî, i. 274; iii. 39, 47.

[3] Ibid. 12. He was succeeded in this office by his son, who held also the government of these two cities on behalf of the *Paşa* of Damascus and was a noted man of letters and poet (cf. ibid. 15).

[4] Cabartî, i. 73/i. 178 (Şeyḫ Muḥammad Ṣanan, a *Şeyḫ el-Azhar*); Murâdî, ii. 33; iv. 69.

[5] Numerous examples will be found in contemporary biographies; e.g. Murâdî, i. 117, 119, 176, 223; ii. 11, 293, 330; iii. 89 (a father's offices divided between his nine sons); Cabartî, i. 74, 388, 417; iii. 555/i. 179; iii. 172–3, 224; vii. 426.

[6] Murâdi, i. 214–15, 310, &c. See also Heyworth-Dunne, 30–31.

[7] Murâdî, ii. 27.

[8] Ibid. iv. 67.

[9] The following portrait of a typical *'Âlim* of an honourable and well-to-do family and of upright character is worth quoting: 'He excelled in law, the rules of inheritance, and calculation, and possessed by heart a great deal of verse of a religious, ethical and didactic character. He was pious and upright; a devotee, frequently spending his nights in prayer; concerned with his own inmost soul; sound-hearted, knowing nothing of deceit or envy; doing good to those who used him ill; of handsome form and cheerful countenance; full of humility and dispensing with formality; with a strong trust in God, truthful in speech and of a happy disposition; an eager reader of works of learning; avoiding what did not concern him; easy and open-handed in his worldly affairs, but strict in matters of religion; preferring solitude and retreat; with no inclinations for high position and no ambitions reaching out towards it.' (Murâdî, ii. 293–4.)

the period than the highly-placed and fortunate minority who belonged to the long-established and honourable *şeyẖly* families of the capital and the great cities. And some of the facts which we have stated in the preceding pages show that, even making all allowance for the exceptions, it cannot be denied that by the eighteenth century corruption had made serious inroads into the higher ranks, at least, of the learned profession.

We are faced, in consequence, with the invidious task of describing some of the causes and results of the deterioration of the religious institution which, as in the ruling institution and for similar reasons, set in about the end of the sixteenth century. The example was set by the hierarchy of the capital. In the first place, as we have already noted, the Sultans' retirement into the seclusion of palace life put an end to the encouragement of learning afforded by their predecessors both directly, by the foundation of *madrasas* for special branches of learning,[1] and indirectly by the maintenance of the Court as to some extent an intellectual centre. In the second place, just as the Janissaries and the grandees of the government desired to secure to their sons and relatives such profitable employment as they enjoyed themselves, so did the *'Ulemâ*. The process consisted in their case, it is true, of the virtual exclusion of all but a certain class of Moslems from at any rate the higher ranks of the profession, whereas the abandonment of the *devşirme* system had broadened the basis of recruitment for the ruling institution. But this was due to the comparative paucity of 'learned' posts. In the third place, here again it was the use of corruption that facilitated the breach by the *'Ulemâ* of the regulations laid down for the granting of diplomas and the distribution of offices.

In the days before decay set in, the *'Ulemâ* enjoyed an almost universal respect for the real learning they displayed and the integrity with which in general they administered justice. Moreover, at this time they usually adhered to an old tradition of Islâm in living modestly,[2] an adherence encouraged by the fact that the scale upon which they were paid was by no means lavish. All three branches then received stipends; and though these were sup-

[1] According to Seyyid Muṣṭafâ, iii. 109, after the millenary the only subjects studied by the *'Ulemâ* were the *Şer'î* sciences and literature. He contradicts this statement, however, on the following pages of his work so far as to say that though some persons still studied 'the philosophical sciences and mathematical arts', they were at a disadvantage in having no facilities for such work.

[2] See Ḳoçu Bey (Behrnauer, 290, 292). This author states that when he first came to Istanbul the *'Ulemâ*, unlike those of the later time of which he writes, had no servants and followers. When a scholar or a professor passed by, everyone would show him honour. The *'Ulemâ* then dressed as other men, without distinctive ornament.

plemented[1] in the case of the judges by the fees they were entitled to charge for their notarial services,[2] the latter did not suffice to make their fortunes. The *'Ulemâ* benefited in their pockets, on the other hand, by being exempt from all taxation, and had this advantage over the members of the ruling institution, that their property was safe from confiscation.[3] These circumstances were to prove of prime importance in guiding the future development of the profession. So long as merit maintained itself, however, against nepotism and corruption as the basis of admission and advancement, they were of minor weight.

Already in the reign of Süleymân the Magnificent, nevertheless, favour and wealth had begun to play a part in the elevation of *Ḳâḍî-'askers*; and the luxury that characterized his court no doubt influenced the *'Ulemâ* as well as the *Ḳapî Ḳullarî*. The subsequent debasement of the coinage also sadly reduced the value of the fixed stipends allotted to them, causing them to look about for other, unauthorized, sources of revenue. The millenary in the reign of Murâd III is again indicated as the epoch of their demoralization,[4] and the Sultan's favourites as to some extent its authors. But the *'Ulemâ* themselves seem to have initiated the process, by procuring the bestowal on their children and followers of the diplomas that rendered them eligible for appointments without their having passed the necessary examinations.[5] The courtiers and powerful members of the ruling institution soon followed their example, and the disposal of posts by nepotism was only a step towards their disposal by sale.[6] Persons without influence continued to enter the profession in the normal fashion, indeed, so that two types of *'Ulemâ* came to be recognized: real and 'official'.[7] But even for these the instruction available in the *madrasas*, being now partly in the hands of ignorant professors, themselves

[1] Apparently from the Treasury. *Muftîs* and mosque ministers also received extra pay from *waḳf* funds; see D'Ohsson, iv. 609, 614–51. D'Ohsson evidently exaggerates the smallness of the salaries received in early times by judges, when he states that even in the reign of Süleymân the Magnificent the *Şeyḫ* received no more than 150 *aḳçes* a day. As noted above (p. 94, n. 5), even in the time of Meḥmed II the chief *Mollâs* received 500 *aḳçes* a day.

[2] See below, p. 125.

[3] D'Ohsson, iv. 599.

[4] Cevdet, i. 112. Ḳoçu Bey (Behrnauer, 291) gives the year 1003 (1594) as that in which the good order of the *'Ulemâ* was first disrupted.

[5] Behrnauer, 291–2: their children would be given *Mevlevîyets*, their followers *ḳâḍîliḳs* and *niyâbets* (office as *Nâ'ibs*). Cf. Seyyid Muṣṭafâ, iii. 109.

[6] Ḳoçu Bey (Behrnauer, 293) declared that to initiate a reform it must be made impossible for *mulâzemets* (certificates of eligibility for office) to be bought. See also Cevdet, i. 112.

A notable example of nepotism is that of Fâḍil Aḥmed, whose father, the famous Grand *Vezîr* Köprülü Meḥmed Paşa, obtained for him the rank of professor (*müderris*) at the age of sixteen; see *Encyc. of Islam*, s.v. 'Köprülü'.

[7] i.e. *'ülemâyî ṭarîḳ* and *'ülemâyî resmîye* (Seyyid Muṣṭafâ, iii. 109).

irregularly appointed, was of a far lower standard than it had been in the past.[1]

Simultaneously there took place a vast increase in the numbers of the *'Ulemâ*, at least of the professors and judges.[2] This was made possible by a resort to frequent changes of appointment, for which corruption had paved the way. It began with the *Ḳâḍî-'askers*, who, like the rest of the profession, had hitherto retained their offices for many years.[3] They were now dismissed, with increasing frequency, to make room for rivals armed with bribes.[4] And as the disposal of most posts in the judicial service lay with the *Ḳâḍî-'askers*, they recouped themselves for the expense they had been put to in securing their positions by accepting contributions from those to whom these posts were granted. By the eighteenth century these changes of appointment had come to be regularized on the following basis: the *Mollâs* held office for twelve and the ordinary *Ḳâḍîs* for eighteen months.[5] The *Muftîs* and *Nâ'ibs* were still appointed for life, since no system of graduation had been established in their case, and these annual or eighteen-monthly changes were closely connected with the graduation system that had always obtained among the judges. But now in every rank of the hierarchy there were large numbers of ex-office-holders (*ma'zûl*),[6] who were eligible when their turn came round for elevation to the offices next higher.[7] Doctorates, at the same time, were granted even more lavishly than judgeships, since, though it was now an understood thing that their recipients too should buy

[1] For the decay of the *madrasas* see below, pp. 150–1.

[2] Ḳoçu Bey (Behrnauer, 293) states that in his time, whenever a place fell vacant, there were always fifteen or twenty applicants.

[3] Ḳoçu Bey (Behrnauer, 290) gives fifteen years as a common term; cf. Cevdet, i. 110. D'Ohsson (iv. 545) seems to be wrong in placing this innovation only at the end of the seventeenth century.

[4] Ḳoçu Bey (Behrnauer, 292).

[5] Already by the time of 'Abdu 'r-Raḥmân Tevḳî'î (1677) the term for *Mollâs* was fixed at one year. That for *Ḳâḍîs* was then two years, according to the *Ḳânûn*; but it is added: 'In our time from two years they deduct four months' (*fî zemânînâ iki seneden dört ay ḳaṣr ederler*). It is notable that the *Ḳânûn* refers to these terms as *'urfî*, i.e. established by the Sultan's arbitrary power; they were not *şer'î*, sanctioned by the Sacred Law. See the *Ḳânûn-nâme*, *Ḳânûn* of the *Mollâs* and *Ḳâḍîs* of Towns; *M.T.M.* i. 541. That two years continued, nevertheless, to be regarded as the proper term for *Ḳâḍîs* is attested by a *ḫaṭṭî hümâyûn* of 1729 addressed to the *Şeyḫü'-Islâm* by Aḥmed III—see Râşid, *Ta'rîḫ* (continuation of Çelebîzâde), iv, fol. 153.

[6] Meaning 'displaced' (Ar. *'azala*, 'set aside, dismiss').

[7] Except those of *Şeyḫü 'l-Islâm* and *Ḳâḍî-'asker* of Rumelia. These offices were generally filled by persons who had already held them. Hence the step from *Ḳâḍî-'asker* of Anatolia to *Ḳâḍî-'asker* of Rumelia was hard to take. No doubt the increase in the latter's power at his colleague's expense (see p. 87 above) was connected with this rule, either as cause or result; cf. D'Ohsson, iv. 545; Juchereau, i. 27–28, 33. To distinguish judges in office from *ma'zûls* the former are referred to in *Ḳânûns* as *bi'l-fi'l* ('actual'); e.g. 'Abdu 'r-Raḥmân Tevḳî'î, *M.T.M.* i. 540.

them, they did so merely to qualify for Mollahood, expecting no immediate return for their money.[1]

The effect of these innovations was, first, to endow the Great *Mollâs* with wealth and power such as they had never possessed in the old days, and, secondly, to make of them an exclusive class. For since the *Şeyḫü 'l-Islâm* was now invariably appointed from among them,[2] all the patronage of the learned profession was theirs to command. So, in the first place, they could amass wealth by means of the payment made by every judge on his appointment and every doctor on receiving his degree,[3] and, in the second place, they could reserve all the best places for their relatives. The charmed circle could be entered by an 'outsider' only by special order of the Sultan. He would exercise this privilege occasionally in favour of the sons of *Paşas* or members of his household, who would then be known as *Bey-Mollâs*,[4] to distinguish them from scions of the true aristocracy.

For an aristocracy it was that these *Mollâ* families constituted, hereditary and privileged, as were no other of the Sultan's subjects. The secular officers of state might momentarily rival or surpass the high *'Ulemâ* in power and wealth; but they were debarred from transmitting these gains to their children on account of their slave status. When they died, if not before, the bulk of their property was seized by the Treasury, whereas that of the *'Ulemâ* was inviolate.[5] While, during the seventeenth century, the learned profession decayed as such, accordingly it gave birth to this new and powerful class which inherited, moreover, the prestige that the *'Ulemâ* of old had deserved.[6] But because very few, if any, of its members were actually endued with light and learning, it offered, regardless of political exigencies, all the opposition it could muster to such innovations as it feared might enhance the power of any other element in Ottoman society. Hence the attachment of the

[1] Ḳoçu Bey (Behrnauer, 292).

[2] See *Encyc. of Islam*, art. 'Shaikh al-Islām'.

[3] D'Ohsson, iv. 610. Each *Mollâ*, for instance, paid the *Şeyḫ* a sum called *Boğça Behâ* on appointment, and so did each of the principal professors on receiving promotion; cf. Seyyid Muṣṭafâ, iii. 77. D'Ohsson states that *Boğça Behâ* means 'prix d'un habit complet', but *boğça* (in modern Turkish spelling *bohça*) usually means 'bundle' or 'cashmere shawl', because these shawls were used for wrapping up. The *Ḳâḍî-'askers* likewise received dues from all *Ḳâḍîs, Nâ'ibs,* and mosque ministers on appointment: D'Ohsson, iv. 611, and see below, p. 123.

[4] So D'Ohsson, vii. 547. Juchereau (i. 26) calls them *Molla Beyis*.

[5] Juchereau, i. 32.

[6] Ḳoçu Bey (Behrnauer, 292), it is true, complains that the *'Ulemâ* were no longer respected when he wrote as they had been in his youth. But it is clear from the evidence which we shall present shortly, as well as from the accounts of D'Ohsson and Juchereau, that even in the eighteenth century they still enjoyed the reverence of the people, as distinguished from educated reformers such as Ḳoçu Bey himself.

'Ulemâ during the latter part of the eighteenth century to the cause of the Janissaries, whom on religious grounds they had no reason to approve.[1] It was not in fact the Janissaries themselves that the *'Ulemâ* regarded with favour, but rather their impotence as an instrument of opposition to their own supremacy. What they dreaded was the creation of a rival force that might be used against them.

The establishment of this learned aristocracy, which was effected simultaneously with the destruction of the old ruling institution, amounted to a real revolution, the transference of power from one class to another. But since the Ottoman Empire had been built up by arms, and by arms alone could be held together, the high *'Ulemâ*, apart from their other shortcomings, were peculiarly ill suited to dominate it. It was to their interest not only, as we have just remarked, to keep the army as nearly impotent as possible, but also to do the same by the Sultans themselves. For owing to their preservation of a right to dismiss the Great *Mollâs*, including the *Şeyẖü 'l-Islâm*, the Sultans formed an obstacle, at least a potential obstacle, to the supremacy of those personages. So the *Şeyẖ* and the *Ḳâḍî-'askers* (whether out of deliberate policy or of instinctive reaction) were on their guard against the Sultan's escape from their supervision, which they could exercise effectually only so long as he remained in Istanbul.[2] Hence, for instance, when Muṣṭafâ III proposed to emulate his ancestors and lead his armies in battle—though a step so well calculated to inspirit them might possibly have affected the fortunes of the war—the *'Ulemâ* would have none of it, and kept him at home.[3]

The actual number of posts in the judicial and professorial, as indeed in the other, branches of the profession had not been increased.[4] But, as we have mentioned, its personnel had become many times larger than in the old days owing to the allocation of these posts to all the holders of any one rank in turn. For every judge and doctor in office, accordingly, there was always a large number out. It therefore became a concern of the corps, especially after it had acquired a class solidarity, to provide for the latter, or at least for those of the *Mollâ* aristocracy. The method adopted was the extension of a system that had been established at an earlier time, prior to the transformation of the *'Ulemâ*. Deserving judges too old or ill to perform their duties had then been given the nominal control of a certain number of *ḳaḍâs* or jurisdictions,

[1] See Juchereau, i. 7 sq., and for the heterodox connexion of the Janissaries, Part I, pp. 63 sqq., and below, p. 191.

[2] Cf. Eton, i. 22.

[3] Ibid.

[4] Indeed, the number of *Mevleviyets*, as was noted above (p. 89), had actually been diminished.

which they administered through deputies with whom they shared the revenues. These holdings, which were called *arpalik*,[1] were now given to all *Şeyhs*, Great *Mollâs*, and *Tahta-Başis* not in office; and other similar holdings, in this case called *ma'işet*, were given to the principal doctors of the *medreses*.[2]

It was thus the Great *Mollâs* who benefited chiefly from this innovation, which was indeed one of the means they used to establish the supremacy of their caste. In the lower ranks of the profession no regular provision appears to have been made for judges awaiting their turn in office. But they were firmly attached by interest to their superiors, in whose hands all patronage lay, and were kept from engaging in other employments which might have rendered them less subservient, since by doing so they forfeited their status.

The same spirit of worldliness and self-seeking, no longer restrained—indeed, even encouraged—by the *'Ulemâ* of the capital, was exemplified in the provinces. The great *şeyhly* families held landed estates (*iltizâms* and *mâlikânes*) and properties in the cities in addition to lucrative religious offices and concessions;[3] we are told of *Şeyhs* who 'loved the world',[4] who had immense fortunes,[5] who were constantly going to Istanbul in order to establish a first claim to vacant posts.[6] Wealth was regarded as an essential requisite for high religious office. There is an illuminating narrative on this point in the annals of Cabartî. He relates that the Egyptian *'Ulemâ*, invited to nominate a successor to the headship of the Bekrî family, hinted that the worthiest candidate was unsuitable on account of his poverty. The *Paşa* rejoined 'Poverty is no disgrace', but immediately furnished him with rich equipment and garments, gave him 80,000 *dirhems*, and a pension of 1,000 piastres.[7] It is not surprising to find bitter satires directed against the *'Ulemâ*,[8] and even mob outbreaks in which they were stoned, sometimes to death.[9]

[1] For *arpaliks* see Part I, p. 188 n. 4. [2] D'Ohsson, iv. 612.

[3] e.g. the Bekrîs, Şarkâwîs, and Cabartîs in Cairo (see Cabartî, *passim*); Murâdî, iii. 207, &c.

[4] Ibid. ii. 215; cf. also i. 285–6, 324; iii. 47; iv. 3, 245; Cabartî, trans. ii. 158, 167, 251, 278, 288; iii. 24; iv. 67, &c. Wealthy merchant *Şeyhs*: Murâdî, i. 175, 250.

[5] A *Hatîb* at Mosul who died in 1734–5 became almost proverbial for his wealth, and once 'entertained seven *Emîrs* with their troops on one day': ibid. iii. 232.

[6] Ibid. ii. 6, 13, 303; iv. 118, 142. Disputes for control of *wakfs*: see below, p. 174.

[7] Cabartî, iii. 210/vii. 92; cf. also iv. 87/viii. 192.

[8] Murâdî, ii. 47; Cabartî, i. 49–50/i. 119–20.

[9] Ğazzî, iii. 293, 297. In one notable instance a *Şeyhü'l-Islâm* himself fell a victim to mob violence. This was that Feydu'llah Efendi (see above, p. 90, n. 3) who, having once been Muştafâ II's *Hoca*, held the post of *Şeyh* throughout that Sultan's reign, from 1695 to 1703. By conferring many of the chief

The relations between the learned and the ruling institutions naturally reflect this state of affairs. On the one hand, the *'Ulemâ* stood for the maintenance of established rights against the tyranny of the governors. Unlike agriculture, industry, and commerce, the religious institution claimed a voice in the government of the state, and its right of participation and control was generally recognized, if not always observed in practice. It was, as we have seen, the one positive link between the governing classes and the governed. However far short it fell of its own ideals of morality and social justice, the secular authorities dared not openly flout it, even if they sometimes despised and circumvented its representatives; and the people in general still looked up to the *'Ulemâ* as their leaders in their relations with the rulers. Although the religious vocation was often hereditary, the equalitarian ideals of Islâm kept its ranks open to scholars of every class and country; and notwithstanding the corruption that tainted the higher castes of the *'Ulemâ*, they remained as a body conscious of their duty to preserve the religious and ethical tradition inherited from generation to generation of their predecessors. No doubt they were bigoted, ignorant (at least of the outside world), and apt, like all such groups, to identify the social content of their doctrine with their own interests. But it would be difficult to prove that any section of the population during the eighteenth century, outside a very small group of persons at Istanbul, was more enlightened or better instructed than were the *'Ulemâ*, and in the last resort their interests concorded to a great extent with the welfare of the Community as a whole. It was probably some obscure appreciation of these facts which was at the bottom of the reverence shown by the people to the *Şeyḫs*.[1] Whereas, moreover, in the preceding cen-

mevleviyets on his sons and other relatives he aroused the hatred of the other chief *'Ulemâ* of the capital, some of whom abetted the rebellion which in the latter year cost Muṣṭafâ his throne. Feyḍu'llah was brought back to Adrianople from the exile into which the Sultan had belatedly sent him, and there tortured and killed by the insurgents; Râşid, *Ta'rîḫ* (ed. 1740), ii, fol. 19.

[1] 'Learning was in a much more flourishing state in Cairo before the entrance of the French army than it has been in later years. . . . Before that period, a shaikh who had studied in the Azhar, if he had only two boys, sons of a moderately rich falláh, to educate, lived in luxury. His two pupils served him, cleaned his house, prepared his food, and though they partook of it with him, were his menial attendants at every time but that of eating; they followed him whenever he went out, carried his shoes (and often kissed them when they took them off) on his entering a mosque, and in every case treated him with the honour due to a prince. He was then distinguished by an ample dress and the large formal turban called a mukleh; and as he passed along the street, whether on foot or mounted on an ass or mule, passengers often pressed towards him to implore a short ejaculatory prayer on their behalf, and he who succeeded in obtaining this wish believed himself especially blessed. If he passed by a Frank riding, the latter was obliged to dismount; if he went to a butcher to procure some meat (for he found it best to do so, and not to send another), the butcher refused to make any charge, but kissed his hand, and received as an honour and a blessing

turies the '*Ulemâ* had lost some of their prestige to the heads of the *ṣûfî* or *dervîş* orders, the universality of *ṣûfî* affiliations and growing prominence of *ṣûfî* families amongst the '*Ulemâ* in the eighteenth century[1] had reinforced their prestige and popular standing.

The *Şeyḫs* on their side were careful to encourage this popular tendency, since it was the chief instrument by which they could bring pressure to bear upon the governors, and they were seldom reluctant to appear in the role of champions and representatives of the people.[2] It was to the *Şeyḫs* of el-Azhar that the populace of Cairo generally had recourse in order to place their wishes or protests before the authorities,[3] and it was the *Şeyḫs* of Damascus who, under pressure from the population, arranged the surrender of the city to Muḥammad Bey Abû Ḏahab after the flight of the *Paşa*.[4] It was one of their principal functions to 'intercede' with the *Paşas*,[5] and the more outstanding personalities held the military authorities in awe of their influence.[6] Since long-established custom had given them a practical immunity from arbitrary execution and punishment, they could afford to brave the displeasure of *Paşas* and *Beys*,[7] although occasional instances of pusillanimity are recorded,[8] and open opposition sometimes entailed dismissal from office or exile.[9] On the whole, however, it would appear from the materials at our disposal that good relations were maintained between the leading '*Ulemâ* and the civil and military authorities.[10]

whatever he chose to give' (E. W. Lane, *Modern Egyptians*, ch. ix); cf. Cabartî, i. 389; ii. 99/iii. 174; iv. 162. Cabartî also refers to the financial privileges and immunities from customs and other duties of highly-placed *Şeyḫs*; though their accounts were duly cast up, the accountants 'would have regarded it as a deadly sin to exact their dues' (iv. 187/ix. 43).

[1] See below, pp. 198–9.

[2] Cf. Murâdî, i. 69; iv. 130; H. Laoust, *Les Gouverneurs de Damas* (Damascus, 1952), 239–40.

[3] e.g. Cabartî, i. 102; iv. 66/i. 238; viii. 143. Even the Sultan of Morocco, writing a letter of protest against the molestation of Moroccan pilgrims by the Beys, addressed it to the '*Ulemâ* of Egypt: Cabartî i. 174/ii. 77–79.

[4] Murâdî, i. 55; and see Part I, p. 221.

[5] e.g. Murâdî, i. 223, 273; ii. 5; iv. 17.

[6] See the biographies of Ş. el-Ḥifnâwî (Cabartî, i. 302/ii. 304), Ş. 'Alî el-Ṣa'îdî (ibid. i. 416/iii. 222), and Ş. 'Abd el-Ğanî el-Nâbulusi (Murâdî, iii. 37).

[7] Judgment given against the *Paşa* in a lawsuit: Cabartî, ii. 124/iv. 224; refusal of the '*Ulemâ* of Alexandria to send a false report at the *Paşa*'s request: Cabartî, iii. 266/vii. 228; and cf. Murâdî, i. 273; iv. 95.

[8] Cabartî, i. 127, 130/i. 293, 301.

[9] Ibid. ii. 18, 51, 98; iii. 210/iii. 268; iv. 62, 162; vii. 92; Murâdî, i. 53; iii. 167. Another instance mentioned by Murâdî (i. 224) is especially interesting. The *Paşa* of Damascus (Süleymân Balṭaci) intended to make a forced loan from the merchants and to institute certain 'oppressive dues', and three prominent *Şeyḫs* opposed the execution of his orders. He thereupon obtained a decree from the Sultan for their exile to Ṣaydâ, but they were recalled three months later, and after a popular reception on their arrival at Damascus the *Paşa* made his apologies and bestowed robes of honour upon them.

[10] Even as landowners, there was little to choose between Mamlûks and *Şeyḫs*; e.g. Cabartî, iv. 191, 234/ix. 52, 149.

Yet it cannot be denied that in maintaining these relations the *şeyḫly* class at times displayed a pliability and a readiness to humour those in power which transgressed even a modest standard of integrity. So ingrained had the habit of submission and of adapting themselves to circumstances become that at moments of decision they showed themselves passive followers rather than active leaders. Preoccupied with their duty of preserving social unity and the solidarity of church and state, they were ready to condone the most glaring breaches by adopting the flimsiest criteria of judgement and in effect sanctioning a double moral standard.[1] A crafty governor could always, by playing on their vanity, find ready tools amongst them, and so reduce the rest to silence,[2] and they too often incurred the suspicion of selling themselves too easily.[3] It is difficult to avoid the impression that in reality the position of the '*Ulemâ* was gravely undermined. Though they still preserved the appearance of power, it was beginning to wear thin; their repeated compromises had shown that in face of

[1] Cf. Cabartî's summing-up of Murâd Bey: 'He was cruel and unjust, but respected the '*Ulemâ*, listened to their intercession, and inclined to Islâm and the Moslems' (iii. 170/vi. 318), and his commendation of Raḍwân Bey (iii. 291/vii. 295–6). Similarly, Murâdî praises the Muğal Sultan Awrangzêb as having 'no equal among the kings of Islâm of this age in respect of upright conduct, fear of God and zeal in religion', yet he relates (without comment) his murder of his brothers (iv. 113–14).

[2] During the prolonged civil struggle in Egypt in 1711, both sides, equally in the wrong, obtained *fatwâs* from the '*Ulemâ* in their favour (Cabartî, i. 108/i. 248). This weakness of moral fibre was by no means confined to the Egyptian *Şeyḫs*, witness the remarkable chapter in the *Prolegomena* of Ibn Ḫaldûn (Book V, ch. 7), in which the author, himself a *Ḳâḍî*, frigidly analyses the relations between the '*Ulemâ* and the secular authorities. See also the following note.

[3] See p. 111, n. 8 above. A still more striking example was given by the '*Ulemâ* of the Holy Cities early in the nineteenth century. There is preserved in Mecca a document containing a lengthy summary of Wahhâbî doctrine, subscribed to on 14th Ḏu 'l-Ḳa'da 1225 (11 Dec. 1810) by the *Şerîf* Ğâlib and others, including the *Muftîs* of the four orthodox rites. The text of Ğâlib's subscription runs as follows: 'I testify that this faith which the Şeyḫ Muḥammad b. 'Abd al-Wahhâb has maintained and which has been propagated by the Imâm of the Moslems, Sa'ûd b. 'Abd al-'Azîz, of declaring the unity of God and rejecting any partner with Him, is the true faith; and that what was practised formerly in Mecca and el-Medîna and is practised in Syria, Egypt, and other countries, of the forms of polytheism which are mentioned in this writing, is infidelity, whereby their blood and property are made lawful [to shed and to seize]; and that whosoever does not enter into this faith and carry out its demands as set forth in this writing is an unbeliever in God and in the Last Day. Written by the *Şerîf* Ğâlib b. Masâ'id, God forgive him.' (Trans. from a photograph of the original document now in Leiden University Library.) In the archives of 'Abdîn Palace, in Cairo, there is preserved a memorial of thanks from the Meccans to Meḥmed 'Alî for their deliverance from the yoke of the Wahhâbîs, 'who have created mischief in the Island of the Arabs and declared their beliefs to be adulterated by incarnation of the Deity and by heresy, and have made lawful to themselves the blood of the household of Islâm and turned back every visitant to the Holy House of God', signed on 10th Muḥarram 1228 (13 Jan. 1813) by the *Şeyḫs* and notables of Mecca, including the identical *Mâlikî Muftî* (Muḥammad 'Arabî el-Bannânî) and the identical *Ḥanbalî Muftî* (Muḥammad b. Yaḥyâ) who had subscribed the former document.

determined action they would yield. The pitiable spectacle which the *Şeyḫs* were to present during the nineteenth century was not solely the result of the rapid overthrow of the old social order. It was the sudden culmination of a long process that had gradually sapped their moral position.

CHAPTER X

THE ADMINISTRATION OF LAW

I. THE NATURE OF ISLAMIC LAW

ISLAMIC law is the deposit of a series of formulations continued over a period of a thousand years. It is not our intention to attempt even a brief synopsis of its provisions, more especially as they are available, in fuller or lesser detail, in a number of authoritative publications.[1] This chapter is more in the nature of a note on certain aspects of the law which have an important bearing on the problems discussed in this and later volumes of our study, and deals in particular with two outstanding features which distinguish it from Western systems of law. In the first place, it is the product of juristic speculation, not statute-law; the state accepted it, and itself derived its legal sanction from it, but had little share in shaping it or determining its methods and decisions. In the second place, the basis of the system is not legal at all, but ethical; it arose out of the *Ḳur'ânic* prescriptions for social conduct, which appeal to the religious duty and conscience of the Believer, and only exceptionally enforce them by specific penalties.

The development of the *Şerî'a* throughout the history of Islamic jurisprudence was conditioned by these two factors. It has already been mentioned in our first chapter that in the early centuries there was much dispute amongst jurists as to rulings and methods of interpretation, and more especially as to the place of rational judgement in meeting new problems. The difficulties which these disputes might have occasioned were surmounted by the acceptance of a dual principle. On the one hand, consensus of opinion (*icmâ'*) was given the rank of a major source of law, little if at all inferior to Revelation and Prophetic Tradition. When such a consensus of opinion was reached on a given point, the door was closed to further controversy on that point. On the other hand, diversity of opinion

[1] Amongst the more important are: J. Schacht, *G. Bergsträsser's Grundzüge des Islamischen Rechts* (Berlin, 1935) (*Ḥanefî*); David Santillana, *Istituzioni di Diritto Musulmano Malichita* (Rome, 1926) (*Mâlikî* and *Şâfi'î*); Th. W. Juynboll, *Handbuch des Islāmischen Gesetzes* (Leiden, 1910) (*Şâfi'î*); E. Sachau, *Muhammedanisches Recht* (Berlin, 1897) (*Şâfi'î*), and numerous translations of Arabic law-books (e.g. C. Hamilton, *The Hedaya* (London, 1791 and 1870 [*Ḥanefî*]). There are more general studies in C. Snouck Hurgronje, *Verspreide Geschriften*, vol. ii (Leiden, 1923); C. H. Becker, *Islamstudien*, vol. i (Leipzig, 1924); and M. Morand, *Introduction à l'Étude du Droit Musulman Algérien* (Algiers, 1921). See also the articles collected in *Law in the Middle East* (ed. by M. Khadduri and H. J. Liebesny), vol. i, Middle East Institute, Washington, D.C., 1955.

was welcomed as 'a mercy from God', and its sting thus removed. Actually, as we have seen, the *Sunnî* jurists gradually enrolled themselves under four different schools, *Ḥanefî*, *Mâlikî*, *Şâfi'î*, and *Ḥanbalî*, each of which recognized the orthodoxy of the others and tolerated their divergences of detail. Hence there is no general 'Islamic law', but four specific orthodox interpretations of Islamic law, with the result that in a given case two, three, or even four different decisions are equally valid, although each judge or jurist might in theory decide only in accordance with the precedents of his own school.

The state, as such, was incapable of altering this situation. It could, and in the Ottoman Empire did, select one school as normative within its territories and limit its official recognition to that one, but it could not prevent the continued activity of the others, nor their validity for their own adherents. Still less could the state combine the rulings of the various schools into an eclectic code, and least of all could it legislate on its own initiative in competition with the *Şerî'a*. For the law, being of divine inspiration, was superior to the state, which existed, in fact, only to execute it. But while this was universally recognized in theory, historical circumstances had conspired to drive a wedge between the state and the law, with unfavourable consequences for both.

During the first century of Islâm, while the *Şerî'a* was still inchoate, ordinary judicial practice was based for the most part on traditional Arab usage, supplemented by the administrative regulations of the Umayyad Caliphs. The beginnings of Islamic jurisprudence coincided with a reaction against the application of such popular and administrative rules, and were dominated by the effort to bring both the practice and the theory of law into conformity with the developing ethical outlook and ideas of Islâm.[1] The established schools of Islamic law represent the victory of this islamizing activity, and the resulting body of legal discussion, constituting the *Şerî'a*, was formally recognized by the 'Abbâsid Caliphs of Bağdâd once and for all as the law administered in the *Ḳâḍî*'s courts (*maḥâkim şer'îya*).

In spite of this, administrative practice still remained outside the control of the jurists, and tended increasingly to trench on the *Ḳâḍî*'s sphere. While the *Şerî'a* remained in theory all-embracing, and its rules continued to be strictly applied in everything that had to do with religious duties and the family, certain branches of civil and penal law were frequently administered by other authorities. Such a limitation of the *Ḳâḍî*'s attributes was not in itself contrary to the *Şerî'a*, since the *Ḳâḍî* is, by definition, the delegate of the civil authority (*Sulṭân*), which is accordingly free to restrict his

[1] See J. Schacht, *The Origins of Islamic Jurisprudence* (Oxford, 1950).

competence,[1] and to delegate the reserved subjects to other tribunals. Thus, from early times, theory and practice came into conflict, and this conflict found expression in the existence side by side of divergent and overlapping jurisdictions. The critical weakness of the *şer'î* courts lay in the conduct of criminal cases and the difficulties sometimes experienced in enforcing the judgments of the *Ḳâḍîs*. To offset this, certain legal powers, or powers of summary punishment, were conferred on the *Muḥtasib*, as inspector of markets and censor of public morals,[2] and on the officers of the *şurṭa* or royal police.[3] Furthermore, the Caliphs of Bağdâd instituted a court of superior instance, called *maẓâlim*, to deal with the more serious civil and criminal cases, especially when they involved administrative and military officers.[4]

It should be observed that none of these institutions and jurisdictions was extra-legal *per se*. The *Şerî'a* itself leaves, in respect of criminal justice, a wide field to the discretion of the sovereign, or of the *Ḳâḍî* acting under the sovereign's direction; and in the *maẓâlim*-court the Caliph or Sultan or his representative (usually sitting with a senior *Ḳâḍî* in attendance) exercised his discretionary powers to award discretionary punishments. The point of departure from the principles of the *Şerî'a* came from their practice, more especially when *Muḥtasibs* and police officers exceeded the strict limits of their jurisdictions and powers, and the *maẓâlim*-courts, through caprice or administrative regulation, or by abusive extension of judicial functions, trespassed upon or violated *Şerî'a* norms. Under the Selcuḳids, the *maẓâlim*, delegated to royal officers, became still further assimilated to administrative courts, and (although evidence on the point is still lacking) presumably still more subject to administrative regulation. With the development of the system of military *iḳṭâ's* or fiefs, some of the regular functions of the *maẓâlim* were transferred to the courts of *Ḳâḍî'l-'asker*,[5] before whom alone the members of the standing military forces were justiciable, and to whose courts, in consequence, suits relating to property were generally referred. The *ḳânûns* of the Ottoman Sultans and the extensive jurisdiction of the *Ḳâḍî-'asker* were the logical end of this process.[6]

This intervention of the state in the administration of law led to a fissure, familiar in human affairs and especially in socio-religious systems, between the uncompromising supporters of the pure ideal

[1] See e.g., E. Tyan, *Histoire de l'Organisation judiciaire en Pays d'Islam*, ii (Beirut, 1943), 19 sqq.
[2] See Part I, pp. 279, 287–8, and Tyan, ii. 436 sqq.
[3] See ibid. 352 sqq.
[4] See Part I, p. 27, and Tyan, ii. 141 sqq.
[5] See ibid., 289 sqq.
[6] See Part I, p. 23, and pp. 119–90 below.

and those who, lest worse might befall, strove to maintain some liaison between the *Şerî'a* and the state. The first class is represented by that great body of Moslem jurists who, uninfluenced by the problems of power and the need of adjustment to practical issues, continued to develop the *Şerî'a* on its now systematically established lines. Juristic casuistry, in the best sense, was from the outset an essential element in their method; but juristic speculation, unhampered by the necessity of applying its conclusions to the facts of daily life, followed the direction taken by much of medieval Islamic intellectual activity. Basing itself upon what were held to be the certain and infallible texts of a verbally-inspired *Ḳur'ân* and Prophetic Tradition, it pushed the method of deduction and logical analysis to its utmost limit. Though the majority of jurists were absolutely sincere, casuistry sometimes declined into sophistry. More and more it came to be recognized that the juristic formulations of the *Şerî'a* were simply an ideal, though the fault was not imputed to the jurists but disguised, as in the passage quoted above from el-Ğazâlî,[1] by attributing all departures from it to the degeneracy of the age.

Yet this ideal system continued to be valid law. The writings of the meanest legist, if they were accepted by his fellows, might determine the practice of the *şer'î* courts throughout the Empire, without requiring any authorization from the Sultan or even from the *Şeyḫü 'l-Islâm*. Indeed, it was a compendium of legal decisions, the *Fetâwâ 'Alemgîrî*, compiled by a commission of jurists in India about the end of the seventeenth century, which was one of the books most widely used in the Ottoman lands in the eighteenth.[2]

That the *Şerî'a* was never elaborated into a formal code is probably, however, due less to this than to the circumstances of its origin. The *Ḳur'ân* is commonly referred to by European writers as a law-book and Muḥammad as a law-giver. It is true, as we have just said, that the sources of Islamic law are to be found in the *Ḳur'ân* and what was accepted as Prophetic Tradition, but the former statement conveys an entirely false idea. There is not much more 'law', in the strict sense, to be found in the *Ḳur'ân* than in the Gospels, and the legal pronouncements ascribed to Muḥammad in the Tradition are admitted, even by Moslem scholars, to be amongst those of more dubious authenticity. For although Muḥammad 'legislated' upon occasion, the basis of his 'legislation' is not legal, but ethical; he does not lay

[1] Part I, p. 31.

[2] Cf. Murâdî, iv. 114: 'They became famous in the Ḥijâz, Egypt, Syria, and Rûm, were universally used, and formed a source upon which the *Muftîs* drew for their *fetwâs*.'

down legal formulas, but indicates what is right conduct and what wrong. Even the most legal-sounding passages in the *Ḳur'ân* are generally accompanied by ethical qualifications and backed up by an appeal to religious feeling.

The spirit of this legislation was shared by those jurists of 'Irâḳ and Medîna who, in the second century, gave its definitive shape to the *Şerî'a*. Their outlook and standards also were ethico-religious, and the effect of their labours was that in all subsequent ages the legal pattern was woven on an ethical warp. The categories into which all actions are juridically classified are moral categories: obligatory, recommended, indifferent, objectionable, prohibited. Thus the *Şerî'a* has been well summed up as 'a doctrine of duties'; for many derelictions the penalties are religious, not civil, and sometimes no penalties are laid down at all.

But while Islamic law, even in its later formulations, never lost this ethical character, it was exposed to a danger which is apt to invade every system in which speculation is not continually referred to the test of practice. The Islamic ideal is, in its conception of Justice itself, nearer to the Equity of the English common law than to the Roman statute law, in that, while the rights of the individual are fully recognized, the claims of the common good are always kept within view. The early law schools took cognizance of this principle under various names,[1] but the stricter jurists of later times, on methodological grounds, attempted either to deny their legality, or to restrict them to a limited number of defined cases. They were not, in fact, entirely successful in this, for reasons which will be seen presently, but the effect of their arguments was to enhance, in the later expositions of the *Şerî'a*, that appearance of rigidity and inflexibility which almost all writers on Islamic law have regarded as its chief feature.

Those students of the law, on the other hand, who accepted the responsibility of administering it in practice, as judges in the *şer'î* courts, were forced to compromise in some degree between this ideal system and the actual circumstances of their place and time, at the price, as we have noted above,[2] of some loss of esteem among their more rigid brethren. Such compromises were not always due to the intervention of the state, but often the result of practical legal issues which forced themselves upon the consideration of the judges. From earliest times Moslem jurists had been forced, even if unwillingly, to pay some attention to the variety of usages current among the peoples who entered into the Islamic Empire. In theory, the *Şerî'a* superseded all such forms of customary law (*'âda*), and it was one of the tasks of the jurists, un-

[1] See *Encyc. of Islam*, art. 'Istiḥsān and Istiṣlāḥ' (Schacht).
[2] p. 82 above.

remittingly pursued, to translate this theory into practice. But the necessities of administration often came into conflict with their ideals, and the officers of the law sometimes found it more equitable (and no doubt easier) to accept ingrained local usages, though they might run counter to the prescriptions of the *Şerî'a*. Thus the practice of the law courts in every region was marked by more or less adaptation to the customs of the country.[1] The consciences of the *Ḳâḍîs* were, if necessary, eased by the admission of qualifying circumstances (*şurûṭ*) and by the so-called *ḥiyal*[2] or interpretations by which the exact letter of the law could be made to permit a particular course of action. The term was less disparaging than it sounds,[3] even if such artifices were spurned by the stricter sort. Very often, however, the application of customary law was not in the hands of the *Ḳâḍîs* at all, but, as will be shown later, in those of different secular authorities.

During the earlier centuries the application of administrative regulations might be justified in the same manner, but as the effective influence of the jurists on administrative practice weakened, the *Ḳâḍîs* were often forced to admit, on the ground of 'compulsion', practices which conflicted more or less openly with the formulations of the *Şerî'a*.[4] Since *Ḳâḍîs* were frequently associated with the other offices and tribunals mentioned earlier in this chapter, the boundary between *şer'î* law and administrative ruling cannot always have been easy to draw; and under the Mamlûk Sultans of Egypt many *Ḳâḍîs* seem to have administered concurrently both *şer'î* law and a more informal penal law, based on public utility, known as *siyâsa*.[5] The novelty introduced by the Ottoman Sultans was simply that the distinction between *şer'î* and administrative law was now codified through the issue of *ḳânûns* and *ḳânûn-nâmes*. And in so doing, though the Sultans showed, on the whole, the greatest concern for the proper organization and working of the *şer'î* courts in their dominions, yet they did not hesitate to introduce, or to sanction, a variety of rules and penal-

[1] This applied especially to contracts and obligations, and its significance must not be overstressed. In all matters of personal law it was much less important than the reverse influence of the *Şerî'a* in moulding the diversity of usages into some degree of uniformity, and in bringing them within the radius of *şer'î* authority. Customary law, as admitted in these courts, thus constituted a kind of outer ring of *şer'î* practice, in which, very often, the principles of the *Şerî'a* were respected even if its explicit rulings were sidetracked.

[2] *Şurûṭ*, pl. of *şarṭ*, 'condition'; *ḥiyal*, pl. of *ḥîla*, 'artifice' or 'quibble'.

[3] 'Evasions are considered as a permissible use of means put at man's disposal by Allah himself': *Encyc. of Islam*; art. 'Sharī'a' (Schacht). See also Ibn Nuceym, *el-Aşbâh wa'l-Naẓâ'ir* (Cairo, 1298), 218 sqq., and J. Schacht, 'Die arabische *ḥiyal*-Litteratur', in *Der Islam*, xv. 211–32.

[4] See for the later juristic admission of 'compulsion' (*ikrâh*) or 'necessity' (*ḍarûra*), C. Snouck Hurgronje, *Verspreide Geschriften*, ii (Leiden, 1923), 318.

[5] Tyan, *Organisation judiciaire*, ii. 161 sqq.

ties that conflicted with the letter of the *Şerîʿa*, as it had been elaborated by the jurists of earlier centuries.[1]

To sum up, then, it may be said that the *Şerîʿa*, in its classical formulations, held up to the conscience of successive generations of Moslems an ideal, ethical even more than legal in the strict sense, of what a true Moslem society should be, while the practice of the courts reflected the measure in which each actual society fell short of that ideal. Yet one must not regard even the *Şerîʿa* as incapable of adaptation and modification to meet new circumstances. True, it was in theory unchangeable; but while ancient rulings were handed down from generation to generation and never disappeared from the law-books, those which were no longer acceptable were allowed to fall into desuetude and newer rulings took their places. A zealous jurist might from time to time revive a discarded rule 'to keep the *Sunna* alive', but his action inspired more mocking comment than appreciation. 'There is probably nothing in Eastern life which appears stranger to the Occidental than this quiet shaping of the law, this entirely unformalistic jurisdiction which is yet so full of form, and this justice which remains free although it never loses sight of circumstances and of the personal sense of right and wrong.'[2] The Islamic legal system, as we have seen, even included a special class of practitioners, the *Muftîs*,[3] whose real function it was to guide and to sanction this process of adaptation. It was the outwardly immutable form in which the *Şerîʿa* is enshrined, combined with the theoretical principles upon which it was constructed, which led European observers—as so often in the case of other Islamic institutions as well—to ascribe to it fixity and lack of adaptability and to regard it as an outworn system and an obstacle to progress. With this last criticism we shall deal in due course; but for our present purposes it is sufficient to note that under its external rigidity Islamic law showed in practice a degree of flexibility which allowed it to meet all the needs of the populations under its jurisdiction.

The ideal, of course, was not always attained, but it was made easier to attain by the corporative structure of Islamic society, upon which we have already so often insisted. Where each group was relatively small, its general interests were more readily grasped,

[1] e.g. the *şerʿî* penalties for theft, adultery, slander, and the drinking of wine were by *ḳânûn* either wholly or partially replaced by monetary fines, a form of punishment foreign to the *Şerîʿa*; see J. Schacht, 'Šarīʿa und Qānūn im modernen Aegypten', in *Der Islam*, xx (1932), 211 sqq. But the limitation of the ancient *şerʿî* penalties for such offences had long been a feature of *Ḥanefî* law; see J. Schacht, *G. Bergsträsser's Grundzüge d. Islam. Rechts*, 97. Cf. also p. 129 below.

[2] A. de Kat Angelino, *Colonial Policy* (The Hague, 1931), i. 73. The whole passage, although referring strictly to customary law, deserves careful study from the standpoint of Islamic law as well.

[3] See Section III below.

and the individual, in his obvious dependence upon the group and the closeness of his relations with its other members, was more fully conscious that his own welfare was bound up with that of the group as a whole. There was thus an intimacy in the administration of Moslem law, a regard for the relevance of each case to the interests of the Community, great or small, which is totally opposed to the impersonality of Western 'Justice', and which, with its moral objects and sanctions, appealed to and as a rule satisfied the moral sense of the people.

II. THE ḲÂḌÎS

It has already been pointed out, in the first chapter, that the establishment and maintenance of the Islamic canon law or *Şerî'a* was one of the ruling principles of the Ottoman Sultanate. During the government of their predecessors in Egypt and Syria the judicial authority of the *Şerî'a* had been sadly diminished. The Mamlûk Sultans, it is true, were careful to surround themselves with *'Ulemâ* and *Şeyḫs*, to nominate chief *Ḳâḍîs* of all four rites, and to carry them in their train on their progresses into Syria, but this external complaisance barely hid the growing encroachment of the royal officers upon the prerogatives of the *Ḳâḍîs* and of 'political law' upon the ordinances of the *Şerî'a*.[1] The substitution of Ottoman supremacy had an immediate and salutary effect; the officers and tribunals of the *Şerî'a* were again given effective jurisdiction (subject, it is true, to some limitation by *ḳânûn*) and endowed with the support and authority of the state.

In describing the organization of the *'Ulemâ* in the preceding chapter, we have had occasion to show how the Sultans reorganized the judicial service in the Empire under a hierarchy culminating in the *Şeyḫü'l-Islâm* and the two *Ḳâḍî-'askers* of Rumelia and Anatolia. Below these, as we have seen, were the 'Great' *Mollâs* who filled the offices of Chief *Ḳâḍî* in the capital, the two Holy Cities, Bursa, Adrianople, Damascus, Cairo, Jerusalem, Smyrna, Aleppo, and other centres.[2] Below these again came the 'Lesser' *Mollâs* in two grades, to the senior of which belonged the *Ḳâḍîs* of Bağdâd and Diyâr Bekir. Lastly came the ordinary *Ḳâḍîs* and their *Nâ'ibs* or substitutes.

[1] See for the relations between the Mamlûks and *'Ulemâ*, Wiet, *Précis*, ii. 239; Gaudefroy-Demombynes, *La Syrie*, pp. lxxvi sqq.; for the encroachments of the *ḥâcib* or Chamberlain upon the *şer'î* administration, Maḳrîzî, *Ḫiṭaṭ*, ii. 219–20 (quoted in R. Levy, *Sociology of Islam*, ii. 246), Tyan, *Organisation judiciaire*, ii. 316–17, and Ibn Ḫaldûn, *Prolégomènes*, tr. de Slane, ii. 17–18.

[2] See p. 89 above. The chief *Ḳâḍîs* in provincial capitals, and more especially in Cairo, were sometimes locally called by the title of *Ḳâḍî-'asker*; cf. Chabrol, 236; Muḥ. Tawfîḳ el-Bekrî, *Beyt el-Ṣiddîḳ*, 61 (quoting the journal of Ş. 'Abdu 'l-Ğanî Nâbulusî).

The subordinate *Ḳâḍîs* were divided into three categories—European, Asiatic, and Egyptian. Those of Asia and Egypt were nominated by the *Ḳâḍî-'asker* of Anatolia, and those of Europe by the *Ḳâḍî-'asker* of Rumelia, who had jurisdiction also over the North African Regencies and the Crimea. The three services were entirely separate; *Ḳâḍîs* were not transferred from one to another. The scheme was typically complicated, each service having a number of grades up which its members worked their way. The European service had nine grades, the ninth and highest being formed by 'The Six of Rumelia' (*Sitte-i Rumeli*). The Asiatic service had ten and the Egyptian service (containing thirty-six jurisdictions in all) had six, the second highest grade in both services being called *mûṣile* ('introductory'), and the highest 'The Six of Anatolia' and 'The Six of Egypt' respectively.[1]

By the middle of the eighteenth century all these posts were held on annual tenures,[2] mainly by Turkish-speaking judges,[3] and all were appointed by and directly responsible to the *Ḳâḍî-'asker* of Rumelia or Anatolia, not to the local Chief *Ḳâḍî*. All *Ḳâḍîs* appointed to office in the provinces were required to reside in their districts except for the two senior *Ḳâḍîs* of each service who resided at the capital, those of Europe acting as counsellors to the *Ḳâḍî-'asker* of Rumelia, and those of Asia and Egypt as counsellors to the *Ḳâḍî-'asker* of Anatolia. They were known as *Taḫta Baṣîs*, 'Heads of the List'.[4] It is noted as a rare exception when an Ottoman *Ḳâḍî* spent his whole life in one post.[5]

No *mîrî* was exacted from *Ḳâḍîs*, but for each category there was a fixed tariff of dues of investiture, or for confirmation if their tenure was extended.[6] These dues, however, established at a time

[1] D'Ohsson, iv. 570; Hammer-Purgstall, *Hist. de l'Empire Ottoman*, trad. Hellert, xvii. 15; Report of el-'Arîşî, *Bulletin de l'Institut d'Égypte*, xviii. 1–18; and cf. generally Chabrol, *Essai sur les mœurs*, esp. 229 sqq. It looks as though each service had originally possessed one top grade, in which there were six *Ḳâḍîs*; that the European service had originally had two lower grades, and the Anatolian service originally eight lower grades. As it was, in the 'Six of Rumelia' grade there were thirteen *Ḳâḍîs* and in the 'Six of Anatolia' grade fifteen. Each grade in the Egyptian service still had six *Ḳâḍîs*.

[2] Originally they were held in perpetuity, but (according to D'Ohsson, 545) were changed to annual tenures at the end of the seventeenth century 'in order to prevent abuses arising from a long stay in the same city and to facilitate the promotion of a multitude of candidates'; see, however, Chap. IX, p. 106, n. 5 above.

[3] But it appears both from Murâdî's biographies and from the names given in el-'Arîşî's report (loc. cit. 7/12), that local *'Ulemâ* were frequently appointed to these posts.

[4] D'Ohsson, iv. 569–73. *Taḫta* means 'a board', and here, it would seem, a board or 'slate' bearing a list of names.

[5] Cabartî, iv. 260/ix. 203. It is remarked even when a *Ḳâḍî* of Damascus held his office for five years: Murâdî, iv. 219.

[6] Hammer-Purgstall, trad. Hellert, xvii. 14. These ranged from 250 *aḳçes* (150 for confirmation) for judges of the first grade to 67 *aḳçes* (24 for confirmation) for those of the ninth.

when the revenues enjoyed by *Ḳâḍîs* were reckoned only in hundreds of *akçes*,[1] in no way corresponded to the sums paid in the eighteenth century by aspirants to judicial office. Like all other official posts they were farmed out, if not actually to the highest bidder, at least for very substantial amounts. The Chief *Ḳâḍî* of Cairo paid 10,000 *paras* a month to the *Şeyḫü 'l-Islâm* in addition to an unspecified sum paid to the *Ḳâḍî-'asker* of Anatolia;[2] and a Chief *Ḳâḍî* of Damascus is said to have paid some 30,000 or 40,000 ducats for his office.[3]

As the school of Abû Ḥanîfa was the official rite throughout the Ottoman dominions, the Ottoman government directly appointed only the Ḥanefî *Ḳâḍîs*, and recognized only their decisions in legal matters. Where a considerable proportion of the local population adhered to another of the four schools (as was, in fact, generally the case in Egypt and Syria),[4] the local authorities seem to have been empowered to recognize one of the leading local jurists of each school as *Ḳâḍî* for members of its own rite;[5] but the limits of the jurisdiction of these *Ḳâḍîs* and their relation to the *Ḥanefî Ḳâḍî* are still obscure. The *Ḳâḍîs* of the dissident (*Şî'î*) groups were apparently on a somewhat similar footing, and in the Lebanon the *Ḳâḍî* of the Druses was appointed by the Druse *Emîr*.[6]

On taking over their offices, each Chief *Ḳâḍî* and *Ḳâḍî* regularly proceeded to appoint one or more judges-substitute (*Nâ'ibs*), the number of these being regulated by usage. It is a striking commentary on the change of spirit in the Ottoman administration that, whereas the *Ḳânûn-nâme* of Süleymân had strictly forbidden the *Ḳâḍîs* to sell to substitutes the right of dispensing justice, and had enjoined the *Paşa* of Egypt to depose summarily all 'who should render themselves guilty of this corrupt practice',[7] the *Ḳâḍî* of Cairo now received on appointment a *fermân* authorizing him to select as many substitutes as he found suitable.[8]

[1] Hammer, *Staatsverfassung*, ii. 389–90; and cf. p. 94 above.
[2] So according to Chabrol, 236.
[3] According to a Venetian report quoted by Lammens, *La Syrie*, ii. 61.
[4] Lower Egypt and a great part of Syria were *Şâfi'î*; Upper Egypt and certain regions in Syria followed the *Mâlikî* school; the *Ḥanbalî* school predominated in the district of Nâblus and had a small following in some other Syrian and 'Irâḳî towns (Damascus, Ba'albek, Bağdâd), but had completely disappeared from Egypt, as is remarked by Cabartî (iv. 229/ix. 139).
[5] *Şâfi'î Ḳâḍî* at Damascus; Murâdî, iv. 126; at Moşul, iv. 69; *Mâlikî Ḳâḍî*, iv. 109; *Ḥanbalî Ḳâḍîs*, i. 219, 254; iii. 8. By the end of the eighteenth century these *ḳâḍî*-ships were no longer filled in Egypt; el-'Arîşî (see p. 103, n. 3) speaks only of 'the' *Ḳâḍî* and four *Muftîs* (p. 24), although Cabartî (iv. 248/ix. 179) dates the withdrawal of recognition from the three non-Ḥanefî *Ḳâḍîs* only from the 'Turkish occupation', i.e. after 1802.
[6] Volney, i. 454.
[7] *Canoun-namé*, ap. Digeon, ii. 260; Barkan, *Z.E.E.*, 382, § 41.
[8] Chabrol, 232; and cf. el-'Arîşî in *Bulletin de l'Institut d'Égypte*, xviii. 7–8/13, 9/15–16 (translation inexact).

Nâ'ibs in the eighteenth century were of various kinds. It seems probable, however, that originally they were employed only to represent the *Mollâs* or *Ḳâḍîs* who appointed them in the various subdivisions (called *nâḥiye*, 'district') of their *mevlevîyets* or *ḳaḍâs*. *Mevlevîyets* sometimes comprised large numbers of such districts. Thus, in the mid-seventeenth century, the *mevlevîyet* of Eyyûb comprised twenty-six, and that of Ğalaṭa no less than forty-four.[1] At Cairo there were eleven *Nâ'ibs* under the jurisdiction of the *Ḳâḍî-'asker*: nine in various quarters of the city, one in Bûlâḳ, and one in Old Cairo, each of whom paid a fixed monthly sum for his office.[2] Almost all other cities also, and even some of the smaller jurisdictions, were divided into several *niyâbas*; at Aleppo, for example, there were four.[3] Such *Nâ'ibs* were called *Ḳaḍâ Nâ'ibis* in later times, to distinguish them from those who then discharged most of their *Ḳâḍî*'s work at his headquarters and were hence termed *Bâb Nâ'ibis*, 'Deputies of the Gate'.[4] Again, when a *Mollâ* or *Ḳâḍî* was absent from his headquarters, he would appoint a special *Nâ'ib* to represent him.[5] Finally, certain *ḳaḍâs* were allotted to retired *'Ulemâ* as *arpalıḳs*; that is to say, such *'Ulemâ* were entitled to draw the revenues derivable from the courts of these places, which they shared with *Nâ'ibs* whom they appointed to discharge their judicial duties.[6]

All *Nâ'ibs* were nominated by the *Mollâs* or *Ḳâḍîs* for whom they deputized, but had to be confirmed in office by one or other of the *Ḳâḍî-'askers*. Their service, unlike that of the regular judges, was thus not organized imperially, and so admitted of no system of promotion such as characterized the others. As they were usually (but not always) local jurists, who bought the confirmation of their office from each new *Ḳâḍî* on his appointment, continuity in judicial administration was maintained in spite of the frequent change of the official holders of the *ḳâḍî*-ships.[7] A separate, and very profitable, office was that of *Ḳassâm*, or Divider

[1] Evliyâ, quoted by 'Osmân Nûrî, i. 300.

[2] According to Chabrol (236), the sum paid by each might amount to 900 *paras* a month; cf. also Cabartî, iv. 248/ix. 178; el-'Arîşî, 9/15.

[3] Murâdî, i. 63; ii. 49, &c.

[4] From the familiar use of *Bâb, Der, Ḳapı*, meaning 'Gate', to signify 'palace' or 'headquarters'; cf. Part I, p. 44, note.

[5] These *Nâ'ibs* were then called *Mollâ Vekîli* or *Ḳâḍî Vekîli*.

[6] D'Ohsson, iv. 573–6.

[7] Chabrol (237) states that although the cost of provincial *niyâbas* was not exactly known, it was apparently not more than 40,000 *paras* per annum for an average charge. Cabartî (ii. 127/iv. 239–40) relates that a certain *Şeyḫ* bought the post of *Nâ'ib* at Abyâr for ten successive years and acquired a large fortune, and that a mamlûk of his held a similar post in other towns. The Damascene historian el-Muḥibbî acted as *Nâ'ib* both in Mecca and in Cairo: Murâdî, iv. 86. A Turkish *Ḳâḍî* at Damascus appointed his own brother as *Nâ'ib*: ibid. i. 32. *Nâ'ibs* might even be 'lay' persons: e.g. Murâdî, i. 196–7 ; iii. 173.

of Inheritances, which was also farmed from the *Ḳâḍî* for a recognized sum.[1]

By immemorial usage the judge was permitted to make a charge of 2½ per cent. on the object of litigation, by way of court expenses.[2] This sum was either deducted from the property in question, when possible, or was paid by the successful party.[3] He had also certain rights on sales or transfers of offices, pensions and the like, and on the division of inheritances, and to a small signature fee on documents of judgments and other matters submitted to him from the various tribunals.[4] The principal *Ḳâḍîs* in each area had in addition the general supervision of the mosques and of the endowments (*waḳfs*) created for their upkeep or for other charitable purposes; and where, as at Damascus, appointments to professorial posts in the *madrasas* were made by diploma, the *Ḳâḍî* assigned vacant posts to candidates, subject to confirmation from Istanbul.[5]

In the Ottoman system, moreover, the *Ḳâḍî* exercised not only judicial functions, but also a degree of general supervision over the conduct of the administration. Thus the *Ḳâḍîs* of the coastal cities in Egypt were enjoined to control the actions of the customs department and to certify the accounts before they were submitted to the *Paşa*.[6] In the frequent disputes between rival factions and even rival *Paşas* they were called upon to act as mediators;[7] occasionally they were authorized to depose a *Paşa*;[8] and in the absence of a regularly-appointed governor they might even take over the government of a city or province.[9]

[1] Cf. Cabartî, iv. 248; Mich. Dam. 21.

[2] Since the clerks, ushers, and interpreters, if required, were in theory paid by the *Ḳâḍî*. Cabartî (iv. 248/ix. 178) remarks that in lawsuits involving *'Ulemâ* and *Emîrs* (i.e. persons of high rank) the fees were fixed by them 'according to their indulgence and desire to do him honour'. See also Lane, *Modern Egyptians*, ch. iv.

[3] This, which was the universal rule in Moslem practice, had the disadvantage of encouraging unscrupulous persons to institute vexatious suits, particularly against non-Moslems, in order to extort money from them by compounding the case; cf. on these 'legal *avanias*' Russell, 121, Thornton, *Turkey*², i. 202–3, and Cabartî, iv. 249/ix. 180 (who signalizes it as an abuse recently introduced).

[4] Cabartî, iv. 248/ix. 178 (the translation is loose). Seyyid Muṣṭafâ (i. 20) states that the salaries originally allotted to *Ḳâḍîs* were so small that in the time of Bâyezîd I they were found to have been supplementing them in undesirable ways. Hence a scale of fees for the notarial services they performed was fixed, and they were authorized to draw them. The recognized sources of income of the *Ḳâḍî* of Cairo are summarized by el 'Arîşî, p. 23.

[5] On occasion, however, the diploma issued at Istanbul conferred the post on a different candidate: Murâdî, i. 251, 260; ii. 151.

[6] *Canoun-namé*, ap. Digeon, ii. 225; Barkan, *Z.E.E.* i. 370. The *Ḳâḍî* of Alexandria also dealt in the first instance with requests to load grain by European merchants: ibid., 221, Barkan, 369.

[7] Ğazzî, iii. 293.

[8] Mich. Dam. 4 (on the deposition of Cezzâr after his first term of office at Damascus).

[9] Mich. Dam. 14: the *Ḳâḍî* of Damascus on the death of Cezzâr. The legal

There were consequently ample means at the disposal of the judges for enriching themselves, and no doubt they were often utilized. It might well seem that the system of appointing foreign judges on annual tenures, and free to buy and sell their offices, was calculated, far from repressing abuses, to create them in the grossest form. There can be no question also that the effects of that general deterioration in the higher ranks of the learned profession, which we have described in a previous chapter, were melancholy in the extreme. The *arpalıḳ-ma'îşet* system, which involved the discharge of judicial duties by substitutes, came in course of time to extend far beyond the ranks of *ma'zûl* officials, for whose benefit it had been created.[1] Now that the sons of Great *Mollâs* obtained their diplomas while they were still children, and by this means became eligible for *maḫrec* rank when no more than five and twenty, they were often so evidently incapable of performing the functions involved, even if they desired to do so, that they usually engaged a substitute for the purpose. Hence the existence of that type of *Nâ'ib* or substitute to which we have already referred, called *Mollâ vekîli* or *Ḳâḍî vekîli*.[2] Nor were such *Nâ'ibs* employed only by judges of *maḫrec* rank. All the Great *Mollâs* whose offices were provincial preferred as a rule to reside in the capital and send these *vekîls* to the cities that should have been the scene of their activities. Among the *şeyḫly* families of the provincial capitals too, the same practice found imitators.[3] Only in the cases of Mecca and Medîna was it considered improper that the judges concerned should not put in a personal appearance. To make matters worse, it appears that a great many of the substitutes employed by the *Mollâs* were persons without any but the most superficial acquaintance with the law, if indeed they were members of the learned profession at all, which was not always the case.[4]

Yet, in spite of the complaints of such reformers as Ḳoçu Bey and of the diatribes of several European observers,[5] the system

status of the *Ḳâḍî* as acting governor in the event of the *Paşa*'s death is asserted also by the *Ḥanefî* jurist Ibn Nuceym (*Risâla* 17, in *Mecmû'at al-Rasâ'il*, annexed to vol. ii. of *el-Aşbâh wa'l-Naẓâ'ir*, Istanbul, 1290, pp. 55–56).

[1] See above, p. 109.

[2] See above, p. 124.

[3] Syrian *Şeyḫs* who held *ḳâḍî*-ships as *arpalıḳs*: Murâdî, i. 176; ii. 128; iii. 3, 47.

[4] See above, p. 124.

[5] e.g. Chabrol, 239: 'Versant l'or à pleines mains pour s'asseoir dans un tribunal, ils ne regardaient le glaive dont la loi les armait alors que comme un instrument de richesse. . . . Tous les grands moyens en leur pouvoir étaient, pour ainsi dire, dirigés vers un même but, celui d'amasser: aussi ne perdaient-ils aucune occasion de grossir leur trésor. Ceux chez lesquels l'amour de la justice et de l'humanité balançait la soif de l'or, se montraient un peu plus équitables; les autres n'étaient retenus que par la crainte de compromettre leur réputation.' Volney (ii. 249) is almost equally eloquent, and still more vague. Russell, 120, is, as usual, fairer in his estimate.

worked on the whole to the satisfaction of public opinion. It will be observed that the judges had as their main direct source of revenue the charges levied upon the object of litigation; and it was in the exaction of these that the principal abuses occurred.[1] The amount levied might be raised on various pretexts to as much as 8 or 10 per cent., but only when the victims were either well-to-do artisans or merchants, or, even more frequently, 'spoilers' themselves, *ḳapı̊ ḳulus*, or Mamlûks. It was probably seldom that this system had the result of making justice too expensive for the poor, since (apart altogether from the fact that it was the winning party that was liable for the costs) sound tradition ensured that a plea of poverty was rarely tendered in vain in the *Ḳâḍî*'s court.[2]

Together with this, it must not be forgotten that the great bulk of the ordinary disputes did not come into the *Ḳâḍî*'s courts at all, whether those of the titular Ottoman *Ḳâḍîs* or of their local substitutes. We have already seen that each village, corporation, and social group had its own arbitral organization, and that internal disputes were dealt with summarily by the *Şeyḫ* of the village or of the relevant guild or corporation; and it will be seen later that when legal advice and arbitration were required, large sections of the population preferred to take the matter before their local *'Ulemâ* and *Muftîs*.[3] Furthermore, certain offences against social convention were punished almost automatically by death without the intervention of any formal judicial or executive authority at all, especially in those groups which still maintained the social traditions of the nomad tribes. The principal offences so dealt with were unchastity and adultery. A village girl found guilty of unchastity was taken out into the desert by her parents

[1] Chabrol, 239–40: 'Les jugemens d'un qâdy obtiennent presque toujours l'assentiment des hommes éclairés, et il serait injuste d'appliquer à ces magistrats, dans toute sa rigueur, le reproche de partialité et de corruption que plusieurs écrivains ont adressé aux juges musulmans en général. . . . Les abus sont plutôt dans l'arbitraire de la taxe, et l'on a toujours murmuré de l'inégale perception des frais de justice.' Cf. Thornton, i. 195–6: 'Generally speaking, the decision of the judges in causes wherein both parties are Mussulmans, is unbiassed. Public opinion, which is nowhere more free or more energetic than among the Turks, checks the voluntary commission of any injustice with respect to them.' Cf. Ğazzî, iii. 293: a *Ḳâḍî* of Aleppo stoned by the populace because he was oppressive and accepted bribes; Cabartî, ii. 159/v. 25–26.

[2] Cabartî asserts that 'the *Ḳâḍîs* who used to come from Istanbul in the days of the Egyptian *amîrs* [i.e. the Mamlûks] never transgressed the established usages and *ḳânûns*' (iv. 240/ix. 198). But he also cites a case (which, however, was in 1807, during the government of Meḥmed 'Alî) of a certain student who was at a disadvantage in a lawsuit 'especially because he was penniless and had none of the money which is now indispensable for commissions and bribes to intermediaries and those who render judgments and to their hangers-on' (iv. 64/viii. 139).

[3] Especially since, as it will be recalled, the courts administered *Ḥanefî* law exclusively, while the bulk of the population in Egypt and many in Syria belonged to the *Şâfi'î* or *Mâlikî* schools.

or relatives and killed without more ado, and an unfaithful wife was often drowned, sometimes with her paramour.[1] This survival of nomadic customary law, in which the social group sets its own standards and maintains their validity in its internal life as against all forms of law imposed by an external authority, is one of the outstanding characteristics of the traditional social structure in Western Asia and North Africa. Yet another of its consequences was the operation of the law of vengeance and the resulting blood-feuds, which frequently gave rise to a state of private war, openly pursued and condoned.[2]

While, therefore, the *Ḳâḍîs'* courts were in theory competent to administer every branch of law (the distinction between civil, penal, personal, and other divisions of law not being recognized by Moslem jurists) and to every section of the population from *Paşas* to beduin, very considerable limitations were, in practice, imposed upon their range of functions by the existence of these group tribunals and customary usages. But such derogations were at least in favour of institutions which themselves partook of the nature of law. A far more serious limitation, inasmuch as it was both illegal in fact and contralegal in principle, was the abuse of penal authority by military and administrative officers. This was the real point of weakness in judicial administration in all Islamic countries. Caliphs and Sultans, as we have seen, had from early times set up special jurisdictions and administrative tribunals, alongside the *Şer'î* courts; and under effective control, when they were confined to the special functions delegated to them by the sovereign, they contributed to the maintenance of good order and government.[3] But the recurrent weakness displayed by all public institutions in face of the encroachments of military authority repeatedly led to abusive extensions of their powers; military commanders, police officers, sometimes even minor officials, would order punishments and executions without the semblance of a trial, and, in the vast majority of cases, without being called to account for their actions. One result had been to create a series of conflicting and overlapping jurisdictions; another, more important for its consequences upon the standards of public morality, was that the infliction of punishment, especially by the military power, involved no moral reprobation, and in no way degraded

[1] That these practices still survive in Egyptian villages is attested by numerous observers, e.g. W. S. Blackman, *The Fellahin of Upper Egypt* (London, 1927), 44–45, and H. Habib Ayrout, *Fellahs* (Cairo, 1942), 121, 123; and cf. Volney, i. 175. For Syria cf. F. Ammoun, *La Syrie criminelle* (Paris, 1929), 165, and for 'Irâḳ E. Main, *Iraq from Mandate to Independence* (London, 1935), 173–4. These practices are not, of course, condoned by the *Şerî'a*.

[2] Chabrol, 277; Agenda de Malus, 154–5; and cf. above, Ch. IV, i.

[3] For the history of these offices prior to the Ottoman period see E. Tyan, *Organisation judiciaire en Pays d'Islam*, ii. (Beirut, 1943).

the recipient, who was more often regarded as the victim of arbitrary officiousness than as one who had received due retribution for his own offences.[1]

As we have indicated above,[2] the Ottoman Sultans by their *ḳânûns* had attempted to put an end to such abuses, and to reform both the administration and the administrative tribunals by defining their powers and codifying the penalties which they were authorized to inflict. The Egyptian *ḳânûn-nâme* of Süleymân could not well be more explicit in its denunciation of 'the barbarity of *Kâşifs*, Arab *Şeyḫs*, and other persons who without reasonable cause put cultivators to death and seize their property'.[3] That a *Kâşif* should inflict even a fine or a corporal punishment upon a peasant is prohibited except with the consent of the local *Ḳâḍî*.[4] Breaches of these regulations were to be investigated by the *Paşa*, and 'the judge who takes the part of the powerful wrongdoer is to be committed to prison and dismissed from his post'.[5] Likewise, the *Ṣubaşî* or prefect of police, although charged with the policing of the city, 'may not judge the cases of individuals, which are to be brought before the *Ḳâḍî*, who will give judgment according to the *Şerî'a*'.[6] The *dîvân* constituted the supreme tribunal in Egypt, and served not only as a military court but also as a court of appeal, administering Ottoman official law, i.e. the *Şerî'a* supplemented by the Sultans' *ḳânûns*.[7]

How long these and similar regulations were observed cannot be determined, but sooner or later they, like all previous attempts to restrain illegality, fell into desuetude. The generality of European observers were struck by the arbitrary conduct and indifference to human life shown by the military and the police.[8]

[1] Cf. Hamont, i. 404: 'Il rentre dans la société, reprend ses habitudes, son commerce, son premier emploi, et souvent . . . les anciens détenus sont promus à des fonctions plus élevées que celles dont ils étaient investis lors de leur condamnation'; also Clot-Bey, *Aperçu*, ii. 105. According to Evliyâ Efendî (trans. Hammer, ii. 169), the assistants of the provost (*Muḥtasib*) on occasions of public procession 'give a good beating to certain men, on the pretext that they do not sell just measure'.

[2] p. 116 above.

[3] Digeon, ii. 262; Barkan, *Z.E.E.*, 383, § 42.

[4] Digeon, ii. 202–3; Barkan, 362, § 13. In all cases fines were to conform to the established tariff; as already pointed out, fines, though not authorized by the *Şerî'a*, were sanctioned by the *ḳânûns*.

[5] Digeon, ii. 262; Barkan, 383. The *ḳânûn* further threatens with the royal displeasure 'any *Paşa* who should have the criminal indulgence to relax in the execution of the present article', although to commit a defaulting *Ḳâḍî* to prison was a further encroachment by *ḳânûn* on the *Şerî'a*.

[6] Digeon, ii. 259–60 (replaces the *Ḳâḍî* by the *dîvân*; but see Barkan, 382, § 41).

[7] In the latter respect (for which see Part I, p. 202) the *dîvân* took the place of the former *maẓâlim* courts of the Sultans or their representatives. The presence *ex-officio* of the *Ḳâḍî* and other *şer'î* representatives as members of the *dîvân* must not, of course, be taken to indicate that the *dîvân* was a *şer'î* tribunal.

[8] e.g. Thornton, i. 204 sqq.; Volney, i. 162; ii. 244.

Conditions in this respect no doubt varied as between provinces,[1] but the impotence of the provincial authorities to protect the population from their tyranny is evidenced by the practice of sending memorials to the Sublime Porte itself,[2] and in Egypt by the action of the *Şeyẖ el-Beled* ʿO̱tmân Bey D̲û'l-Fiḳâr in reviving, about 1743, the custom of *maẓâlim*-courts, two of which he set up in his house, one for men and one for women.[3]

The ordinary procedure in the hearing of cases in the *Ḳâḍî*'s court is described by E. W. Lane as follows:[4]

'When a person has a suit to prefer at the Mahkémeh [Tribunal] against another individual or party, he goes thither, and applies to the Básh Rusul (or chief of the bailiffs or sergeants who execute arrests)[5] for a "Rasool" to arrest the accused. The Rasool receives a piastre or two, and generally gives half of this fee privately to his chief. The plaintiff and defendant then present themselves in a great hall of the Mahkémeh, which is a large saloon, facing a spacious court, and having an open front formed by a row of columns and arches.[6] Here are seated several officers called "Sháhids",[7] whose business is to hear and write the statements of the case to be submitted to judgment, and who are under the authority of the "Básh Kátib" (or Chief Secretary). The plaintiff, addressing any one of the Sháhids whom he finds unoccupied, states the case, and the Sháhid commits it to writing, and receives a fee of a piastre or more; after which, if the case be of a trifling nature, and the defendant acknowledges the justice of the suit, he (the Sháhid) passes sentence;[8] but otherwise he conducts the two parties before the Náïb, who holds his court in an inner apartment. The Náïb, having heard the case, desires the plaintiff to procure a "fetwa" (or judicial decision) from

[1] Instances are cited of protests made by the *Ḳâḍî* of Damascus against summary executions by military authorities, and with some success (Mich. Dam. 30, 37).

[2] Examples of memorials to the Porte are not infrequent, e.g. Ǧazzî, iii. 304; Mich. Dam., 4; *Recueil de Firmans*, Nos. 3, 5, 10.

[3] Cabartî, i. 179/ii. 87–88.

[4] *Modern Egyptians*, ch. iv. Though Lane's description refers to the reign of Meḥmed-ʿAlî, there is no reason to suppose that the procedure was in any way different in the eighteenth century; and cf. D'Ohsson, iv. 582–3.

[5] On the *Ḳâḍî*'s ushers (*ʿawn* or *rasûl*) see E. Tyan, *Organisation judiciaire en Pays d'Islam*, i (Paris, 1938), 383.

[6] Such a saloon is still to be seen in the traditional 'Ḳâḍî's House' (*Beyt el-Ḳâḍî*) in Cairo and in a former Mamlûk residence outside the Bâb Zuweyla.

[7] The term *şâhid* (literally 'witness'), technically applied to those persons whose testimony is accepted in the Islamic courts, became in time the name of a subordinate class of legal officers, of a lower educational standing than the fully-qualified *Ḳâḍîs* and *Muftîs*. A synonym is *ʿadl*, literally 'one possessed of moral responsibility', or more often *kâtib*, 'clerk, notary'. Such *kâtibs* often held responsible judicial positions, especially as dividers of inheritances (*ḳassâm*: Murâdî, ii. 118, 164, 184; iv. 228–9), and sometimes acquired a considerable fortune, not always honestly, from their practice; cf. Cabartî, ii. 267/v. 224, and Murâdî, iv. 5, 206. On the history of this class see E. Tyan, *Le Notariat . . . dans la Pratique du Droit musulman* (Lyon, 1945).

[8] The relevant documents being countersigned by the *Ḳâḍî* for a trifling fee: Cabartî, iv. 248 (not in the translation).

the Muftee of the sect of the Hanafees,[1] who receives a fee—seldom less than ten piastres, and often more than a hundred or two hundred. This is the course pursued in all cases but those of a very trifling nature, which are settled with less trouble, and those of great importance or intricacy. A case of the latter kind is tried in the private apartment of the Kádee, before the Kádee himself, the Náïb, and the Muftee of the Hanafees, who is summoned to hear it and to give his decision; and sometimes, in case of very great difficulty or moment, several of the ʿUlama are, in like manner, summoned. The Muftee hears the case and writes the sentence, and the Kádee confirms his judgment, and stamps the paper with his seal, which is all that he has to do in any case'.[2]

Apart from the exaction of unauthorized fees, some of the principal abuses of justice arose from the conception of evidence current in the Moslem courts. Both parties are required to present themselves before the court, but in the normal procedure evidence is given on one side only. The plaintiff is called upon to produce at least two witnesses, who are required to be men of good character: written or documentary evidence is excluded except in specified cases. If the evidence given on the plaintiff's behalf is sufficient to carry conviction, decision must be given in his favour; if not, the defendant is not required to produce witnesses, but to clear himself by oath, and when he does so the case is dismissed. The procedure may be varied according to the discretion of the judge, but in general any 'conflict of evidence' is avoided. The volume of oral evidence is thus a decisive factor in any case, and difficulties were created by restrictions as to the persons whose evidence could be admitted. Thus the testimony of close relatives is generally rejected, and likewise that of slaves, or even of a master in favour of his slave. The evidence of two women is reckoned as equal only to that of one man; that of non-Moslems against Moslems is occasionally but grudgingly admitted, and on serious charges not admitted at all.

The principles underlying such restrictions are indeed respectable, but they sometimes amounted in effect to a denial of justice, especially as the taking of an oath was very lightly regarded in all except pious circles. A still more flagrant abuse was the suborning of false witnesses, which was apparently a common enough practice in all countries.[3] The *ḳânûns* of Süleymân contain several provisions intended to prevent such miscarriages of justice through

[1] On the office and function of the *Muftî* see the following section.

[2] Chabrol (202–3) asserts a different view: 'Il est rare qu'un qâdy très-versé dans la jurisprudence demande l'opinion d'un moufty, et encore plus qu'il s'en tienne à ses décisions; mais, s'il n'est pas fort habile, comme il arrive assez souvent, il demande toujours l'avis du moufty avant de prononcer.'

[3] Lane, loc. cit.; Murâdî, i. 206: the *Muftî* of Damascus with the *Ḳâḍî*'s connivance procured a sentence against a student by means of false witnesses, 'all of whom [it is added] died within a short time'.

the manœuvres of dishonest persons on pain of the *Ḳâḍî*'s dismissal and punishment.[1] The conduct of certain judges towards litigants, especially those of humble station, seems also to have been open to reproach, and a curious record is preserved of a *Ḳâḍî* of Aleppo who was removed from office in 1813 on the ground that 'he treated the nobles and notables of the town, and even the governor himself, as if they were common people', and so far forgot himself on one occasion as to strike the *Muftî* on the face.[2]

Since the *Ḳâḍî* was concerned not only with the settlement of disputes but also with civil contracts of all kinds, he or his *Nâ'ib* acted as notary-public, registrar, and procurator, officiated at marriages of notables, and looked after the property of orphans and minors. The business of the *Şer'î* courts was therefore extensive and often complicated, but by law and usage no provision was made for more than a single judge in each court. The decision of the first court before which any case was heard was final, no one court having in theory a status higher than another. But although the practice of taking a case decided in one court to another court for retrial is strictly contrary to Islamic law, it evidently existed in Egypt, since in 1786 the *Ḳaptan Paşa* Ḥasan published an order prohibiting it,[3] and at the time of the French occupation the court of the *Ḳâḍî-'asker* served occasionally as a court of appeal against the decisions of his substitutes.[4]

Although, as the preceding pages have shown, the giving of decisions contrary to law in the interests of a more powerful or better-paying party was, from all accounts, not unknown, the available evidence suggests that it cannot have been so common or widespread as European writers have usually assumed. The conduct of the *Ḳâḍîs* was in fact subjected to two controls, an outer and an inner. The outer was supplied, not so much by the official measures of supervision, whether by the civil authorities or by superior officers in the judicial service, as by the jealous surveillance of their potential rivals and of the *'Ulemâ*. A certain degree of latitude was tacitly allowed, but misdealing that became too persistent or extravagant generally resulted in the offender forfeiting both place and reputation, and often his ill-gotten gains to boot.[5] From a very early date the *Şeyḫs* had adopted a critical attitude towards the *Ḳâḍîs*, regarding them often as little better than hypocrites and time-servers; and the stricter sort, with the *Ṣûfîs* generally, echoed el-Ğazâlî's counsel to have nothing to do with them.[6] In the Ottoman system the gap between *'Âlim* and *Ḳâḍî* in the Arab

[1] Digeon, ii. 260–1; Barkan, 382–3.
[2] Ğazzî, iii. 320.
[3] Cabartî, ii. 124/iv. 232.
[4] Chabrol, 235–6. See also p. 129 above.
[5] Murâdî, iv. 24–25; Ğazzî, iii. 304; Mich. Dam. 21.
[6] See A. Mez, *Die Renaissance des Islams*, 209–10; and cf. above, p. 82.

provinces was widened by the former's ignorance of Turkish, and though there is mention of friendly relations between *Ḳâḍîs* and the local *ʿUlemâ* in all our sources,[1] they give evidence also of the survival of the traditional attitude.[2] And yet another check upon arbitrary action lay in the facts that custom and tradition had long since settled the precedents in almost every possible case, and that the *Ḳâḍî*'s 'decisions' were often little more than an authentication of the rulings supplied by the *Muftî*.

But in the last resort the principal safeguard was the moral conscience of the judges themselves and of the community. Those who may be disposed to regard this as an illusory and ineffective protection may doubtless point to many examples which confirm their distrust, but the very maintenance of the system itself to the general satisfaction of the people suggests that these incidents are not to be taken as typical of its general working.[3] We shall revert to this aspect in dealing with the spirit and the ideals fostered by the system of religious education; at this point it is sufficient to conclude that that spirit and those ideals cannot have been entirely without effect in the ordinary operation of the religious courts.

III. THE MUFTÎS

The Islamic legal system included, alongside the *Ḳâḍîs*, a second class of practitioners, known as *Muftîs*. We have already seen that the *Şerîʿa*, so far from constituting a fixed code, consisted rather of a discussion of the duties of Moslems, formulated over the centuries in a vast literature of legal argument. In the early days, when this literature was still in its beginnings and many doubtful questions called for authoritative rulings, a number of eminent jurists met this need by 'exerting themselves' to discover, from the recognized sources of revealed law and the application of analogy, what the appropriate rulings should be. Such doctors were accordingly called *Muctahids*,[4] and from their sometimes divergent decisions sprang the various 'schools' or 'rites' of orthodox *Sunnî* Islâm. But once these schools were established, the *ʿUlemâ* were progressively restricted in their liberty of interpretation, having now

[1] e.g. Murâdî, i. 222.

[2] Murâdî, ii. 59; and note also the relatively small part played by the *Ḳâḍîs* in Cabartî's chronicle.

[3] Cf. Chabrol, 235: 'Ainsi l'opinion et la morale imposaient en quelque sorte des bornes à l'avidité des juges. On remarquait même assez communément que le qâdy a'skar, homme d'un caractère grave et imposant, entouré de la considération publique, se contentait de ce qui lui était offert, sans jamais rien exiger de lui-même, pour conserver l'estime des grands et l'affection du peuple.'

[4] Active participle from the Arabic verb *ictahada*, 'exert oneself'.

to reconcile their decisions with the particular principles of the school to which each adhered. Within a few generations, indeed, this liberty was entirely abolished by the tacit operation of *icmâ'* or 'consensus'; and since, in the traditional phrase, 'the Gate of interpretation was shut',[1] those *'Ulemâ* of whom pronouncements on legal points were demanded were no longer *Muctahids* but *Muḳallids*, 'imitators',[2] in the sense that in reaching their decisions they were required to follow closely the precedents laid down by their august predecessors.

These precedents were, of course, contained in the fundamental texts of each school, with the copious commentaries and expositions added by later generations.[3] The *'Âlim* or *Faḳîh* from whom a statement on a point of law was demanded had only, therefore, to be sufficiently well versed in these works to be able to adduce the appropriate precedent on any given occasion. The questioner formulated his problem in precise terms, and received in reply a *fetwâ*, or statement of the legal position, often consisting of nothing more than the single word, 'yes' or 'no'. In theory, every qualified doctor of the law was competent to deliver such an opinion, orally or in writing; but as the volume of legal literature and the compilation of *fetwâs* and discussion of precedents continued to expand, the study of them constituted a specialized branch of learning, and those jurists who devoted themselves to it professionally were distinguished by the formal appellation of *Muftîs*, i.e. jurisconsults.[4] Theoretically again, as we have just said, a *Muftî* could not innovate, but merely frame his reply on the basis of established rules and precedents; in practice, however, the *Muftîs*, by selecting appropriate precedents and neglecting those which were no longer applicable, could and did adapt the *Şerî'a* to new circumstances.

In contrast to the *Ḳâḍîs*, who held office by delegation of authority from the temporal ruler and could be dismissed at will, the *Muftîs* retained in general a private and voluntary status. But the needs of government required the services of 'official *Muftîs*', and a number of qualified scholars accordingly received some measure of official recognition. Under the Mamlûk Sultans of Egypt, a *Muftî* of each rite was officially appointed to sit in the judicial college, called *Dâr el-'Adl* or 'Hall of Justice', set up in each pro-

[1] See Part I, p. 22.

[2] From Arabic *ḳallada*, 'put on a necklace', hence 'accept the authority of another person'.

[3] For a general survey of this literature see N. P. Aghnides, *An Introduction to Mohammedan Law and a Bibliography* (Columbia Univ. Studies in History, Economics, and Public Law, No. 166), New York, 1916.

[4] *Muftî* is the active participle from *aftâ*, 'deliver an opinion or *fetwâ*'. The position of the *Muftî* is often, but not very exactly, compared to that of counsel in English judicial practice; cf. Hammer-Purgstall, trad. Hellert iii. 431, n. vii.

vincial capital, these *Muftîs* having precedence next below the *Ḳâḍî-'askers*.[1]

In the Ottoman state, the *Muftî* of Istanbul was, as we have already noted,[2] promoted to be the first religious dignitary in the Empire, with the title of *Şeyḫü 'l-Islâm*. About the same time, in the reign of Süleymân the Magnificent, the organization of the *Ḳâḍîs* on an imperial scale was supplemented by a parallel organization of *Muftîs*. But since the *Muftîs* received no official salaries, and were not (being all theoretically equal in rank) graded like the *Ḳâḍîs* in classes with promotion from one to the next, their organization remained looser and relatively more independent. Each of the chief cities of the Empire had its official *Muftî*, appointed by the *Şeyḫü 'l-Islâm*,[3] and likewise most *ḳaḍâs* in the provinces—the nomination in the latter case being confirmed either by the *Şeyḫ* or by the local authorities, according to local usage. Provincial *muftîliks* were open not only to those *'Ulemâ* who had completed part of the full training in the *madrasas* of Istanbul required for the attainment of 'Great' Mollahood, but also to those trained in the *madrasas* of other cities. In principle, all *Muftîs* held office for life.[4]

Since the Turks had always favoured the *Ḥanefî* school of law, there were few adherents of the other schools in any parts of the 'original' Empire, that is to say in the provinces it comprised before the conquests of Selîm I. In Syria, Egypt, and the Ḥijâz, however, it was otherwise. Consequently, though no city to which a *Muftî* was posted at all was left without one of the *Ḥanefî* persuasion, in the more important cities of these provinces the people were provided also with *Muftîs* of the other three schools. *Muftîs* everywhere ranked below *Ḳâḍîs*, though above their *Nâ'ibs*. In smaller places to which no *Muftîs* were posted *fetwâs* were given, when required, by the *Ḳâḍîs*.[5]

The degree of freedom which the *Muftîs* retained varied considerably as between provinces. Generally speaking, it seems to have been greater in the Arabic-speaking provinces, and most of all in Egypt. Here the principal *Muftîs* of the *Ḥanefî* and *Şâfi'î* schools, at least, were nominated by their respective corps of

[1] See Gaudefroy-Demombynes, *La Syrie*, pp. lxxvii, 162, &c.; W. Björkmann, *Beiträge zur Geschichte der Staatskanzlei im islamischen Ägypten* (Hamburg, 1928), 100, 154, 158.

[2] See above, p. 84.

[3] The *Şeyḫ*'s immediate jurisdiction included Adrianople and Bursa, as well as Istanbul. The two former cities, accordingly, had no *Muftîs* of their own, but delegates of the *Şeyḫ*.

[4] As the ordinary *Muftî* held no appointment, he could not be dismissed, but he might be suspended or interdicted; D'Ohsson, iv. 586. Murâdî mentions *Şeyḫs* who officiated as *Muftîs* for forty or forty-five years in the same city: ii. 303; iv. 84.

[5] D'Ohsson, iv. 584–6.

'Ulemâ, and officially confirmed and recognized by the civil authorities. They had their delegates or representatives in all the principal towns, though possibly towns which possessed a large local body of *'Ulemâ* nominated their own *Muftîs*.[1] Several instances are recorded of the removal of *Muftîs* by the civil power,[2] but it would appear that this action was taken only with the agreement of the principal *Şeyhs*.[3]

In Syria, the *Ḥanefî Muftîs*, though generally (but not always)[4] local *Şeyhs*, were to a much greater extent functionaries of the state. Although they were nominated, usually from among the leading families, by the *Şeyhs* and notables, the choice had to be submitted to Istanbul for confirmation, and occasionally the Porte substituted another candidate.[5] Presumably, the nominee had to support his claim by the usual presents to the *Şeyhü'l-Islâm*, and several instances are cited of candidates who went to Istanbul to solicit office in person, and who even succeeded in obtaining appointment over the head of the *Muftî* in office.[6] On one occasion, however, when a rival succeeded in obtaining a sentence of exile against the *Muftî* of Damascus, the populace rose in revolt and the *Paşa* hastily revoked the order.[7] But such incidents seem to have been rare. There was a tendency for the office to pass by heredity; at Damascus it was held in the latter part of the century by three generations of the Murâdî family,[8] and before that by the 'Imâdî family.[9] In the provincial towns also, the *Muftîs* were generally local *Şeyhs*, those of the *Ḥanefî* school being presumably confirmed in office by the Porte, and those of the other schools by the local governors.[10] It is noteworthy that the local corporations of *Şerîfs*[11] had their own *Muftîs*, each according to their own schools.[12]

[1] Chabrol, 203; for the *Ḥanefî*, *Şâfi'î*, and *Mâlikî Muftîs* of Alexandria, Olivier, ii. 12. It is probable that direct delegates of the chief *Muftîs* bought their appointments for a given period.

[2] Cabartî, ii. 18, 51/iii. 268; iv. 62. Imprisonment of a *Ḥanefî Muftî*: ibid. ii. 18/iii. 270.

[3] Cabartî, iv. 100/viii. 223 (this was in 1809).

[4] e.g. Murâdî, ii. 101.

[5] Ibid. 84.

[6] Ibid. 6, 13. A rare instance is noted of a *Şeyh* who was appointed *Muftî* of Damascus 'without solicitation of any kind': i. 257. On the other hand, Ṣâliḥ b. Ibrâhîm (d. 1170/1757), though admitted to be the best *Ḥanefî* legist of his time, never held any legal post: ii. 208–9.

[7] Murâdî, ii. 282. A *Muftî* at Ba'albek assassinated: ibid. iv. 53.

[8] The historian was the second of the line; the third was assassinated in 1803 by order of Cezzâr Paşa, who was called to account for his action by the Porte and allowed his representative at Damascus to be put to death in retaliation: Mich. Dam. 12–13.

[9] Murâdî, ii. 11–19, 282; iii. 196; iv. 17–18. At Medîna the Seyyid family of Üsküdâr held the office of *Muftî* for several generations: ibid. i. 222–3; iii. 134–5; iv. 34, 58–59.

[10] Murâdî mentions, e.g., *Muftîs* at 'Akka, Gaza, Nâblus, and Ḥomṣ. An exceptional case of a *Şeyh* who combined the offices of *Ḥanefî* and *Şâfi'î Muftî* at Aleppo: ibid., iv. 10, and cf. i. 24.

[11] See above, p. 93.

[12] Murâdî, ii. 66, 80, 172, &c.

The fact that the office of *Muftî* carried with it no salary as such emphasized, in the eyes of the religious, its superiority to that of the *Ḳâḍî*. In practice, however, the *Muftî* generally exacted a fee for delivering a *fetwâ*, proportioned to the wealth of the petitioner,[1] and it is comparatively rare to find mention of *Muftîs* who consistently refused to accept any fees for their services.[2] Such fees, probably supplemented by an income from teaching or other minor religious office, provided a sufficient income for the lesser *Muftîs*, but the chief *Muftîs* in the principal cities held a much more privileged position. The Ottoman authorities appear to have made a practice of maintaining some financial control over them by the grant of pensions and of various administrative posts and honorary religious offices. It seems to have been usual for the chief *Ḥanefî Muftî* at Damascus to hold the title of *Ra'îs* of the city,[3] and there are frequent references to *Muftîs* who held *mâlikânes* in addition to holding *Ḳâḍî*-ships as *arpalıḳs*.[4] There were even instances of *Muftîs* acting as *Nâ'ibs* in the local tribunals.[5] It is not surprising, therefore, to find some of them acquiring vast wealth, and falling sadly short at times of the ideals which it was their duty to maintain.[6] Their actual functions were frequently delegated to *wakîls*, or were carried out by junior assistants, called *amîn el-futyâ*, who corresponded to the *fetvâ-emîni* of the *Şeyḫü 'l-Islâm* at the capital.[7] In such circumstances (and although it is recorded that a certain *Ḥanefî Muftî* at Damascus used solemnly to warn his assistant against taking bribes), the control which the *Muftîs* were able to exercise over the administration of justice in the religious courts is likely to have been fluctuating and capricious, even if we beware of attributing to a whole class the faults of a few.

Finally, and in spite of the marked tendency in the Ottoman system to circumscribe the freedom of the *Şeyḫs* and jurists, and to limit the judicial function to those who were officially recognized, it was impossible to eliminate the traditional usages altogether. In Egypt, at least, it still remained a common practice for local *Şeyḫs* to act unofficially as judges and *Muftîs* in their own districts (some,

[1] See above, p. 131.

[2] e.g. el-Mahdî (see Lane, *Modern Egyptians*, ch. iv); also Cabartî, iv. 77/viii. 168.

[3] See above, Part I, p. 279.

[4] e.g. Murâdî, i. 63, 176; ii. 184. From about 1723 the *Şâfi'î Muftî* of Jerusalem was assigned a pension on the revenue from the three Christian convents there: ibid., iii. 209. For *arpalıḳs*, see above, p. 109.

[5] Murâdî, i. 63 (Damascus); iii. 83 (Medîna). Another *Muftî* at Medîna, however, resigned his office on taking up an appointment as *Nâ'ib*: ibid., iv. 240.

[6] Ibid., i. 206; ii. 13; iv. 24–25.

[7] Ibid., iii. 42, 229; iv. 245 (a *Mâlikî Muftî* who had previously served as *amîn ul-futyâ* to the *Ḥanefî Muftî* at Damascus). For the *fetwâ-emîni* see above, p. 86.

indeed, made their livelihood in this way), and it would appear that the mass of artisans and villagers preferred this method of settling their disputes to the intervention of the regular courts,[1] even to the extent of appealing to them to retry cases already decided by the *Ḳâḍî*.[2]

[1] Cf. Cabartî, i. 369, 375; ii. 60, 71, 165 (a particularly interesting case), 263; iv. 77, 260/iii. 127, 143; iv. 84, 99; v. 40, 219; viii. 168; ix. 204. An instance in Syria (relating to a problem of inheritance): Murâdî, i. 145.

[2] Cabartî, iv. 77/viii. 168.

CHAPTER XI

EDUCATION

THE mainspring of the religious institution and the principal source of its influence over the secular authorities is to be found in the system of education. During the early centuries of Islâm, the theologians had maintained a long and finally successful struggle to monopolize the control of education; and from the time when the Ottoman Empire was founded—if not from a much earlier period—the sole type of education accessible in the Islamic lands was one not only based upon but consisting almost exclusively of religious instruction. The *Ḳur'ân* schools supplied the universal basis upon which all further education—military, administrative, and technical, no less than theological or mystical—was superimposed, and that the importance of their function was recognized is evident from the care with which successive generations of benefactors in all walks of life provided for their foundation and maintenance. Nor, probably, is there any other social institution in which the universalist spirit of Islâm had so completely succeeded in imposing uniformity throughout the length and breadth of its territories, for the traditional subjects and methods of elementary education were pursued alike by Niger, Nile, and Indus.

The social education of the child was, of course, carried out in the home, where, despite differences of rank and class, discipline and respect for elders were universally inculcated.[1] This social foundation of education in the narrower sense must not be overlooked, for it predetermined the whole attitude of the pupil towards his teacher and the subjects of his study, and gave his mind that cant towards acceptance of authority which characterized all branches of Islamic learning. In well-to-do houses, the beginnings of formal education also were given at home by a tutor, or visiting *Şeyḫ*,[2] but this instruction can seldom have differed in any way from the type of instruction given in the *Ḳur'ân* schools.[3] Since these have remained in existence down to our own day, they require no fresh description.[4] The pupil was taught to recite some portions of the

[1] Cf. S. Lane-Poole, *Social Life in Egypt*, 80. Elementary religious instruction also was given in the home, not in school.

[2] Cf. Murâdî, iii. 202.

[3] We use this term to designate the *Kuttâb* (or *Mekteb*) instead of the usual French term 'primary school', since the latter was used at a later date to signify a totally different kind of school, with a different educational policy.

[4] See especially Ṭâhâ Ḥuseyn, *An Egyptian Childhood* (tr. E. H. Paxton, London, 1932); Lane, *Modern Egyptians*, ch. ii; S. Lane-Poole, 81–82 and plate; and note Denon's sarcastic caption (*Travels*, iii. 242, plate xlvii): 'they here learn to read the Koran and to receive the bastinado on the soles of their feet'.

Ḳur'ân from memory, and at most to read and write; simple arithmetic may sometimes have been taught, but was more often learnt from the public weigher (*ḳabbânî*) or village land-measurer (*massâḥ*).

Ḳur'ân schools were generally numerous in the towns and were often situated in the upper story of the public fountain (*sebîl*) attached to a mosque. In the villages the mosque itself served, when required, as a school. But the private teacher could hold his class in any suitable place, and neither teachers nor buildings were in any way supported by the government. Such buildings as existed for this specific purpose were due to the munificence of the rich, who founded them and assigned endowments for their upkeep, in some cases sufficient also to feed and clothe a number of poor scholars.[1] Where the teacher (or *Fiki*) was dependent on his earnings, the parents paid him a small weekly sum, ranging from 3 to 20 *paras*.[2] There appears to have been no system of inspection and control of the instruction given by the *Fikis*; when the school was endowed, its direction and the appointment of teachers was in the hands of the administrator of the endowment, usually a descendant of the founder, and the *Ḳâḍî* had a general right of supervision, but in both cases the control exercised was probably limited to matters of finance. It seems to be generally agreed that the average *Fiki* was ignorant and venal, and the profession was despised by the higher *'Ulemâ*,[3] although it was still held in some respect by the general population.

Any general computation of *Ḳur'ân* schools and of the numbers of children who attended them is probably impossible.[4] According to Chabrol, between a quarter and a third of the population of Cairo could read and write, but it is certain that elsewhere and in the country as a whole the percentage of illiteracy was much higher. The situation in Syria was probably similar to that in Egypt.[5]

[1] Jomard, *Description de l'Égypte*, ii. 2, 681–2, remarks that these endowments were usually 'religiously respected'.

[2] See generally Chabrol, 62–66. The term *fiki* is apparently a colloquial contraction of *faḳîh*, 'student of law', applied to men of religion generally. The *Fiki* was not as a rule a 'graduate' of any theological seminary, although he might have attended elementary classes at el-Azhar or some other *madrasa* for two or three years.

[3] There is, exceptionally, a notice of a teacher in Murâdî's work (i. 73): 'Abû Yezîd of Ḥalab, a chaste and saintly devotee, used to educate children in a mosque in the Muṣaraḳa quarter. All who saw him loved him; the people looked on him as a source of blessing, and used to obtain amulets from him and to experience their blessed power. . . . He possessed a majesty, light, and dignity which astonished those who looked upon him', &c.

[4] Jomard's figure of 'over a hundred' schools in Cairo is too uncertain, both in itself and in regard to what it includes, to be satisfactory as a basis.

[5] Explicit references to village schools in Syria are, of course, seldom found, but casual notices (e.g. Murâdî, i. 134 and 259) indicate their existence in most (if not all) districts. Rousseau's statement (p. 16) that at Bağdâd there were no

It was probably very rarely that any child not destined for the scholastic life or for administration continued his studies after leaving the *Kuttâb*. Yet, however open to criticism the *Kuttâb* may have been from the point of view of efficiency and intellectual training, it is important to observe that both in method and in content it fulfilled adequately the tasks demanded of it. Those who were proceeding to a higher education were familiarized with the classical language (though not yet capable of understanding its grammatical structure, for to explain Arabic grammar was probably beyond the power of the average *Fiki*) and were exercised in the task of memorizing, which was to constitute their main activity in the theological colleges. Those whose formal education finished at this stage had received a grounding of religious culture and ethic which prepared them to take their place in the Moslem community in accordance with their station in life. In most cases they passed into the guilds and corporations, whose traditional obligations and *ṣûfî* rituals finally imposed upon the young apprentice the characteristic religious discipline of Islâm, the conception of duty bound up with the tradition of the elders, as mediated through the teachings of the great mystics.[1]

From any but a purely religious standpoint, and even to some extent from that, the *Ḳur'ân* schools that were founded in all the Ottoman 'homelands' from early times were educationally more inadequate to the needs of their Moslem inhabitants than the schools of the Arab provinces to theirs. For although the children who attended the latter were not taught the classical Arabic of the *Ḳur'ân* and the prayers they were made to memorize, Arabic was at least their native tongue, whereas it was not that of the vast majority of the Moslem inhabitants of the homelands. These schools may be said indeed to have achieved their purpose in that they provided means whereby Moslem children in those provinces might acquaint themselves with sacred texts and learn how to perform their ritual prayers. But since in no *mekteb* of the homelands was Arabic, classical or vernacular, taught as a language,[2] and since little attempt seems to have been made by the teachers employed in them to interpret the texts their pupils got by heart, even though the abler among the latter might succeed in memorizing long pas-

schools for children is obviously inexact, since the *madrasas* (cf. Murâdî, ii. 9; iii. 84–86, 179) must have been fed from *Ḳu'rân* schools; for Moṣul and Kirkuk see below, p. 156. Even in Arabia Niebuhr attests the existence of many schools and several colleges (1774, pp. 91–92).

[1] Cf. the diploma of admission to the guild of bow-makers quoted by Cabartî (ii. 214–15/v. 136–9).

[2] The first imperial *mekteb* in the *waḳfîye* (see below, p. 143) of which provision was made for the teaching of Arabic and Persian—but not Turkish—was founded in 1781 (past the end of our period) by Sultan 'Abdü 'l-Ḥamîd I —see 'Oṣmân Nûrî Ergin, *Türkiye Maarif Tarihi*, i. 72.

sages, if not the whole, of the *Ḳur'ân*,[1] they might yet possess little, if any, idea what its sonorous verses might signify. A grasp of their meaning seems, indeed, to have been regarded as of less moment than an ability to recite the sacred words correctly, these being held by the vulgar to possess an almost magic power. Furthermore, in their ignorance of Arabic these pupils derived no such benefit from getting classical texts by heart as accrued to those in such provinces as Egypt; and if, as it appears they usually did, they learnt the Arabic alphabet, this can have been of use to them only as an aid to memorization. For although Ottoman Turkish was of course written in the Arabic character, they were not taught that either. In the second quarter of the eighteenth century a *mekteb* was founded at Ğalaṭa by the mother of Sultan Maḥmûd I (1730–54), at which (apparently for the first time in the history of Ottoman *mektebs*) the pupils were taught to write.[2] But the art in which they were instructed was rather calligraphy than common orthography; and since they were taught neither Arabic nor Turkish, although they might leave such establishments—for calligraphy was later included in the curricula of other *mektebs*[3]—capable of copying manuscripts and inscribing texts in a variety of beautiful styles, they might yet have no notion how to compose or spell the shortest letter or message.[4] The teaching of calligraphy had indeed quite another object than that of enabling pupils to record or communicate their personal thoughts or those of anyone else. It, too, was purely religious: it enabled them to commit to paper, *ad majorem Dei gloriam*, the sacred sentences and prayers that they otherwise spent their time in getting by heart from their *ḫocas*.

The *mektebs* of the Ottoman homelands, accordingly, though they fulfilled the purpose for which they were founded, did little towards supplying the children who attended them with even the elements of a general education. What further knowledge they acquired, such as the rudiments of mathematics, they must pick up from their families or their employers. The vast majority of the population, particularly, of course, in the country-side, hence remained entirely illiterate; and it was on this account that anyone who could read or write, and still more the *'Ulemâ*, enjoyed a general respect that, in a more book-learned society, their attainments might not always have won for them.

As in the Arab provinces, so in the homelands, all *mektebs* owned their existence to private beneficence. Some, it is true, were

[1] Ibid. 70, n. 2, where a passage is quoted from the reminiscences of İhsan Sungu, born in 1882, who had learnt the whole *Ḳur'ân* by heart without being able to read.

[2] Ibid. 70.

[3] e.g. that founded by 'Abdü'l-Ḥamid I and referred to above.

[4] Ibid. 71.

founded by Sultans; but in founding them such Sultans acted, as it were, as private persons. Their *mektebs* were in no sense state schools. They differed from those founded by inferior persons, such as *Ḳadîns* and *Paşas*,[1] only in being larger and better provided. That the foundation of *mektebs* was a 'good work', comparable to the provision of hostelries for wayfarers or the building of bridges and fountains, is clearly shown by, for instance, the *waḳfîyes*—that is, the *waḳf* 'deeds'—of the *Ḳur'ân* schools established in Istanbul by Sultans Meḥmed II and Bâyezîd II, the first of which indicates that Meḥmed's school was intended for the education of orphan children or, failing enough of them, children of the indigent, while the second stipulates that before dispersing for the night the children shall pray for the founder.[2] As in many such schools in the Arab provinces, the pupils in those of the homelands were generally furnished with clothes and food. Rather in the manner of the trade-guilds they were also, once a year, given an outing. In *mektebs* founded in conjunction with an *'imâret*, or kitchen for the distribution of food to the poor, such as the imperial *mektebs* of the capital, they were given meals morning and evening. In ordinary *mektebs* the founder usually made provision for them to receive a daily allowance of money instead.[3] *Mektebs* in general were evidently intended for children whose parents could not afford to have them instructed privately, the more affluent being expected to do so from their own resources.[4] The typical *mekteb* building consisted of a large domed saloon, leading off which was a small room for the *ḥoca* and his assistants. The pupils were all taught together, and instead of being placed in rows, sat each crosslegged on a mattress with a low desk in front of him.[5]

Higher education in all the Islamic lands was given in college-mosques and *madrasas*,[6] greatly differing in size, staffing, and importance, according to the extent of their endowments.

[1] Ergin, i. 75–76, lists 47 *mektebs* founded by *Ḳadîns* in Istanbul, 37 by *Paşas*, 45 by *Beys*, *Çelebis*, and *Efendis*, 59 by guilds (*eşnâf*) and *Ağas*, i.e., with 10 founded by Sultans, 198 in all. These were institutions still existing and known by their founders' names at the beginning of the present century. In some provincial cities the number of *mektebs* was sometimes very considerable. For instance, Evliya Çelebi records the existence (in the second quarter of the seventeenth century) of 120 in Bosna-Sarayî (Sarayevo)—see art. 'Bosna-Sarayî' in *I.A.*

[2] Ergin, i. 69, 73.

[3] Ibid. 73–74. The *waḳfiye* of Bâyezîd II mentions the provision of morning and evening meals, that of Süleymân the provision of 10 *aḳçes* for the pupils' clothes, which they were given twice a year, while the *waḳfiye* of a school founded near the end of our period, in 1755, lists precisely what clothes each pupil was to receive.

[4] Cf. D'Ohsson, iv. 477.

[5] Ergin, i. 76.

[6] Pronounced *medrese* in Turkish.

The foundation of such colleges soon became a concern of the early Ottoman Sultans, a monastery at Iznik̦ (Nicaea) being converted into one after its conquest by Orḫan in 1331.[1] In Bursa, which soon displaced Iznik̦ as the Ottoman capital, *medreses* were founded by Murâd I and his next three successors;[2] and the last of these, Murâd II, not only turned another monastery in the citadel of Adrianople, the next Ottoman capital, into a *medrese*, he also added one to the 'Üç-Şerefeli'[3] mosque he built in one quarter of the city, and founded a third in another quarter. The wife of one of his *Paşas* founded a fourth; and after him Meḥmed II, Bâyezîd II, and Selîm I all founded others, while the buildings of the great mosque of Selîm II, designed by the famous architect Sinân, included not only two *medreses* proper[4] but a 'Readers' House'[5] and a boys' *mekteb*.[6] Apart from these the city was furnished by private persons with at least two other colleges, and so for its size was well appointed as a centre of learning.[7] Partly on that account, but also as pertaining to a former capital, the *medrese* organization of Adrianople, together with that of Bursa, retained a special status, the professors of its colleges ranking, indeed, below those of Istanbul, but above those of *medreses* founded or already existing elsewhere.[8]

Elsewhere in the homeland provinces all the chief towns were also provided with *medreses*; and in the provinces that had been in Moslem control before the Ottoman conquest some of these were of pre-Ottoman foundation, as at Ķonya, the capital of the Selcuķids of Rûm,[9] Diyârbekir and Amasya, which were both notable centres of learning,[10] Anķara and Ķastamonu. But in these and other cities of Anatolia many more were built under the Ottoman régime, as also in those of the European provinces, such as Belgrade and Bosna-Sarayî.[11]

Istanbul itself was, naturally, the most abundantly furnished of all. All the Sultans who built imperial mosques there also built a number of *medreses* in connexion with them. Aya Ṣofya, after its conversion into a mosque, was likewise provided with one;[12]

[1] *I.A.*, art. 'Iznik̦'.
[2] Ibid. art. 'Bursa'.
[3] That is, 'having minarets with three galleries'.
[4] Called *Dârü 'l-Ḥadîs̱* (cf. below, p. 145) and *Dârü 'l-Tedrîs*—'Tradition-house' and 'Teaching-house'.
[5] *Dârü 'l-Ķurrâ'*—the Readers in question being specialists in the recitation, punctuation, and vocalization of the *Ķur'ân*.
[6] Called *Dârü 'l-Ṣubyân*.
[7] *I.A.*, art. 'Edirne'.
[8] Hammer, *Staatsverfassung*, ii. 405.
[9] *Encyc. of Islam*, s.v.
[10] G. Perrot, *Souvenirs d'un voyage en Asie Mineure* (1861), 453, describes Amasya as 'the Oxford of Anatolia'.
[11] See the arts. on these cities in *I.A.*
[12] See *T.O.E.M.*, No. 13, p. 20, for a reference to it in the *Ķânûn-nâme* of Meḥmed II.

and so were many large mosques built by private benefactors,[1] till in the eighteenth century there were at least 275 in various parts of the city.[2] The most important of these foundations were the *medreses* built by Meḥmed II, Bâyezîd II, and Süleymân the Magnificent. Apart from those attached to Aya Ṣofya Meḥmed built no fewer than sixteen round his mosque, generally called *Fâtiḥ* ('The Conqueror's') after him; and some seventy years later Süleymân surrounded his, the Süleymânîye mosque, with others. It was in these two groups of *medreses*, together with the *medreses* of the mosque of Bâyezîd II, that all the principal *'Ulemâ* were trained, and they consequently possessed a special importance. Meḥmed II built his in two stages. He first built four to the north and four to the south of his mosque. These were known as the '*Medreses* of the Courtyard',[3] and the courtyard, on their account, as the 'Courtyard of the Eight'.[4] But he later found it necessary to build eight more, similarly grouped, which were called, since they were devoted to preliminary studies, either 'Introductory to the Courtyard',[5] or 'Supplementary'.[6] Those of the first group, whose chambers were domed, each contained, besides a main hall, in which at first instruction was given, fifteen single rooms for students, two rooms for assistant teachers, and two others for door-keepers and servants, whereas the accommodation provided in the Supplementary *medreses* was more modest. Each of these *medreses* contained only eight rooms, not domed, each of which housed three students. Altogether, therefore, Meḥmed II's *medreses* could lodge 312 students at a time.[7] Of the *medreses* that formed part of the Süleymânîye foundation two were devoted to special studies, a *Dârü 'l-Ḥadîs̱* for the study of Tradition, and a *Dârü 'l-Ṭibb* for the study of medicine.[8] The *medreses* at the mosque of Bâyezîd were wholly devoted, at least eventually, to the study of law.[9]

[1] See, for instance, the list of *medreses* built by Sinân in Aḥmed Refîḳ, *Mimar Sinan*, 67–68. According to this he built no fewer than fifty-five in all, of which a large number in Istanbul were for persons other than Sultans.

[2] Hammer, *Geschichte*, ix. 145, lists that number.

[3] *Ṣaḥn medreseleri.*

[4] *Ṣaḥnî S̱emân.*

[5] *Mûṣilei Ṣaḥn.*

[6] *Tetimme.*

[7] Ergin, 82–86.

[8] In addition to five other *medreses*, called *Ḫavâmisi Süleymânîye*. So the last-cited author in his *Maarif*, 86, and his earlier *Belediye*, i. 269. At the same time in the latter work, 271, he also describes the foundation as consisting of four *medreses*, the *Dârü 'l-Ḥadîs̱*, and an unspecified number of preparatory *medreses*, which went collectively by the name of *Mûṣilei Süleymânîye* (cf. *Mûṣilei Ṣaḥn*). In this he seems to be following Cevdet, i. 110, who further states that the four *medreses* were those in which students attained the eleventh stage in their advancement, the stage called simply '*Süleymânîye*'. If so the *Ḫavâmis* must have been others; and Cevdet, i. 111, in fact mentions these too, as no longer existing in his day. Aḥmed Refîḳ, 67, lists only six *medreses* as having been built by Sinân at the Süleymânîye.

[9] D'Ohsson, ii. 470, iv. 487; Hammer, *Staatsverfassung*, ii. 402–3.

It was after the construction of the Süleymânîye *medreses* that the teaching provided in all these establishments was finally organized in twelve grades.[1] Every student, at each stage of his progress through the first eleven, must obtain a licence (*icâze*) declaring him fully conversant with whatever works he had been studying from the masters concerned, before moving up to the next grade. When he had thus passed into the sixth grade, that of the Courtyard of the Eight, he was allowed, while continuing his studies in the higher *medreses*, to act as an assistant in the lower by taking the students attending them through what they had already learnt from their teachers, and was hence called *mu'îd*, or 'recapitulator'.[2] It was at this point too that he ceased to be a *softâ*, as beginners were called, and became a *dânişmend*.[3] Thereafter, if he saw any hope of attaining the highest offices in the judicial hierarchy, he must graduate through most, if not all, of the remaining six stages and so, as a preliminary, become a master, or *müderris*,[4] himself. Moreover, having become one, he must start at the bottom again and work his way, as a teacher, through at least nine of the twelve grades towards the top again. Only then was he eligible for a 'great' *mevleviyet*;[5] and since influence, as well as academic proficiency, played a part in his obtaining one, comparatively few of the *softâs* who entered the lowest *medreses* remained to complete the course. Instead, after at some stage attending the *medreses* of the Bâyezîd mosque, they would elect to become *Nâ'ibs*, ordinary *Ḳâḍîs*, or provincial *Muftîs*, posts that were all open also to 'graduates' of other *medreses*, outside this 'central' scheme.[6] Those

[1] They were called: 1. *Ibtidâi Ḫâric* ('Outside Beginning'). 2. *Hareketi Ḫâric* ('Outside Remove'). 3. *Ibtidâi Dâḫil* ('Inside Beginning'). 4. *Ḥareketi Dâḫil* ('Inside Remove'). 5. *Mûşilei Ṣaḥn* ('Introductory to the Courtyard'). 6. *Ṣaḥnî Semân* ('Courtyard of the Eight'). 7. *Ibtidâi Altmişlî* ('*Altmişlî*—see below—Beginning'). 8. *Ḥareketi Altmişlî* ('*Altmişlî* Remove'). 9. *Mûşilei Süleymânîye* ('Introductory to the *Süleymânîye*'). 10. *Ḫavâmisi Süleymânîye* ('The *Süleymânîye* Five'). 11. *Süleymânîye*. 12. *Dârü 'l-Ḥadîs*—see Ergin, *Belediye*, i. 270, *Maarif*, i. 85. D'Ohsson, iv. 487, shows only ten grades, omitting grades 8 and 12 as shown above. The *Ḳânûn-nâme* of 'Abdu'r-Raḥmân Tevḳî'î (*M.T.M.* i. 539) shows only seven (for purposes of precedence), further omitting the two other *Ḥareket* grades (2 and 4) and grade 10. But in any case, although each *müderris* had his own *medrese*, these grades did not, it seems, exactly correspond to particular colleges or groups of them, and were rather distinguished by the books expounded by the teachers and by the latters' emoluments. The *Altmişlî* grades were thus apparently so called because the *müderrises* concerned received (originally at any rate) 50–60 *akçes* a day—see Hammer, ii. 404.

[2] Ergin, *Belediye*, i. 267.

[3] Ergin, *Maarif*, i. 84. The word *softâ* is usually derived from the Persian *suḫta*, meaning 'burnt'—i.e. consumed with zeal for learning. Ergin, loc. cit., however, derides this derivation, which indeed seems far-fetched, and proposes instead (though not very plausibly either) one from the Greek *sophos*. *Dânişmänd* is Persian for 'learned'.

[4] *müderris*, *medrese*, and *tedrîs* are all from the Arabic *darasa*, 'he studied'.

[5] See p. 89 above.

[6] It was only after passing out of the Bâyezîd *medreses* that *dânişmends* could

who persisted and obtained *müderrisliks* in the 'central' *medreses* thereby became dignitaries of sufficient importance to attend the receptions held by the Grand *Vezîr* before the Friday *dîvân* and the receptions held by both the Grand *Vezîr* and the *Şeyḫü 'l-Islâm* at *Bayrams*.[1] These *müderrisliks* were themselves, however, divided into three classes. The lowest *müderrislik* from which a 'great' *mevleviyet* was obtainable being one of the ninth grade, the highest class was composed of the *müderrises* of this and the grades above it, headed by the *müderris* of the *Dârü 'l-Ḥadîs̱*. The next class comprised the *müderrises* of grades six, seven, and eight; and the third class the remainder.[2]

The occupation of teaching posts in these particular *medreses* of Istanbul was thus regarded primarily as a preparation for judicial office. In the fifteenth century *müderrisliks* were also stepping-stones to certain clerkly employments in the ruling institution, such as those of *Nîşâncî* and *Defterdâr*.[3] Afterwards, however, the latter seem nearly always to have been filled by *Ḳapî Ḳulus*; and *müderrisliks* then led only to enrolment in the order of *Mollâs*. This development went hand in hand with a narrowing in the scope of the teaching offered by these *medreses* and perhaps *medreses* in general. For it would appear that from the reign of Meḥmed II to that of Süleymân the Magnificent what were known as the 'rational'[4] as well as the 'religious' sciences were to some extent studied in them, but that from the middle of the sixteenth century the '*Ulemâ* normally devoted their whole attention to the latter, and in particular to theology and jurisprudence.[5] Those who continued to study such subjects as mathematics, astronomy, and natural history, did so out of personal rather than professional interest, with the result that such studies progressively languished.[6] It seems doubtful, indeed, precisely how far they ever formed part of the regular studies pursued in *medreses* under the Ottoman régime. The head of the first Ottoman

become *mulâzims*, that is to say, candidates for office. If they chose to persist in their studies and become *müderrises*, they must face another seven years' training in the higher colleges. But on becoming *mulâzims* they began receiving salaries —Ergin, *Belediye*, i. 267–8; D'Ohsson, iv. 486–9; Juchereau, i. 29.

[1] *M.T.M.* i. 503, 539–40 (*Ḳânûn-nâme* of 'Abdu 'r-Raḥmân Tevḳî'î). The attendance of *müderrises* (and Great *Mollâs*) before *dîvâns* was, however, dispensed with in 1656, on the accession to the Grand Vezirate of Köprülü Meḥmed Paşa, owing to pressure of business. For their attendance at *Bayrams* see op. cit. 520.

[2] Ergin, *Belediye*, i. 270–1. *Müderrises* of the two higher classes, but not those of the third class, took part in the *bey'at* ceremony, at which allegiance was sworn to a new Sultan—D'Ohsson, iv. 550.

[3] Cases in point are Ḳaramânî Meḥmed Paşa in the reign of Meḥmed II and Ca'fer Çelebi in that of Bâyezîd II—*Encyc. of Islam*, s. vv.

[4] '*aḳlî*, from Arabic '*aḳl*, 'mind'.

[5] See, e.g., D'Ohsson, ii. 466; Seyyid Muṣṭafâ, iii. 109.

[6] D'Ohsson, iv. 476.

medrese at Iznik̦ is said to have cultivated the 'rational' sciences.[1] From the reign of Orḫan to that of Murâd II some half-dozen Ottoman *'Ulemâ* composed, or in one case translated, works on mathematics, astronomy, and natural history,[2] and it may be that they also taught them. Under Meḥmed II, who was himself of an inquiring mind and a student of Ptolemy's *Geography*,[3] a certain 'Alî K̦uşcu, a native of Transoxania, where he had become director of an observatory at Samark̦and, was installed at the *medrese* of Aya Ṣofya as a professor of astronomy and mathematics, and composed treatises on astronomy, arithmetic, and algebra, which are said to have been long used in *medreses* as standard works on those subjects.[4] Under Bâyezîd II, again, a mathematician and astronomer was appointed to one of the Courtyard *medreses*. But, despite the Sultan's favour, he was eventually executed as a free-thinker at the instance of some of the bigoted among his fellow *'Ulemâ*;[5] and in the sixteenth century, though works on some of the 'rational' sciences continued to be composed,[6] the only science in which much notable activity was shown was geography.[7] Interest in this had been stimulated, even in the isolation of the Ottoman world, by the discovery of America and the Cape route to the east; and several works that broke new ground, such as the *Baḥrîye* of the *k̦aptan* Pîrî Re'îs, made their appearance.[8] But it seems improbable that the teaching in the *medreses* was much, if at all, affected by such compositions; and it is at least doubtful whether any of the *medreses* founded by Süleymân were, as is sometimes alleged, intended especially to promote the study of any of the 'rational' sciences except medicine.[9] That the wrath of the *'Ulemâ* was easily aroused against unfamiliar investigations was shown under Murâd III, when the first Ottoman observatory, erected on the heights above the *Ṭopḫâne* in Ğalaṭa, in which a narrow pit, 40 foot deep, served as a primitive telescope for the observation of the heavens by day, was summarily destroyed with all its contents at the instance of the then *Şeyḫü 'l-Islâm* on the pretext that astronomical observations were unlucky.[10]

The only non-religious science that was regarded with some favour by the more rigid of the *'Ulemâ* was medicine, perhaps on account of its charitable aspect. The foundation of hospitals had long ranked among laudable 'good works'. In the Ottoman homelands there existed hospitals dating from Selcuk̦id times in at least

[1] Abdülhak Adnan, *La Science chez les Ottomans*, 9–10.
[2] Ibid. 12–13, 19. [3] Ibid. 26. [4] Ibid. 33–34. [5] Ibid. 45.
[6] Notably by a certain Mîrim Bey, a grandson of both 'Alî K̦uşcu and of another mathematician-astronomer, the K̦âḍî-zâdei Rûmî (d. 1412)—ibid. 12, 47.
[7] Cf. ibid. 55. [8] Ibid. 63–74.
[9] See Ergin, *Maarif*, i. 127. [10] Adnan, 78–79.

seven cities of Anatolia;[1] and these were supplemented by Sultans and others throughout the area of the Ottoman conquests. Medicine seems to have been included in the subjects taught originally in the Courtyard *medreses* founded by Meḥmed II;[2] and one of the Süleymânîye *medreses* was certainly devoted to it under the name *Dârü 'l-Ṭibb*,[3] the foundation also comprising a hospital.[4] But what was taught seems at best to have dated from the medieval heyday of Islâm;[5] and though at least one work exhibiting some originality was composed early in the sixteenth century,[6] a decline in fact set in after the establishment of Süleymân's college, for a paradoxical reason: its professorships were so well endowed that they became sought after by fortune-hunters and were too often bestowed on the unworthy.[7] The systematic pursuit of medical studies was not perhaps helped by the fact that the Sultans' *Ḥekîm Başîs*, far from being professional physicians, were ordinary members of the high *'Ulemâ* who might, both before assuming this position and after leaving it, perform some quite other duties.[8] Nevertheless, at least three of the *Ḥekîm Başîs* of Meḥmed IV (1648–87) wrote medical treatises, in one of which experiment, as well as adherence to traditional method, is advocated, and in the other two of which reference is made to European medical innovations.[9] During the latter part of the reign of Aḥmed III (1703–30), again, when European influences were for a time relatively powerful, the medical theories of Paracelsus had a vogue among some Moslem physicians at Istanbul. But their adoption so far met with official disapproval that one of Aḥmed's *Ḥekîm Başîs* induced him to require practitioners of this 'new' medicine to undergo an examination before being allowed to treat patients, while foreign physicians were at the same time forbidden to practise altogether; and although this ban seems soon to have been lifted, towards the end of the reign another *Ḥekîm Başî* was instructed to supervise all doctors without, however, any particular reference to these theories.[10] It seems probable that medicine was somewhat less bound by tradition than other learned pursuits because the existence of

[1] Ergin, *Maarif*, i. 124; Adnan, 18.

[2] Though Ergin, *Maarif*, i. 86, omits any reference to it in his description of the courses in these *medreses*, Adnan, 36, states that one of the Courtyard *medreses* was devoted to medical studies and had a hospital attached to it. Ergin, *Maarif*, 124, also refers to this hospital.

[3] Ergin, *Maarif*, 86, 125, cites the *wakfîye* of the foundation. Some of the original apparatus is still preserved in the college.

[4] Ergin, *Belediye*, i. 269.

[5] See Ergin, *Maarif*, i. 125.

[6] The *Yâdgâr* of Ibn Şerîf—Adnan, 53–54.

[7] Ibid. 85.

[8] Ergin, *Maarif*, i. 125.

[9] Adnan, 94, 96, 98–99.

[10] Ibid. 128–30. According to Russell, *Natural Hist. of Aleppo*, 97, a licence to practise was obtained from the *Ḥekîm Başî* 'for a few sequins'.

hospitals everywhere favoured experiment in treatment; and it is notable that inoculation against the smallpox was practised in Turkey before its value was recognized in the West.[1] On the other hand, Moslem physicians were gravely handicapped by being forbidden to dissect dead bodies; and so even religious prejudice was not strong enough to deter well-to-do Moslems, headed by the Sultans themselves, from preferring the ministrations of Europeans or European-trained Greeks.[2]

From the second half of the sixteenth century not only did the teaching given in *medreses* become almost wholly restricted to law and theology, but its quality deteriorated. Just as in the ruling institution from the reign of Murâd III the regulations governing the appointment of office-holders were relaxed and many unsuitable and ignorant persons thereby admitted into it, so in the order of the *müderrises*. Students in the *medreses* were still subjected to examination, but at the turning-point in their progress towards the status of teacher, when, after completing their studies in the *medreses* of Bâyezîd, they might be granted *mulâzemets*, they now found these conferred more and more frequently on rivals who had undergone no such arduous training as themselves but were related, or in some other manner connected, either with powerful members of the learned profession itself or with still more powerful courtiers or government officials. In due course, accordingly, the chief *müderrisliks* came often to be occupied by such persons, quite ignorant though they were of the subjects they were supposed to teach. Their aim was, of course, to secure *mevleviyets*; but in the meantime they were able to draw the salaries that went with these teaching posts. As they were unfitted to discharge the duties these entailed, however, they engaged substitutes from among the 'graduates' of the *medreses*; and a complete breakdown in the system was thus prevented. These substitutes, who were known as *ḫocas*,[3] succeeded in maintaining it to a tolerable extent. But the honour in which *müderrises* had earlier been held was no longer accorded to them. *Müderrisliks* indeed came increasingly to be regarded as mere sources of income; and their holders are said often not even to have known the whereabouts of the *medreses* they were meant to teach in, and even to have been appointed in certain instances to *medreses* that no longer existed. The number of 'central' *müderrisliks* came also to be much increased in the grades below the Courtyard, in which there continued to be no more than eight; and since the extra *müderrises* concerned were unprovided for by the original foundations, they were granted *ḳaḍâs* to live on, which they again caused to be administered by deputies. This increase

[1] Adnan, 136.
[2] D'Ohsson, i. 347.
[3] Cf. p. 94 above. See D'Ohsson, iv. 491.

in turn brought about so strong a pressure for advancement that promotions became automatic rather than dependent on attainments. The eight highest *müderrises*[1] were then regularly granted *mevleviyets*[2] annually, for a year's tenure, and replaced by the next eight on the list.[3] In the eighteenth century *dânişmends* who had completed the studies that qualified them to become *müderrises* were sometimes appointed, pending their attainment of judgeships, not only (in the regular fashion) to *medreses* of the twelve grades, but also to posts in the office of the *Şeyḫü 'l-Islâm*, the *Ḳâḍî-'askers*, and the *Ḳâḍî* of Istanbul,[4] and to teach *softâs* and children of the poor in mosques.[5] By that time, indeed, it had become usual for all teaching to be conducted in the mosques round which the *medreses* were built rather than in the *medreses* themselves, which were by then devoted solely to accommodating students.[6] By the eighteenth century, again, *müderrises* appear largely to have regained the esteem of the people,[7] partly no doubt because of the greater influence exercised by the high *'Ulemâ* in general at that period.

Already in the sixteenth century, before this decline set in, the *'Ulemâ* had shown signs of a growing bigotry. Thus after the death of Süleymân they insisted on the replacement of certain standard works that had formed the basis of the study of law in the *medreses* by others, free of the 'philosophy' they detected in the former.[8] In the latter half of the century three 'learned men' were executed for free-thinking, one of them a *müderris* in a *medrese* at the capital who maintained the eternity of the world and the predetermination of events.[9] Any chance that the Ottoman world would benefit by contemporary European advances in knowledge was precluded by a ban on the import of printed books.[10] Moreover, printing (by Moslems) itself was forbidden down to early in the eighteenth century; and this alone almost ensured that Ottoman learning should not progress. Nevertheless, even in the seventeenth century the composition of works on mathematics, astronomy, geography, and medicine continued.[11] Their authors, however, were not as a rule *medrese*-trained. The most celebrated of such authors was Muṣṭafâ ibn 'Abdillah, known as Ḥaccî Ḫalîfe or the Kâtib Çelebi,[12] who

[1] i.e. the *müderris* of the *Dârü 'l-Ḥadîs*, the *müderrises* of the four Süleymânîye *medreses*, and three others.

[2] The eight lowest, which were hence called *maḫrec* (i.e. 'outlet', these being the posts into which they 'emerged').

[3] Ḳoçu Bey, *Risâle* (trans. Behrnauer, *Z.D.M.G.* xv (1861), 290 sq.). Cf. Cevdet, i. 112–15; Ergin, *Maarif*, i. 271–2.

[4] Such as those of *Fetvâ Emîni* and *Telḫişçi*.

[5] D'Ohsson, iv. 490.

[6] Ergin, *Maarif*, i. 85.

[7] D'Ohsson, iv. 494.

[8] Ergin, *Belediye*, i. 270.

[9] Adnan, 88–89.

[10] Ibid. 87.

[11] Ibid. 91 sq.

[12] He was called Ḥaccî Ḫalîfe because he had performed the Pilgrimage and was *ḫalîfe* (*ḳalfa*) in his government department.

was the son of a 'standing' cavalryman and himself a secretary in one of the bureaux of the Porte. He deplored the neglect of the 'rational' sciences by the *'Ulemâ* of the *medreses*, and contrived to acquire from other sources a wide knowledge of physics, astronomy, geometry, and geography; to give lessons in them himself; and to compose a number of remarkable works. Whereas he was disdained by the *'Ulemâ* for his lack of *medrese* training, he was in fact the first Ottoman learned man to acquaint himself with European scientific thought and attempt to introduce it into the Sultans' dominions.[1] It is evident, indeed, that though the *medreses* declined into mere inefficient religious seminaries, the study of many subjects they neglected was in fact pursued elsewhere.

The schools provided for the *'Acemî Oğlans* and *Iç Oğlans*[2] of the Sultan's Household, for instance, were in some respects superior to the *medreses*. In them, too, pupils were instructed in the 'religious' sciences; Evliya Çelebi regarded the religious instruction received by the *Iç Oğlans* of his day (and he was one himself) as better than that of the contemporary (mid-seventeenth-century) *medreses*. As well as Arabic both Persian and Turkish were taught not only in the Enderûn but also in the *'Acemî-Oğlan* schools; and though much of the pages' time was consumed in acquiring the manual accomplishments required in the various palace services, and in perfecting their horsemanship, archery, and lance-throwing,[3] they learned how to converse in a cultivated fashion, to write prose and verse, and to compose and perform musical pieces. It was in these schools also that the architects, sculptors, and painters, the annalists and calligraphers, who have left so many fine works for our admiration, seem for the most part to have been formed;[4] and it was the *'Acemî-Oğlan* schools and other military and naval institutions such as the *Ṭopḫâne* and the *Tersâne*[5] that produced the cannon-founders, ship designers and builders, &c., who were required for the Sultan's armed forces. Some of the *dervîş tekkes* also fulfilled an educational purpose. Thus the *Bektaşî tekkes* were centres for the cultivation of music among the people, while the *tekkes* of the *Mevlevîs* were resorted to by the educated not only for the study and performance of music of a more sophisticated type, but also for instruction in the works of the great Persian mystics and particularly, of course, in the famous *Mesnevî* of Mevlânâ Celâlü'd-Dîn Rûmî himself.[6]

Down to early in the eighteenth century, although Ottoman

[1] Adnan, 103–20.
[2] See Part I, index.
[3] The throwing of the palm-branch lances or darts called *cerîd*; see Oppenheim, 'Der *Djerīd* und das *Djerīd*-Spiel', *Islamica*, ii (4), 590–617.
[4] Ergin, *Maarif*, i. 8–11, 23, 28.
[5] See Part I, index.
[6] Ergin, *Maarif*, i. 20.

Turkish poetry was based on Persian models and some knowledge of Persian was indispensable for the Turkish poets, it was entirely excluded from the curriculum of the *medreses*. There was a reason for this. Persian was disliked by the more rigid of the *'Ulemâ* for its particular association with mysticism; and among the more ignorant and fanatical *softâs* was even characterized, quite solemnly, as the 'language of Hell'.[1] After the conclusion of the Treaty of Passarovitz in 1718, however, for some twelve years the government was directed, under Aḥmed III, by the Grand *Vezîr* Damad Nevşehirli Ibrâhîm Paşa; and in the *medrese* founded in 1720–1 by this interesting and enlightened minister provision was made for the teaching not only of Persian but also of mathematics.[2] This all too short period, known pleasantly as *Lâle Devri*—the Age of Tulips (because the cultivation of tulips then became a fashion among the well-to-do)—might well have led to an Ottoman renaissance, had it not been brought to a sudden end in 1730 by the revolution that cost Aḥmed III his throne and Ibrâhîm Paşa his life. But while it lasted Ibrâhîm gave all the encouragement he could to men of learning. He set up a commission of twenty-five scholars to translate Arabic and Persian historical works into Turkish. He caused scientific and literary works to be made available in unexampled abundance in the public libraries, five of which were opened at this time;[3] and—most important of all—it was he who encouraged the foundation of the first Ottoman Moslem printing press by the Transylvanian convert, Ibrâhîm the Muteferriḳa. There already existed Ottoman Greek, Armenian, and Jewish presses, some of which printed works in the Arabic character. But until the Tulip Age the *'Ulemâ*, as we have mentioned, had set their faces against the printing of books by Moslems. Even when Ibrâhîm the Muteferriḳa was finally authorized to create his press —in collaboration with a certain Sa'îd Meḥmed Efendi who, having accompanied his father[4] on a diplomatic mission to Paris, had returned much impressed with western culture—it was laid down by *fetvâ* that he might publish only dictionaries and scientific and historical works: he was forbidden to publish any that might be classified as religious. The hostility of the *'Ulemâ* also perhaps accounts partly for the fact that after his death in 1745 the enterprise was more or less abandoned until revived towards the end of the century. But it was in truth very much a 'one-man show'. Ibrâhîm was not only its founder and manager, but also its moving spirit, himself designing and cutting the characters, writing intro-

[1] Ibid. 133–4.
[2] Ibid. 122, 128, 134.
[3] Adnan, 126. Cf. E. Z. Karal, art. 'Ahmed III' in *I.A.*
[4] Strangely named *Yirmi-sekiz* ('Twenty-eight') Meḥmed Çelebi—see Karal in art. cited.

ductions to the works published, furnishing them with contents lists, drawing maps to illustrate them, and above all choosing them. He published only seventeen works in all, the most important perhaps being the Kâtib Çelebi's cosmography, the *Cihânnümâ*, and the additions to it he himself composed, in which he drew upon European sources and even made circumspect reference to the systems of Copernicus and Tycho Brahe, Galileo and Descartes. In referring to the Copernican theory he remarks that no one is obliged to believe in such doctrines. On the contrary, he says, the Moslem doctors can refute them and so fortify the opinions of Ptolemy, which they admit as valid.[1]

This indicates clearly enough how unready the high *'Ulemâ* then were to allow the diffusion of any new ideas among the Moslems of the Empire; and in fact Ibrâhîm's enterprise seems to have proved quite ineffective in enlightening the Ottoman ruling classes to any appreciable extent during the eighteenth century. According to the Baron de Tott, who was sent by the French government to advise the Porte at the very end of our period, the Ottoman ministers were then so ignorant of European geography, for instance, as to suppose that no Russian ships could enter the Mediterranean from the west;[2] and although we may perhaps discount some of his adverse comments as due to misunderstanding and exasperation, it seems probable that he does not greatly exaggerate in depicting the Ottoman Moslems of that time as in general profoundly and complacently ill-informed.

As regards the Arab provinces, there is ample evidence of an active educational tradition in 'Irâḳ and Syria no less than in Egypt. It is a totally mistaken view that concentrates upon the college mosque of el-Azhar at Cairo as the only institution of the kind, although it was undoubtedly the most important (because it was the richest) in the Arabic lands. It was at this period tolerably well staffed and endowed, had some sixty to seventy professors (exclusive of junior teachers and officials),[3] and a great number of students drawn mostly from Cairo itself and the provinces of Egypt, but also from all other Moslem lands. Owing to its great reputation, the other *madrasas* and college mosques of Cairo[4] had become its satellites, and though they retained a certain independence in the matter of their endowments, the teaching posts were held as a rule

[1] T. Halasi Kun, art. 'Ibrâhim Muteferrika', in *I.A.* Cf. Adnan, 131–5.

[2] *Memoirs*, iii. 14.

[3] Chabrol, 67–70; he gives forty to fifty professors, but during the French occupation the numbers were considerably reduced, owing to the flight of many and the execution of others. Napoleon's own estimate is sixty (*Commentaires*, ii. 362–3, quoted Chauvin, *Légende*, 22).

[4] Cabartî mentions about twenty *madrasas* and as many mosques where teaching was given; in some there may have been no more than a single teacher, but one or two were quite notable institutions.

by *Şeyḫs* of the Azhar. In addition, there were some eighteen or twenty towns in Egypt with college mosques, varying in number from one to seven or so. In these again the principal teachers were generally local *Şeyḫs* trained at el-Azhar, but in return they supplied the latter with many of its most prominent scholars.[1] Of these provincial schools the most active were at Rosetta, Damietta, Desûḳ, Maḥalla, Manṣûra, and Ṭanṭa in the Delta, and at Ṭahṭa in Upper Egypt.[2]

Education in Syria was less centralized, since in addition to the two main centres of Aleppo and Damascus there were important provincial schools at Jerusalem and Nâblus, and college mosques in all towns.[3] Besides the cathedral mosques of Damascus and Aleppo, which, in accordance with the old tradition, were their central teaching institutions, both cities had a number of mosque schools and *madrasas*, some associated with and some independent of the principal mosque. Murâdî mentions no less than forty-five *madrasas* in Damascus, exclusive of mosques, during the eighteenth century, and their number in Aleppo was probably not much less.[4] Syrian scholars were apparently more inclined than those of Egypt to travel outside their borders; many, of course, went to el-Azhar, where the Syrian *riwâḳ* was one of the most active,[5] some to the Holy Cities, and a considerable number, especially of the more ambitious, to Istanbul, to seek enlistment in the Turkish cadres.[6] On the other hand, Damascus was a favourite centre for scholars from other countries, probably because of its attractive situation on the Pilgrim Road.

ʿIrâḳ was in a less fortunate position, having with difficulty preserved a tradition of education through the troubled centuries that followed the Mongol conquest of 1258. Nevertheless, there were *madrasas* capable of producing recognized scholars in Bağdâd[7] and

[1] It is noteworthy in this connexion that not one of the Head *Şeyḫs* of el-Azhar in the eighteenth century was of Cairene origin.

[2] References in Cabartî and materials in ʿAlî Paşa Mubârak, *el-Ḫiṭaṭ el-Tawfîḳîya*.

[3] For Jerusalem note especially Murâdî, i. 175, which implies that a full education could be obtained there; Nâblus was a chief centre of Ḥanbalî learning (cf. Murâdî, i. 82, 191–2; iii. 41; iv. 31–32). Amongst the towns in which colleges are mentioned are Ramleh, Ḥoms, Ğazza, Ṣaydâ, Hâmah, Idlib, ʿAkka, Tripoli, and Baʿalbek.

[4] Volney's remarks on learning amongst the Moslems of Syria ('A Damas, les gens de loi ne font aucun cas de leur propre science': ii. 296) and his absurd statement about libraries (ii. 91) must be entirely discounted, since it is clear, especially from chapters xxxiv and xxxv of his work, that he was kept in ignorance of the internal life of the Moslem population. Russell (96 sqq.) presents a much more trustworthy picture of intellectual activities at Aleppo

[5] On the *riwâḳs* see p. 157 below.

[6] Murâdî, i. 22, 50, 51, 69, 107, 176, 206, 260 (a *Şâfiʿî*, exceptionally); ii. 27, 73 (became *Ḳâḍîʿasker* of Anatolia), and *passim*.

[7] Cf. Murâdî, i. 272; iii. 84–86, 179. The second of these passages relates to Şeyḫ ʿAbdallâh b. Ḥusayn el-Suwaydî (1692–1756), who gained a great reputation

Moṣul—indeed, some of the first wits of the eighteenth century were Moṣulîs[1]—and others are mentioned in Baṣra, Şehrizôr, and elsewhere. Moreover, the great *şî'î* colleges of Nejef and Kerbelâ attracted *şî'î* students, not only from Persia, but also from India and Syria; but the strained relations between *Sunnîs* and *Şî'îs* put any educational contacts out of the question. Lastly, Medîna and Mecca were still centres of some educational activity, maintained both by resident and by visiting *Şeyḫs* from other countries.[2]

Practically all *madrasas* and teaching posts were kept up by endowments of land and buildings, constituted by generations of former donors. The primacy of el-Azhar was derived from its wealth and variety of endowments, in addition to which it received certain grants from the government,[3] an exceptional privilege shared only by Mecca and Medîna. Frequently, also, gifts were made to the *'Ulemâ* by Amîrs, Beys, and wealthy citizens,[4] and an annual present was received from the Sultan of Morocco.[5] The founder of a *madrasa* always constituted at the same time the necessary endowments for its maintenance and for that of the students as well, but not always for that of the teachers. The conditions of the latter were widely different; some enjoyed a large income from the revenues or administration of endowments,[6] but the majority probably gained little directly from teaching, and lived on the in-

by the success with which he presided at the conference held at Ḥilla in 1743, in the presence of Nâdir Şâh, to reconcile *sunnî* and *şî'î* doctrine (see L. Lockhart, *Nadir Shah*, London, 1938, 232–3, and A. E. Schmidt, 'Zur Geschichte der sunnitisch-schiitischen Beziehung' (in Russian), in *'Iḳd al-Cumân* (Barthold-Festschrift), Tashkent, 1927, 67–107). Several of the literary works of 'Abdallâh el-Suwaydî have been printed, including his travels in Nejd. The 'Irâḳî scholar Maḥmûd Şukrî el-Alûsî, in his biographical notes on 'Irâḳî scholars, entitled *el-Misk el-Aḏfar* (Bağdâd, 1930), follows up his notice of Şeyḫ 'Abdallâh (60–64) by notices of a number of his sons, grandsons, and great-grandsons (65–86) who also distinguished themselves as scholars and writers. Cf. also C. Brockelmann, *Geschichte der arabischen Litteratur*, Supplementband ii (Leiden, 1938), 501, 508, 785.

[1] Murâdî, ii. 7–8, 106, 230–1; iii. 117, &c.

[2] e.g. Murâdî, iii. 203. Scholars, before or after making the Pilgrimage, frequently spent some months or years in the Ḥijâz, engaged in learning and teaching.

[3] According to Chabrol, 68, 5,600 *ardebbs* of grain were given annually to the mosque for distribution to the students. The teachers did not receive provisions, but were given some small pensions. The financial statement given by Estève (377–8) shows a special entry of 598,296 *paras* for el-Azhar, divided as follows: 576,030 for the *'Ulemâ* (i.e. teachers), 1,777 for candles, and 20,489 for the annual distribution of rice and honey to the poor and blind during the month of Ramaḍân. The *Şeyḫs* probably shared also in the distribution of the 1,295,534 *paras* appropriated under the heading of '*Şeyḫs* and *'Ulemâ*', but paid, like other appropriations, in discredited paper (see p. 64 above).

[4] e.g. Cabartî, iv. 160, 161/viii. 361, 364.

[5] Ibid. ii. 148/iv. 490.

[6] In Syria, at least, appointment to these offices (called *tawâlî* and *tadârîs*) was made by diploma from the appropriate office in Istanbul; but there is no indication that appointments to paid teaching offices in Egypt were referred to Istanbul.

direct sources of income opened up to them by virtue of their office.[1]

There is no indication of serious decline in the standards or means of education in the Arabic provinces during the eighteenth century as compared with the seventeenth or sixteenth. It is true that there was a constant fluctuation in the fortunes of the *madrasas*, corresponding to the productivity of their endowments and the probity of their supervisors. But while some *madrasas* declined or shut their doors for these reasons,[2] the wastage was made good on the whole by new foundations. In this, as in other respects, the Mamlûk Beys maintained their ancient tradition of patronage of religion and learning,[3] although their benefactions were sometimes recalled or reduced by their successors, especially in the last quarter-century.[4]

The student, on entering the college mosque or *madrasa*, was generally attached to a foundation from which he was supplied with rations or a small stipend or both. In most *madrasas* the students appear to have been lodged in or adjacent to the building, under the control of the superintendent. At el-Azhar, however, owing to their large numbers,[5] they were distributed amongst the various endowed hostels or *riwâḳs*, which were recruited on a geographical basis for the most part, each having its own *Şeyḫ* and teaching staff, and forming a separate corporation.[6] The principal foreign *riwâḳs* were those of the Turks, the Syrians, and the Mağribîs, and one of the largest was that for blind students. Feuds between the *riwâḳs* were not unusual, and the students in general often engaged in violent demonstrations.[7]

In no college or *madrasa* was there a fixed course of studies. Since the majority of students entered at an early age and with no

[1] There is only one mention of a *Şeyḫ* demanding fees from students, namely, the mathematician Ḥuseyn al-Maḥallî (Cabartî, i. 219, foot). Cf. also Chabrol, 68–69.

[2] See Ch. XII below for a general discussion of *Waḳf* administration, and Russell, 97.

[3] See S. Lane-Poole, *The Story of Cairo* (London, 1906), 297–302, for a summary of the new buildings and restorations of this period.

[4] Thus the revenues affected by Muḥammad Bey Abû Ḏahab to his new *madrasa* (described by Lane-Poole, 301) were seized by the Mamlûks after his death in 1775, and the school rapidly fell into decay (Cabartî, i. 418–19/iii. 227–30).

[5] The total number of students at el-Azhar during the eighteenth century is almost impossible to estimate, but was probably not less than 3,000, of whom perhaps 1,000 were from outside Egypt.

[6] There were probably some twenty-five *riwâḳs* at this time; amongst them were *riwâḳs* for Kurds, Turks, 'Irâḳîs, Takrûrîs (from the Niger territories), Bornuans, Somâlîs, Indians, Javanese, Afğâns, and Ḫorâsânîs, and a number for students from the different provinces of Egypt, from Syria, and from Arabia. (See also Lane's *Modern Egyptians*, ch. ix.)

[7] Cabartî, ii. 93, 102/iv. 151, 171. The blind students were particularly unmanageable.

grounding other than that given by the *Ḳur'ân* schools, the first few years were generally spent in preliminary studies (including that of the language) under junior teachers.[1] At a more advanced stage, the student would attend the lectures of the principal *Şeyḫs* in the particular branches of theology and law which he wished to learn. The range of studies was, as in most religious seminaries,[2] relatively narrow, being confined to the Arabic linguistic sciences (including rhetoric and prosody), theology, religious jurisprudence, logic, and the elements of mathematics; in Syria and Arabia, and in the *madrasas* belonging to the religious orders, *ṣûfî* works were studied also.[3] Those who intended to become clerks and secretaries also went through a good deal of the ordinary theological range, but finished with a special course of studies under calligraphers.[4] Other students dropped out as they finished acquiring the necessary groundwork for their careers as *Imâms* of mosques, *Ḳâḍîs*, *Muftîs*, and the like. A minority went on, to become at length teachers and professors themselves after some preliminary tests by their future colleagues. There were, of course, no general examinations or diplomas. Each student who read through a book with a teacher received from him an *icâza* or licence to teach that book, but before being permitted to teach in el-Azhar some sort of authorization was apparently required from the Head *Şeyḫ* of el-Azhar, who was the head of the corporation of *'Ulemâ* in Egypt.[5]

Except in so far as custom and convention imposed some limits, there seems to have been a good deal of freedom in the colleges. The teacher, having established his claim to a place in the mosque or *madrasa*, taught from a given text either by dictation or commentary to all who cared to attend,[6] and for the benefit of genuine students the lesson was generally gone over again by a *mu'îd* or repeater. During the lesson, the auditors were at liberty to question or argue with the teacher;[7] it was, in fact, very largely by their success in such arguments that young teachers made their reputation.

Seen thus in perspective, the *madrasa* system of education had many good features.

[1] It would appear that in Syria at least some of the teachers of Arabic were not *Şeyḫs* but laymen: cf. Murâdî, iii. 86. Probably also each *riwâḳ* at el-Azhar had its own staff of teachers for the junior students.

[2] Even el-Azhar is not, and never was, a university in the western sense.

[3] Cf. the biography of 'Abd el-Ğanî el-Nâbulusî in Murâdî, iii. 30–38. Reference is made below to some of the rarer specialized branches of learning.

[4] Cf. Murâdî, i. 73, 97, &c. The calligraphers formed a highly important corporation, of which the *Şeyḫ* and probably most of the members were Turks (cf. Cabartî, i. 384; ii. 211/iii. 165; v. 130).

[5] Chabrol, 70.

[6] Instances are reported where one professor had a class of 500 listeners (Murâdî, iii. 272; iv. 50). On the other hand, one hears of 'teachers' in el-Azhar who often had not a single student (Cabartî, ii. 99/iv. 164).

[7] Chabrol, 69.

'The constitution of the Azhar University [writes one observer in the late nineteenth century] is ideally perfect. The poorest youth who comes to it will be immediately welcomed, and will be taught all that the professors know. . . . He will receive the highest education that a Moslem can receive, by Moslem methods, without being called upon to pay a single piastre.'[1]

But there was much to offset against this ideal picture. A proportion of the students may have been enrolled in el-Azhar or other *madrasas* simply for the sake of the free distribution of food enjoyed by the pupils. But while in theory a *madrasa* education was open to all seekers after knowledge, the *Şeyḫ*ly profession was, in practice, almost exclusively hereditary, and the impression left by the sources is that it was even more so in Egypt than in Syria, where the looser organization made the path easier for the outsider.

For the same reason family connexions generally counted for more than the personal merits of the student. Nor were the teachers themselves exempt from the defects of a semi-hereditary system. The historian Murâdî remarks that scions of noted families were often appointed to teaching posts without qualifications, and did no teaching at all, and that although *Paşas* would issue strict injunctions that all titular professors must teach regularly or have their work done by substitutes, things soon fell back into the old state. The scandal could even go so far that a professor had his lectures corrected for him in advance by members of his audience; he would then read them out, 'and when he gave vent to an incorrect statement on any question or committed an error, no one would put him right, but all of them being worthy and honourable men they listened in silence, because he used to make generous gifts to them and they were unwilling to disgrace him'.[2] A further widespread abuse was that of pluralism; an influential *Şeyḫ* might hold several teaching posts simultaneously and draw their revenues, but either neglect the duties altogether or have them performed by substitutes.[3] The most serious ground of criticism, however, is the limitation of both subjects and outlook. It is important to appreciate the narrowly vocational and technical character of the training given at el-Azhar and all similar institutions. Neither teacher nor pupil regarded it as anything other than the acquisition of a certain amount of 'knowledge', all such knowledge being a known or

[1] S. Lane-Poole, *Social Life in Egypt*, 84.

[2] Murâdî, ii. 282–3.

[3] Ibid. 239; iv. 121. Of the same sort were the abuses attaching to the grant of 'honorary' *icâzas*, originally made as a compliment to noted scholars (e.g. Murâdî, i. 168; iii. 31). Leading *'Ulemâ* then began to beg them for their sons (ibid. ii. 26, 202, 209, &c.), and it is recorded even that a Moroccan *Şeyḫ* asked for one on behalf of his son then aged two (ibid. iv. 91).

knowable quantity with strictly defined boundaries. To overstep these boundaries or to question them in any way was to incur the suspicion and disapprobation of one's fellow 'knowers' (to translate literally the term *'Ulemâ*), and in certain cases even the penalty of expulsion from their corporation and loss of livelihood, as well as of reputation. The inevitable result of such a system, over which no quickening breath had blown since at least the beginning of the sixteenth century,[1] was to intensify both the narrowness of the educational range itself and its narrowing effect upon the minds of the educated.[2] The biographies of *Şeyḫs* and scholars include lengthy lists of books and pamphlets which show no decline in quantity from the literary output of earlier centuries, but even within the fields of study still most cultivated—those of law and theology—it is doubtful if more than a fraction preserved a trace of the ancient quality.[3] If the dead-point of a society is reached when the educational forces are no longer effective to influence or to direct its development, it must be admitted that the dead-point was long since passed in Islamic society. Education had ceased to set before itself even the hope of moulding society in the direction of its ideals, and had sunk to the level of merely holding society together by the inculcation of tradition.

Yet there remains something to be set upon the other side. Making all allowances for the defects of the hereditary system and the rule of thumb of vocational training, there is still to be seen, amongst a substantial proportion of the learned, a genuine zeal and

[1] The reformist movement of Muḥammad b. 'Abd el-Wahhâb in Central Arabia, though initiated as far back as 1744, attracted little notice outside. The first mention of the Wahhâbîs by Cabartî is under date May 1802 (iii. 220/vii. 107), in terms which represent it as a very recent development but express no opinion either for or against it. This was not the first movement of the kind in the eighteenth century. Cabartî relates (i. 48–49/i. 116–19) that in 1123/1711 a Turkish preacher in Cairo declaimed against the worship of saints and urged that the cupolas over saints' tombs should be destroyed. His audience, mostly Turks, took up arms and set about tearing down the flags over the tombs of saints. The *'Ulemâ* of el-Azhar, however, issued a *fatwâ* declaring that saints are able to work miracles after their death, and called upon the *Paşa* to punish the preacher. The latter was exiled, and those implicated in the disorders were punished. Popular opinion in Egypt evidently sided with the *Şeyḫs* against the preacher, although the poet Ḥasan el-Ḥijâzî wrote a poem satirizing the worship of hallucinated men as saints and the acceptance of this belief by the *'Ulemâ* (Cabartî, i. 78–79/i. 187).

[2] The principal question which was debated in theological circles during the seventeenth and eighteenth centuries was the lawfulness of smoking: cf. Murâdî, i. 254; Cabartî, i. 415/iii. 221. One *Paşa* of Egypt even prohibited smoking in public: ibid. i. 151/ii. 24.

[3] The literature of this period is considered more fully below, pp. 163–4. Actually, of the thousands of works mentioned in the sources, the number still preserved appears to be very small—an indication that they were little read, on the whole, and probably in many cases never went beyond the author's manuscript. For this reason also, it must be admitted that the judgement passed in the text is based on inference rather than on detailed personal investigation.

devotion to learning. The typical Moslem *'âlim* remains a student to the end of his days, and whether he travels to Cairo, Mecca, or Istanbul, or remains at home, he always seeks out the most noted scholars and attends their lectures. The travelling *Şeyḫ* receives a warm welcome from his brethren, and is sure of a lodging either in their houses or in a *madrasa*.[1] Thus continuity of contact is ensured, and a strong sense of solidarity maintained amongst the *'Ulemâ*, which makes for keeping up the professional standard. While some of their intellectual activities may have been misdirected and their initiative stifled by the cramped sphere in which they moved, the historian must recognize that it was due to them, and to the work of the religious brotherhoods, that the civilization of Islâm did not founder in the cataclysms of the later medieval centuries. Seen in this light, even their narrowness and unyielding grip of tradition becomes understandable and justified, since their task was indeed to hold society together in a period of confusion and economic decline, when it could not afford to take the risk of intellectual adventure.

While the social function of education must, therefore, be given full recognition, its intellectual quality must finally be judged by the character of its products. In this connexion, however, it would be unjustifiable to criticize the 'medievalism' of the Islamic world in itself; in its isolation from the rest of the civilized world, and lacking any but the most superficial contact with Western Europe (and that only in Istanbul), it inevitably retained all those medieval characteristics which were then being overcome but slowly even in the West. Amongst these was the belief in astrology and divination, of which numerous examples could be given,[2] and the closely allied occult literature, divided into some half-dozen 'sciences'. The popular and thaumaturgical practices of Ṣûfism powerfully aided the spread of occultism, with such success as practically to silence all criticism and opposition. Many *Şeyḫs* were indeed highly esteemed for their writings on these subjects, and for their skill in amulets and charms, not only by the vulgar but also by the learned.[3]

The real gravamen of the criticism to be brought against Islamic intellectual culture in the eighteenth century is that it had fallen so far below even its own medieval standards, and appeared to be quite unconscious of the decline. Perhaps the most striking

[1] Cf. Murâdî, iv. 61.

[2] e.g. Murâdî, i. 9; iii. 154. At the same time there was still a certain amount of scientific astronomical compilation; see Brockelmann, *Ges. d. arab. Litt.* ii. 357–60.

[3] e.g. Cabartî, i. 159–60, 161/ii. 39–42, 43; Murâdî, i. 45; iii. 59 (a *Ḥanbalî Şeyḫ*), 105, &c., and see Lane, *Modern Egyptians*, ch. xi. On talismans for agriculture see 'Abd el-Ğanî el-Nâbulusî, *'Ilm el-filâḥa*, 220 sqq.

example is given by the theory and practice of medicine. At the beginning of the seventeenth century, something still remained of the medieval science of Islâm,[1] although it was already bound up with astrology and magic, and medical treatises and compendiums continued to be written in both Egypt and Syria.[2] Murâdî cites the eulogy of a physician astronomer at Moṣul by one of his fellow citizens:[3]

'champion in the company of letters, victor in the contest between the worthiest of Arab and non-Arab; Hippocrates of the Wisdom was his slave-boy, and Plato of the Wisdom but one of his servants; he expunged the memory of Ptolemy by his wonderful works, and ground the Sinai of Ibn Sînâ to fragments when he displayed the flash of his lightnings; el-Fârâbî was but a drop from this well, and el-Abharî but a trickle from this sea; he removed the putrefaction of the humours of ignorance by the electuaries of his science, and rectified the constitution of virtue and breeding by the humours of his understanding.'

At the same time Volney was writing of medicine in Egypt and Syria: 'À peine trouve-t-on un homme qui sache saigner avec la *flamme*; quand il a ordonné le cautère, appliqué le feu, ou prescrit une recette banale, sa science est épuisée: aussi les valets des Européens sont-ils consultés comme des Esculapes.'[4]

The truth, as usual, seems to lie between the two extremes, if perhaps a little nearer to Volney than to the master of Hippocrates. The medical craft was, like other crafts, largely hereditary, which gave some guarantee against the complete disappearance of the old science. On the other hand, it is not uncommon to find a *Ḳâḍî* or *'Âlim* as the head of the corporation of physicians,[5] and other men of religion practising medicine.[6] But the true bearing of these facts is rendered difficult to discover by the existence, alongside the scientific study of medicine derived from the Greeks, of what is called 'Prophetic Medicine',[7] namely, the study of the medical information contained in the Traditions of the Prophet, and hence included in the religious sciences. The first firm ground is supplied here, as elsewhere, by the *Description de l'Égypte*, to which Rouyer contributed a careful account of the Egyptian medical science of

[1] See the article on al-Anṭâkî (Dâ'ud b. 'Omar) (d. 1599) in *Encyc. of Islâm*.

[2] The most interesting of these would probably be a medical work which was translated from Turkish into Arabic by a physician of Gaza (d. 1718): Murâdî, iv. 59.

[3] The subject was a certain Muḥammad el-'Abdalî, part of whose studies were made in Egypt; he died in 1753: Murâdî, iv. 125.

[4] Volney, ii. 291–2. The English M.D., Alex. Russell, is, though critical, somewhat less contemptuous: *Natural Hist. of Aleppo*, 97–99.

[5] e.g. Murâdî, ii. 230; iv. 37, and cf. Evliya Efendî, tr. Hammer, ii. 116. At Damascus, however, the chief of the physicians was a layman: Murâdî, iv. 264–5.

[6] Murâdî, iv. 34–35; Russell, 96–98; and cf. p. 125 above.

[7] *El-ṭibb el-nabawî*.

the day.[1] From his explicit statements, it is evident that pharmaceutical science was in fact much decayed;[2] and the same conclusion emerges from all the information available on the methods of the surgeon-barbers (who formed a separate corporation) and the conditions of the public hospital or *Mâristân*,[3] which was at once hospital and lunatic asylum. Yet a doubt remains whether in Syria, owing to its closer relations with Istanbul, the theory and practice of medicine may not have been somewhat higher than they were in Egypt, though the difference, if any, cannot have been very marked. Already by the end of the eighteenth century, however, European physicians and pharmacies were already to be found in Cairo and Damascus, and in the former place, at least, were resorted to by a certain number of Moslems and Copts.[4] Moreover, at least two European works of medicine had been translated into Turkish and Arabic.[5]

The literary production of the eighteenth century shows as a whole the same characteristic degeneration, although here too the barrenness of the period has been greatly exaggerated. This decline is sometimes accounted for by an excessive concentration upon scholastic and religious works, which is, however, no more than part of the truth. The scholastic output was indeed enormous, and of small originality. But little else could be expected, for the cultivation of profane literature depended largely upon the encouragement of patrons, and the subjection of the Arabic provinces to Ottoman control deprived them of this support except to a limited extent.[6] The main causes of the literary decline are rather to be looked for in the conditions of its existence, and more especially in the absence of fruitful contact with the outside world. Lacking any healthy stimulus or criticism from without, it was suffering from a kind of introversion and living on its own past. Its links even with the contemporary literature in Turkish and Persian were of the slightest, except possibly in Aleppo. A second cause of weakness was the narrowness of the literary circle, with the inevitable

[1] *Notice sur les médicamens usuels des Égyptiens*: i. 1217–32. See also Clot-Bey, *Aperçu*, ii. 383–4.

[2] He notes also that the principal demand was for fattening and aphrodisiac drugs (222).

[3] See Bowring's *Report*, 141 (from Clot-Bey).

[4] Rouyer, 222–3: there were three pharmacies in Cairo, one run by Greeks and two belonging to Venetians; their clients were mostly Europeans and Syrian Christians. The French doctor (Chaboceau) at Damascus was the only European resident in that city (1794): Olivier, ii. 255.

[5] See C. E. Daniëls, 'La Version orientale, Arabe et Turque, des deux premiers livres de Herman Boerhaave', in *Janus* (Leiden, 1912), 295–312.

[6] For an instance of patronage of scholarship among the Mamlûk Beys see Part I, p. 226, n. 4; and on Egyptian education and literature in general in the eighteenth century, J. Heyworth-Dunne, *Introduction to the History of Education in Modern Egypt*, 1–87.

consequence of artificial standards, which put a premium upon style and discouraged invention and originality.

There is, however, a distinction to be drawn between literary production in Egypt and that in Syria. Except for some few poets, the literature of Egypt was exclusively the work of *Şeyẖs*, whereas in Syria, and to some extent also in 'Irâķ, the educated lay classes of clerks and secretaries took a prominent share in both poetry and *belles-lettres*, and even members of the military families made a literary reputation for themselves.[1] The Syrians, also, as has already been noted, were more active travellers than the Egyptians, and several amongst them wrote narratives of their travels. Moreover, while Egypt was to a very large extent self-contained and self-centred, Syria was in close touch with the Turkish and other Arabic lands. This preserved a certain openness of view among Syrian writers,[2] and even within the framework of religious learning allowed an exceptional scholar and poet, such as the *Ṣûfî* Şeyẖ 'Abd el-Ğanî el-Nâbulusî (d. 1731), to display a certain measure of creative originality.[3] The biographical tradition in particular, which had been established in Damascus since the thirteenth century, and is represented by Murâdî and his predecessor Muḥibbî, was a living and vital branch of letters, inspired by a dignified conception of the historic mission and continuity of Islâm.[4] To deny all significance or value, therefore, to the Arabic literature of the eighteenth century, is unjustifiable. One may even go further and say that it confirms the general impression of a society which had exhausted its own resources, and was waiting for some fresh stimulus to restore it to productive activity.

[1] e.g. Murâdî, i. 97–106, 183–4; iv. 166.

[2] It is very evident, for example, on a comparison of the works of Murâdî and Cabartî, although it must be remembered that the latter was writing primarily a history of Egypt.

[3] See *Encyc. of Islam*, new edition, s.v., and p. 198 below.

[4] Cabartî himself makes no secret of the fact that it was at the urgent entreaty of Murâdî, backed up by the Turkish *'Ulemâ*, that he undertook the composition of his history.

CHAPTER XII

RELIGIOUS ENDOWMENTS (*AWKÂF*)

IN spite of the very close relations maintained between church and state in the Islamic, and more especially the Ottoman, system, it had never been held to be any part of the duty of the state to provide for the upkeep of religious edifices and services. The expense entailed would obviously have been prohibitive. Their upkeep therefore fell primarily upon the shoulders of those to whom they ministered. From relatively early times, it is true, Caliphs and Sultans had made a practice of devoting some part of the revenues of the privy purse to religious objects. But the bulk of the revenues of the religious institutions were derived from private charity, principally in the form of permanent endowments of land and other immovable property by a deed of 'restraint' (*wakf*—*vakîf* in Turkish—or *habs*). The property so restrained (*mawkûf*, *mahbûs*) was thereby withdrawn from all further transfer of ownership, and its usufruct devoted to a specific object designated by the donor. Such endowments (*awkâf*—*evkâf* in Turkish) had been created by innumerable governors and private persons from the earliest centuries of Islâm for the benefit of mosques, *madrasas*, convents, and charities of all kinds, and were by theory valid in perpetuity.

In the homelands of the Ottoman Empire the provinces that had been ruled by Moslem potentates before their acquisition by the Sultans abounded in pre-Ottoman foundations, whose terms were respected by the new rulers;[1] and in the provinces first incorporated by them in the Domain of Islâm religious and charitable institutions and purposes were everywhere, except in the purely tributary dependencies, provided for in the same way. The system, as far as charity was concerned, consorted indeed with practices current among some of the Turkish peoples before their conversion to Islam;[2] and under the Ottoman régime, as under that of earlier Islamic rulers, *Dimmîs*, as well as Moslems, were entitled to form *awkâf* and did so, the only restriction on their entitlement being that the object of their foundations should not be anything, such as the building, upkeep, or service of churches or monasteries, incompatible with those of Islâm.[3]

[1] See, e.g., A. Süheyl Ünver, 'Büyük Selçuklu Imparatorluğun zamanînda vakîf hastanelerin bir kîsmîna dair', in *Vakîflar Dergisi*, i. 21–22.

[2] Halim Baki Kunter, 'Türk Vakîflarî ve Vakfiyeleri', in *Vakîflar Dergisi*, i. 104, 117–18.

[3] Heffening, art. 'Wakf' in the *Encyc. of Islam*. See Kunter, 120–1, for two *wakfs* founded by *Dimmî* women, one in aid of a Mevlevî *tekke*. Cf. D'Ohsson, ii. 552, and Belin, 'Propriété foncière', in *J.A.*, Série V, xviii. 514–15.

One kind of property with the revenues of which *awḳâf* were endowed was agricultural land. But perhaps because the term 'state land' (*arḍî memleket*) was unknown to the *Şerîʿa*, and the terms *ʿuşr* and *ḫarâc* were in Ottoman usage applied to the dues collected from peasants inhabiting such land (whereas in their original use the land whose inhabitants had paid them was private property), already by the sixteenth century there seems, as regards agricultural land, to have been considerable doubt among the Sultans' subjects over what might, and what might not, be lawfully assigned to *awḳâf*, and a considerable infringement of the principles then reiterated by the *Muftîs* whose rulings on the subject were sought.[1] One principle was that only private property might be so assigned; and since in general agricultural land was declared *not* to be private property but to be state land, it followed that the only lands already lawfully assigned to *awḳâf* were those which the reigning Sultan and his predecessors had either so assigned themselves or else presented as private property to favoured recipients, who had then used them for this purpose.[2] It also followed that agricultural land could be lawfully assigned to *awḳâf* in future only by one or other of these processes. The process by which land might be assigned to a *waḳf* after first being converted into private property by the mere will and motion of a Sultan is illustrated by the foundation of Ḫâdim Ibrâhîm Paşa, a brother-in-law of Süleymân the Magnificent. Süleymân first presented him with seven villages in Rumelia: and the *Paşa* then devoted their revenues to a number of foundations in Istanbul, among them two mosques, a *medrese*, and three *mektebs*.[3] But it seems probable that most of the existing *waḳf* lands had been assigned by Sultans direct; and it is evident that they were already very extensive.[4] *Reʿâyâ* who inhabited *waḳf* land were in much the same position as those who inhabited fiefs. *Waḳf* lands were regarded, however, as being 'let' to them: the payment called *ṭapu* in the case of fiefs was in their case called 'advance rent',[5] and their recurrent payment of dues 'periodical rent'.[6] Their security of tenure was similar, but they were if anything more strictly bound to the soil.[7]

[1] See the *Ḳânûn-nâme* of Süleymân (with later additions) in *M.T.M.* i. 51 sq.

[2] Cf. Seyyid Muṣṭafâ, i. 16.

[3] Abdülkadir Erdoğan, 'Hadim Ibrâhim Paşa Camii', in *Vakiflar Dergisi*, i. 31 sq.

[4] *M.T.M.* i. 53—'moreover the lands placed in *waḳf* by former Sultans are many'.

[5] *icâre(i) muʿaccele.*

[6] *icâre(i) muʾeccele.* See *M.T.M.* i. 54, 61, 77, 95. Sometimes the form *ücret* is used for 'rent' instead of *icâre*, and sometimes *ṭapu* is actually used in relation to *waḳf* land.

[7] Ibid. 305.

In later times it appears that a good deal of what had originally been state land was irregularly converted into private property and that a high proportion of this was assigned by its owners to *awḳâf* for prudential motives that we shall explain.[1] What was even stranger was the assignment to *awḳâf* by private persons of the yield of certain taxes and dues, the right to 'farm' which they had contracted for.[2] In this, it is true, they were only following imperial example, since Meḥmed the Conqueror had assigned the yield of a customs due, or rather toll, in Istanbul to one of his foundations.[3] But such assignments by private persons were obviously irregular and were indeed regarded as so being. Most at least of the smaller, private, foundations at all periods, on the other hand, seem to have depended on revenues drawn from urban, or semi-urban, property that had originally been legally *mulk*, such as houses, rooms, shops, baths, coffee-houses, flour-mills, vineyards, and plantations of fruit-trees. These are the types that figure most frequently in the *waḳfîyas* or deeds of foundation.[4]

The objects for which *awḳâf* were founded are almost innumerable. Apart from specifically religious institutions such as mosques and *tekkes*, and educational institutions such as *medreses*, *mektebs*, and libraries, virtually all 'public works' such as roads, pavements, bridges, aqueducts, water-conduits, and lighthouses were provided by this private means, as were also such more evidently charitable institutions as hospitals, hostels, houses for widows, kitchens, and laundries. Nor was this all. Many *awḳâf* were founded for the supply of money to the needy: dowries for orphan girls, the payment of their debts for imprisoned debtors, the payment of fees for the release of penniless prisoners, aid for the inhabitants of particular villages and quarters of towns in the payment of *'urfî* taxes.[5] Others were founded for the supply of assistance in kind: clothes for aged villagers, food and clothing for school-children, rice for birds, food and water for animals. Some *awḳâf* again had as their object the provision of excursions for children in spring-time and burial of the indigent, while still others were founded in aid of the armed forces: the equipment of soldiers,

[1] See the *Risâle* of Ḳoçu Bey (ed. Istanbul, 1303), 82. He asks, writing in the second quarter of the seventeenth century, how it could be right that favourites of the Sultans had been allowed first to appropriate state lands and then to place some of them in *waḳf*. He recommends that villages placed in *waḳf* within the previous 200 years should be regranted to *Sipâhîs*, except such as had been assigned to the upkeep of mosques, *medreses*, &c. State land had been improperly assigned to *awḳâf* as early as the reign of Süleymân: see Belin, 'Histoire économique', *J.A.*, 1864, iv. 281.

[2] Seyyid Muṣṭafâ, iv. 105.

[3] Kunter, 115. Cf. Belin, 'Histoire économique', 348, for the assignment in this way under Süleymân of the Gypsy *'cizye'* (for which see above, p. 16).

[4] *vaḳfiye* in Turkish. See Kunter, *passim*.

[5] For *'urfî* taxation see above, p. 2.

the financing of the construction and maintenance of fortresses and other fortifications and of ships for the Ottoman fleet.[1]

All such types of foundation were appropriately called *awḳâf ḫayrîya*,[2] which we may translate perhaps as 'foundations for public benefit', to distinguish them from another type called *awḳâf ahlîya* or *awḳâf ḏurrîya*—'family foundations'.[3] Family foundations had been permitted in Islâm from early times.[4] The founder would allocate property in the same way as for other *awḳâf*; but the revenues accruing from it would provide solely for the livelihood of his descendants as long as any remained. They formed, indeed, family trusts from which succeeding generations might benefit, in principle unobjectionable though in practice widely abused, as we shall explain. Such pure family trusts, however, were perhaps less common than foundations in the *waḳfîyas* of which the founders allowed for the enjoyment by their descendants only of any revenue that might remain yearly after the cost had been met of whatever 'beneficial' purpose the foundation was designed to further. *Awḳâf* might also serve another purpose that was personal rather than charitable, by providing for the recital of Scripture on behalf of the founder (during his lifetime) and for the souls of his (or her) defunct relatives. Thus an extant *waḳfîya* of 1588, constituting a foundation made by a certain Zeyni Ḫâṭûn of Istanbul, provides with nice discrimination for the daily recitation of three sections (*cuz'*) of the *Ḳur'ân* for herself, of five sections for the soul of her son, of one section for the soul of her mother, and of two sections for the soul of her daughter, each reciter to be paid 1½ *aḳçes* a day. In addition this *waḳf* provides 1 *aḳçe* a day apiece for three 'good religious men' to recite the chapter of the *Ḳur'ân* called *Iḫlâṣ* a hundred times a day, but is otherwise of the family type, furnishing an income for the foundress's descendants until they die out.[5]

The only persons among the Sultans' subjects who were tempted, and indeed able, to abuse the institution of the family *waḳf*, were their slaves, the *Ḳapî Ḳullarî*. Other people could not abuse it because they were entitled to assign any property they possessed to endowments. But the *Ḳapî Ḳullarî* were in an equivocal position as regards the ownership of property since, according to the *Şerî'a*, slaves were incapable of it. There had always been some doubt about their status; and after the abandonment of the *devşirme*,

[1] See in particular the lists of the objects of *awḳâf* in Kunter, 110–11. Cf. D'Ohsson, ii. 542, and Belin, 'La Propriété foncière', 509 sq.

[2] *evḳâfi ḫayrîye* in Turkish, from the Arabic *ḫayr* (good), meaning 'beneficial'.

[3] *evḳâfi ehlîye* and *evḳâfi ḏürrîye* in Turkish, from the Arabic *ahl* (meaning 'family', 'household') and *ḏurrîya* (meaning 'children', 'descendants').

[4] *Encycl. of Islam*, s.v. 'Waḳf.' Foundations of this kind, however, are legally valid only if the ultimate object is of a charitable nature.

[5] Kunter, 120–1. Cf. D'Ohsson, ii. 542.

when few, if any, of them were other than free men, it was evident that they had every right to own property, and so to use it for endowments, except in so far as by entering the Sultan's service they had become in some sense his slaves. Those among them who attained to high office, however, were exceptionally well placed to acquire property, and few among them neglected the opportunity of doing so. Hence in later times, when the Treasury was almost always in desperate need of revenue, the government was tempted, and often succumbed to the temptation, to confiscate such an official's property either when he was dismissed or when he died. There was a case for this procedure. It was clear that some of the possessions of such officials had been acquired by them in virtue of their appointments. The government was not altogether unjustified, therefore, in regarding such property as really appertaining to the state and the officials' right to use it as ending with their employment. We have already referred to the seizure of such property when considering the finances.[1] Here we need do no more than note the uncertainty in which the possibility of confiscation left rich officials: they could never be sure how much of what they possessed would be regarded as rightfully theirs. Nothing was more natural, therefore, than that they should assign some of their property to a foundation, after which the government would be powerless to seize at least this without infringing the Sacred Law; and the 'family' *waḳf* system enabled them to ensure that not only they themselves, but also their descendants, would remain in enjoyment of such revenues as the property so assigned might yield. This device was much resorted to; so much that it came to be commonly thought that the whole object of 'family', if not other, *awḳâf* was to prevent the state from seizing the possessions of the well-to-do,[2] whereas in fact it was to provide the founder and his descendants with an income, while preventing the latter from dissipating the 'capital' transmitted to them, and at the same time circumventing the rules of the *Şerî'a* for the distribution of inheritances. In later times, indeed, the government declined to recognize *awḳâf* founded by officials without first examining each case to determine whether any of the property assigned could be claimed as legally its own.[3] By this means a kind of equilibrium was established between the claims of the government, with their tendency to be exorbitant, and the attempts of officials or their heirs to retain for themselves more private property than they were rightfully entitled to.

[1] Above, p. 28.
[2] Kunter, 105; Cf. Seyyid Muṣṭafâ, ii. 103 sq., who devotes much space to demonstrating the error of this opinion.
[3] D'Ohsson, ii. 530.

In the *waḳfîyas*, or deeds, of both types of foundation, 'beneficial' and 'family', the properties the revenues from which were to maintain them and all the persons appointed to administer and serve them, together with their emoluments, were minutely particularized. All *awḳâf* had two persons designated to assure their execution in perpetuity: an administrator, called *mutawallî*, whose appointment was called *tawliya*,[1] and a supervisor, called *nâẓir*. But other persons were frequently designated too. Thus the *waḳfîya* of Ḫâdim Ibrâhîm Paşa, to which we have already alluded, provides in connexion with one of his mosques for a *Ḫaṭîb*, an *Imâm*, four *Mü'eẕẕins*, a *Mu'arrif*,[2] two *Ḥâfiẓes*, two *Ḳayyims*, and others, as well as for a *Müderris* at his *medrese*, and for one *Mu'allim* or *Ḫoca* and one assistant teacher at each of his three schools, all to receive appropriate salaries.[3] For *awḳâf* supported by extensive properties it was also sometimes necessary for the founder to provide for the employment of a secretary and a collector and, when buildings were involved, for an architect, a 'repairer',[4] and even for a functionary to ensure that the walls did not remain defaced with *graffiti*.[5]

The persons appointed as *Nâẓirs* were usually important government servants or religious dignitaries, since it was a necessary feature of the arrangement that in contrast to the *Mutawallîs*, who were more often than not descendants of the founder, the *Nâẓirs* should be in a position to control the actions of the *Mutawallîs* and, if the family died out, to choose suitable persons as their successors. If, therefore, the *Nâẓirs* had not generally acted as such *ex officio*, the founder would have had either to designate the particular persons who should replace them as time went on (an impossible task), or leave it to each *Nâẓir* in turn to appoint his successor. Sultans Meḥmed II, Selîm I, and Süleymân the Magnificent appointed the Grand *Vezîr* to be *Nâẓir* of the *awḳâf* of their mosques; whereas Bâyezîd II and Aḥmed I appointed the *Şeyhü 'l-Islâm*.[6] In later times, however, the supervision of nearly all mosque foundations, imperial and private, was confided, strangely enough, to the *Ḳizlar Ağasis*, no doubt because of the intimate association of those eunuchs with the Sultans themselves.[7] Despite the fact that neither *Nâẓirs* nor *Mutawallîs* were supposed to draw any

[1] Pronounced *mutevellî* and *tevliyet* in Turkish.

[2] The duty (in mosques) of *Mu'arrifs* was to recite prayers for the Prophet, his Companions, the founder, and all Moslems. See M. F. Köprülü, 'Vakf'a ait tarihî istilahlar meselesi', in *Vakiflar Dergisi*, i. 136.

[3] Erdoğan, 32.

[4] *Meremmetçi* (from Arabic *maramma*, 'repair').

[5] *Mâḥî'n-nuḳûş*, 'obliterator of drawings': Kunter, 115–16.

[6] Seyyid Muṣṭafâ, iv. 99, and D'Ohsson, as below.

[7] In succession to the *Ḳapî Ağasis*, the Chief White Eunuchs, whom they had superseded from the end of the sixteenth century; cf. Part I, p. 76.

emoluments from *waḳf* funds except small fees known as 'boot-price',[1] the supervision of these foundations was extremely profitable to the *Ḳizlar Ağasis*, though it involved them in much work. By the eighteenth century they were responsible for the *awḳâf* of as many as 500 mosques alone; and to consider the affairs of these institutions and others used to preside over weekly meetings of the *Mutawallîs* concerned at what was called the *Ḥarameyn Dîvânî*, since the *Ḳizlar Ağasis* were then also *Nâẓirs* of all the *awḳâf* of the Holy Cities. To assist them they had as inspectors an *'Âlim* entitled *Ḥarameyn Müfettişi*[2] and two deputies, one resident at Bursa and one at Adrianople. But under Muṣṭafâ III, the Sultan reigning at the terminal date of our survey, the Grand *Vezîr* Râğib Paşa virtually deprived the *Ḳizlar Ağasis* of their authority in this sphere by placing responsibility for the collection of these *waḳf* revenues, which had long been effected by tax-farm, in the hands of the *Defterdârs*, at the same time dismissing many unsuitable persons who had been appointed as *Mutawallîs*. The result was a swift increase in the revenues; and as long as this new arrangement lasted—which was no more than a few years—the *Ḳizlar Ağasis* and their deprived colleagues were indemnified out of the surplus thus achieved for the loss of the perquisites that had previously come their way.[3]

The founder of a *waḳf*, who was called the *wâḳif*, was free to appoint anyone he wished as *Mutawallî*.[4] The *Mutawallîs* of imperial foundations, as well as their *Nâẓirs*, were usually government servants, appointed, however, not *ex officio* but personally; and one of the reasons for the frequent maladministration of these *awḳâf*, particularly in the seventeenth century, was the granting of their *tawliyas* to such unsuitable persons as *Sipâhîs* of the standing army.[5] As regards ordinary *awḳâf*, it was quite in order, as we have already indicated, and very usual, for a *Wâḳif* to appoint himself *Mutawallî*,[6] providing for the *tawliya* to pass on his death to his descendants;[7] and if in such a case the family died out, since it fell to the *Nâẓir* to choose a *Mutawallî*, further opportunities occurred for 'slaves of the sultanate',[8] whether suitable or not, to assume *tawliyas*. On the other hand, the *Wâḳif* might from the first leave

[1] *Çizme paha*, *çizme* meaning a 'top-boot' or 'riding-boot'.

[2] Inspector of the Two Sanctuaries.

[3] D'Ohsson, ii. 526, 535–6; Belin, 'Histoire économique', in *J.A.*, 1864, iv. 305.

[4] D'Ohsson, ii. 524.

[5] Belin, 304, 306–7.

[6] D'Ohsson, ii. 529. Ḫâdim Ibrâhîm Paşa, for instance, appointed himself: see Erdoğan.

[7] D'Ohsson, ii. 543. Cf. Seyyid Muṣṭafâ, iv. 99.

[8] *Bendegânî Selṭane*, the phrase used by 'Abdu'r-Raḥmân Şeref, *Ta'rîḫi Devleti 'Osmânîye*, ii. 510; i.e. *Ḳapi Ḳullari*.

it to the *Nâzir* to appoint a *Mutawallî*; and it was no obstacle to the appointment that the *Mutawallî* should have another occupation: mosque ministers were in fact often chosen.[1] The *Mutawallî* was in all cases obliged to render a yearly account of his stewardship to the *Nâzir*.

At the time of the Ottoman conquest of Syria and Egypt, the number and extent of *awkâf*, both of lands and of other property, was very considerable. In all old-established Moslem countries the problem set by the accumulation of *awkâf* was a serious one, and in Egypt and Syria the tables had not been razed (as in al-ʿIrâk and the East) by Türkmen and Mongol invasions. Various methods (all, no doubt, strictly illegal) were adopted from time to time to restore a substantial proportion of the tied lands to free circulation, and the Circassian Mamlûk Sultans had already suppressed many *wakfs*. The Ottoman Sultans appear to have taken immediate steps to regulate the situation. The former royal (*sulṭânî*) *wakfs* affected to the upkeep of the Holy Cities were maintained and placed, together with their own new (and extensive) imperial *wakfs*, under the direction of the finance departments.[2] The 'private' (i.e. ordinary charitable) *wakfs* of former Sultans, Beys, and other persons were investigated by an administrator-general sent from Istanbul; those for which valid deeds could be produced were confirmed, but in all cases subjected to *mîrî*, and an attempt was made to bring derelict *wakf* properties back into cultivation.[3] In the following centuries fresh *wakfs* were frequently constituted by *multazims*, who affected part of their estates (but only after obtaining the consent of the *Paşa* and with the restrictions which we shall mention presently) to the upkeep of specific mosques or to other religious purposes. These *wakfs* also were assessed for *mîrî*, which was paid by the heirs or successors of the *multazims* from whose estates they had been constituted, but they were exempt from all other taxes.[4] Where an entire village was constituted in *wakf*, the mosque or other beneficiary institution

[1] D'Ohsson, ii. 527. It is noteworthy that women also were eligible for this office.

[2] i.e. of the *rûznâmecî*: Digeon, 267. Similarly the extensive *wakfs* constituted in 1500 by ʿAlâ el-Dawla of the Du'l-Kadr dynasty in northern Syria were confirmed (Ġazzî, ii. 528–33).

[3] *Canoun-namé*, ap. Digeon, ii. 263–4, 267, 269; Barkan, 383–4. The old registers and archives in Egypt were burned shortly after the Ottoman conquest, probably in 1525 or 1526 (see the discussion by Deny in *Sommaire des Archives*, 22), and a large number of the *wakfs* still in existence were suppressed by a new decree in 1550 (de Sacy, i. 131–4). As already noted above (Ch. VII, p 42) an appreciable sum, amounting to over 13 million *paras* (equivalent in the seventeenth century to about £20,000 gold), was affected from the revenues of Egypt to the upkeep of mosques, convents, and hospitals, possibly to compensate for loss of revenue from suppressed *wakfs*.

[4] Cabartî, iv. 209/ix. 93.

held the *iltizâm* of the village in perpetuity, and became liable for payment of the assessed *mîrî*.[1]

The Ottomans introduced two important innovations relating to *awkâf*. One was the consequence of the new land system, which vested the ownership of the land in the Sultan alone, and thus prevented any alienation of land except with the consent of the Sultan or his representative. In Egypt, a parcel of land affected to a religious endowment was technically known as *rizka* (plural *rizâk*), and a *multazim*, though rarely permitted to alienate the land itself as an endowment, was able (with the *Paşa*'s consent) to create '*rizâk* in cash', i.e. annual rents or charges in perpetuity from the revenues of a given estate, and payable to the beneficiary of the *wakf* by all subsequent *multazims* of that estate.[2] Nevertheless, in spite of the restrictions imposed on the constitution of new landed *awkâf*, their number steadily increased. In Syria two very extensive *wakfs* are particularly noteworthy: that of Muḥammad, son of the famous Sinân Paşa, created in 1574 and known as the '*wakf* of Ibrâhîm Ḫân',[3] and that constituted by Aḥmad Paşa Küçük in favour of Damascus, Jerusalem, and the Holy Cities, out of the estates of the Druse chief Faḫr el-Dîn ibn Maʿn, which were granted to him by Sultan Murâd IV on the capture and death of Faḫr el-Dîn in 1635.[4]

The second innovation was an attempt to centralize the supervision of *awkâf*. Detailed regulations are laid down in the Egyptian *kânûn*: the accounts of all *wakfs* are to be examined and audited annually in the presence of the *Paşa*, and a copy of the receipts and expenditure of each to be sent to Istanbul; when there is a vacancy in the intendance of a *wakf*, the *Kâdî* is to make a formal written recommendation to the *Paşa* in favour of some 'poor person of upright character and good knowledge', sealed also by the Treasurer (after he has verified the existence of the vacancy), and the candidate is to be duly installed pending the arrival of the formal 'deed' (*berât*, Arabic *barâ'a*) from the appropriate office in Istanbul.[5] In each of the Syrian provinces there was a central 'department of *awkâf*', which dealt similarly with the appointment of intendants, and also, apparently, with the distribution of the revenues from landed endowments to the beneficiaries.[6]

[1] Lancret, 239; Estève, 304. Mosque lands were generally administered like *waṣîya* lands, but were never cultivated by *corvée* (Lancret, 243). Their *mîrî* was frequently paid in kind, especially in Upper Egypt.

[2] Estève, 304. In 1607 the administration of these *rizâk* was centralized at Cairo and the amount of them added to the sums due from the district; at that time they amounted to about a hundred purses: de Sacy, i. 142–3.

[3] Abstract in Ğazzî, ii. 516–28.

[4] See Murâdî, ii. 60. For Faḫr el-Dîn see Part I, p. 222, n. 1.

[5] Digeon, 265–6; Barkan, 383. Before being installed the new intendant was required to pay the fee for 'dispatch of the *berât*', but the actual dispatch was delayed until some forty or fifty had been collected for transmission together.

[6] Ğazzî, ii. 513; Murâdî, iv. 185.

Since all *awḳâf*, even when constituted by non-Moslems, were registered in the *şer'î* courts, it would be possible by examination of the extant archives of the various provincial *maḥkamas* to obtain detailed and exact figures of the number, destinations, and character of *waḳf* foundations created during the Ottoman period. In the absence of a complete survey, the following figures relating to the province of Aleppo may be taken as representative of the general situation.[1] Between 1718 and 1800 some 485 new *waḳfs* were registered; of these only 32 were composed exclusively of lands, and a further 30 included both lands and other immovable property; the remainder were buildings (shops, workshops, mills, baths, &c.). The precise area of land affected is not quoted. Of the total number 237 were family *waḳfs*, either in whole or in part. The beneficiaries of the charitable *waḳfs* were mosques, *madrasas*, convents, *dervîş tekkes*, fountains, water-channels, *ḫâns*, the sanctuaries of Mecca, Medîna, and Jerusalem,[2] the holders of specific religious offices, the poor generally, and miscellaneous charities. While each *waḳf* might be, and in general was, relatively small, the total amount of property conveyed as endowments was thus very considerable.

As so often in this period, however, the excellent intentions of the Ottoman regulation were nullified by official corruption. The obvious candidates for posts as intendants were the poorer *'Ulemâ*, and many of them were indeed enabled to make a livelihood by these means. But every student of the period will be struck by the large numbers of *waḳfs* held by the wealthy families, not only of the religious classes but also of civil and military officers. There was keen competition for the control more especially of the larger *waḳfs*,[3] with all the resulting intrigues, bribery, and other abuses. Rival claimants appealed to Istanbul, and it appears to have been not uncommon for existing intendants to be evicted in favour of more influential candidates.[4] Cabartî bitterly criticizes

[1] These figures are based on the abstract of *waḳfîyas* at Aleppo published by Kâmil al-Ġazzî, ii. 534–630; those relating to the period 1130/1718–1216/1800 are contained on pp. 538–69. No similar abstracts appear to exist for other provinces. It may be noted that these *waḳfs* include a number of Christian foundations for the benefit of the Greek and Maronite churches in Aleppo, and even for convents in Lebanon, although (as we have already noted) such foundations were regarded as strictly illegal.

[2] The revenues of the *awḳâf* affected to the sanctuary of Jerusalem were collected annually by one of the *Şeyḫs* of the Ḥaram or his representatives: Murâdî, iii. 166.

[3] Exclusive of the *sulṭânî awḳâf*, which were administered by the *Ağas*.

[4] Cf. *Recueil des Firmans*, No. 1; Murâdî, i. 41. Apparently the status of the confirming office made a great difference; one of the Keylânî family obtained the intendance (*tawliya*) of part of a family *waḳf* by a *berât* from the *Ḳâḍî-'asker*. He then got it transferred to the Holy Cities account (*muḥâsabet el-ḥarameyn*; see p. 175, n. 8, below), and finally, by using influence, obtained a *Ḫaṭṭî Şerîf* for it from Sultan Maḥmûd I: Murâdî, iii. 138. Other imperial *fermâns*: *Recueil*, Nos. 4, 7, 9, 12, 13, 15.

the administration of rich *waḳfs* by 'highly placed' personages, and asserts that 'the greater part of the administrative expenses, luxuries, and hospitalities of the notables of the districts were derived from *waḳf* lands, which they held without any right.'[1] Although many intendants were doubtless honest and upright in their administration, even *Şeyḫs*, *Ḳâḍîs*, and *Muftîs* were not immune from abusing their positions of trust in similar ways, but they were occasionally detected and punished by the authorities.[2]

Awḳâf were in principle irrevocable and constituted in perpetuity,[3] and their provisions were unalterable. Nor, though the jurists differed on this point, might a *waḳf* be designed to take effect only at the founder's death; he must relinquish his ownership of the dedicated property from the date at which the *waḳfîya* became valid.[4] If the object of the foundation ceased to exist, if, for instance, a hospital or a *medrese* were destroyed, the revenues were supposed to be applied to some other charitable purpose, which was in many cases specified in the *waḳfîya* itself.[5] *Waḳfîyas* were authenticated by *şâhids* at a *Ḳâḍî*'s court,[6] and engrossed in either book or scroll form on paper or parchment. Sometimes, if the object of the *waḳf* were a building, an epitome of the *waḳfîya* would be carved in stone on some part of its walls.[7] All *waḳfîyas* were likewise registered in one or other of the three bureaux of the Finance Department that dealt with these foundations at Istanbul,[8] or in the provincial Finance Departments.[9]

If the revenues forthcoming from the properties assigned to a foundation exceeded the necessary expenditure—and those of the imperial mosques habitually did so[10]—the balance was supposed to form a reserve fund called *dolab*.[11] From this fund other properties

[1] Cabartî, iv. 210/ix. 94; cf. Murâdî, iii. 192, 280.

[2] Murâdî, i. 41; iv. 24–25, 185.

[3] *Encyc. of Islam*, s.v. 'Waḳf'; Kunter, 109.

[4] In Ottoman practice if a man declared, without completing the formalities necessary for the establishment of a proper *waḳf*, that at his death some of his possessions were to be *mevḳûf*, it was regarded as an ordinary testamentary disposition and could hence apply to no more than one-third of what he left: D'Ohsson, ii. 546, and Belin, 157 sq.

[5] Ünver, 21; Kunter, 124.

[6] *Encyc. of Islam*, s.v. 'S͟hāhid'; and see p. 130 above.

[7] Kunter, 116.

[8] The *Ḥarameyn Muḥâsebesi*, the *Ḥarameyn Muḳâṭa'asi*, and the *Küçük Evḳâf Muḥâsebesi*. See Part I, index.

[9] See p. 173 above.

[10] See D'Ohsson, ii. 538, for the revenues in his day of the chief imperial mosques at the capital.

[11] A Persian word of various meanings, used in Turkish to signify among other things a 'cupboard'. But its use in this case for 'treasury' comes perhaps from its Persian meaning of a revolving cylinder set in an opening in the wall of an institution such as a hospital for the reception of alms: see Steingass, *Persian Dictionary*, s.v.

might be acquired. Sometimes they were bought outright; but a special system was also much used, whereby *Mutawallîs* would pay no more than half the purchase price of a property to its vendor, and often much less, on condition that the vendor then leased it from the foundation, to which he must furnish both an advance rent and periodical rents, like the *re'âyâ* on *wakf* lands. This served the interests of both parties, since it gained the *wakf* a sound security cheaply, whilst enabling the lessee to continue in the enjoyment of what had been his property, which was now protected by its *wakf* status from being distrained upon for debt. The lessee could also dispose of his lease to another, on which the *wakf* again benefited by the fee payable on such a transfer, or he could bequeath it to descendants untrammelled by the heritage provisions of the Sacred Law.[1] If any lessee died without heirs, the property passed wholly into the possession of the foundation.

The *Harameyn Dolabi*, the treasury of the imperial *awkâf*, owing to the accumulation of surplus revenues accruing from the properties assigned to them, usually contained very substantial sums; and though such transfers were deplored, from the seventeenth century the government from time to time, when particularly hard pressed, borrowed from this source to meet its commitments.[2] A commoner and even less laudable use of the surplus (and even of ordinary) revenues of these and other *awkâf*, moreover, was their partial appropriation by the *Nâzirs* and *Mutawallîs* responsible for them. Indeed, the main cause of the disorders that were rife in the management of *awkâf* in later times would seem to have been the negligence, or worse, of the *Nâzirs* in exercising their authority.[3] Although, as we have noted, irregularities in management were occasionally punished,[4] administrators had little to fear in so misapplying these funds except from their successors in office, who could usually be relied on to raise no complaints, since silence would enable them to follow a similar course.[5] Founders were, indeed, and with good reason, conscious of the possibility that the revenues that they assigned to their foundations would be misused; and *wakfîyas* often contain a minatory clause in which those who so misuse them are threatened with retribution on the

[1] D'Ohsson, ii. 552 sq., followed by Belin, 516 sq., classifies these supplementary holdings as 'customary *awkâf*'. Cabartî (iv. 209–10/ix. 93–94) notes that the occupation of *wakf* lands was coveted more especially by the cultivators, since the very small tax with which they were burdened could not be increased.

[2] Instances are noted by Belin (*J.A.*, 1864, iv. 296, 330, 360) as occurring in 1622, 1655, 1698. Cf. D'Ohsson, ii. 541.

[3] Seyyid Muṣṭafâ, iv. 100; 'Abdu'r-Raḥmân Şeref, 511.

[4] Above, p. 175. D'Ohsson perhaps exaggerates in saying that the state took no cognizance of the details of *wakf* administration, beyond insisting that the objects of their founders should not be neglected (ii. 547–8).

[5] D'Ohsson, ii. 538–9.

Day of Judgement'.[1] That the *Ḳizlar Ağasis* derived so much profit from their supervision of *awḳâf* was no doubt due to misappropriation on a large scale, which by the eighteenth century had developed into a recognized and tolerated abuse. Yet D'Ohsson states that the *awḳâf* under the *Ḳizlar Ağasis'* control were those in the administration of which fewest irregularities occurred.[2]

Apart, in fact, from the misappropriation of their revenues, the maintenance of the *waḳf* properties themselves was constantly threatened from two directions. On the one hand, wealthy and influential intendants, or even persons of lower rank who held their posts by virtue of long hereditary tenure, were inclined to transform *waḳf* property into private property by force, bribery, or guile.[3] It was one of the express duties of the administration to prevent the illegal occupation or absorption of *waḳf* property, and in Egypt, for example, each *rizḳa* was registered by a special *Efendi*.[4] Yet there can be little doubt that many *rizâḳ* had, by the end of the eighteenth century, become to all intents and purposes private property, both lands and revenues being disposed of by the administrators as they chose,[5] with the result that at this time *waḳf* lands were at a premium.

Nevertheless, the incentive supplied both to cultivators and to *Nâẓirs* towards maintaining *waḳf* property in good condition did not outweigh the effects of lack of personal ownership, and in particular of the continued application of capital which, even in Egypt, is needed to maintain land in full productivity. Although it was the duty of the central administration, aided by the local *Ḳâḍîs*, to see that all *waḳf* properties were kept productive and in full repair, the almost inevitable fate of *waḳf* lands was to be starved, under-cultivated, and finally left derelict. The only remedy which received full legal recognition was the permission to alienate them on long lease, the lessee paying a lump sum in advance and a small annual rent thereafter.[6] While the law tolerated such a sale only when the properties were in bad condition, and on the understanding that the sum realized might be used only to purchase other properties for conversion into *awḳâf*,

[1] e.g. the *waḳfîyas* published by Kunter, 120–1.

[2] D'Ohsson, ii. 539.

[3] e.g. Murâdî, iv. 185.

[4] Lancret, 240. His honesty is not highly commended by Cabartî (iv. 77/viii. 169).

[5] Cabartî, iv. 208–9/ix. 94. Earlier complaints of withholding of *waḳf* revenues: ibid. i. 26/i. 61. Lancret mentions (239) that several proprietors of *waḳfs* paid a small duty to the *Paşa* for protection in recovering their revenues.

[6] This contract was known as *icârateyn*, its effect being to produce a situation similar to that of *waḳf* lands 'let' to *re'âyâ*, see p. 166 above. Lancret (239) states that the lease was usually granted for ninety years.

it will be seen how readily this system opened the way to arrangements designed to evade the law, provided that the connivance of the *Ḳâḍî* could be secured. *Waḳf* lands, however, probably suffered less from these abuses than *waḳf* property in buildings. The experience of many centuries and in all countries proved that *waḳf* properties rapidly fell into ruin. To meet this contingency, a semi-legal device was found in the 'exchange' of *waḳf* property for other property of equal value, the former passing into the possession of the previous owner of the latter, now become a *waḳf*.[1] But already by the sixteenth century this had become so flagrant a device for the seizure of *waḳf* property that the *ḳânûns* of Sultan Süleymân expressly forbid the alienation either by sale or exchange of ruined buildings belonging to *awḳâf*, even if it should appear to be to the advantage of the *waḳfs* concerned, because of the prevarications committed on this pretext; and further that in case of contravention of this *ḳânûn* both seller and buyer should be severely punished.[2] The cure prescribed by the Ottoman lawgiver was to spend part of the revenue on repairs, even if it should be necessary to curtail in consequence the pensions payable from the endowment,[3] and to hold the *Nâẓirs* responsible before the courts for maintaining the property in good condition.[4] Nevertheless, a regulation so rigid in pursuit of logical consistency at the expense of public utility was obviously unworkable in the long run, and by the eighteenth century properties assigned in *waḳf* might, by imperial *fermân*, be exchanged for others.[5] By this time, however, the corruption in the administration of *awḳâf* in general had gone so far that it is not surprising to find its better regulation among the first measures of reform undertaken by Sultan Maḥmûd II at the beginning of the nineteenth century, and a still more drastic operation carried through in Egypt by his viceroy Meḥmed ʿAlî.

[1] Such an exchange was called *istibdâl*.

[2] Digeon, ii. 267–8; Barkan, 384.

[3] Digeon, ii. 265–6: 'If necessary, only the *Nâẓir*, *Imâm*, *Mü'ezzin*, and *Ḫaṭîb* may be paid, and the rest given up to repairs' (cf. 270).

[4] Cf. *Recueil des Firmans*, No. 2.

[5] D'Ohsson, ii. 548; cf. Belin, 'Propriété foncière' (*J.A.*, Série V, xviii. 411).

CHAPTER XIII

THE *DERVÎŞES*

WE have now examined the main organisms of the official religious institution in the Ottoman Empire; but there remains another highly important class of persons whose status resembled that of the *'Ulemâ* in that it likewise was religious, and who have often been mentioned in the preceding chapters, namely, the *dervîşes*. The Persian word *därvîş* is used in that language and in Turkish (in the form *dervîş*) as the equivalent of the Arabic *faḳîr*, 'poor man', in the sense of a holy man living a life of voluntary poverty. The holy men to whom it is applied are the practitioners of mysticism (*taṣawwuf*), or *Ṣûfîs*.

In describing the general features of the religious institution in Chapter VIII, we have already outlined the history of the *ṣûfî* movement within Islâm and its relations with the *Sunnî 'Ulemâ*.[1] Before considering the position occupied by the *dervîşes* and their social influence in the Ottoman Empire, however, we must discuss in somewhat fuller detail certain features within the movement which contributed to characterize its later development within our period.

The earlier Moslem mystics in no wise conceived that their practices might come to be held by theologians to conflict with those ordained by true belief. They were 'searchers of the heart',[2] who sought by fervent devotion and ascetic discipline to prepare themselves for illumination. But at a certain point the emphasis which they placed on the dictation of the conscience led some of them to value this illumination and its discipline above the prescriptions of the *Şerî'a*; worse still, some of them took to the metaphysical speculation that was the fashion of the age. The first clash with the *'Ulemâ* led to the execution for blasphemy and heresy of a

[1] See further, *Encyc. of Islam*, art. 'Darwīsh' (Macdonald), artt. 'Shadd', 'Ṭarīḳa', and 'Taṣawwuf' (Massignon); R. A. Nicholson, *The Mystics of Islam* (London, 1914); A. J. Arberry, *Sufism* (London, 1951); and the numerous books and studies of L. Massignon. Apart from the information given by D'Ohsson, no general account of *taṣawwuf* in the Ottoman Empire has yet been written. Specific studies on certain movements are cited in their places below, but these are few, and the survey which we attempt in this chapter can do little more than indicate the importance of the *dervîşes* in the religious and social life of the people and the immense field which remains to be investigated in detail.

[2] The expression was actually used in a ritual sense in later ages. Among the *Melâmîs*, for instance, there was a personage called *Ḳalba Baḳici*, 'a looker into the heart', whose duty it was to examine the conscience of aspirants to holiness, an operation that was called *gönül bekleme*, which likewise means 'heart-searching': Abdül Baki, *Melâmilik ve Melâmiler*, 192; Köprülüzade Mehmet Fuat, *Les Origines du Bektachisme*. For the *Melâmîs*, see p. 180 below.

certain Manṣûr el-Ḥallâc in A.D. 921;[1] and thereafter the *ṣûfî* movement may be said, generally speaking, to have broken into two wings: one, centred at Bağdâd, which remained in fairly close relations with orthodoxy; the other, centred in Ḫorâsân (though with adepts in other countries as well), which tended towards more extreme attitudes.

Among the *Ṣûfîs* of Ḫorâsân and the East, moreover, these tendencies took two distinct directions, both of which were to exert a great influence on some of the *dervîş* orders which came into existence in later centuries, and especially upon the Turks, who were, precisely at this period, entering into the Moslem community. One of these characteristics was represented by the groups known as *Melâmetîya* or *Melâmîya*.[2] They were distinguished by their detestation of hypocrisy in religion. By hypocrisy they meant the belief that the discharge of the duties prescribed by the *Şerî'a* was enough, particularly if that discharge were ostentatious. Hence their name, which implies that they were willing to incur censure for nonconformity; nevertheless, they were careful to avoid ostentation in nonconformity itself, and in order to do so would perform the more obvious duties, inefficacious though they held them to be. They would also wear no special dress and would pursue ordinary callings, so that the generality should observe in them nothing peculiar. Finally, they would neither preach nor hold meetings for the recital of litanies, like the other mystics, nor above all attract the admiration of the ignorant by wonder-working. The ideals of the *Melâmetîs* were to represent in the later history of Moslem mysticism perhaps its purest ethical element, and in two later periods were to win many adherents.[3] At the same time, it was not to be expected that all who professed the *melâmetî* doctrine would be careful to avoid infringing the *Şerî'a*, for the antinomian tendency that pervaded all *ṣûfî* circles was to be found among them also and laid them open to severe criticism both from the theologians and from their fellow *Ṣûfîs*.[4]

The second feature of Ḫorâsânî *taṣawwuf* was an intense attachment to el-Ḥallâc, who became the symbol of the ecstatic 'martyr of love'. This enthusiasm was even more displeasing to the orthodox since, along with the theosophical tendencies that it implied, there went an overt repudiation of the *'Ulemâ*, who were held

[1] L. Massignon, *La Passion d'al-Hallaj* (Paris, 1922).

[2] From Ar. *malâma*, plur. *malâmât*, 'blame'.

[3] Abdülbaki, 22–26.

[4] See, e.g., Arberry, 40, 70. It would seem, however, that these reproaches were addressed less to the *Melâmetîs* proper than to the extroverts who took their name and were afterwards known as *Ḳalenderîs*: see below, p. 188, and Suhrawardî, *'Awârif ul-Ma'ârif*, on margin of el-Ğazâlî's *Iḥyâ*, ii. 2–4.

responsible for his execution.[1] Entering into the lyrical productions of the great Persian poets of the pre-Mongol century, *Ḥallâcî* Ṣûfism gained a wide influence, not only amongst Persians, but also amongst the Turks, including the first and greatest of the eastern Turkî poets, Aḥmed Yesevî (d. A.D. 1166).[2]

There was yet a third antinomian element which had also begun to affect the *ṣûfî* movement. Among the various branches of Şî'ism which spread throughout the Islamic countries in the ninth and tenth centuries, the most active was that of the Ismâ'îlîs, whose revolutionary propaganda gave birth to the Fâṭimid Caliphate, the Carmathians, the Druses, and at a later date the 'Assassins' of northern Persia and Syria. The adherents of these doctrines were called *Bâṭinî*, because they asserted that the *Ḳur'ân* should be interpreted allegorically (*bâṭin* meaning 'interior', 'internal', as opposed to *ẓâhir*, 'exterior', 'external'). We have already noted that Ṣûfism and Şî'ism alike gained their most numerous following in the early centuries amongst the dissatisfied urban populations, although the solutions sought for the problems of social injustice by the *Bâṭinîs* and *Ṣûfîs* respectively were different. The attitude of the *Ṣûfîs* was too other-worldly to attract the *Bâṭinîs*, who aimed at a mundane revolution. The doctrine and method of allegorical interpretation adopted by the *Bâṭinîs*, however, exerted an immense and lasting influence on the mystics, who had, in any case, a further link with the *Şî'a* in their attachment to the memory of 'Alî and his descendants.[3]

The acceptance of Ṣûfism by the *Sunnî* doctors in the twelfth century did not, of course, give an automatic *droit de cité* within Islâm to these more aberrant forms. It did, however, make it more difficult for the doctors to draw the line in a theological sense; while, simultaneously, political developments in the eastern and northern provinces removed, for several centuries, any possibility of their exercising an effective political control over the local religious movements. In these areas, it would appear that the continued frontier warfare against the unbelievers and the heathen had in the course of time led to the formation of local associations of *ğâzîs* or 'Warriors for the Faith' who, under the influence of Persian knightly ideals, called themselves *fityân* and their association *futûwa*.[4]

[1] See L. Massignon, 'L'Œuvre Hallagienne d'Attar', in *Revue des Études Islamiques*, 1941–6, 117–44.

[2] Id., 'La Légende de Hallâcé Mansur en pays turcs', in *Revue des Études Islamiques*, 1941–6, 67–73.

[3] It should be noted, however, that doctrinal Şî'ism was still more hostile to Ṣûfism than were the early *Sunnîs*, since by laying stress on the immediate relation between God and man the *Ṣûfîs* denied the distinguishing tenet of Şî'ism, that salvation depends upon devotion to an Imâm of the house of 'Alî.

[4] *Fityân* is the plural of Ar. *fatâ*, already associated in Arabic literature with

These associations found imitators in other quarters also, especially in the cities, where gangs of toughs, calling themselves *fityân*, met the violence and tyranny of the Sultans and their officers with counter-violence.[1] The *Ṣûfîs* in turn patronized similar associations, to which they endeavoured to impart a moral rather than political content, aiming to induce a sentiment of solidarity among their members by the pooling of resources and the inculcation of the virtues of generosity, hospitality, and the protection of the weak. So widespread was their appeal that at the end of the twelfth century an ʿAbbâsid Caliph (el-Nâṣir, reigned A.D. 1180–1225) even promulgated an aristocratic *futûwa* order and prohibited all others, in an attempt to re-establish the decayed authority of the Caliphate.[2]

We must now return to the Turkish tribes who migrated into the lands of Islâm from the eleventh to the thirteenth centuries. While still outside the sphere of Moslem civilization, various branches of the Turks had at different times embraced Christianity, Zoroastrianism, Buddhism, and Manichaeism. There were also ties between the Oğuz, the branch from which the invaders mostly derived, and the Khazars, who had been converted to Judaism. Nevertheless, those Turks, the majority, who were to maintain their tribal life during and after the migrations, remained attached to their own primitive religion, in which a leading part was played by the holy men known as *Ḳam Ozans*. Now certain restrictions imposed by Islâm, the prohibition of wine-drinking and the seclusion of women in particular, together with the whole apparatus of regulated worship, appealed to these nomads no more than they had appealed to the beduin of Arabia. Islâm was from the beginning a religion not of the desert but of the city, or at any rate of the settlement; and all the superstructure built upon its early foundations was the work of townsmen. In view of its great prestige, however, in the lands overrun by the Turks, there was no question but that they should turn Moslem, even if only in name, especially since the tribesmen of the earliest movement had auto-

the beduin ideal of manliness, courage, and generosity, and popularly applied in a special sense to ʿAlî; see *Encyc. of Islam*, artt. 'Futuwwa', 'Shadd'; H. Thorning, *Beiträge zur Kenntnis des islamischen Vereinswesens* (Berlin, 1913); F. Taeschner, 'Das Futuwwa-Rittertum des islamischen Mittelalters', in *Beiträge zur Arabistik, Semitistik und Islamwissenschaft* (Leipzig, 1944). The common outward characteristic of all *futûwa* associations was an initiation ceremony which involved a drink of salt water and investiture with a girdle and the 'trousers of manliness'.

[1] How far these associations grew out of the former guilds is still uncertain, and although *bâṭinî* influences have been suspected in their formation, no proof of this has yet been established. In the modern colloquial language of Egypt, *fatâ* still has the sense of 'a tough, an apache'.

[2] References in note 4, p. 181; also P. Kahle in *Festschrift für Georg Jacob* (Leipzig, 1932), 112 sqq., and G. Salinger in *Proc. of Amer. Phil. Soc.*, 1950, 481 sqq.

matically followed their leaders in adopting the new religion. But they and their successors in migration had many brands of Moslem practice from which to choose. Their choice, inevitably, fell upon the *ğâzî* brand of *futûwa* associations, the more so that, in the first place, they occupied the northern frontier territories of Islâm from beyond the Oxus to the heart of Anatolia, and, in the second place, in adopting these they conserved, along with their tribal life, many of their native religious customs. The former *Ḳam Ozans* were replaced by, or transformed into, Moslem holy men, under the name of *Babas* (fathers), and these in turn were strongly influenced by the Ṣufism of Ḫorâsân, both orthodox and (still more) unorthodox.[1]

The combination of *futûwa* organization with *ṣûfî* leadership proved to be the most vigorous and effective social institution in the troubled centuries between the battle of Manzikert (1071) and the rise of the Ṣafavid state in Persia (1500). The Turkish conquest of Asia Minor was accomplished by organizations of this type, operating on their own account; after the catastrophic Mongol invasions of Persia it served as the pattern on which the damaged tissues of Islamic life and culture were slowly reconstructed, with infinite effort and in face of repeated hurricanes of devastation; and both the Ottoman sultanate and the rival Ṣafavid empire were built upon the same foundations. The Selcuḳid Sultans of Anatolia, following the evolution characteristic of all Moslem dynasties, became the champions of orthodoxy against heterodoxy; to master the anarchical independence of the tribal *ğâzî* organizations they strove to build up an orderly centralized administration; and they transplanted into Anatolia the urban culture which these policies demanded by attracting Moslem doctors, lawyers, merchants, and artisans from Syria and Mesopotamia.[2] So successful were they that when they in turn were enfeebled by Mongol intervention, new *futûwa* corporations sprang up in the cities, under the name of *aḫis*, to whose influence on the institutions of the nascent Ottoman Empire we have frequently had occasion to refer.[3] These associations of merchants and artisans not only held the Selcuḳid

[1] Köprülüzade Mehmet Fuad, *Anadoluda Islâmiyet*, 42 sq. It may be of some significance for the later history of Islâm that to the Turks, as a nation or a group of peoples, early Moslem orthodoxy was known only as a formal or imperial system, and that their own religious experience within Islâm was from the first of a mystical or sufistic type.

[2] The violent antagonism aroused by this policy amongst the tribesmen found vent in their half-political, half-religious rising in 1239 under a *Ḳalenderî Şeyḫ* named Baba Isḥaḳ. Although the revolt was suppressed, this *Baba'î* movement was the forerunner of the *Bektâşî* movement: see below, pp. 188–90.

[3] See Part I, index, s.v.; also Köprülüzade; P. Wittek, *The Rise of the Ottoman Empire* (London, 1938); Mustafa Akdağ, in *Belleten* of the Türk Tarih Kurumu, vol. xiv, part 55 (1950), pp. 319 sqq.; Ibn Baṭṭúṭa, *Travels in Asia and Africa* (London, 1929), 125–6 and note; *Encyc. of Islam*², s.v. 'akhī'.

administrators at bay, but constituted little republics whose chiefs, thanks to their dual economic and religious authority, exercised some control over the neighbouring country-side also.

By the end of the thirteenth century, therefore, it is possible to distinguish (formally, if not always in practice, owing to innumerable cross-currents) three main divisions in Ṣûfîsm. One was the moderate and generally orthodox mysticism of the school of Bağdâd, transplanted to the cities of Syria and Egypt by Nureddin, Saladin, and their successors, and with which the *ʿUlemâ* were increasingly associated. At the other extreme were the 'rural' associations, *ğâzî* in practice or principle,[1] but all of them latitudinarian in varying degrees and shading into heresy. In between were the artisan or popular urban associations, more orthodox than the latter, less intellectual than the former, interpreting the 'Holy War' in socio-ethical terms and addicted to ecstatic exercises under the supervision of local *Şeyḫs*.

During the following centuries, while these differences persisted, there was, in some respects, a gradual lessening of the distance between them, owing partly to the spread of a common doctrine, and still more to the adoption of a common type of organization. As regards doctrine, *ṣûfî* speculation had not ceased, and came to a head with the system propounded by the famous Spanish-Arab teacher Ibn el-ʿArabî (1165–1240). This system has been described as 'Existential Monism'; and it was to remain, with but few modifications, the metaphysical theory of most Moslem mystics.[2] The stricter orthodox might well denounce it; for whereas earlier *ṣûfî* speculation had been reconcilable (at a pinch, and excluding aberrations) with orthodox theology, this was almost exactly contradicted by the monism of Ibn el-ʿArabî. Orthodoxy proposed a completely transcendent God; Ibn el-ʿArabî one wholly immanent. Worse still, if existence is a divine unity, evil can be no more than apparent. The learned mystics who expounded the doctrine were moved by an intense love of God, and they could not admit any real imperfections in a universe that had emanated from the divine essence. This adoration inspired innumerable poets to sublime creation, and a still vaster number of devotees to lives of contemplation and renunciation. But the effect on morals of the doctrine depended upon the spirit in which it was entertained. For the generality of orthodox Moslems, as of Christians, morality had depended upon a system of supernatural sanctions: good would be

[1] The *ğâzî* principle was not confined to the Turks, though most prominent amongst them. The *Bedawîya* (or *Aḥmedîya*) congregation formed by Şeyḫ Aḥmed el-Badawî in Lower Egypt was also inspired in the first instance by the defence of Egypt against the Crusaders.

[2] See A. E. Affifi, *The Mystical Philosophy of Muḥyid Dín-Ibnul ʿArabí* (Cambridge, 1929).

rewarded and evil punished in a world to come. But if everything, despite appearances to the contrary, was good, the whole system collapsed. If, therefore, the doctrine were adopted by persons in whom its concomitant mystical call to adoration found no echo, it was inevitable that, in so far as it was not counteracted by a simultaneous and inconsistent belief in the orthodox moral code, it should produce in them two main effects: a conviction that they might do what they would with impunity, and a fatalistic endurance of suffering.

Equally important from the social standpoint was the growth and expansion of the *dervîş* orders.[1] This new organization (in which, as we shall describe shortly, *ṣûfî* congregations in many different centres and countries were attached as branches or lodges to one or other of a number of systems, each with its own discipline and rule) was largely responsible for the hold gained by Ṣûfism on all classes of Moslem society during the Ottoman period.[2] Not only did these provide the schools of mysticism with permanent centres such as had not existed hitherto, but it became an almost universal custom for 'laymen' to affiliate themselves to the orders.[3] We thus have the curious spectacle of what were really two mutually contradictory systems of religion existing side by side and being generally regarded as one. To the great bulk of the people the inconsistency was of no moment, was indeed scarcely apparent. The *'Ulemâ* alone were thoroughly conversant with the *Şerî'a* and its orthodox interpretation; and the *'Ulemâ* were townsmen. Those who came within their orbit of influence compromised with a performance of the prescribed ritual of worship and an adherence to a strongly 'Sufistic' system of belief. Those outside it tended, according to the strength or weakness of governmental control over their actions, to dispense with even the forms of orthodoxy. Thus there was reinforced the contrast between the urban and rural forms of *taṣawwuf* that was due in the first place to the difference in origin and character of the respective sections of the population by which they were adopted.

What we have hitherto referred to as the 'orders' of the *dervîşes* are called in Moslem parlance 'paths' (in Arabic *ṭarîka*, in Turkish *ṭarîḳat*). The term had been used in early times in the sense of 'a method of moral psychology for individuals with a mystic call'.

[1] A list of orders is given by L. Massignon in *Encyc. of Islam*, art. 'Ṭarīḳa'. See further J. P. Brown, *The Darvishes*, ed. by H. A. Rose (London, 1927); O. Depont et X. Coppolani, *Les Confréries religieuses musulmanes* (Alger, 1897).

[2] The degree of popular support enjoyed by the *dervîş* orders and their saints is brought out by H. J. Kissling, 'The Role of the Dervish Orders in the Ottoman Empire', in *Studies in Islamic Cultural History, American Anthropologist*, Memoir No. 76, April 1954.

[3] D'Ohsson, iv. 172–3; *Encyc. of Islam*, art. 'Darwīsh'.

But when the *Ṣûfîs* took to forming societies, it came insensibly to connote the body of special rules that the members of each of these societies were called upon to obey. These rules varied as between the orders, but were alike in their general character. The members lived in, or, in the case of certain 'wandering' orders, paid periodical visits for retreats to, monasteries called *tekye* or *tekke* in Turkish, *ḫânḳâh* in Persian, and *ribâṭ* or *zâwiya* in Arabic.[1] In order to become an adept, when only he might rank as a *dervîş* or *faḳîr* proper, the novice (*murîd*), after a course of training under an elder, would receive initiation from the head of the monastery (called *Şeyḫ*, *Pîr*, or *Baba*), in the presence of other office-holders, by means of a ceremony of binding, or girding, or oath-taking. After his initiation the *dervîş* was invested in the frock (*ḫirḳa*) and padded cap (*tâc*) by which mystical devotees were distinguished. Their shape and colour varied according to the order.[2]

Dervîşes regarded themselves as the spiritual descendants of earlier *Ṣûfîs*. Each was instructed in his spiritual genealogy. The existence of such a practice was perhaps connected with one like it that had been in vogue among early Traditionists, who on citing a Tradition invariably gave the name of the authority from whom they had received it, together with a 'chain' (*silsila*) of names leading back to the apostolic age. In any case the *dervîş* genealogies were likewise termed *silsila*. The *silsilas* of the orders were naturally different each from the others in their later links; but in all but three of them the earlier links were the same: their 'chains' all led back to the Caliph 'Alî.[3] And though orthodox opponents were able to show that the earliest four personages that figured in the list had never encountered one another, *dervîş* faith in its validity was unshaken.[4] Especially prominent in each chain was the founder, or reputed founder, of the order. Its parent *tekke* was usually built at his tomb, which formed a centre of pilgrimage. For the mystical exercises of the *Ṣûfîs* were directed towards the attainment of contact with the divine, which they conceived to result in the reception of 'graces' (*karâmât*) by the devotee. These graces endowed him

[1] *tekye* is from the Arabic *takîya* (plural *takâyâ*), a late formation from *ittakâ*, 'he sat upright' and also 'he ate'. The usual spelling *tekke*, with the *y* omitted, is perhaps due to the pronunciation of 'ke' as 'kye'.

[2] *Encyc. of Islam*, artt. 'Ṭarīḳa' (Massignon) and 'Derwīsh' (Macdonald); D'Ohsson, iv. 632–9, 661–4.

[3] So D'Ohsson, iv. 626, where it is stated that the *Bisṭâmîs*, the *Naḳşbendîs*, and the *Bektaşîs*, all attributed their origin to the Caliph Abû Bakr. Cf. *Encyc. of Islam*, art. 'Bektāsh' (Tschudi). A *ṣûfî* doctrine taught in comparatively late days, though possibly held in earlier times, distinguished between an outward and an inward transmission of the Caliphate from the Prophet to his successors. The outward transmission was to Abû Bakr, &c., the inward to 'Alî—see Abdül Baki, 198–9.

[4] *Encyc. of Islam*, art. 'Taṣawwuf'. Cf. the *Ḫalwetî silsila* given in Sadik Vicdanî, *Halvetiye*, iv. 7.

with supernatural powers: in the eyes of the generality, therefore, who had no doubt that such claims were well founded, the *ṣûfî* adept enjoyed the reputation of a saint. Whilst alive his blessing was eagerly sought; and after his death his tomb would be visited as the place in which his intercession might most effectually be invoked.

In the later history of Islâm the veneration of saints is a particularly widespread and notable feature of the religion; but its genesis is entirely due to the conquest of the faithful by *ṣûfî* conceptions. It is true that the Pilgrimage to Mecca provided, as it were, a sanctioned precedent for the belief in the efficacy of visitation; and that the attribution by the *Şî'a* of semi-divinity to the *Imâms* paved the way to the later development. But this development itself is *ṣûfî* in origin; and duly aroused the contempt and wrath of those who prized the primitive above this later interpretation of the religion; hence, for example, the hostility of the Wahhâbî 'puritans' of Arabia to the visitation of tombs.

The saints themselves were known as 'the Friends' (*Awliyâ*, *Evliyâ* in Turkish), that is to say the Friends of God. Among them were included all the Prophets from Adam to Muḥammad, as well as the *Ṣûfîs* of later times. Furthermore, the belief in this quality of sainthood led to another: that there were always alive in the world a certain number of such saints, known as the 'People of the Unseen',[1] graded in a hierarchy headed by one supreme saint called the 'Axis', the mystical axis of the world.[2] The number of living saints, it was believed, was always kept constant by the admission to this hierarchy of fresh members when others died. But their identity was a secret known only to the living saints themselves. Their importance in the *ṣûfî* outlook was supreme, however. It was believed that the world continued in being only by reason of their intercessions.[3]

Owing to the penetration of *ṣûfî* ideas into all but a very small circle of the rigidly orthodox, this conception of the governance of the world by occult personages, like the belief in the miraculous power of saints and their tombs, was very widely entertained. But before describing the effect of these ideas on the outlook and character of the Moslem subjects of the Sultans in the eighteenth century, we propose to consider some of the *dervîş* orders from which they radiated.

At one time and another a very large number of *ṭarîḳas* flourished in the Empire. But there is no need to describe, or even to name, them all here, since the five or six most important, to which we

[1] *ahl el-ğayb.*
[2] *ḳuṭb. Encyc. of Islam,* art. 'Taṣawwuf'.
[3] D'Ohsson, iv. 671–2.

must give some space, were representative of the rest. What is most interesting from our point of view, moreover, is rather the general effect of the spread of *ṣûfî* doctrines among the people than the peculiarities of the different orders. The distinction that we drew above between 'rural' and 'urban' associations becomes, in this context, of less importance than that between 'regular' and 'irregular' orders, of which the latter were, as the term suggests, not only loose in organization, but also extravagantly loose in doctrine and practice. Since, however, their devotees continued to enjoy scarcely less (and possibly even more) respect among the populace of both town and country-side than the *Şeyḫs* of the 'regular' orders, we shall begin, by way of sketching in the background of popular Ṣûfism, with such an 'irregular' order, that of the *Ḳalenderîs*, familiar to generations of English readers of the *Arabian Nights* as 'Calenders'.[1]

The *Ḳalenderîs*, who spread during the twelfth century over almost all parts of the eastern Moslem world, appear to have been inspired by the teaching of the *Melâmetîs*. But they differed very strikingly in their conduct from those practitioners of secret devotion. They went out of their way to 'incur censure' by wandering about with their hair, beards, and eyebrows shaven, and openly disregarded every precept of the Sacred Law. They would travel on foot from place to place with flags and drums, attracting crowds by their strange appearance and behaviour. They begged for a living, had no worldly interests, and took no thought for the morrow. Being mostly drawn from the lower classes, they were quite uneducated and incapable of understanding the niceties of *ṣûfî* philosophy. Their doctrine, such as it was, was pantheistic; they were said to believe in the endless repetition of events and the transmigration of souls, and to account no action unlawful, and thus belonged to the extreme *bâṭinî* wing of *taṣawwuf*.

The *Ḳalenderîs* are of interest to us, moreover, because it was *dervîşes* of their type, though often called by other names, that appealed to the Turkish tribes of Anatolia and elsewhere, and took the place, under the name of *Baba*, of their heathen priests. It was, also, 'active' *dervîşes* of this type—which contrasted strongly with that of the secluded contemplatives of the towns—who played a leading part in inspiring the Turkish tribesmen and other immigrants to the 'frontier' territories to engage in the holy wars by means of which the Empire was brought to birth. Hence it came about, as we observed at the beginning of this introduction, that the Ottoman adventure was started mainly by men professing a highly unorthodox form of the Faith. And hence again there was

[1] See *Encyc. of Islam*, art. 'Ḳalandar'; D'Ohsson, iv. 684–5; Abdül Baki, 25–26.

to occur that divergence of religious opinion to which we have also referred between the Sultans and many of their Moslem subjects, when the former, as during the fourteenth century they gradually adopted a civilized palace life, came more and more under orthodox influences.

During the hundred years that saw the establishment of the Ottomans in the Balkan peninsula,[1] the influence of the *aḫîs* in the towns and of the *dervîşes* among the tribesmen of Asia Minor had remained almost without opposition. For it appears that the principal rival dynasty in Anatolia, the princes of the Ḳaraman-oğlu dynasty, had also gained their position with the aid of the heterodox tribesmen, and that, unlike the Ottoman Sultans, they remained true to their original faith.[2] All this accounts for the difficulty experienced by the Ottoman Sultans in subjecting Asia Minor to their rule and in their endeavours to set up centralized orthodox institutions, by which the authority of the chiefs of the *aḫîs* was supplanted by that of the officially appointed *Ḳâḍîs*.

It is significant again that the interregnum that followed the defeat and capture of Bâyezîd I by Tîmûr was followed by another rising, this time in Europe, also led by a *Baba* of the *Ḳalenderî* type, who supported one of the sons of that Sultan in his attempt to secure the throne. The defeat of this movement by another son, who then succeeded as Meḥmed I, naturally intensified the bias of the Sultans against heterodoxy, and widened the breach between them and those of their subjects who looked to the *Babas* for religious leadership. In the end the Sultans were, outwardly at any rate, to have a final triumph at the beginning of the sixteenth century, when Selîm I proscribed Şî'ism in his dominions and massacred all its adherents on whom he could lay hands—this because many of them had taken part in a formidable rising in Anatolia, which had as its aim the extension over that country of the power of Şâh Ismâ'îl, the founder of the *şî'î* Ṣafavid Empire in Persia. These partisans of Şâh Ismâ'îl were known as *ḳizilbaş* (red-heads) because of the red *dervîş* caps they affected as a token of their allegiance to the Imâms;[3] and since that time the term *ḳizilbaş* has been applied in Turkey to all adherents of rural heterodoxy. But from the time of its proscription by Selîm, the political importance of this type of heterodoxy declined, though another rebellion that

[1] 'For the activities of the *dervîşes* in 'colonizing' the European provinces see Barkan, 'Istilâ Devrinin Kolonizatör Türk Dervişleri', in *Vakiflar Dergisi*, ii (Ankara, 1942).

[2] Köprülüzade, *Les Origines du Bektachisme*, 20; *Anadoluda Islâmiyet*, 63–64; Wittek, *Rise of the Ottoman Empire*, 37.

[3] Cf. E. G. Browne, *Literary History of Persia*, iv. 48. For the varieties of caps (called *kulâh*, Persian) worn by the different orders see Brown, *The Darvishes*, 59–62, and for their significance, ibid. 99–104.

took place almost a century later seems to have marked a temporary recrudescence of its appeal.[1]

Meanwhile, however, an order of *dervişes* that professed tenets virtually indistinguishable from those of the *Ḳalenderîs*[2] had found its way into the heart of the Ruling Institution and won for heterodoxy, though in a different form, some of the political power these rebellions had failed to achieve for it. When precisely the *Bektaşîs* formed themselves into an order, with *tekkes*, a hierarchy, and all the rest of the apparatus characteristic of 'urban' dervishhood, is uncertain. It was probably about the beginning of the fifteenth century.[3] But the date is not of great importance, since they had long been active in the lands newly acquired by the Ottoman Sultans under the name of *Abdâlânî Rûm*.[4] This name was merely one of those by which some of the inflammatory *Babas* that we have referred to were characterized. The *Abdâlân* were intimately connected with the whole enterprise of military conquest in so far as this was undertaken by the tribesmen among whom they practised, and even after the chief part in that enterprise had been assumed by the Sultan's standing army, manned by slaves, they contrived to establish and maintain a no less close connexion with this too.

It seems probable that the *Abdâlân* first came generally to be known as *Bektâşîs* when they established themselves as a 'settled' order, since they were then obliged, by convention, to adopt some adept of the past as their patron and supposed founder. And nothing was more natural than that they should choose for the purpose Ḥâccî Bektâş, since it has been all but proved that this personage was a disciple of Baba Isḥâḳ, whom he succeeded as leader of the *bâṭinî-ṣûfî* movement among the tribes of Anatolia in the mid-thirteenth century, after the suppression of their first great rebellion against the Selcuḳids.[5] In any case, choose him they did, and built their mother-*tekke* beside his tomb at Ḳirşehir between Anḳara and Ḳayseri in central Anatolia.

Now part of the 'classical' account of the foundation of the Janissaries brings this Ḥâccî Bektâş into the picture. He is said to

[1] Köprülüzade, *Anadoluda Islâmiyet*, 81–85. Cf., too, ibid. 89 sq. for a brilliant account of the growth of subterranean *şî'î* movements in Persia prior to the foundation of the Ṣafavid kingdom and the consequences of the invasion of Tîmûr.

[2] Köprülüzade, *Les Origines du Bektachisme*, 13, 22; J. K. Birge, *The Bektashi Order of Dervishes* (London, 1937), 32.

[3] Köprülüzade, 21; Birge, 51 sqq. It is to be noted that even after this partial metamorphosis the members of the *Bektaşî* order spent much of their time wandering about begging, a habit that was forbidden to other orders (D'Ohsson, iv. 664) except, apparently, the *Rifâ'îs* and some 'foreign' orders. These wandering *dervişes* were known as *sayyâḥ*.

[4] 'Madmen of Rome' (i.e. of the East Roman Empire)—Köprülüzade, 24.

[5] Köprülüzade; Birge, 33 sq.

have blessed the new corps by placing his sleeve on the head of one of its members; and for this reason to have been regarded thereafter as the Janissaries' patron saint. This account is certainly legendary—Ḥâccî Bektaş, apart from anything else, died long before the Janissaries were ever thought of. But it evidently enshrines a truth, that the *Abdâlân* took the new infantry under their spiritual protection, as they had hitherto taken the warrior tribesmen. For the Janissaries did, in fact, ever after, look upon Ḥâccî Bektâş as their patron, so much so that an alternative name for them was 'the Bektâşî soldiery'. The story of the sleeve was invented to account for the peculiar Janissary head-dress, a felt tube fitted on to the head and falling down below the waist behind. For this head-dress was really a shocking witness to the prevalence of Bâṭinism at the time of the corps's foundation. It was, almost certainly, derived from that of the *Aḫîs*.

The formation of the Janissaries was itself to some extent a consequence of the growing 'civilization' of the Sultans. As we observed earlier, the notion of a slave corps was attractive to them partly because they might be assured of its exclusive attachment to themselves. The first enrolment of the corps occurred just at the point where the Ottoman enterprise began definitely to take on a dynastic, opposed to the popular religious, character that it had hitherto displayed. Whether consciously or not, therefore, the *Abdâlân-Bektâşîs* delivered a master stroke in carrying their influence into this new sphere. And it was probably almost the last moment—before the Sultans turned definitely orthodox—at which they could have managed it. It seems probable, indeed, that the formation of their order was in the nature of a politic camouflage; for compared to the 'active' *Babas*, the 'settled' orders were held to be respectable.

The heterodox Ṣûfism of earlier centuries had appealed to the Turkish tribesmen, as they first immigrated into the lands of Islâm, on account of its latitudinarianism. But the Janissary corps was manned by men in a similar case, of more or less compulsory conversion; so the same doctrine, preached now by the *Bektâşîs*, was admirably framed to appeal to them. The Janissaries, as long as they remained a slave corps, were almost to a man of Christian origin. It is not surprising, therefore, to find that Bektâşism has several features of a quasi-Christian character, such as the belief in a Trinity—Allah, Muḥammad, and 'Alî—and a belief in the efficacy of confession and absolution.[1] It was a tenet of the whole

[1] Similar beliefs and practices were characteristic of the heretical sect of the Ḥurûfîya—see *Encyc. of Islam*, art. 'Ḥurūfīs' (Huart). L. Massignon relates these practices to survivals or resuscitations of *Ḥallâcî* Ṣûfism in both *Ḥurûfî* and *Bektaşî* circles, as shown by the poems of the celebrated *Bektaşî* poet Yûnus Emre (d. *c.* 1340) and the *Ḥurûfî* poet 'Imâd Nesîmî (d. 1417), and by the prominent

ultra-*bâṭinî-ṣûfî* movement that all religions are equally valid; so that the adoption of such beliefs and practices did not involve any compromise of its original character. Indeed, some of the Christian-like features that Bektâşism displayed were common to other branches of the movement. And in the later centuries of Ottoman rule over what had formerly been the orthodox Christian world, the prevalence of a more or less disguised heterodoxy of this type —outside the actual sphere of Bektâşism—among all the lower classes of the Moslem population led to a curious development. The veneration of saints and a belief in the magical efficacy of sites and objects connected with them was perhaps the most marked feature both of Orthodox Christianity and this heterodox Muhammadanism in their more popular forms. It came to pass, consequently, that throughout the Balkans and Asia Minor many saints and shrines were venerated and visited in common by the adherents of both religions. But their complete amalgamation was prevented, partly by the maintenance of language differences as a badge of religious distinction, and the existence in each camp of upper classes that upheld the 'exclusivist' claims of their respective faiths. Even more important in this respect, perhaps, was the political organization, in the mid-fifteenth century, of all the *Ḏimmîs* in separate confessional communities—a matter with which we shall deal in the next chapter. For this created a situation in which it was to the interest both of the Ottoman government and of the communities themselves to guard against the reception of *Ḏimmîs* into the fold of Islâm on any considerable scale. Onwards from the early sixteenth century, moreover, when Syria, the Ḥijâz, and Egypt were incorporated in the Empire, there appears to have been an influx from those countries into Istanbul of Ḥanefî doctors, who still further stiffened the Sultans and their government in orthodoxy. This rendered finally impossible any hopes that might have existed until then of an assimilation of Christian and Moslem. Indeed, it was a strong contributing factor to the development that we shall notice, of a growing antagonism between them.

Perhaps because of this increased attachment of the Sultans to orthodoxy, the *Bektâşîs* maintained, in later times at any rate—we do not know enough of their early history to say whether they had always done so—that they, like all the other orders of the Ottoman Empire, were a *Sunnî* order, and paraded a reverence for the immediate successor of the Prophet, Abû Bakr, since it was characteristic of heterodoxy to execrate his memory, together with that of the next two Caliphs, 'Umar and 'Uṯmân. In private, on

place taken in the *Bektaşî* ceremony of repentance by the space called the 'gallows of el-Ḥallâc' (*Dâr-e Manṣûr*); 'La Légende de Hallacé Mansur en pays turcs', in *Revue des Études Islamiques*, 1941–6, 67 sqq.; and cf. Birge, 170.

the other hand—and the *Bektâşîs* were secretive to a far greater extent than most *dervîş* orders[1]—they professed a doctrine that conserved many *şî'î* features;[2] and whether because their dissimulation was effective, or because their connexion with the Janissaries preserved them from persecution by the *Sunnî* authorities, they escaped the general ban upon their co-religionists, and maintained their heretical hold on this vital part of the Ruling Institution. The connexion was close. Thus the Master-General of the Order held the honorary rank of *Çorbacî* in one of the Janissary companies; and eight *Bektâşî dervîşes*, lodged in the Janissary barracks at Istanbul, were charged with the duties of daily reciting prayers for the prosperity of the Empire and its arms, and on occasions of ceremony of preceding the *Ağa* on foot, dressed in habits of green cloth, with folded hands, crying out responses in chorus. But it appears that official recognition to the *Bektâşî*-Janissary connexion was not accorded until near the end of the sixteenth century. If so, it presumably became closer than ever thereafter. And as the lower classes of Moslems from whom the Janissaries gradually came exclusively to be recruited during the seventeenth century were in any case traditionally inclined to heterodoxy, if of a less pronounced kind than theirs, the *Bektâşîs* can only have increased their influence as a result of this process. It is remarkable, in any case, that though, after the destruction of the Janissaries (if we may look into the future from the point of view of our survey), the government took stern measures also against the *Bektâşîs*—the orthodox doctors heaping epithets of abuse upon them as scandalous heretics—until this time no word was uttered, still less was any action taken, against them. On the contrary, their 'Master-General', whose post, by the eighteenth century, had for some time been hereditary, was confirmed in it, like the Masters-General of other orders, by the *Şeyhü 'l-Islâm* himself.[3]

So much for the *Bekṭâşîs*. We may now consider the other *ṭarîka* that occupied a special place among the Ottoman Turks—the *Mevlevî*. The *Mevlevî* is perhaps the order best known in Europe; for it is that of the Dancing Dervishes. This picturesque but misleading name has of course been given on account of the striking and peculiar exercise that its members perform as part of their discipline. It consists in each adept's revolving on his right foot

[1] Theirs was the only order that held its exercises in private—see D'Ohsson, iv. 657.

[2] It is notable, for instance, that they observed the characteristic *şî'î* ceremony of the '*Aşûrâ*—D'Ohsson, iv. 655; Birge, 169.

[3] D'Ohsson, iv, 667–8, 673–5; *Encyc. of Islam*, art. 'Bekṭāsh'; Köprülüzade, op. cit., and *Anadoluda Islâmiyet*, 52 sq., 85–88.

till dizziness gives way to ecstasy. This so-called dancing is therefore nothing more than the particular method adopted by the order for the inducement of this state, as others have adopted the repetition of words and even the consumption of drugs.[1] This is not to say that the efforts of any of the orders to attain to mystical illumination have been confined to such mechanical means. Their use has invariably been accompanied by practices, more generally recognized as religious, such as prayer and fasting.[2] But as the former exercises are the more peculiar, so they have attracted greater attention. They have always been regarded with distrust by the strictly orthodox, however, particularly when Ṣûfism itself has not been accepted as legitimate. And the *Mevlevî* turning-exercise has had the additional defect in the eyes of such orthodox observers of being accompanied by the performance of music and the recitation of poetry, activities only less frivolous and reprehensible than dancing itself.[3]

Nevertheless, the *Mevlevîs* under the Ottoman régime, in its later stages at any rate, enjoyed an incomparably greater favour with the authorities than the *Bektaşîs* and their like. For the *Mevlevî* order was of 'urban' origin; its members were not of the active type of *dervîş*; its doctrine was far too intellectual to appeal to the tribesmen; and consequently it inspired no revolutionary movements. Indeed, it always did its best to keep on the right side of the government.

Celâlü'd-Dîn Rûmî, the great thirteenth-century poet and mystic, from whose title *Mevlânâ*, 'our lord', the order took its name, settled at the Selcuḳid court of Ḳonya, where he attracted a large following not only among the *Ṣûfîs* and *Aḫîs*, but also among government servants and even theologians and men of the law. That he should have been on good terms with the latter is the more remarkable in that he adopted the metaphysical system of Ibn el-ʻArabî, to which, as we have remarked, they had good reason to take exception. But the particular favour with which he was regarded by the Selcuḳid prince of the time no doubt compelled their complaisance to some extent. Also the chief cleavage of religious opinion at this period was between the two types of *taṣawwuf*, the 'rural' and the 'urban', rather than between *taṣawwuf* and strictly orthodox theology. In any case the result of this cleavage was that the activities most deprecated by Celâlü'd-Dîn were those of the *Babas*, among whom, dramatically enough in view of the future, was Ḥâccî Bektaş himself. Now Mevlânâ did not, any more than

[1] Cf. *Encyc. of Islam*, art. 'Ṭarīḳa'.

[2] See for a description of *dervîş* fasting D'Ohsson, iv. 658–60.

[3] Cf. D'Ohsson, iv. 670, and the very extensive literature in Arabic and Turkish on the lawfulness or illegality of music in religious exercises.

Ḥâccî Bektaş, found an order, the foundation of the *Mevlevî ṭarîḳa* being the work of his successors. But the members of the order in the centuries that followed retained his antagonism to the *Abdâlân* and later to the *Bektaşîs*. They threw in their lot with the government and did all they could to emphasize their orthodoxy, keeping in the shade those features of their doctrine that were calculated to displease the orthodox theologians.[1] Perhaps on this account their *ṭarîḳa* attained its greatest prestige in the later centuries of the Ottoman régime; for, as we have seen, the Ḳaraman-oğlu dynasty of Ḳonya, which remained the *Mevlevî* headquarters, was inclined to favour the 'rural' *dervîşes* above the 'urban'. At any rate the *Mevlevîs* were in high favour with the Ottoman authorities by the end of the sixteenth century. In 1634 Murâd IV made the assignment that we have mentioned of the Ḳonya *cizya* to the mother *tekke*;[2] and during the reign of his successor, Ibrâhîm, the *Mevlevîs* seem to have acquired so influential a position as to have been able to bring about the deposition of that eccentric Sultan and to claim for their 'Grand Master' (the *Çelebi* or *Mollâ Ḫünkâr*, as he was most often called) the right, which, lapsing in the interval, came in the nineteenth century to be generally acknowledged, of girding the Sultan on his accession with a sword—the ceremony corresponding to coronation.

We thus observe both the *Bektaşîs* and the *Mevlevîs* to have become more closely associated with the Ruling Institution in the time of its decay. The explanation appears to be that the *Mevlevîs* were resorted to by the Sultans to counterbalance the influence of the *Bektaşîs*, as the latter's protégés, the Janissaries, became more and more unruly. Unhappily this increased influence of the *dervîş* orders seems to have come too late to check another development of the age: a growth of Moslem fanaticism and a worsening of the relations between Moslems and *Ḏimmîs*—for the *Mevlevîs* were scarcely less broad-minded than the *Bektaşîs* in respect of other religions. The development can be accounted for to some extent by the growing fear of Christian Europe among the Moslems. Also the abandonment of the *devşirme* system may, paradoxically, have contributed to it, by drawing a sharper line between the communities. Finally, it is possible that, as they came to terms with it, orthodoxy induced a more rigid spirit among the *dervîşes* themselves. But this fanaticism seems to have been more prevalent in the towns than in the country. As we have seen when dealing with the trade guilds, it showed itself in their sphere. And by this time Bektaşism had become almost as 'urban' in its range of influence

[1] Köprülüzade, *Les Origines*, 17; *Anadoluda Islâmiyet*, 67 sq.
[2] The *Mevlevîs* were the best endowed of all the orders—D'Ohsson, iv. 665–6.

as the orders that were urban in origin. The Moslem country people and particularly the nomad tribes, the *yürüks*, remained no less heretical than before, though no longer apt to revolt: they were still *ḳizilbaş* in the general estimation, though in some places names such as *taḫtaci*, 'woodcutter', indicative of a tribal calling, were applied to them.

The number of *dervîş* orders continued to increase right down to the eighteenth century. D'Ohsson, writing at the end of that century, enumerates no less than thirty-six, but other sources double or even quadruple this figure.[1] The great majority of these were offshoots of older *ṭarîḳas*, formed during the Ottoman period, and important chiefly as an indication of the immense extension of their influence to embrace all classes and regions. Many outstanding *Şeyḫs* formed their own sub-orders, some of which had a purely local appeal or rapidly disappeared, but others survived and even spread to neighbouring provinces and regions. We cannot, however, leave the great *ṭarîḳas* altogether unnoticed, since, although they played no political role comparable to that of the *Bektâşîs* and *Mevlevîs*, their members were far more numerous, and their spread in the Ottoman dominions was a social factor of the greatest importance in that, unlike these two orders, they embraced both Turks and Arabs.[2]

The *Ḳâdirî* is actually the oldest regular order of all still in existence, having been founded in Bağdâd about A.D. 1200,[3] and the most widely spread in the Moslem world. Since it was regarded as the most orthodox of all *ṭarîḳas*, it may be significant that it was introduced into Asia Minor and Europe only in the course of the sixteenth century, but it quickly gained a large following at the capital and elsewhere.[4] The second important order of 'Irâḳî origin, the *Rifâ'î*, was, by contrast, remarkable for the tortures to which its devotees subjected themselves—the *Rifâ'îs* being the so-called Howling *Dervîşes*, whose practice it was to stab and burn themselves without coming to harm. It spread into Anatolia in the thirteenth and fourteenth centuries,[5] and later into Bosnia, but was more popular in the Arab provinces, and especially in Egypt, where a sub-order, the *Aḥmedî* or *Bedawî*, founded in the

[1] D'Ohsson, iv. 616 sq.; cf. Brown, *The Darvishes*, 80–84. Evliyâ Efendi (tr. Hammer, vol. i, part ii, p. 29) reckons over 140; el-Ṭawîl, *el-Taṣawwuf fî Miṣr*, 75, speaks of nearly eighty in Egypt in the Ottoman period.

[2] The *Mevlevîs* had *tekkes* only in Aleppo, Damascus, Cairo, and other towns where there was a resident Turkish population (cf. Murâdî, i. 329; iii. 116). The *Bektâşî* order had scarcely even a footing in Egypt (Cabartî, ii. 144/iv. 282–3), apart from the famous Ḳayğusuz *tekke* south of the Citadel.

[3] *Encyc. of Islam*, art. 'Ḳādirīya' (Margoliouth).

[4] Brown, 474–7, lists 37 *tekkes* of this order in Istanbul.

[5] Köprülüzade, *Ilk Mutasavviflar*, 228 sqq. Brown, 477–8, lists 18 *tekkes* in Istanbul.

thirteenth century,[1] became itself the mother of some score of sub-orders.[2] It was the *Şeyh̲* of another *Rifâ'î* sub-order, the *Sa'dî*,[3] who performed the celebrated ceremony of the *dôsa* at Cairo,[4] in which he rode on horseback over the prostrate bodies of his *dervîşes* and others; and this sub-order apparently eclipsed the other *Rifâ'î* congregations in popularity at the capital.[5] A powerful rival to these orders in Egypt was the North African orthodox *Şâd̲ilî* order, with its dozen or so sub-orders, but they had a relatively small following in the Asiatic provinces (except Arabia) and in Turkey.[6]

The two other *ṭarîḳas* which claim our attention were of Central Asian origin, and did not appear in the Ottoman Empire until late in the fifteenth or early in the sixteenth century. Both of them appear to have strong orthodox leanings, in opposition to the latitudinarian or heterodox tendencies of the older Turkish orders, and they were especially favoured by the *'Ulemâ* in consequence. It is not surprising, therefore, to find them making such rapid progress in Turkey that already in the seventeenth century Evliyâ Efendi could write, 'Well-informed men know that the great *Şeyh̲s* may be classed in two principal orders—that of *Ḫalwetî*, and that of *Naḳşbendî*.'[7]

The *Naḳşbendî* order was founded originally in Transoxania[8] and seems to have been introduced into Turkey by *Şeyh̲s* from Boh̲ârâ. It had a strong footing also in India, where it enjoyed the support of the Muğal emperors, and thus constituted a link with the other great *Sunnî* empire; and although the relations between the Indian and Ottoman branches are still obscure, the Syrian lodges of the order were, in fact, founded by a missionary from India.[9] In the eighteenth century the order acquired a great

[1] See p. 184, n. 2 above.

[2] None of these appear to have had any following outside Egypt; but Brown, 459, lists two Bedawî *tekkes* in Istanbul.

[3] Founded by the Syrian *Şeyh̲* Sa'd el-dîn el-Cibâwî in the fourteenth century.

[4] Ar. *dawsa*, 'trampling'; see Lane, *Modern Egyptians*, ch. x, for a description of the ceremony.

[5] Cf. D'Ohsson, iv. 676. Brown, 478–80, lists 27 Sa'dî *tekkes* in Istanbul.

[6] *Encyc. of Islam*, art. 'Shādhilīya' (Margoliouth). Brown, 480, lists only two *Şâd̲ilî tekkes* in Istanbul. Among the Egyptian sub-orders one of the most influential was the *Wafâ'î*, a 'reformed' sub-order founded in the fourteenth century by a family of *Şerîfs*. The *Şâd̲ilî* order also produced the most remarkable figure among the later Arabic mystics, 'Abd el-Wahhâb el-Şa'rânî (d. 1565); see Arberry, *Sufism*, 123–8.

[7] Tr. Hammer, vol. i, part ii, p. 29.

[8] Here it had, curiously enough, an early link with the very different *Bektâşî* order in the person of Aḥmed Yesevî: Köprülüzade Mehmet Fuat, *Ilk Mutasavvîflar*, 123.

[9] Murâd el-Boh̲ârî (d. 1720), the great-grandfather of the historian Murâdî (so frequently cited in these pages): see *Encyc. of Islam*, *Supplement*, art. 'Murādī'.

reputation in Arab Asia through the journeys and writings of the Damascene *Şeyḫ* ʿAbdu'l-Ġanî el-Nâbulusî, who ranks among the greatest of the later *Ṣûfîs*.[1] Its followers were enjoined to neglect none of the observances prescribed by the Sacred Law, and their chief exercises (in which some observers have detected Indian influences) were the practice of silent meditation and 'holding of the breath'. According to D'Ohsson, Naḳşbendism was much affected in his day by laymen of every class, who engaged themselves to pray in private every day and in community once a week; so that, in his eyes, it differed from all the other orders in having the character of a mere religious association, the members of which were not distinguished by any special dress.[2]

During the eighteenth century the *Naḳşbendîs* became allied to some extent with the other order mentioned by Evliyâ Efendi—the *Ḫalwetî*, so called because of their practice of 'retreat' for periods of up to forty days, fasting from dawn to sunset in a solitary cell.[3] The early affiliations of the order were peculiarly unpropitious from the orthodox and Ottoman point of view, since it began as a sub-order of the 'illuminationist' *Suhrawardî* order,[4] and spread first in Şîrwân and among the Türkmens of the 'Black Sheep' in Āẕerbâycân, in close contact with its sister sub-order, the heterodox *Ṣafawî*. After the conquest of Istanbul it gained a powerful following among the population and in the Ottoman military forces. Sub-orders were founded in many parts of Anatolia and Syria, and two of its leading *Şeyḫs* devoted themselves to the spiritual welfare of the *ocaḳs* in Egypt after the conquest.[5] Their activism and dubious orthodoxy brought the *Ḫalwetîs* at first under suspicion of the authorities and into controversy with the *ʿUlemâ*, but they appear to have moved gradually towards the relatively orthodox brands of Ṣûfism. In the seventeenth and eighteenth centuries the *Ḫalwetî* was the most active and enterprising order, sustained by a succession of outstanding *Şeyḫs* and scholars, such as Niyâzî Miṣrî, whose bold attempts to stem the corruption at court led to repeated exile, and Muṣṭafâ el-Bekrî, a Damascene *Şeyḫ* (d. 1749),

[1] d. 1731: Murâdî, iii. 30 sqq.; Brockelmann, *Ges. d. Arab. Litt.* ii. 345–8; *Encyc. of Islam*², s.v.

[2] D'Ohsson, iv. 627–9; cf. Köprülüzade Mehmet Fuat, *Anadoluda Islâmiyet*, 127; *Ilk Mutasavviflar*, 66, 68, note to 124–5, 187; Murâdî, i. 107, 172 and *passim*. Brown (470–3) lists 52 *Naḳşbendî tekkes* in Istanbul.

[3] Ar. *ḫalwa*, 'solitude', from *ḫalâ*, 'he was alone'. The epithet was given to the original founders of the order. The *Ḫalwetî* order is to be distinguished from the *Celwetî*, also of *Suhrawardî* origin, but of *Ṣafawî* descent through the *Bayramîs*: see p. 199, n. 5 below.

[4] The *Suhrawardîs*, though a powerful order in ʿIrâḳ and India, were represented in Istanbul and Anatolia chiefly by a sub-order, the *Zeynî*, founded at Aleppo by Zeyn el dîn Ḫwâfî (d. 1435).

[5] S. Muḥammad Demirdaş (d. 1524) and S. Ibrâhîm Gulşenî (d. 1527), both of whom founded important sub-orders.

through whose missionary journeys and labours the order gained a large, though temporary, extension in Syria and Egypt.[1] Several of the most influential Egyptian *Şeyḫs* founded, under his inspiration, *Ḫalwetî* sub-orders,[2] and the head of the order became, early in the nineteenth century, hereditary Chief *Şeyḫ* (*Şeyḫ el-Meşâyiḫ*) of the *ṣûfî* orders in Egypt. Judging by the number of convents and *tekkes* belonging to the order, the *Ḫalwetî tarîka* was by far the most popular in Istanbul and Anatolia.[3]

Besides the 'regular' and 'irregular' orders which we have surveyed, there was another *dervîş* movement which is mentioned neither by D'Ohsson nor by the other eighteenth-century writers, for the good reason that it was esoteric in their time. This was a revival of Melâmetism, now called Melâmism.[4] Its original author was a certain Ḥâccî Bayrâm, who flourished in the mid-fifteenth century at Anḳara.[5] Ḥâccî Bayrâm and his successors resembled the *Melâmetîs* of old in cultivating no special dress, in living 'normal' lives, and in scorning hypocrisy. In spite of their unostentatious habits, consequently, their candour soon got them into trouble with the authorities. For this candour obliged them openly to preach the monism that the *dervîşes* in general subscribed to but had the tact to disguise. Public attention was drawn to the new *ṭarîḳa* by a series of imprisonments and executions. But these merely attracted fresh adherents and during the sixteenth century, after a further stringent reform,[6] the doctrine was propagated all over Rumelia, but particularly in Bosnia and in the Adrianople

[1] Murâdî, iv. 190 sqq. and *passim*; Depont et Coppolani, *Les Confréries*, 369–82; Brockelmann, ii. 348–51. There is an Arabic history of the Bekrî family, *Beyt ul-Ṣiddîḳ*, by Muḥ. Tawfîḳ el-Bekrî (Cairo, 1905).

[2] The most important of these was that founded by S. Muḥ. el-Ḥifnî, *Şeyḫ* of el-Azhar 1757–67 (Cabartî, i. 289–304/ii. 284–305), one of whose Algerian students, Muḥammad b. 'Abd el-Raḥmân (d. 1794), became an active missionary of Ḫalwetism in his own country, where he founded the *Raḥmânî* sub-order: Depont et Coppolani, 382 sqq.; L. Rinn, *Marabouts et Khouan*, 452–80.

[3] Brown (462–9) lists 67 *tekkes* in Istanbul for the main order, exclusive of those belonging to the sub-orders, of which the *Sunbulî* alone had fifteen (ibid. 480–2). Evliyâ Efendi (tr. Hammer, ii. 8) notes the preponderance of *Ḫalwetî tekkes* at Bursa.

[4] We use the term 'movement' of Melâmism advisedly, since it was not an order properly speaking, for not only did members of other orders sometimes belong to it, but it had no *tekkes*, &c., or particular ceremonies of its own: Abdül Baki, esp. 190–3, 194. See also Brown, 225–41, where he gives a translation of a *Melâmî* treatise.

[5] See Evliyâ Efendi, ii. 231, 233–4. The order which he founded was a reformed branch of the *Ṣafawî* sub-order of the *Suhrawardîs*.

[6] By Ş. Ḥamza of Bursa; hence the *Melâmis* were generally ḳnown as *Ḥamzâwîs*. Whether the *Ḥamzâwîs* separated from the *Bayramîs* seems to be uncertain. The reform of Ş. Ḥamza may have been intended to reorganize the original *Beyramî* congregations after the formation by Pîr Uftâda (d. 1580) of a new sub-order, called *Celwetî*, which appears to have been strongly influenced by Ḫalwetism, and is sometimes reckoned as a *Ḫalwetî* sub-order. Its most notable representative was the poet and scholar Ismâ'îl Ḥaḳḳî of Bursa (d. 1724).

area. Moreover, it was adopted by the *Bölük* cavalry, the 'standing' *Sipâhîs*, apparently in imitation of the Janissary adherence to Bektâşism, and contributed, so it seems, to exacerbate the rivalry that existed between them.[1]

Even more remarkable was the *ṭarîḳa*'s history during the first half of the seventeenth century, when, besides spreading to Arabia, it came to number a Grand *Vezîr*[2] and actually a *Şeyḫ ü 'l-Islâm*[3] among its adherents. But in 1662 its then head came to attract so many followers as to arouse the jealousy of other *dervîş Şeyḫs* and certain learned men; and though he was then over ninety years old, he and forty of his disciples were publicly strangled and their bodies thrown into the sea.[4] After this the directors of the order changed their tactics. They concealed their identity, and pursued their activities in secret.[5] But it continued in being right up to and past the time of our survey, and still gained adherents in high places. Early in the eighteenth century indeed the actual leadership was held first by another *Şeyḫ ü 'l-Islâm*[6] and then by another Grand *Vezîr*.[7]

Apart from general indications of the relative 'orthodoxy' of the main orders, we have not, in the preceding account, attempted to define at all closely the distinctive doctrines of each. This would, in fact, be a most difficult and delicate task; for even were we to set out the precise views of the founders of each *ṭarîḳa*, it by no means follows that in the course of centuries these views remained intact. On the contrary, all the evidence suggests that their chief characteristic (as was to be expected from the individualist and experiential basis of Ṣûfism) was an extreme flexibility. Several which began as 'heterodox' orders ended up as pillars of orthodoxy, just as, conversely, the *Ṣafawî* organization which converted Persia to Şîʿism had begun as an 'orthodox' order. But such external transpositions, however important, present only one aspect of this process. Whereas, at the beginning of this chapter, we were able to distinguish several strands in early Ṣûfism, these had, by the time with which we are concerned, become so interwoven as to be inseparable. The assimilative process was carried further by the growing custom of combining membership of more than one *ṭarîḳa*. Multiple affiliations were the rule among the learned, and

[1] Abdülbaki, 169–71.

[2] Ḫalîl Paşa, d. 1630, after having held office under four Sultans—Aḥmed I, Muṣṭafâ I, ʿOṣmân II, and Murâd IV: Abdül Baki, 136.

[3] Muṣṭafâ Efendi Ebu 'l-Meyâmîn (1546–1605): ibid. 135.

[4] These executions were ordered by the second of the Köprülü Grand *Vezîrs*, Fâḍil Aḥmed Paşa, under Meḥmed IV.

[5] Abdülbaki, 173.

[6] Paşmaḳçi-Zâde Seyyid ʿAlî Efendi, d. 1712.

[7] Şehîd ʿAlî Paşa, killed in battle 1716, under Aḥmed III (notice in ʿAṭâ, *Ta'rîḫ*, ii. 84–100).

already in the sixteenth century an illuminate like el-Şa'rânî could boast that he had been regularly admitted into twenty-six.[1] Every new order or sub-order probably represented yet another eclectic or syncretic rearrangement of the diverse pieces. Islâm in the eighteenth century was like a richly coloured tapestry into whose pattern had gone not only *Ḳur'ân* and *Ḥadîṯ*, *şer'î* puritanism, *melâmî* ethics, *Ḥallâcî* exaltation,[2] *bâṭinî* interpretation, the monism of Ibn el-'Arabî, the aesthetic sensibility of Rûmî, and the hypnotic or thaumaturgic rituals of the ecstatic orders, but also astrology, divination, wonder-working, and, above all, the cult of saints, dead and alive.

The conception of a hierarchy of living saints with whom lay the direction of the world (referred to earlier in this chapter) was common to all those, and they were now the vast majority, if not totality, of the Moslem population, who subscribed to *taṣawwuf* in its various forms, though the adepts might not agree on the identity of the persons composing it. In thc eyes of the generality, accordingly, the saints living and dead were paramount in the world and its history. No secular authority could compete with them for the allegiance of believers. But the very fact that the saintly hierarchy was known as 'People of the Unseen' implied that its composition was a secret at any rate to the profane. Anyone might be a saint in disguise; and evidences of saintship were eagerly looked for. Naturally, the best-placed candidates were, among the living, the 'professional' practitioners of *taṣawwuf*, and, among the dead, apart from Patriarchs, Prophets, and *dervîşes* revered as saints in their lifetime, those whose tombs were found, often by accident, to repay visitation for cures and favours. In fine, the band of saints was a large one, and their cult on the whole more vital than that of the mosque.

But again, by this date, as we have pointed out, we cannot always clearly distinguish the mosque from the *tekke*. The *'Ulemâ* themselves were convinced believers in saintship, and even candidates for its honours. They, no less than the *ṣûfî Şeyḫs*, expounded the mysteries of absorption in God (*fanâ*) and monism (*waḥdat el-wucûd*) to the faithful; they, no less eagerly than the populace, devoured the literature and oral reports of miracles and wonders and, if perhaps with more circumspection, practised the *ṣûfî* rituals. The few who dared to contradict the claims or pretensions of the saints were censured by their fellow *'Ulemâ* and sometimes in danger of their lives from mob violence and official zeal.[3] *Taṣaw-*

[1] El-Ṭawîl, *el-Taṣawwuf fî Miṣr*, 75, quoting *el-Manâḳib el-Kubrâ*, 66.

[2] Turkish piety had found a means of reconciling even this with a justification of *şer'î* puritanism: see the *ḥikâya* quoted by L. Massignon in *Revue des Études Islamiques*, 1941–6, 82.

[3] See above, p. 160, n. 1; and cf. Murâdî, ii. 325.

wuf, as we have remarked, had by transforming Islâm given it new life and above all a social cohesion which puritan orthodoxy had been unable to supply. The effects were universal and cumulative; amongst Moslems of every occupation and class the room of the soul was warmly, perhaps even too cosily, furnished.

But the rank luxuriance of the *dervîş* institution had to be paid for, both literally and figuratively, and in both cases the price was a heavy one. In addition to the young men from both cities and villages who thronged the *medrasas* and, in default of better occupation, constituted the unruly bands of *softâs*, thousands of others entered the *tekkes* as postulants, and their services were lost to the community. The harder life became for the cultivators, the greater the temptation to find the easy way out. *Tekkes* multiplied in the towns; already in 1638, according to the official enumeration quoted by Evliyâ Efendi, there were 557 'great *ḫânḳâhs*' in Istanbul and 6,000 smaller *dervîş* cells and rooms.[1] For the maintenance and endowment of these establishments, Sultans, *Vezîrs*, and officials and wealthy men of all ranks constituted *waḳfs* of land and urban property, and as time went on the number of such *waḳfs* grew inordinately.[2] The strains which this imposed on the economic welfare of the Empire and the problems to which it was to give rise have been indicated in the preceding chapter.

The spiritual cost was possibly heavier still. Every institution carries within it the germ of its own corruption; and while we cannot assent to the unreserved condemnation which modern Moslem reformers pour upon the *ṣûfî* movement, the evidences of its corruption by excess are overwhelming. For genuine mystical experience was, of course, of comparatively rare occurrence, nor could the *ṣûfî* discipline be guaranteed to induce or develop it in all its practitioners. 'Not every *dervîş* is a *Ṣûfî*', says the saint-loving Evliyâ Efendi, 'although [he adds] he may be a true unitarian *dervîş*.'[3] What the people, on the look-out for sainthood, most valued were evidences of supernatural powers in the adepts.[4] The literature of the seventeenth and eighteenth centuries teems with saintly personages of all types and classes and with instances of their miraculous or prophetic powers and their special 'graces'.[5] But

[1] Tr. Hammer, vol. i, part ii, p. 103. The same census gives 74 'great mosques of the Sultans', 1,985 'great mosques of the *Vezîrs*', 6,990 'small mosques of the town quarters', and 6,665 'other mosques great and small'. Evliyâ himself reckons 300 *ḫânḳâhs* in Brusa; ibid. ii. 8.

[2] Cf. Mustafa Akdağ in *Belleten*, xiv, no. 55, p. 363.

[3] Vol. i, part ii, p. 99. His nickname of *Evliyâ* (plural of *velî*, 'saint') was given to him because of his 'affection for the saints'.

[4] D'Ohsson, iv. 677, 679.

[5] For example, a Rifâ'î *dervîş* at Damascus who wore iron rings sunk into his arms and fingers claimed that they represented the cities of Islâm. One day a ring was pulled off by force, and shortly afterwards news arrived that 'a great

such evidences could not be produced to order; and so the temptation to produce them by fraud was irresistible. Already the juggleries and impostures of the *dervîşes* were bringing the orders into disrepute among the more enlightened of the *'Ulemâ* and the laity.[1] But meanwhile the 'man in the street', and even more the 'man in the field', had come to place their faith far more in the efficacy of *dervîş* miracles than in the discharge of their devotions as prescribed by the law. Islâm in practice was riddled with superstition,[2] and so in no very brave trim to withstand contact with ideas from another sphere, where superstitions of a not dissimilar character had already been largely exploded—even if others were taking their place.

The mentality of the Moslems, and to some extent, by contagion, that of their non-Moslem fellow subjects, were thus very largely influenced by *şûfî* teaching. But since the real incompatibility of much of this teaching with the Sacred Law, as it represented the earlier traditions of Islâm, was not recognized, and since, as we have observed, Islâm now embodied two antagonistic systems masquerading as one, the attitude to life and the conduct that one of these systems would otherwise have induced were modified by the competing prestige of the other. The prestige of the *Şerî'a* was on the whole stronger among the upper classes, the 'rulers'; the prestige, or at any rate the influence on conduct, of *taşawwuf* among the lower, the 'ruled', with certain social consequences which we may, in conclusion, attempt to sum up.

First, *şûfî* 'latitudinarianism' seems to have allowed the people to indulge in certain pleasures upon which the *Şerî'a* frowns—for instance in musical performances. As regards the 'home-lands' of the Empire—Rumelia and Anatolia—at any rate, the Chevalier D'Ohsson remarks on the passionate addiction of the people of these provinces to music, the *Mevlevî dervîşes* being the most sought-after performers. The use of a musical accompaniment to their exercises—though it was not, in fact, confined to their order[3] —had been adopted by the founders of the *Mevlevî ṭarîḳa*, indeed, largely because the people of Anatolia were known to be so much addicted to the art.[4] Then in the matters of wine-drinking, coffee-drinking, tobacco-smoking, and the consumption of opium and *ḥaşîş*, the prohibitions of the Sacred Law seem to have been very

city in Europe' had been seized by the Christians: Murâdî, ii. 4. See also Evliyâ, vol. i, part ii, pp. 25–28.

[1] Cabartî, i. 48–50, 78–80/i. 116–120, 187–9; and cf. D'Ohsson, iv. 648.

[2] D'Ohsson, 672, 679–83.

[3] For instance, it was used by the *Rifâ'îs* (see Ibn Baṭṭûṭa's account of a performance at the mother convent of the order in the 'Irâḳ in the late thirteenth century, ii. 4, 5), and is said to have been actually introduced as a *dervîş* practice by the founder of the *Ḳâdirî* order—see D'Ohsson, iv. 656. Cf. Abdül Baki, 25.

[4] D'Ohsson, iv. 414 sq.

widely disregarded. Coffee and tobacco, of course, are unknown to it; and caused the *'Ulemâ* much searching of heart. In both cases they appear to have felt that the spirit of the *Şerî'a* was against the consumption of these commodities. But as on this point there was no letter to appeal to, in the end they bowed to popular demand. How far this demand was merely human, how far it was influenced by *dervîş* broad-mindedness, is hard to say. But in the case of wine and drugs the *dervîşes* certainly led the way. The prohibition of wine has always been flouted in Moslem countries—the annals of the Caliphate are full of references to wine-drinking, and many of the best poets, Arabic, Persian, and Turkish, have lavished their talents on the composition of verse in its praise. Yet it has always been considered disreputable, and for this very reason the *Ṣûfîs* in speech and writing used wine as a metaphor for divine grace, just as they used erotic images to express their love of God. In this convention innumerable lines of highly equivocal poetry came to be composed. Is Ḥâfiẓ speaking now of mystical wine—and love—or real? It is often impossible to say. And such confusion was inevitably carried over into practice. Dispensation from the obligations imposed by the *Şerî'a* has always been characteristic of Ṣûfism: it was their disregard of these in particular that aroused the wrath of the orthodox in early days;[1] and among the obligations pleasantest to dispense with was abstinence from wine. D'Ohsson states that whereas the Sultans never drank wine in his day, and government officials and the *'Ulemâ* drank it only with the utmost caution,[2] the lower classes, particularly soldiers and sailors, did so with a freedom circumscribed less by conscience than by the vigilance of the authorities; and the *dervîşes* drank it most unrestrainedly of all.[3] The attitude of the *'Ulemâ* towards the use of narcotics was less definite; they disagreed upon its legality, though most condemned it. Consequently it was much more general, even among the strait-laced, than the use of wine. Indeed, many who desired to give up wine cured themselves of the taste by taking to opium or other drugs. As for the *dervîşes*, some orders used stimulants, as we have mentioned, to further their aim of ecstatic experience, and, in so far, consecrated their use in the eyes of their followers.[4]

Other results of the awe and reverence in which saints and *dervîşes* were held, were the respect generally paid to madmen and the very widespread belief in magic, fortune-telling, predictions, and

[1] Cf. *Encyc. of Islam*, art. 'Ṭarîḳa'.

[2] The famous Grand *Vezîr* Köprülü Fâḍil Aḥmed Paşa is said to have died prematurely from habitual drinking—*Encyc. of Islam*, s.v.

[3] Drinking-houses existed only in quarters inhabited by Christians and were shut on the eve of every feast by the police—D'Ohsson, ii. 231, iv. 52–67.

[4] Ibid. 67–76.

astrology. For madmen were held to be permanently in that state of abstraction from earthly concerns to which the *dervîşes* attained only from time to time and at the cost of a long and painful discipline: they were natural *evliyâ*, so to speak.[1] And as for astrology, fortune-telling, &c., though the practice of such arts was explicitly forbidden by the Law, yet it was universally indulged in, even by the government and the Sultans. The most that the Law countenanced in the way of inquiry into the future was the drawing of omens from the *Ḳur'ân*, and prayer to Heaven for a sign. But its prohibition of astrology had always been even less effective than its prohibition of wine-drinking. As late as the second half of the eighteenth century, major issues of policy were often decided in accordance with the advice of the Head Astrologer; and how little his activities were then held to be illegal may be judged from the fact that this official was actually appointed from among the *'Ulemâ* themselves.[2] The *dervîşeş* cannot perhaps be said to have contributed very much to the belief in astrology—it had no need of their assistance—but the wonders with which they astounded their admirers, the tales of miraculous foresight and divination that fill all the biographies of their saints, their sale of talismans to ward off evil and effect cures, created an atmosphere in which belief in magic and miracles, in superstitions of the most extravagant description, flourished to the almost total exclusion of common sense.

But of all the effects produced by the vulgarization of *taṣawwuf* perhaps the most impressive is one that we have already mentioned —namely, the prevalence of irresponsibility and fatalism. As we have seen, there were economic causes for the growth of corruption in Ottoman society during the seventeenth and eighteenth centuries. But it is noteworthy that these centuries also saw at once a decline of culture and learning, largely as a result of this corruption, and a permeation of the upper classes, among whom corruption had its greatest scope, by *dervîş* influences. And it is hard to avoid the conclusion that these developments were connected: it looks as though the Sacred Law had lost ground in the sphere of morality to its *dervîş* rival. These centuries, it is true, saw the triumph of the high *'Ulemâ* as an aristocracy; and the *'Ulemâ* were the representatives of the *Şerî'a*. But their power was rather political than moral; indeed, many of them were shining examples of corruption. Moreover, by the eighteenth century, as we have seen, it is difficult to draw a line between *dervîşes* and *'Ulemâ*. These circumstances would appear to account very well for another noted by D'Ohsson: that in his day contempt of the Law was held to be a far more

[1] Ibid. i. 313–14. Cf. also the frequent notices of demented 'saints' in Murâdî (i. 43–44, 250, ii. 103, 183, &c.).

[2] D'Ohsson, i. 333–422.

heinous offence, and was punished with far greater severity, than its transgression.[1] Certain practices contrary to the Law indeed were, as we have seen, generally connived at; and negligence and corruption in the administration of justice on the part of the *'Ulemâ* themselves were frequent, if not universal. Yet they insisted with great rigour on the punctual discharge by the people of their religious duties, construing any failure in this respect as evidence of infidelity.

As for the prevalence of fatalism, no European observer of the Ottoman Empire in the eighteenth century fails to dwell on it. For it produced striking results: whole quarters of Istanbul were perpetually being burnt down; every few years the population would be decimated by plague. Yet nothing would make the Moslems build their houses of anything but wood, or take the slightest precautions, for themselves or their families, against infection. They were, it is true, quite inconsistent: for instance they would call in a physician to treat a patient and would do their best to extinguish these conflagrations: what constituted flying in the face of Fate was settled rather by convention than otherwise. The one unpardonable blasphemy was to complain of misfortune: for this was to imply either that an event might occur otherwise than by the will of God, or else that the will of God was unjust. The correct response was an immovable calm and a reference to *Ḳismet* or *Taḳdîr*.[2]

The effects of this attitude to events were not wholly bad. It gave the Moslems an almost incomparable capacity for bearing misfortune with equanimity. And in all the misfortunes that were to befall them this was no mean advantage. But this very contentment with things as they were precluded the possibility of their striving to better their lot. Hence it is that all reforms were to be imposed from above, by leaders infected with another spirit—and not, as is sometimes stated, because the Sultans alone enjoyed political power, and held down a population of slaves under their despotism. In the eighteenth century, as we have remarked, the most powerful elements in the Empire were the Janissaries—now composed almost entirely of artisans and representative of popular Ṣûfism—and the *'Ulemâ*. In the face of a combination between the two, the Sultans were to have the utmost difficulty in imposing their will.

[1] D'Ohsson, i. 170, 328–31.
[2] Arabic *ḳisma*, 'division'; cf. Hughes, *Dictionary of Islam*, s.v. 'Predestination'. See D'Ohsson, i. 166–76; iv. 385 sq.

CHAPTER XIV

THE *ḎIMMÎS*[1]

ḎIMMÎ, as will already be apparent, is the term applied, in the vocabulary of the Sacred Law, to the non-Moslem subjects of a Moslem ruler. It is so applied because their relations with him are held to be regulated by a contract (*ḏimma*), entered into at the time of the incorporation of the country concerned in the Domain of Islâm.

Like everything else in the Sacred Law, the principles upon which non-Moslems are to be dealt with by Moslem rulers were evolved in the early centuries of Islâm, and are variously defined by the four orthodox schools. But they have their roots in the attitude of the Prophet to the other religions with which he was acquainted, and to the problem of opposition to his mission. He appears to have been acquainted with five religions: the Jewish, the Christian, the Sabian, the Zoroastrian, and the polytheistic cults of Arabia. But the Jewish and the Christian religions had a special place in his conception of the world. Whatever view may be held of the origin of the *Ḳur'ân*, it is evident that its subject-matter is composed to a very large extent of what are recognizably Old and New Testament topics; and Muḥammad himself claimed to have had Mûsâ (Moses) and 'Îsâ (Jesus) as predecessors in prophecy. Jews and Christians were better, therefore, in his eyes than polytheists. They at least had Books of their own to excuse them for not receiving his; and so, with the Judaeo-Christian Sabians,[2] they are given a special name in the *Ḳur'ân*, 'the People of Scripture'.[3] The Zoroastrians are mentioned only once in the Sacred Volume, and then in such an ambiguous way that it is impossible to say whether they are to be classed with the People of Scripture or with the polytheists.[4] The worst curses of the *Ḳur'ân* are directed against the latter, with whom the People of Scripture are contrasted. Hence the Sacred Law eventually laid it down

[1] First-hand materials for the study of the subject of this chapter are very seldom to be found in the sources which we have utilized for our examination of Moslem institutions. The original sources in this instance include not only the Ottoman archives, but also those of all the non-Moslem religious communities inhabiting or in relations with the Ottoman Empire. It appeared to us, however, that we could not exclude from our survey a chapter devoted to these communities, even if it had to be based on secondary sources to a much greater extent than the other chapters. We take this opportunity to express our thanks to Dr. Alford Carleton, who kindly allowed us to make use of his unpublished dissertation on *The Millet System*.

[2] Identified by (later) Moslem tradition with the Mandaeans of Mesopotamia.

[3] Arabic, *Ahl al-Kitâb*.

[4] *Ḳur'ân, Sûra* xxii. 17: 'Those that believe and those that are Jews and the Sabians and the Christians and the Zoroastrians and those that are idolaters, verily God shall distinguish between them on the Day of Resurrection.'

that whereas on the conquest of new territory by Moslem armies polytheists must accept Islâm or die, the People of Scripture, as long as they do not take up arms against the invader (in which case they may be slain or enslaved), shall be permitted under special conditions to practise their religions as before. These conditions are embodied in the contract that we have mentioned. The People of Scripture thus became *Dimmîs*, tolerated infidels.

The Prophet looked on the People of Scripture as benevolently as he did largely because he compared them to their advantage with the polytheists that were his chief butt. But the polytheists were destined to disappear from the Islamic scene either by extermination or conversion. In the long run, therefore, the *Dimmîs* were to lose the comparatively worthy status they had enjoyed in the Prophet's eyes, and become in those of the faithful the sole representatives of infidelity. In some countries, it is true, toleration had to be extended to persons that were not strictly speaking 'of Scripture' at all, as in Persia, where the doubtful verse was interpreted in favour of the Zoroastrians, or in India, where the polytheists were so many that the mass of them could neither be converted nor exterminated. But both were tolerated on precisely the same footing as the Christians and Jews, and so did nothing to restore these two communities, as it were, to their lost intermediate rank. Throughout the Islamic world, accordingly, society came to be divided simply into believers and infidels, Moslems on the one hand and *Dimmîs* on the other.

By the terms of his contract with the *Dimmîs*, the Moslem ruler guarantees their lives, their liberties, and to some extent their property, and allows them to practise their religion. The *Dimmîs* in return undertake to pay the special poll-tax, called *Cizya*, and the land-tax called *Ḫarâc*, and agree to suffer certain restrictions that mark them out as a caste inferior to that of their Moslem fellow subjects. These restrictions are of various kinds. In the first place *Dimmîs* are at a disadvantage legally in comparison with Moslems: for instance, their evidence is not accepted against that of a Moslem in a *Ḳâḍî*'s court; the Moslem murderer of a *Dimmî* does not suffer the death penalty; a *Dimmî* man may not marry a Moslem woman, whereas a Moslem man may marry a *Dimmî* woman. In the second place, *Dimmîs* are obliged to wear distinctive clothes so that they may not be confused with true believers, and are forbidden to ride horses or to carry arms. Finally, though their churches may be, and in practice frequently have been, converted into mosques, they are not to build new ones. The most they may do is to repair those that have fallen into decay.[1]

[1] *Encyc. of Islam*, art. 'Dhimmīs'; A. S. Tritton, *The Caliphs and their Non-Muslim Subjects* (Oxford, 1930), 5–17.

The movement of expansion that led to the formation of the Ottoman Empire resembled in some ways that other movement which had led to the formation of the Caliphate, the first great Moslem state. Both had the effect of bringing large territories hitherto Christian into the Domain of Islâm and so of presenting the Moslem rulers with vast numbers of Christian *dimmî* subjects. But both Christendom and Islâm were changed in the interval between them. Christendom was split by the great schism between Orthodoxy and Catholicism. Islâm, as we have seen, was transformed by the operation of *ṣûfî* influences. The schism, indeed, placed the Orthodox in a situation that again somewhat resembled the situation of the Christians who had been overcome by the first Moslem conquerors. For most of these, in Syria, Mesopotamia, and Egypt, had been heretics of various kinds, Nestorian or Monophysite, and so antagonistic to the still united Orthodox-Catholic Church,[1] just as the Orthodox of the later period were hostile to the Catholics. In both cases, therefore, large numbers of the Christians who thus became *Dimmîs* did so with the greater readiness in that it offered them a means of escape from unwelcome attentions on the part of those that regarded them as heretical. Down to the end of the fifteenth century the limits of the Ottoman conquests in Europe corresponded fairly exactly with the limits of Orthodoxy. The only considerable Orthodox community that remained outside them was the Muscovite. And though its Tsars from the first regarded themselves as the heirs of Byzantium,[2] Muscovy in the early days of the Empire was not strong enough to attract the attention of Orthodox within it.

As for the attitude of the early Ottomans to the non-Moslems they fought and overcame, this, it appears, was far from being conventionally Moslem. But it again, oddly enough, had some resemblance to the attitude of the early Moslem conquerors of Syria, who were better disposed to the infidels and of more liberal views than their successors. The Ottoman conquerors, like the Arabs, were largely inspired by covetous motives, by the hope of acquiring land and booty, but partly also by religious enthusiasm; and the religious ideas most widespread among them were of the *bâṭinî-ṣûfî* order. Now Ṣûfism is inclined to place all religions on a level, and Bâṭinism to preach doctrines of a semi-Christian flavour.[3] It is not surprising to find, therefore, that the relations subsisting between Moslems and Christians during the early centuries of Ottoman rule were much more cordial than they had been under

[1] In Egypt, for instance, the Monophysite Copts actually aided the Arabs in their conquest of that country.—*Encyc. of Islam*, art. 'Ḳibt'.

[2] The Tsar Ivan III married the daughter of Constantine IX, the last Emperor.

[3] See p. 191 above on the *Bektâşî* doctrines.

earlier orthodox *Sunnî* dynasties,[1] or were to be later, after the Sultans had turned to orthodox Sunnism. Thus in the Ottomans' earliest campaigns they were supported by many Christian allies; and several of the earlier Sultans took Christian princesses to wife. During the invasion of the Balkans, moreover, large numbers of Christians turned Moslem; and though this may not seem to be evidence of good Moslem–Christian relations, it is to some extent so in fact, since it shows that the transition—if we are to judge by the frequency with which it was performed—was less painful at this period than it became later, when Moslem orthodoxy forbade any compromise in belief. Indeed, if this return to, or adoption of, orthodoxy had never occurred, it seems possible that the veneration of shrines in common[2] by the adherents of the two religions might have ended in their sinking their differences and evolving a syncretic faith—a Sufistic Christianity.

The turn to Moslem orthodoxy seems to have begun after the restoration of the Sultanate under Meḥmed I—which was effected by the suppression of a *bâṭinî* rising[3]—and, because of the growing estrangement of the Sultans from their original supporters,[4] had as one of its results the establishment of the *Devşirme* system. This system, by which Christian boys were recruited for the Sultan's slave-household and army, often no doubt inspired the *dimmî* parents thus bereaved with a hatred of their Moslem masters. Yet actually the *Devşirme* was a gate to the highest positions in the state. During the fifteenth and sixteenth centuries these were occupied exclusively by the Sultan's convert slaves, most of whom had been recruited by *Devşirme*; and often enough these high officers and officials would use their power to benefit their *dimmî* relatives. At this period, then, it was actually for those ambitious of worldly greatness an advantage to have been born a *Dimmî* eligible for conscription; so much so that it was common for parents to contrive the selection of their sons even when these were not eligible,[5] and that the born-Moslem population came to resent their exclusion from the management of affairs. There succeeded therefore to the first period, when the prevalence of Moslem heterodoxy allowed its practitioners to maintain close and friendly relations with the Christians, another, when the influence of Moslems and *Dimmîs* in the Empire was nicely balanced

[1] On the ambivalent attitude of the *Ğâzîs* of Anatolia (out of which the Ottoman state developed) towards the Christian population see P. Wittek, *The Rise of the Ottoman Empire* (London, 1938), 28–29, 43; and on the attitude of the Selcuḳids, O. Turan, 'Les Souverains seldjoukides et leurs sujets non-musulmans', in *Studia Islamica*, i (Paris, 1953), 65–100.

[2] See p. 192 above.

[3] See above, p. 189.

[4] See above, Part I, pp. 42 sq., 175, and Part II, p. 27.

[5] Cf. Part I, pp. 179 sq.

by the paradoxical reservation of high office in this Moslem state to persons of *ḍimmî* birth.[1]

So far we have spoken of the *Ḍimmîs*, at least the Christian *Ḍimmîs*, as if they formed a single community. But this was not so. Actually all we have said about the *Devşirme*, for instance, and the part played by the *Ḍimmî*-born in the state at its most flourishing period, applies only to the Orthodox community, and not even to the whole of this. But in early times the vast majority of the *Ḍimmîs* did in fact belong to it; and the attitude of the Moslems and the government towards the other *Ḍimmîs* even later was largely determined by their attitude to the Orthodox.

It will be remembered that the Ottomans acquired the principal territories that made up their Empire roughly in the following order: the north-west corner of Asia Minor; most of the Balkan peninsula; the rest of Asia Minor; Constantinople; central and southern Greece; Syria, Egypt, and the Ḥijâz. This is to say that, whereas all this territory, except the Ḥijâz, had once been Christian, they began in part of it that was still so, extended their rule next into part that had been in Moslem hands for some 300 years, and finally added the remainder, all of which, except for the interlude of the Crusades, had all been in Moslem hands since the seventh century. Now, partly because some of the Christian inhabitants of these lands had been under Moslem dominion longer than others, partly because the early Church in the east had been prolific of heresies, and partly because early missionaries had been apt to endow local churches with rites that differed from what came to be regarded as Orthodox, there were many different communities of Christians to be found in the Ottoman Empire by the time that it attained its greatest extent. The policy of the Sultans towards each community was determined by the circumstances in which it had come under their control. And since when once determined these policies were not modified for the sake of uniformity, they exhibited some inconsistencies. In order to trace their causes we propose to deal with the situation of the *ḍimmî* communities at three different stages. We shall first consider them at the stage when the Empire consisted virtually of only Rumelia and Anatolia, then at that when it had come to include the 'Arabic-speaking' countries, and finally at that when it fell into decline.

Before doing so, however, we may pause to emphasize the fact that the Ottoman government did usually deal with *Ḍimmîs* of all denominations as members of a community, not as individuals. This was a consequence, partly of the general organization of Ottoman society, which, as we have seen, was essentially 'corporate', but partly too of the nature of the Sacred Law. For

[1] This does not of course apply to offices of the learned profession.

though the Sacred Law regulates the relations of *Dimmîs* with both individual Moslems and the Moslem state, yet, for the very reasons that it *is* a sacred law, and that the distinction drawn between *Dimmîs* and Moslems is a religious one, it cannot provide for the relations of *Dimmîs* with one another. They are outside its scope, which includes only Moslems—except in so far as these come into contact with non-believers, or as *dimmî* litigants may agree to be judged in accordance with its provisions. It therefore leaves these 'internal' relations of the *Dimmîs* to be regulated by its rivals, the laws of the religions to which they adhere. Hence again, it comes to regard the adherents of each of these religions as forming a community controlled by the guardians of its sacred traditions. Individual *Dimmîs* will be obliged by the Moslem ruler to behave in accordance with such rules as those described above; but in other matters the ruler will be inclined to deal with each *dimmî* community as a whole: in such dealings the community will be represented by its leading ecclesiastical functionaries—its patriarchs or rabbis; and these functionaries in turn will have the ruler's support in enforcing discipline on their flocks. The status of the individual *Dimmî*, in short, derives exclusively from his membership of a protected community.

Such a community was called in Ottoman usage a *millet*,[1] and the officer responsible to the state for its administration was entitled *Millet-başi*. Although some of the administrative details (and possibly also the special significance of the term) were innovations of the Ottomans, the system itself was not. Its roots lay in the universal practice of the Roman and medieval empires to allow subject communities to retain their own laws and to apply them amongst themselves under the general jurisdiction of some recognized authority who was responsible to the ruling power. Under the Sasanian kings of pre-Islamic Persia, the Catholicos of the Nestorian Church was formally invested with the headship of all Christians in the Empire,[2] and that his successors preserved the same legal powers under the Caliphs is attested by an abundance of secondary evidence, by the surviving document of appointment of a Nestorian

[1] The Arabic word *milla*, apparently derived from Syriac *meltâ*, is used in the *Ḳur'ân* in the sense of 'religion' (especially in the phrase *millat Ibrâhîm*, 'the religion of Abraham') and retains this meaning in later Arabic usage. But since the abstract term 'religion' is never clearly divorced from the body of its adherents, it implies also 'religious community', and in medieval Islamic literature it is applied particularly to the religion and community of Moslems in contradistinction to the *ahl el-dimma* or protected communities: see *Encyc. of Islam*, s.v. The Ottoman usage thus appears to have been an innovation. The present Turkish use of *millet* in the sense of 'nation' dates only from the nineteenth century.

[2] See the remarks by W. A. Wigram (*An Introduction to the History of the Nestorian Church*, London, 1910, 95–96) on the Council of Isaac, traditionally dated in A.D. 410.

Catholicos in 1138,[1] and by the existence of numerous law-books of the various Christian communities.[2] The Jewish community (or rather communities, for the Rabbanites and Karaites were separate) were similarly administered by Chief Rabbis at Bağdâd and later at Cairo.[3] In the Byzantine Empire also the Armenians at Constantinople had a parallel organization,[4] as well as the Jews.[5]

The dispositions relating to the non-Moslem communities in the *Şerî'a*, therefore, though influenced in detail by Moslem attitudes, can properly be regarded as reproducing in general an established principle. It is important, however, in view of frequent misunderstandings on the subject, to distinguish the legal status and autonomy of *Dimmîs*, i.e. non-Moslem communities subject to Moslem rule, from the later practice of the grant of capitulatory rights to communities of foreign merchants, who are not subjects of the Moslem ruler. The latter, technically described in the *Şerî'a* by the term *musta'min* (i.e. one who is granted *amân* or security), were in the early centuries of Islâm generally placed on the same footing as *Dimmîs*. Only from the twelfth century onwards were merchant communities organized under the civil and legal jurisdiction of consuls of their own nations, with specific privileges relating to taxation and rates of customs duties under the terms of agreements negotiated individually with their governments. Such agreements thus fell generally into the sphere of *ḳânûn* rather than of *Şerî'a*, and, indeed, disregarded the views of the legal schools on a number of points, the most important being the concession that cases in which a Moslem was the plaintiff should be tried in the consular courts. The origin of these agreements is evidently to be sought in the expansion of commercial relations with the Italian city-states; and such agreements with Moslem rulers were again anticipated by similar agreements with the Byzantine emperors and the Crusading states, the model of which they followed closely.[6]

We should be entitled to assume, therefore, even had we no

[1] Studied by H. F. Amedroz in *J.R.A.S.*, 1908, 449–52 (text 467–70); see also A. S. Tritton, *The Caliphs and their Non-Muslim Subjects*, 86–88. The document cited appoints him to be 'Catholicos of the Nestorian Christians in Baghdâd and the other lands of Islam, and head of them and of the others, Greeks, Jacobites and Melkites, in the whole land', with the duty of 'managing their affairs, settling their policy and doing justice between the strong and the weak'.

[2] See C. A. Nallino, *Raccolta di Scritti*, &c., iv (Rome, 1942), esp. 546–81; Graf, *Gesch. d. christlichen arabischen Literatur*, vol. ii (Vatican City, 1947).

[3] Tritton, 96–97; cf. also R. J. H. Gottheil, 'Dhimmis and Moslems in Egypt', in *Old Testament and Semitic Studies in Memory of William R. Harper*, vol. ii (Chicago, 1908). For Jewish courts in the Sasanian empire see S. Funk, *Die Juden in Babylonien*, vol. i (Berlin, 1902).

[4] S. Runciman, *Byzantine Civilization* (London, 1933), 93, 289.

[5] See below, p. 217.

[6] See, for a discussion of the legal development of the status of foreigners in Moslem law and practice, W. Heffening, *Das islamische Fremdenrecht* (Hanover, 1925), M. Khadduri, *War and Peace in the Law of Islam* (Baltimore, Md., 1955).

direct evidence, that the Ottoman Sultans did not introduce the *millet* system into their Empire only on the capture of Constantinople, but were already applying its principles to the non-Moslem communities under their rule. Sufficient, even though fragmentary, evidence has, however, survived from the earlier period to make the fact certain, both as regards the Orthodox[1] and as regards the Jews.[2]

The Balkan peninsula and Asia Minor were in the original Ottoman view inhabited by three kinds of *Dimmîs*, the Orthodox, the Armenians, and the Jews. They rightly distinguished between the Orthodox and the Armenians, the Church of the latter, which was of very early independent foundation, being Monophysite and so gravely heretical in the eyes of the former: indeed, the doctrinal decisions come to from time to time in the Armenian Church had been framed largely out of hatred for the Orthodox. We now propose, therefore, to consider in turn their attitude to, and the manner in which they dealt with, these three communities.

To begin with the Orthodox. Most of these territories had in earlier times been included in the jurisdiction of the Patriarchate of Constantinople.[3] But since its foundation the greater part of the Balkan peninsula had been transformed ethnologically by the successive invasions of Slavs and Bulgars, none of whom were converted to Christianity till the ninth century. Apart from Greece, including Thrace, the only area in the peninsula in which the original inhabitants survived in any purity was Albania; and although the south of that country had meanwhile been brought under the control of the Byzantine Emperors, the north had become subject to chieftains of the Serbian race, which had settled in the north-western corner of the peninsula in the sixth century.[4] Other Serbian princes had meanwhile extended their rule south-eastwards, and had acknowledged Byzantine overlordship. But the most powerful of these peoples at the time of the conversion was the Bulgarian, which had meanwhile become so far Slavicized as to lose its original language. The first Bulgarian Empire was then growing yearly in might and extent, till at the end of the ninth century it stretched from the Danube to Thrace, and from the Black Sea to the Adriatic. When Tsar Boris accepted Christianity in 864, accordingly, he was able to insist that the Bulgarian Church should be autocephalous, its primate being later raised to the rank of Patriarch. Moreover, the conversion of both the Bulgarians and the Serbs was brought about by the disciples of Saints Cyril and

[1] See the references cited by Bréhier in *Camb. Med. Hist.*, iv. 625.
[2] G. Young, *Corps de Droit ottoman*, ii. 123–5.
[3] *Encyclopaedia Britannica*, art. 'Orthodox Eastern Church'.
[4] Ibid., arts. 'Albania' and 'Servia'.

Methodius, who endowed their churches with a liturgy in the Slavonic dialect of Macedonia;[1] and though early in the eleventh century the whole peninsula except northern Albania was brought again under Byzantine rule, the Bulgarian Patriarchate and this distinctive liturgy were allowed to persist. The seat of the Patriarchate had meanwhile been repeatedly moved owing to political exigencies; but it was finally established at Ochrida in western Macedonia.[2] At the end of the twelfth century, however, a second Bulgarian Empire was brought into being with its capital at Trnovo, in the east; and this resulted in the formation of a rival and independent patriarchate with its centre in that city.[3] Finally, the early fourteenth century witnessed the sudden and short-lived flowering of a Serbian Empire whose monarch, Stephan Dushan, formed yet another patriarchate at Ipek.[4] At the time of the Ottoman conquest, therefore, the Slavonic branch of the Orthodox Church in the Sultan's dominions included no less than three separate patriarchates—of Ochrida, of Trnovo, and of Ipek.

Now these churches, though their liturgy was Slavonic, were separated from Greek Orthodoxy by no doctrinal differences. But they had come into being as the result of movements that were partly racial, partly dynastic, and so formed centres of national feeling. For these reasons Meḥmed the Conqueror, when he was at length in a position to consider his policy as regards the Orthodox Church as a whole, placed all its adherents without exception under the authority of the Oecumenical Patriarch. The Patriarchate of Trnovo was actually suppressed; and though those of Ochrida and Ipek were maintained, together with their Slavonic liturgy, they were subjected to Constantinople.[5]

This unification was effected immediately after the conquest of Constantinople in 1453, when it first became feasible. For though the Sultans had long possessed more Orthodox subjects than the Emperors, they had been obliged hitherto to control them through their local bishops.[6] Now, however, with the Patriarch at his beck

[1] Ibid., art. 'Roman Empire, Later'. It may be noted that the Bulgarians decided in favour of Orthodoxy as against Catholicism largely from political motives, and that during the reconciliation between the ninth and the eleventh century the Bulgarian Emperor and Patriarch were recognized by the Pope—Steen de Jehay, *De la situation légale des sujets ottomans non-Musulmans* (Brussels, 1906), 148.

[2] Actually in the *vilâyet* of Monastîr.

[3] Ochrida being outside the boundaries of the second Empire: Steen, 150. *Encyc. Brit.*, arts. 'Bulgaria' and 'Ochrida'.

[4] Situated in the later to be celebrated *Sancaḳ* of Novibazar (Turkish, *Yeni Pazar*). *Encyc. Brit.*, arts. 'Ipek' and 'Servia'. The first Patriarch was proclaimed in 1351, but it was only in 1376 that the Oecumenical Patriarch recognized the Church as autocephalous—Steen, 175. The Church of Montenegro was dependent on this Patriarchate—ibid. 180.

[5] *Encyc. Brit.*, art. 'Bulgaria'. Cf. Steen, 152.

[6] *Camb. Med. Hist.* iv. 625.

and call, the Conqueror organized the whole Orthodox Church as a *millet* under the Patriarch's authority and the name of *Rûm milleti*, 'the Roman community', *Rûm* in Moslem usage signifying 'East Roman' or 'Byzantine'. The Patriarch was duly installed with as many of the traditional ceremonies as might be performed in the absence of an Emperor; he was assigned the ceremonial rank of a *Paşa* with three *ṭuğs*;[1] and he was allowed his own court and prison in the Phanar quarter, with all but unlimited civil jurisdiction over and responsibility for the *Dimmîs* of his church.[2] Even in the matter of taxation, though the amount to which the *millet* was subject as a whole was ascertained by officials of the Porte in collaboration with its local religious authorities, its apportionment between communities and individuals was left to the Patriarch, who supervised its collection and was responsible for its payment.[3]

The citizens of Ğalata, however, being Genoese, were granted a separate decree, which guaranteed them security of their possessions and freedom of trade and travel, subject to the payment of the legal *ḫarâc*,[4] and the same decree confirmed their enjoyment of their 'capitulatory' rights, 'according to the established régime'.[5]

[1] F. Giese, 'Die geschichtlichen Grundlagen für die Stellung der christlichen Untertanen im osmanischen Reich', in *Der Islam*, xix. 274. For *ṭuğs* see Part I, p. 139.

[2] No documentary record has survived of the formal grant of such powers and privileges to the new Patriarch, Gennadius, who was installed by the Sultan a few months after the conquest—although in view of what has been said above, the fact itself is scarcely open to question. Dr. A. Carleton, in the dissertation cited *supra*, p. 208, n. 1, has subjected the contemporary evidence, that of two Greek historians, George Phrantzes (d. 1477) and Marcus Critobulus, and one Turkish historian, Âşiḳpaşazâde (d. 1495), to a fresh examination. In the light of this study, the version given by von Hammer (*Ges. d. osmanischen Reiches*, i. 426–8; 2nd ed. (Pest, 1828), ii. 1–2) is shown to be confused in detail, and the alleged translation of the same by Hellert (*Histoire de l'Empire ottoman*, 3rd ed., iii. 3–5) to contain misleading and unwarrantable additions, which have not only been accepted by the majority of later European and modern Turkish historians, but have acquired on the way still further embellishments. See also F. Giese, *Der Islam*, xix. 264–77. It seems doubtful whether any document which Gennadius may have received from Meḥmed II could, in any case, constitute a 'charter' of liberties or privileges, since no action of the Conqueror could bind his successors in their relations with the Patriarchs. There is some evidence, indeed, that in the reigns of both Selîm I and Süleymân the Magnificent the question whether Constantinople was 'voluntarily surrendered'—which alone, according to Islamic law, could justify the grant of *dimmî* rights to its Orthodox inhabitants—was referred to the legal authorities and vouched for by two Janissary veterans, survivors of the siege; see Giese, 273–6 (citing Crusius, *Turcograeciae* (Basel, 1584) and a *fetwâ* of the *Şeyḫü 'l-Islâm* Abu 'l-Su'ûd Efendi). As will be noted presently, it is admitted that the Jews and certain other communities were administered as *millets* for centuries before being formally recognized as such.

[3] Steen, 84–90, 94.

[4] i.e. poll-tax, see Part I, pp. 250 n., 278 n.

[5] *T.O.E.M.* v. 52–53. The document is dated 'at the end of the fifth month of 857', i.e. at the beginning of June 1453, and thus probably antedates the appointment of Gennadius as Patriarch. On the *Comunità* of Péra see also Young, *Corps de Droit ottoman*, ii. 123–5.

So much for the Orthodox in our first period. Almost simultaneously the Jews were tacitly recognized as forming another *millet*.[1] The Conqueror permitted them to settle in Istanbul, and appointed a *Ḥaham Başî*, or Chief Rabbi,[2] with powers, similar to those enjoyed by the Patriarch, over all his co-religionists in the Empire. The Chief Rabbi was actually given precedence over the Patriarch next to the head of the *'Ulemâ*;[3] and the position of the Jews was altogether improved. Under the Byzantine régime they had indeed been treated in theory much as were the *Dimmîs* by the Ottomans: Justinian had laid it down that disputes arising among members of their faith should be dealt with in their own courts, and had debarred them both from giving evidence against Christians and from holding public offices or enjoying public honours.[4] They had thus been regarded as outcasts in Byzantine society, of which their community formed but a small section. In Ottoman society, on the other hand, the *dimmî* communities (before the conquest of the Arabic-speaking countries) surpassed the Moslems in number, and so, despite the disabilities to which they were subjected, were preserved from the particular odium attaching to a small minority of dissidents. Moreover, the Jews had already won the favour of earlier Sultans. Murâd II had started the fashion of employing one as his personal physician and had given others important positions at court.[5] Nor did he insist on their dressing in a particular manner, but allowed them to live as they pleased.[6] Later, when *Sunnî* standards were applied to all departments of Ottoman life, the Jews, like the Christians, were forced to conform to th sumptuary laws, and came altogether to enjoy a less favoured position. At the time of the conquest, however, the conditions under which they were permitted to live in the Ottoman Empire contrasted so strikingly with those imposed on them in various parts of Christendom that the fifteenth century witnessed a large influx of Jews into the Sultan's dominions.[7] During the first half of the century persecutions had occurred in Bohemia, Austria, and Poland; but it was the measures taken against them in Spain, culminating in 1492 in their expulsion, that gave the greatest

[1] *Encyc. of Islam*, arts. 'Turks' and 'Naṣâra'. Steen, 92, gives the impression that until 1461 all the *Dimmîs* were subordinated to the Oecumenical Patriarch. It was not until 1839 that the Jews were formally recognized as a *millet*: G. Young, ii. 143.

[2] *Jew. Encyc.*, art. 'Turkey'. A certain Moses Kapsali was the first to fill this office, but it is uncertain whether his appointment was made before 1461.

[3] Ibid., also Young, ii. 141 sq., and Franco, *Essai sur l'histoire des Israélites de l'Empire Ottoman* (Paris, 1897), 32.

[4] *Encyc. Brit.*, art. 'Jews'.

[5] Franco, 30.

[6] *Jew. Encyc.*, art. 'Turkey'.

[7] Franco, 34. See Gallanté, *Turcs et Juifs* (Istanbul, 1932), 24, for a letter written to their countrymen early in the fifteenth century by two German rabbis who had sought refuge in the Ottoman Empire, extolling its beauties and advantages.

momentum to this migration.[1] As Spain had been for centuries the most advanced centre of Jewish life, those refugees that sought an asylum in the Ottoman Empire brought with them a valuable tradition of culture. They were received with the greater enthusiasm in that their banishment was coincident with and chiefly due to the fall of the Moslem emirate of Granada, so that they were accompanied by many 'Moorish' fugitives. A Venetian observer of the sixteenth century declares even that these Jews and their Moslem compatriots 'have taught and are teaching every useful art to the Turks; and the greater part of the shops and arts are kept and exercised by them';[2] and though this is an absurd exaggeration, there is no doubt that these immigrants contributed notably to the short-lived flowering of Ottoman civilization under Selîm the Grim and Süleymân the Magnificent. Indeed, there seems to have been something sympathetic to the Jewish nature in the culture of Islâm. It is a fact, at any rate, that, despite their condemnation to a *dimmî* status, from the rise of the Caliphate till the abolition of the ghettos in Europe the most flourishing centres of Jewish life were to be found in Moslem countries: in the 'Irâḳ during the 'Abbâsid period, in Spain throughout the period of Moorish domination, and thereafter in the Ottoman Empire.[3]

There came to be four main divisions of Jews in the Ottoman Empire as it then existed. For the 'original' communities—that is to say those that had been resident in these countries before the immigrations of the fifteenth century—were divided doctrinally into Rabbanites, those that revered the Talmud, and Karaites,[4] those that did not. The Karaite schism had originated in Mesopotamia early in the 'Abbâsid period, when an 'Exilarch' elect[5] had fallen foul of the *Geonim*, the heads of the theological colleges, and after being imprisoned had migrated to found a synagogue in Palestine. The Karaite doctrine, we may note, is said to have been affected by the teaching of Abû Ḥanîfa, the Moslem theologian and jurist, whose 'school' was that followed officially in the Ottoman Empire—a contemporary and fellow prisoner of the Karaite founder. However that may be, from Palestine it had spread into various parts both of Asia and of south-eastern Europe, though its adherents seem never to have even rivalled the Rabbanites in numbers.[6] Many of the immigrants from Europe

[1] Franco, 35 sq.
[2] Lybyer, 241—from Romberti, *The Affairs of the Turks.*
[3] Cf. S. W. Baron, *The Jewish Community* (Philadelphia, 1945), i. 157.
[4] A name derived from the same Semitic root, meaning 'to read', as the word *Ḳur'ân.*
[5] Exilarch was the name given to the head of the community in Mesopotamia.
[6] *Encyc. Brit.*, art. 'Qaraites'. Graetz, *History of the Jews* (English trans., London, 1892), iv. 291 sq.; Franco, 33–34; Baron, i. 178.

are to be classed with the Rabbanites. Those from Germany, however, formed a distinct class, the Ashkenazim—our third division. The fourth division was that of the fugitives from Spain and Portugal, who were known as Sephardim.

The news that Jews were welcome in the Ottoman Empire travelled quickly about the Jewish world. Apart from the countries we have already mentioned immigrants began to arrive from Hungary, Moldavia (not yet Ottoman), the Crimea, and parts of Asia, Rabbanites and Karaites alike. Nor were their meetings always amicable. As well as the Rabbanite-Karaite quarrel, another broke out in 1460 among the Karaites themselves. Moreover, when the Sephardim came in turn to swell the numbers of the *millet*, they kept themselves aloof from their co-religionists, maintaining their own congregations with a distinctive ritual.[1] They did not even form a solidary community themselves, but split into small bodies each preserving the customs and regulations of the place from which its members had originally emigrated.[2] The internal differences of the Jews, therefore, were many. Nevertheless, they were not enough to compromise the unity of the *millet*, the affairs of which continued to be controlled by the *Ḥaḥam Başîs*. All the *Ḥaḥam Başîs* but the first, moreover, were elected by the Jews themselves, and confirmed in office by the Porte.[3]

The expulsion of the Jews from Spain occurred in the reign of Bâyezîd II, the successor of Meḥmed the Conqueror. Bâyezîd was particularly well disposed towards them, and issued a decree enjoining their good treatment in his dominions.[4] Indeed, it appears that the Moslems favoured the Jewish above the Christian *Dimmîs* at this period, since the latter were already suspected of regarding the powers of Christendom with undue sympathy.[5] The immigrants from Spain and Portugal consisted partly of the so-called *Maraños*, Jews that had outwardly turned Christian for the advantages offered by conversion or to escape persecution. But it appears that on finding an asylum in the Empire these usually abandoned their disguise and so became merged in the Sephardic congregations. The chief centres in which the Sephardim settled were Istanbul, Salonika, Adrianople, and Nikopolis in the European provinces; Bursa, Amasya, and Toḳat in the Asiatic provinces. Istanbul, indeed, soon came to harbour the largest community of Jews in the whole of Europe; and Salonika became a predominantly Jewish city.[6] The influx of Sephardim was on so large a scale that

[1] Graetz, iv. 415 sq. Cf. Franco, 38.
[2] Graetz, iv. 430; Franco, 40.
[3] Kapsali was succeeded on his death by Elias Mizrakhi: Graetz, iv. 430–1; Franco, 45; *Jew. Encyc.*, art. 'Turkey'.
[4] Graetz, iv. 390.
[5] Ibid. 428.
[6] Ibid. 430, 433, 434; Franco, 40–41.

they outnumbered the other congregations in all the larger cities of the Empire and so set the tone for the whole *millet*. As we have indicated, *Dimmîs*, Jews and Christians alike, in these early times enjoyed membership, jointly with Moslems, of the industrial and commercial guilds: and of the Jews the *Maraños* particularly became celebrated as manufacturers of weapons of war.[1] Others engaged in large-scale trade by land and sea. Sephardim of the medical school of Salamanca were also much in demand as doctors; and much of the favour which they enjoyed down to 1700 was due to the influence of the court physicians.[2] Finally, Jews were very commonly employed, on account of their connexions with and knowledge of Europe, as interpreters.[3]

To turn now to the third community, the Armenian. The Armenians were not formally recognized as a *millet* until 1461.[4] The Porte was faced with a problem in their case that did not arise in those either of the Orthodox or of the Jews. For whereas the Patriarch was the most prominent ecclesiastical figure in the Orthodox Church,[5] and the Jews had no spiritual director universally recognized as supreme, the head of the Armenian Church, its Catholicos, was not resident within the borders of the Ottoman Empire. In fact the position of the Armenians was similar to that of the Orthodox before the conquest of Constantinople.

The Armenian Church was, as we have mentioned, Monophysite and so heretical from the Orthodox standpoint.[6] It is generally called Gregorian (to distinguish its adherents from their fellow countrymen who are in communion with the Church of Rome) after its reputed organizer of the third century, Gregory the Illuminator.[7] In early times it had been extremely powerful, not only in Armenia proper but also throughout the country immediately south of the Caucasus range, the churches of Georgia and Arrân owing their existence to and being dependent upon it. But the first had been converted to Orthodoxy in the sixth century, and the second had been wiped out during the Selcuḳid invasion of the eleventh. Earlier in the same century, moreover, the hitherto independent kingdom of Armenia had been absorbed in the Byzan-

[1] Franco, 39.

[2] Young, *Corps de Droit ottoman*, ii. 142. Cf. Franco, 46, and B. Lewis, 'The Privilege granted by Meḥmed II to his Physician', *B.S.O.S.* xiv. 550 sq.

[3] Graetz, iv. 429–30; Franco, loc. cit.

[4] Lybyer 34, note; G. Young, ii. 73 sqq.

[5] Though not its supreme head; cf. below, p. 224.

[6] Though the authorities both of this Church and of the Jacobites denied that their doctrine was Eutychian. They maintained that their explanation of the nature of Christ was that of Dioscorus, namely, that the two impersonal natures of Christ reunited in one personal nature—Steen, 32, 45.

[7] It is only since the Peace of Türkmençay (1828), however, that the name Gregorian has been applied, as it then was by the Russian government—Steen, 46.

tine Empire, certain princes of the Bagratid line accepting lands in Cappadocia and Cilicia in exchange for their original possessions, so that the latter might be brought under the direct control of Constantinople in order to strengthen the eastern borders of the Empire against Turkish attacks. This exchange of territories was accompanied by a considerable migration of Armenians to southern Asia Minor, and eventually resulted in the creation of the kingdom of Little Armenia. Henceforward, therefore, there were two Armenian centres: one here in the Taurus region and the other in the mountains to the east of Anatolia.

The original seat of the Armenian Catholicos was Echmiadzin in Erivân.[1] But during the Selcuḳid period it was moved first to Sîvâs and then to Little Armenia. After the invasion of Tîmûr, however, the Armenian provinces of the east fell into the hands of the Türkmen dynasties of the Black and White Sheep;[2] and Little Armenia having by now, after a period of Crusader rule, been incorporated in the Mamlûk Empire, the Catholicos of the time returned to Echmiadzin. At the time of the formation of the *millets*, however, neither the Armenian provinces of the East, nor Little Armenia, had as yet fallen to the Ottomans. When creating the Armenian *millet*, therefore, Meḥmed II chose the Gregorian bishop of Bursa, Horaghim, to control it, naming him Patriarch of Istanbul, with powers similar to those conferred on the Orthodox Patriarch and the *Ḥaḫam Baṣî*.[3]

A curious feature of the Armenian *millet* was that besides Armenians proper it was held to include all the subjects of the Sultan otherwise unclassified.[4] Presumably, therefore, the widespread Bogomil or Paulician[5] sect was so included; and, if so, this inclusion was appropriate, since the sect was actually of Armenian origin. The Paulician doctrine was far more radically heretical than that of the Armenian Church itself from the Orthodox standpoint. For it was not only Adoptionist, but also Manichean: that is to say it asserted, on the one hand, that Jesus was a man who for his perfection of holiness had been 'adopted' by God and elevated to divinity, and, on the other, that there were two divine principles,

[1] It was removed from Dvin to Echmiadzin in 893 (V. Minorsky, *Studies in Caucasian History* (London, 1953), 118).

[2] *Ḳara Ḳoyunlu* and *Aḳ Ḳoyunlu*.

[3] *Encyc. Brit.*, art. 'Armenia'; Steen, 45 sq. It may here be noted that owing to the vicissitudes through which the Armenian Church had passed, by the date of the formation of the *millet* there were no less than five Armenian patriarchs, three of whom—those of Echmiadzin, Sis, and Aghtamin—bore the title of Catholicos. The other two were the patriarchs of Jerusalem and Constantinople.

[4] Lybyer, 35, note, says all 'who were not Moslem or Greek Orthodox', ignoring the Jewish *millet*, which had undoubtedly been recognized earlier. Cf. Steen, 61–62, note, who states that the Jews were at first included in the Armenian *millet*.

[5] So called after Paul of Samosata.

one good and one evil, of which the universe was the battlefield. The doctrine was first brought into Europe in the eighth century, when certain Armenians professing it settled in Thrace; and in the tenth century others, who had been transported to the neighbourhood of Philippopolis by the Emperor, converted to it large numbers of Bulgarians, against whom they had been meant to form a barrier. These Bulgarians were the original Bogomils, a name probably derived from that of an early leader; and as heretics they were duly persecuted by the national Orthodox Church, established in the previous century.[1] Hence the adherents of the sect fled to the more inaccessible of the mountain districts, and as time went on, by way of the ranges and trade routes, sent missionaries north and west so that the doctrine was spread abroad in many parts not only of the Orthodox, but also of the Catholic world. In the west the sect was represented notably by the Albigenses and Waldenses (in Provence and Piedmont);[2] in the east by the Patarenes of Bosnia, its adherents in Serbia as well as in Bulgaria preserving their original name. When the Balkans were overrun by the Ottoman armies many are said to have accepted Islâm (though this assertion has the air of an Orthodox apology). Most of the converts in Bosnia, for instance, where a much larger proportion of the people turned Moslem than elsewhere, were alleged to be Patarenes. Nevertheless, many of them in their original home round Philippopolis retained their peculiar faith under Ottoman rule. They were known as Pavleniki.[3]

Another community not formally recognized as a *millet* was the Catholic. The number of Catholics in the Empire as constituted at the time of the Conquest was not large. But at the capital itself there was, for instance, a Genoese colony established at Ğalata; and this the Sultan allowed to continue in being.[4] Other Catholics became subjects of the Porte on the final[5] conquest of central Greece in 1456 and that of the Morea four years later. Ever since the Latin conquest of Constantinople these territories had been ruled by Western Catholics of various provenance, though for a short space at the beginning of the fifteenth century the Byzantine

[1] See above, p. 215, and on the Bogomils generally, D. Obolensky, *The Bogomils, a study in Balkan Neo-Manichaeism* (Cambridge, 1948).

[2] Waldenses were also to be found in northern France and Flanders, see *Encyc. Brit.*, art. 'Anabaptists'.

[3] i.e. Paulicians. *Encyc. of Religion and Ethics*, ii. 784, art. 'Bogomils'.

[4] See above, p. 216. The Conqueror, Meḥmed II, is said to have diverted himself by visiting the Catholic churches in Ğalata to observe the ceremonial—*Encyc. of Islam*, art. 'Constantinople'. The Genoese had been established as a self-governing community in 1261 by Michael VII Paleologos on the restoration of the Empire—ibid.

[5] Ottoman expeditions or threats had earlier reduced almost the whole of Greece to a tributary status.

Emperors had regained control of most parts of the peninsula. Consequently a Catholic hierarchy had been set up, and the Orthodox subordinated to it. Catholicism, nevertheless, made few converts among the people; and when on the Ottoman conquest the Latin rulers were dispossessed, the Orthodox Church was given a position of supremacy.[1]

Of the three *millets* originally recognized by the Ottoman government the Orthodox was distinguished, as we have mentioned, by what may be regarded either as a disability or as an advantage. It was the only *millet* whose members were subjected to the *Devşirme* conscription. The Armenians and Jews were thus debarred from becoming *Ḳapî Ḳullarî*, and so from all the opportunities that this employment offered to the ambitious. Their exclusion, however, was actually, and not surprisingly, held to be a privilege—as may be judged from the fact that after the conquest all the *Ḏimmîs* resident in Istanbul, of whatever faith, were likewise exempted. The *Devşirme* was after all based, though arbitrarily, on the provisions of the *Şerî'a* regarding slave prisoners of war, and so savoured initially of degradation. Moreover, it involved its subjects in separation from their parents at an early age, in all but forced conversion, and in a hard and tedious training. The privilege of the Armenians and Jews dated from before the conquest of Constantinople and the institution of the *millets*, perhaps from the first adoption of the *Devşirme* itself. Its grant may have been due to the fact that there were comparatively few Jews and Armenians in the provinces then incorporated in the Empire; for the immigration of Jews to which we have referred had not yet taken place, nor were the Armenian 'home-lands' yet Ottoman. Hence most of the Sultan's Armenian subjects were townsmen, as were all the Jews; and it was children of peasant stock that were desired for enrolment. Another reason for the exemption was that the Sultans, in instituting the *Devşirme*, sought to give it a colour of legality by alleging that they were merely exercising the right allowed by the *Şerî'a* to the İmâm of reserving for his own service a proportion of captives taken in war with the infidel. This subterfuge obliged them to restrict the conscription to the European provinces, which had recently enough formed part of the Domain of War, in contrast to the Asiatic, which had for centuries been included in that of Islâm. But the conquering armies of the Faith had met with opposition only from the Orthodox of various races. The Jews and Armenians, therefore, could not by any stretching of the law be represented as deserving of penalization on this score for the sins of their fathers. Later, it is true, the Orthodox of Anatolia were subjected also to the *Devşirme*, but by this time its legality

[1] Miller, *Latins in the Levant*, 438 sq.

was taken for granted. The privilege of the Jews and Armenians was maintained, however, possibly because they were not considered likely to make satisfactory soldiers. Nor was the net of the *Devşirme* cast over the 'Arabic-speaking' countries acquired by Selîm and Süleymân.

The conquest of these countries brought about a great change in the situation of the *Ḍimmîs*. In the first place, their populations were predominantly Moslem, so that, whereas the *Ḍimmîs* had hitherto outnumbered the Moslems, henceforward the Moslems outnumbered the *Ḍimmîs*. The Ottoman Empire now for the first time acquired the Moslem majority that had long been usual in the states of the Islamic world. Secondly, as a natural, though perhaps not an inevitable, consequence of this change in the composition, regarded from a religious standpoint, of the population of their dominions, the inclination of the Sultans to a strict Sunnism, which had already been all but forced on them of political necessity, was intensified. Thirdly, each of the *ḍimmî* communities was swollen by the acquisition of more or less large numbers of co-sectaries resident in the conquered territories. And, finally, various new types of *Ḍimmîs* were brought under the Sultan's rule.

To take the third of these points first. By the conquest first of Syria and Egypt, and later of Cyprus, Crete, and what were to be the North African Regencies, the Ottoman Empire came to include all the territory in which the Orthodox Church had ever flourished, and particularly the three ancient patriarchates of Antioch, Jerusalem, and Alexandria.[2] All three had now been under Moslem rule since the seventh century, except during the period of Crusader rule in Syria and Palestine (which, since the Crusaders as Catholics were fitfully hostile to the Orthodox Church and all its ways, did little to improve the lot of the two patriarchs concerned). Moreover, even before the Moslem conquest these countries had been the principal theatre of heresy in the East Roman Empire. Hence the number of Orthodox to be found in them was, relatively, small.

The constitution of the Orthodox Church differed from that of the Catholic in that it had no supreme head. It was governed by an oligarchy of patriarchs each of whom enjoyed a position within his diocese like that of the Catholic Pope.[1] The reunion of the four patriarchates in one political state, therefore, did not involve any difficulties in the matter of church government. The Oecumenical Patriarch, indeed, remained head of the *millet* in the eyes of the

[1] The Alexandrian patriarchate came next in precedence to the Oecumenical: Steen, 128.

[2] Steen, 81; *Encyc. Brit.*, art. 'Orthodox Eastern Church'.

Porte, but shared spiritual jurisdiction with his fellows as formerly. The supremacy of the Greek element in the Syrian provinces was, however, ensured by a regulation attributed to the Patriarch Germanos shortly after their conquest by Selîm I, which excluded Arabophone natives of Syria and Palestine from entering Greek monasteries, thus rendering them incapable of attaining the higher ecclesiastical dignities and confining them to the ranks of the secular clergy.[1]

As well as the three patriarchates the Ottoman conquests of the sixteenth century brought two other Orthodox bodies into the *millet*, namely, the churches of Cyprus and Sinai. The latter, however, consisted only of the celebrated monastery of Saint Catherine[2] —all that remained of the ancient Church of Arabia; and the former had virtually to be reconstituted. The Church of Cyprus had been recognized as an autonomous body from early times.[3] It was governed by the metropolitan of the capital, styled Archbishop of all Cyprus. But when, during the Third Crusade, the island became the seat of a Latin kingdom and a Catholic hierarchy was established, the archbishopric was abolished, the Orthodox bishops were obliged to do homage and swear fealty to the Latin Church, and the Orthodox sees were reduced from some twenty to four. The Catholic supremacy was maintained by the Venetians who succeeded to the Lusignan dynasty in 1475. The conquest of Cyprus just a century later by the Ottomans, therefore, was regarded as a liberation by the Orthodox. The Catholic hierarchy vanished; their Cathedral at Nicosia was turned into a mosque; and though the Orthodox sees that had been suppressed were not revived, an archbishop was reinstated in his former authority.[4]

The *millet* of the Jews also received a great accession of strength by the Asiatic conquests of Selîm and Süleymân. For in addition to the communities that had always existed in these provinces, when the Jews of Europe learnt of the paradisiacal life awaiting them in Turkey, many of them set out for Palestine. The Rhineland, Styria, Hungary, and Moldavia are mentioned as centres from which this migration took place; and though it was somewhat checked by the Franciscans of Jerusalem, who talked the Pope into forbidding the Venetians to carry Jewish passengers to the Holy Land, it appears to have been considerable.[5] Moreover, on

[1] Whether such a regulation actually existed or not, it is certain that from the sixteenth century the Orthodox hierarchy of Palestine was chosen exclusively from the 'Brotherhood of the Sacred Tomb', the membership of which was confined to Greeks: see G. Graf, *Gesch. d. christlichen arab. Lit.*, iii. 28.

[2] It owned, however, in later times at least, property in various parts of the Empire. Its independence was always doubtful: see Steen, 144–6.

[3] Actually at the Council of Ephesus (431): Steen, 143.

[4] *Encyc. Brit.*, art. 'Cyprus'; Steen, 143.

[5] Graetz, iv. 293 sq.

the expulsion of the Jews from Spain and Portugal, though most of the refugees from these countries who sought refuge in the Ottoman Empire made for its European provinces, a large number settled not only in Palestine but also in Syria and Egypt.[1] In Palestine Jerusalem itself and the town of Ṣafed in Galilee were the chief centres of settlement, in Egypt Alexandria and Cairo, in Syria, Damascus.[2] As in the European provinces the Sephardim soon came to dominate their co-religionists in these parts; and in Egypt, though they had but just escaped from persecution themselves, were disposed to use it with those that differed from them in matters of religion. After his conquest of Egypt Selîm laid down new ordinances for the Jewish community, which, curiously enough, effected within it a process exactly the opposite of *millet*-making. For hitherto the Egyptian Jews had been controlled by a Rabbi and prince-judge, called *Nagîd* or *Reîs*, whose authority was almost precisely similar to that conferred on the *Ḥaḫam Başî* of the capital. The office of this personage resembled that of the 'Exilarchs' that had ruled the Jewish community in Mesopotamia during the early Middle Ages: it was a minor sovereignty. Perhaps on this account, perhaps because it was feared that his authority would clash with that of the *Ḥaḫam*, Selîm abolished it and decreed that thenceforward every congregation should rule itself. Nevertheless, in the reign of Süleymân we read of the then *Ḥaḫam Başî* as representing all the Jews of the Empire. So it would seem that the local self-government of the congregation was limited.[3]

The reign of Süleymân saw an innovation in the governance of the Jewish *millet*. This was the appointment of a *Kâḫya* to represent its interests with the government, rather after the manner of the *Kâḫyas* of the guilds. The *Kâḫya* was himself a Jew. But he had right of access to the Sultan and the ministers of the Porte, to whose notice he would bring cases of injustice suffered by his co-religionists at the hands either of provincial governors or of fanatical Christians.[4]

The conquests of Selîm the Grim included not only the whole Mamlûk Empire but the greater part of Armenia proper, which fell to him after his deafeat of Şâh Ismâ'îl the Ṣafevid in 1514. Hence both the Armenian 'home-lands' were incorporated in the Ottoman dominions during his reign, and with them the seat of the Catholicos at Echmiadzin. The affairs of the *millet* seem still to have been managed as they regarded the government, however,

[1] Graetz, iv. 424; Franco, 42–43, 44. It will be remembered that the expulsion occurred before the incorporation of Syria and Egypt in the Empire.

[2] Graetz, iv. 427.

[3] Ibid. 421–2; Franco, 44.

[4] Graetz, iv. 432; Franco, 46–47. The first *Kâḫya* fell foul of the *Ḥaḫam Başî* for interfering in *millet* affairs that were not his proper concern.

by the Gregorian Patriarch of Istanbul.[1] In any case Echmiadzin again became Persian rather more than a century later, when Erivân was ceded by the Porte to Şâh ʿAbbâs.

The Armenian provinces had long been distracted by wars, invasions, and raids. The Selcuḳid invasion had been followed by the Mongol, the Mongol by that of Tîmûr. The Türkmen dynasties of the Black and White Sheep had ravaged the whole country and fought out their quarrels with grievous consequences to its prosperity. The numbers of the Armenians had been greatly depleted both by sudden death and emigration; and into the lands thus vacated enterprising Kurdish tribes from the south and south-east had pushed their way, till the more southerly parts of what had been Armenia had become as much Kurdish as Armenian in population. When this region was acquired by Selîm he found it a prey to local feuds, and determined to reorganize it. In the anarchy much of the arable land in the valleys and plains had been abandoned by its inhabitants, who had sought refuge in the mountains. The Ottoman policy was to re-people the vacant lands with Kurds; to divide the whole area up into small *sancaḳs*; and to place those that were easily accessible under the control of officials appointed by the Porte, leaving the rest in that of local chieftains. This was to favour the Kurds, who had aided Selîm against Ismâʿîl, because the latter had sought to control their depredations. Although, therefore, the Ottoman conquest restored some tranquillity to the region, it was in the long run deleterious to the Armenians, since it added to their disabilities as *Dimmîs* a dominance by their mortal enemies, the Kurds. As long as the central government remained strong enough to maintain some kind of control through its officials, a certain balance was maintained between the two races. But in later times the Kurds had matters all their own way and the Armenians suffered accordingly.

The new kinds of *Dimmîs* who, as we have mentioned, were brought under Ottoman rule by the conquests of Selîm and Süleymân, were all Christians adhering to various churches regarded by the Orthodox as heretical. We may therefore deal with them in the order of their foundation.

The first church, then, is the Nestorian. Its Christological difference from Orthodoxy is precisely the opposite of the Monophysite. Whereas Orthodoxy decided—in the fifth century—that Christ had two natures, one divine and one human, but only a single person, the Nestorians maintained that he had two persons each with its

[1] The Patriarch of Istanbul was in later times, at any rate, recognized as having jurisdiction over all Ottoman Armenians, though the Catholicoses of Sis and Aghtamin remained ecclesiastically subordinate only to the Patriarch of Echmiadzin—Steen, 64–65.

nature. When this doctrine was condemned by the Council of Ephesus its adherents met with such obloquy and later persecution at the hands of the Orthodox that they migrated eastwards into the dominions of Persia. The Sasanian Emperors welcomed them as rebels from Rome; and though the Zoroastrian priesthood raised objections to their toleration, tolerated they were, and grew in numbers, power, and area of influence until at the time of the Moslem conquests they formed the largest Christian community in the Caliphate. Throughout the ʿAbbâsid period (i.e. until 1256) they remained a considerable body despite their *ḏimmî* disabilities, their patriarch residing at the capital, Bağdâd; but their missionary enterprise, which had resulted in the foundation of Nestorian churches even in India and China, was now confined to the inner regions of Central Asia beyond the pale of Islâm. They were involved, however, in irretrievable disaster by the Mongol invasion of the thirteenth century. It is true that many of the Mongols themselves, including some of their Ḫâns, were actually converted to Nestorianism. But this was not enough to make up for the ruin brought on the centre of the Church in the ʿIrâḳ; moreover, on second thoughts the Mongols decided in favour of Islâm as their religion. The Nestorians' days of prosperity were over. The only considerable community to be found in the territories comprised in the Ottoman Empire was that of the district east of the middle Tigris and in the mountains of Kurdistan between Moṣul and Vân. It was that commonly called the 'Assyrian' (whose woes have more recently attracted the attention of the world). It was (and still is) controlled by a hereditary patriarch, the Mâr Ṣimʿûn, Catholicos of the East, then resident in a village to the north of Moṣul. The office of the Catholicos descended from uncle to nephew. Throughout our period the Nestorian community was in a state of extreme cultural and economic decay, and suffered further from the establishment of a rival patriarchate at Kotṣannes, on the Turco-Persian frontier, from the middle of the seventeenth to the beginning of the nineteenth century.[1]

The second heretical church was the Monophysite (whose distinguishing tenet was, as its name implies, that Christ had not only one person but one nature as well).[2] This was split into two branches, the Jacobite[3] of Syria and the Coptic of Egypt. Both were the object of persecution by the Orthodox down to the time of

[1] Steen, 26–33. *Encyc. Brit.*, artt. 'Church History' and 'Nestorians'; G. Graf, *Geschichte der christlichen arabischen Literatur*, iii (Vatican City, 1949), 61–64.

[2] Though it denied the imputation of Eutychianism: see p. 220, n. 6 above.

[3] So called from the name of the bishop, Jacob Baradeus (Bar ʿAddai), who restored it after persecution early in the sixth century.

the Moslem conquests; but both secured the allegiance of the bulk of the population, so that the Orthodox in Syria and Egypt alike were known as Melkites—King's men. Hence it was that when the Arabs began their raids, very many of the Syrians and Egyptians were by no means loath to exchange the sovereignty of the Emperor for that of the Caliph. In Egypt, indeed, whereas the 'Melkite' community was composed almost entirely of Greeks and other foreigners resident in Alexandria, the native Egyptians were with but few exceptions Monophysite, and actually aided the Moslems to effect their conquest. In both countries the Melkite community all but disappeared, though their three patriarchates remained in being with a handful of adherents, as we have indicated.

The Jacobite Church was not confined to Syria. It had spread in early times into the south of Asia Minor and into Mesopotamia, thus 'overlapping' its Nestorian rival. It again had a patriarch, styled of Antioch, who in the time of its greatest prosperity, in the early Middle Ages, headed a hierarchy of 150 bishops. For a time, beginning in the eighth century, the Jacobites effected a temporary union with the Armenian Church which, as we have noted, was likewise Monophysite; but they were less successful than the Nestorians in maintaining their numbers in face of the temptation to turn Moslem; and these gradually dwindled. The Crusades, too, affected them adversely, since the Crusaders, who were everywhere eager missionaries for Rome, were even worse disposed towards dissidents from Orthodoxy than towards the Orthodox themselves; and the first Crusade duly led to a considerable emigration of Jacobites from Syria to Egypt. In the sixteenth century, not long after the Ottoman conquest, the Jacobite population of Syria was estimated at about 50,000 families. Other congregations continued to exist in Mesopotamia, however, notably one at Bağdâd; and in later times the Patriarch has usually resided in the Jezîra.[1]

The Coptic Church, similarly, was not confined to Egypt. Besides that country its jurisdiction originally extended to Jerusalem, Pentapolis, Nubia, and Abyssinia. Very early, however, it acquired the character of a national church in Egypt, and perhaps for that reason, except for its connexion with Abyssinia, lost all influence elsewhere. It, too, was governed by a patriarch, resident in early times at Alexandria, later (on its foundation) at Cairo. After the Moslem conquest the Coptic Church gradually lost adherents through conversion to Islâm, largely because of the economic and social advantages that conversion brought with it. Nevertheless,

[1] At the monastery of Deyr al-Za'farân, near Mârdîn: Steen, 34–42. *Encyc. Brit.*, artt. 'Jacobite Church' and 'Church History'. The Jacobite Church also suffered from a rival patriarchate, at Ṭûr 'Abdîn: G. Graf, iii. 52–53. For the literature of the Jacobites in the Ottoman period, see Graf, iv (Vatican City, 1951), 3–41.

Copts continued down to and throughout our period to be employed in official positions, particularly in connexion with the finances. Although the laws designed to mark off *Dimmîs* as an inferior caste were sometimes applied to them with great rigour, they maintained themselves in relative prosperity until the thirteenth century. During the period of Mamlûk rule, however, most of the Coptic churches and monasteries were destroyed; the adherents of the Church dwindled to the small minority—about one-tenth—of the population that it has remained ever since; and the Coptic language, directly derived from that of ancient Egypt, fell out of use. Such, indeed, was the Church's distress that in 1439, presumably because he desired to obtain some support from the outside world, the then patriarch sent a delegate to the Council of Florence to participate in the proposed reunion of the Christian churches. This gesture, which seems to have been no more than a political move, produced little but controversy, and in spite of later negotiations[1] the Coptic Church retained its independence of Rome.[2]

The heretical character of the third church, the Maronite, was less definite at the date of the Ottoman conquest of Syria. But in earlier times, from the seventh to the twelfth centuries at least, its adherents, who inhabited the Lebanon, the anti-Lebanon, and Mount Hermon, had adopted the doctrine known as Monothelism: the assertion that Christ has but one will, as against the Orthodox dogma that he has two, one for each nature.[3] The heresy appears to have been imported into these regions shortly after 680, when it was condemned at the Council of Constantinople, by refugees fleeing from persecution. The Maronite Church was affected even more than the others that we have described by the rule of the Crusaders in Syria. Some of its bishops are said to have submitted to Rome late in the twelfth century; and it was formally united with the Roman Church in 1445, after the Council of Florence. Nevertheless, the patriarch and the bishops failed to carry the lower clergy or the people with them in this movement and for another three centuries they remained recalcitrant, although the connexion with Rome was never repudiated.[4] From the point of view of the Ottoman government, then, the Maronites at the time of the Conquest constituted a community of a kind slightly different from any other in the Empire. For there was only one other community in communion with Rome: the Uniate Armenians of Cilicia, that

[1] See below, p. 248.

[2] *Encyc. Brit.*, art. 'Copts'; Steen, 43–44, 129–30; E. L. Butcher, *The Story of the Church in Egypt*, vol. ii (London, 1897); G. Graf, iv. 114 sqq.

[3] See p. 227 above. The evidences for this earlier heterodoxy are controverted with much ingenuity by later Maronite apologists: see G. Graf, iii. 361 sqq., and the article 'Maronite' in *Dict. de Théologie Catholique*, vol. x (Paris, 1927).

[4] G. Graf, iii. 41 sqq.

is to say, Armenian congregations of that province which under the influence of the Crusaders[1] had in 1335 adopted the dogmas of the Roman Catholic Church and had been formally received into it, again by the Council of Florence, in 1439. Their position differed, however, from that of the Maronites in being quite unambiguous.

There were of course ordinary 'Latin' Catholics, as we have mentioned. Indeed the numbers of this community were much increased by the conquests of the sixteenth century. The only compact Catholic populations were on the north-western borders of the Orthodox world, beyond which the Ottoman Empire was thrust out by the enterprise of Süleyman, in northern Albania, Croatia, and Hungary. But both Cyprus and the Aegean islands that had hitherto formed the Latin Duchy of the Archipelago were conquered from Catholic rulers, who left behind them at least some adherents of their faith. In Cyprus, certainly, they appear to have been few, since the Latin hierarchy that had been dominant under the Lusignans and Venetians was abolished.[2] In the islands, on the other hand, the community was numerous enough to justify its retention, despite the agitations of the Oecumenical Patriarch.[3] As for the Asiatic accessions, after the reconquest of Jerusalem by Saladin the Latin clergy introduced by the Crusaders had been expelled; and few Catholic Christians, except the subjects of foreign powers, had, it appears, remained in any part of Syria. The Franciscans, however, maintained a regular mission in Jerusalem from 1336 until 1571, when they were ejected from their monastery on Mount Sion and removed to Aleppo.[4] The jurisdiction of the Franciscans in Jerusalem extended also to Egypt; but most of the early attempts to establish hospices in that country were frustrated by Moslem opposition. In 1697 Upper Egypt was placed under a separate Vicar Apostolic, and by the beginning of the eighteenth century the Franciscans had nine establishments in Upper Egypt in addition to hospices in Cairo, Alexandria, and Rosetta, which maintained relations with the Uniate (Catholic) Copts.[5]

The precedent set by Meḥmed the Conqueror of organizing the various communities of *Ḏimmîs* into recognized *millets* was not followed by his successors. They simply maintained the three

[1] The native kings of Lesser Armenia welcomed the Crusaders and established trading relations with the Italian republics. Later, moreover, the kingdom passed to a branch of the Lusignan dynasty which reigned from 1342 down to the Mamlûk conquest. In this and the following centuries a considerable number of Uniate Armenians migrated into Syria and Mesopotamia: G. Graf, iii. 59–60.

[2] See p. 225 above.

[3] W. Miller, *Latins in the Levant*, 635. The conquest was effected in 1564, although the Duke had for some time before paid tribute to the Sultan.

[4] G. Graf, iv. 169 sqq.

[5] For the Uniate Copts see p. 248 below.

original *millets* and classified all their non-Orthodox Christian subjects as Armenians. Indeed, the Armenian became as it were the *millet* of Heretics, into which such incompatibles as Catholics, Nestorians, and Jacobites were thrown together. The Armenian Patriarch had, officially, civil jurisdiction over them,[1] though in practice they seem to have been dealt with locally through their ecclesiastical dignitaries. The recognized communities, however, undoubtedly enjoyed an advantage over the others. They were able at any rate to protest with effect when attempts were made by other churches to proselytize their members.

Having enumerated the *ḏimmî* communities that were to be found in the Ottoman Empire at the time of its greatest extent, we may now consider the effect produced on the relations between them and the Moslem community by the conquests of the sixteenth century. The most notable, as we have indicated, was the shift in the balance of population, in which the Moslems now came to outnumber the *Ḏimmîs*, whereas before they had been outnumbered. This affected the whole Moslem outlook. In the first place the bulk of the new Moslem subjects of the Sultans were much more strictly *Sunnî* than the old. The result was an intensification of the leaning towards a strict Sunnism that had by now characterized the Sultans and their government for over a century, and induced a spirit of growing intolerance towards non-Moslems. The *Ḏimmîs* were, it is true, protected within definite limits by the rules laid down for their control in the Sacred Law. But their actual treatment depended, of course, on the spirit that animated their Moslem masters. In the second place the preponderance of Moslems in the population of the Empire made the reservation of high office to persons of *ḏimmî* birth seem far more illogical, and even preposterous, to the Moslem population than before. Hence there came about the Moslem revolt against this reservation that ushered in the period of decline.

This, as we have mentioned, is generally held to have begun at the millenary of the Hegira. It is indication enough of the growth of ill-feeling towards the *Ḏimmîs* by this date, that the millenary was expected to herald a defeat of Islâm by Christendom. This defeat was to be effected, probably, by hostile Christian powers, but with the aid of *ḏimmî* Christians. The latter were thus regarded as the natural allies of the external enemy. No doubt this view had always been held to some extent. It had been encouraged by the attempts of the fourteenth century on the part of popes and monarchs to launch crusades for the recovery of the Balkans. Then, however, it had been very obviously disproved by the evident preference of the Orthodox, if they might not conserve their in-

[1] See, for the Nestorians, Steen 28; for the Jacobites, ibid. 37.

dependence, to be ruled by Moslems rather than by Catholics. But by this time the existence of this antagonism can hardly have been remembered by the Moslem generality, to whom Christians of all colours were much alike.

In dealing with the *Dimmîs* during the period of decline we may begin, as before, with the Orthodox. They indeed were more affected than any other *dimmî* community by the Moslem capture of the 'Ruling Institution', since, as we have remarked, they alone had had access to it. The gradual abandonment of the *Devşirme* was no doubt greeted by them with relief. Yet they had been far from unconscious that enrolment was a door to glory, and in so far must have regretted its shutting. From the standpoint of the Ottoman polity the abandonment was undoubtedly deplorable: not only because it involved the disruption of the admirable order that had hitherto distinguished the Ruling Institution by peopling it with unruly Moslems; but because the *Devşirme*, by in some sort linking together the Moslem community and the most numerous and important community of *Dimmîs*, had formed a substitute for what would have been better still, the assimilation of the two. Islâm, in fact, fell between two stools. Its interests had been on the whole well served by the genuine toleration of the *Dimmîs* on the part of the earlier Sultans, and might also have been served by their forcible conversion, as Selîm the Grim had desired, but was prevented from attempting by the opposition of the *'Ulemâ*. But the contemptuous half-toleration with which the *dimmî* communities were treated in the later centuries rendered impossible any real co-operation and growth of a feeling of unity. Even while religious allegiance remained more important than national, the existence of unassimilated communities within them was always at least a potential danger to Moslem states;[1] and with the growth in modern times of national feeling this danger was enhanced. The Moslems of the 'original' provinces of the Ottoman Empire, few of whom had much, and most of whom had no Turkish blood, came to be regarded, wherever they had abandoned their local languages in favour of Turkish, as Turks—at least by Europe and the *Dimmîs*

[1] It is worth noting that the history of the older Moslem states in Asia and Africa offered more than one example of this; for instance, the association between Mardaites and Greeks in Syria in the seventh century, between Maronites and Crusaders in the eleventh, and between Nestorians and Mongols in Mesopotamia in the thirteenth. Consciously or unconsciously, therefore, the Moslem authorities had been driven to a policy of steady pressure upon the non-Moslem communities which, while rarely proceeding to the extreme of active persecution, had the effect of relegating the bulk of them to isolated areas, generally in the mountainous regions. Thus, by the time of the Ottoman conquest, the non-Moslems actually living amongst the Moslems in Asia and Egypt were for the most part small 'remnant' bodies, whose presence was indispensable, or at least desirable, for the economic activities of Moslem society.

—and so to be separated from the latter by a 'racial' as well as a religious barrier. This largely false racial distinction, therefore, came to intensify the contrast between governing Moslems and subject *Dimmîs* that the capture of the Ruling Institution and the consequent abandonment of the *Devşirme* initiated.

The Orthodox *millet* consisted of Greeks, Serbs, Bulgarians, Rumanians,[1] Bosnians, and the inhabitants of southern Albania. The Ottoman government, however, took little or no cognizance of these national or racial differences. To it they were all of the '*Rûm milleti*'; and since *Rûm* also denoted Greek,[2] they tended all to be regarded more or less as Greeks. The authority over the whole Church conferred on the Oecumenical Patriarch, moreover, resulted actually in a considerable graecizing of the Slavs. In Bulgaria, for instance, the Constantinopolitan clergy monopolized the highest places in the Church and filled the parishes with Greek priests. In the schools supported by the *millet*, moreover, only Greek was taught, so that Greek soon became the language of the better-to-do Bulgarians that attended them. Finally, the Slavonic liturgy was suppressed; and though this was no less unintelligible to the unlettered Bulgarians than the Greek that replaced it, its suppression swept away another 'national' distinction. Similar developments seem to have taken place in the territories inhabited by the Serbs. The maintenance of their independence by the prince-bishops of Montenegro, who were consecrated by the patriarchs of Ipek, encouraged the Serb *Dimmîs*, however, to think of themselves as a distinct people.[3] It was only in areas where either the Moslems were distinguished by a provincial name—such as Bosnia and Albania—or where a special régime was in force—such as the Principalities—that the *Dimmîs* were recognized as being of a race distinct from the Greek. And in the case of the Bulgarians so complete was their absorption in the Greek *millet* that in the first place there is actually no mention of them by name in Ottoman official documents until after the period of our survey,[4] except as *Voynuks*,[5] and, in the second, their very existence as a people was almost unknown in Europe even to students of Slavonic literature as late as the beginning of the nineteenth century.[6]

As for the real Greeks, they turned their privileged position to

[1] Including those known as *Kutzovlaks* living outside the Principalities in various parts of the Balkan Peninsula, particularly in southern Macedonia—Steen, 194 sq.

[2] The Greek language, called by the Greeks themselves Romaic, being referred to in Turkish as '*Rumca*'.

[3] *Encyc. Brit.*, artt. 'Montenegro' and 'Orthodox Eastern Church'.

[4] Aḥmed Refîķ, *Türk Idaresinde Bulgaristan.*

[5] See Part I, p. 54.

[6] *Encyc. Brit.*, art. 'Bulgaria'. Indeed the Bulgarian alphabet was invented only at this time—see Steen, 153.

good use. While the other Orthodox *Dimmîs* were all but forgotten by Europe, they attracted its attention as the Christians of the Empire *par excellence*, and on their side kept in touch with developments in the West, particularly, as was natural at the time, in the sphere of religion. The most outstanding and important instance of this interest is afforded by the career of the Cretan Cyril Lucaris, who after travelling in Italy and visiting Geneva, became Patriarch successively of Alexandria and Constantinople (the latter in 1621). In Geneva Lucaris came under the influence of Calvin, and returned to the Levant imbued with a desire to reform the Orthodox Church on Calvinistic lines. To this end he sent a number of young Greek theologians to study in Switzerland, Holland, and England, and in 1629 published a *Confession*, in which he dressed up Calvinistic propositions in Orthodox guise. The book caused a *furore*, not only in the Orthodox *millet*, but in Europe, where it was forthwith translated into several languages. Lucaris, as Patriarch, was in a strong position. But he failed to carry many of his subordinates with him, and had, moreover, to face the opposition of certain Jesuit missions, who preferred the single error of the Orthodox to the legion of the Protestants. Lucaris was at length, in 1637, accused to Murad IV of plotting to stir up certain Cossacks to rebellion, and was executed. But the question of his proposed reform continued to agitate the Orthodox Church throughout the seventeenth century.[1]

His doctrine was finally condemned in 1691. But the controversy it provoked had meanwhile proved of incalculable value to Orthodoxy. In the first place it had obliged the Orthodox to consider their position afresh and so had revitalized their faith: the confession promulgated by the Synod of Jerusalem in 1672, at which the propositions of Lucaris were refuted article by article, is said to have been the most vital statement made by the Greek Church for a thousand years.[2] In the second, it diverted from Orthodoxy itself part of the attack launched by Rome in the early seventeenth century, chiefly by means of the Jesuits. And in the third it brought about a closer collaboration than had hitherto existed between the hierarchy of the Empire and that of Russia.[3] With the Catholic attack we shall deal in detail later when considering the position of the Catholic *Dimmîs*. But here we may mention that, though it was only very moderately successful in achieving its main object, conversion, it resulted in the penetration

[1] Jorga, iv. 23–31. *Encyc. Brit.*, art. 'Orthodox Eastern Church'.

[2] *Encyc. Brit.*, artt. 'Jerusalem, Synod of', and 'Lucaris, Cyrillos'.

[3] See Jorga, iv. 30, for a meeting of Greek, Rumanian, and Russian clergy in 1644 to subscribe to the confession of Peter Movila and to determine the position of the metropolitan Church of Kiev and the Patriarchate of Moscow; and ibid. 173 for other contacts.

of higher Greek society with European ideas—so that the 'Westernization' of the Greeks began quite a century before that of the more educated Ottoman Moslems.[1] Hence in the new era that opened with the Peace of Carlovitz in 1699 the Greeks were ready to play an ever more important role in the governance of the Sultan's dominions.

The Peace of Carlovitz marks a turning-point in Ottoman history. Not only did it provide for the first large cession of territory in Europe to Christian powers, but it rendered the Ottoman Empire, whose rulers had hitherto been able virtually to do what they would, dependent for the future on the changes of European politics. Both these circumstances were important for the *Dimmîs*, particularly the Orthodox. For the first implied that the whole Orthodox world (always excepting Russia) was no longer Ottoman, and the second forced the Porte to consider foreign policy in a fresh light, and to turn for help to those of its subjects that were the best versed in European affairs.[2] It is true that the Greeks thus called in to aid in negotiations with foreign powers were those of a very small class, resident in the quarter of the Phanar in Istanbul,[3] and that the Moslem ministers and officials held the services that they performed, as Dragomans, to be quite menial—so that in reading Turkish annals one is scarcely aware of their existence. Nevertheless, the enhanced importance of the Phanariots redounded in some degree to the credit of the whole *millet*, and was further marked by the government's decision in 1716 thenceforward to appoint Phanariots as Hospodars of the Principalities.

By the Peace of Carlovitz, Hungary, Transylvania, and Podolia were lost for ever to the Sultans. But the Venetian occupation of the Morea, which it also provided for, was only temporary. It lasted until 1718, when the Treaty of Passarovitz put an end to it. Venice, however, still held certain tracts of what had formerly been Ottoman territory in Albania and Dalmatia. Moreover, this same peace gave the Belgrade region and Little Wallachia to Austria. Austria in turn lost them at the Peace of Belgrade in 1739. But by that time the mischief, from the Ottoman point of view, had been done: Greeks, Serbians, and Rumanians had had a taste of foreign

[1] It became common during the seventeenth century for Greek students to attend the colleges founded for their benefit at both Rome and Venice. Others studied in Padua, Naples, and the Ionian Islands. See Jorga, iv. 20. For the missions sent by Lucaris to Germany, Switzerland, and England, see p. 235 above.

[2] Even before the second siege of Vienna a Greek, Panagiotes Nikussios, played an important part in Ottoman foreign policy; but the most notable of the early Phanariots was Alexander Mavrocordato, who was habitually consulted by the Grand *Vêzir*, Rami Paşa, at the turn of the century—see Jorga, iv. 281, 283 sq.

[3] See Jorga, iv. 280; also 282—only some fifty families were well enough off to assert themselves. They depended on banking for their wealth.

rule,[1] and though it did not by any means universally appeal to them, the experience was unsettling: it turned their thoughts to the possibility of independence.[2] This was something new. Except during the early years of the conquest the Balkan peoples had never made any serious attempt to throw off Ottoman rule. And this was not merely because during the heyday of the Empire they had been too weak to do so: they really seem to have been moderately content with their lot, because then they had been justly ruled. During the seventeenth century, however, provincial administration in nearly every part of the Empire had grown more and more disorganized. The *Paşas* and their subordinates, obliged to pay large sums for office, oppressed the peasantry, Christian and Moslem alike, in attempts to recoup themselves.

The European provinces also suffered sadly at the end of the seventeenth century and the beginning of the eighteenth from the depredations of the Ottoman armies, in which by this time discipline had greatly decayed. This was true especially of Bulgaria, since all forces setting out northward from Istanbul were bound to pass through it. On the re-establishment of Ottoman rule in the Morea, again, the Porte had sought to repopulate the country, which had lost very large numbers of its inhabitants in the wars, by colonizing it with Albanians who proved far from friendly neighbours to the Greeks.[3] A notable result of these various happenings was to encourage the hardier *D̲immîs* all over the peninsula to take to brigandage, a way of life that its geography had always favoured. Among the Greeks these brigands went by the name of *Klepht*, among the Slavs by that of *Hayduk*.[4] Their principal object was robbery; but their natural enemies were the Ottoman troops sent from time to time to put an end to their activities; and these, partly through the encouragement of foreign powers, gradually took on a political aspect: their banditry and violence were now held to be forms of legitimate and even sanctified revolt against the tyranny of their Ottoman masters. Under the *millet* system the Sultans had allowed local *D̲immîs* a considerable measure of self-government. Their representative headmen were known as *Ḳoca Başîs* (head elders), who apparently dealt in

[1] See Jorga, iv. 326 sq. Both the Greeks of the Morea and the Rumanians of Little Wallachia disliked Venetian and Austrian rule respectively—the first largely because of the Venetians' Catholicizing activities, their interference with long-established trade relations, the high taxation they imposed, and their policy of colonization; the second because of the introduction by the Austrians of distressingly regular taxation. The Serbs, on the other hand, prospered under and welcomed Austrian rule at this period.

Miller, *The Ottoman Empire and its Successors*, 24, admits that Venetian rule was unpopular while it lasted, but states that it was actually an improvement on that of the Ottomans.

[2] *Encyc. Brit.*, art. 'Greece'.

[3] Ibid.

[4] *Encyc. Brit.*, art. 'Bulgaria'. *Haydut* in Turkish.

the provinces with the *Subaşîs*. To cope with the *Klephts* and *Hayduks* they used a similar method, enrolling bands of loyal *Dimmîs* from the villages that suffered from the marauders. Members of these armed bands, however, were always inclined on slight provocation to join the brigands that they were out to suppress; and with the rebirth of 'nationalist' feeling among the *Dimmî* peoples they became less and less dependable.

It will be clear from what we have related that the Orthodox *millet* cannot be regarded as by any means a homogeneous body. For apart from its racial divisions, which were practically ignored, the Phanariot Greeks that headed it were in a position altogether different from that of its other members. From about the middle of the seventeenth century, and especially after the Peace of Carlovitz, they set themselves in general against any attempt to overthrow Ottoman rule in favour of any foreign power: their aim became rather to improve their position in the state and ultimately to control it and convert it into a reborn Byzantine Empire. In order to attain this aim they sought to enhance the prestige both of the Orthodox Church and of the Principalities, and to use their position of influence in Ottoman diplomacy to improve its direction.[1] During the eighteenth century the Phanariots did much to achieve these purposes. They did not, however, pursue them single-mindedly: they wavered at times towards falling in with foreign, especially Russian, designs of conquest. The Tsars aimed also at a restoration of the Byzantine Empire—with themselves, of course, on its throne;[2] and the Phanariots, because the Ottoman Orthodox and the Russian clergy maintained close relations, sometimes inclined to this scheme for the repair of their fortunes rather than to their own scheme, and in doing so damaged their prestige with the Moslems. Nevertheless, the Greeks greatly improved their position both in the Ottoman government and in the Orthodox *millet* during the eighteenth century. Thus many more of them than before were employed in the Ottoman administration; and their hold over the *millet* was much strengthened by the appointment everywhere of Greek priests.[3] In 1766 and 1767, indeed, the patriarchates of Ipek and Ochrida were actually abolished.[4] Now, therefore, there was but one Orthodox Patriarchate in the European provinces, the Oecumenical.

[1] See Jorga, iv. 280 sq.

[2] This aim of the Tsars had been formulated at least as early as the mid-seventeenth century, as it was then divulged to the Porte by a Pole—Jorga, iv. 175–6.

[3] *Encyc. Brit.*, art. 'Greece'.

[4] Ibid., art. 'Orthodox Eastern Church'. The last patriarch of Ochrida abdicated voluntarily—Steen, 147. The see of Ipek was forcibly suppressed, the Oecumenical Patriarch paying the Porte 65,000 *akçes*—ibid. 176–7. The sup-

If the Phanariots had pursued their policy of gradually obtaining control of the Ottoman Empire with pertinacity, and had conducted themselves with such integrity as both to win the confidence of the Moslems and to introduce sensible improvements into the administration, their hopes might possibly have been fulfilled. But, as for integrity, their influence was largely acquired by judicious corruption; and as for pertinacity, they were not always capable of withstanding the blandishments of foreign powers. Down to the terminal date of our survey nationalist feeling, which was in the end to prove fatal to their policy, had made but little headway among the *millet* at large. But the provincial administration steadily deteriorated, so that local insurrections grew more and more common and provided an ideal ground for the subversive propaganda of foreign agents. In so far, therefore, as the Phanariots identified themselves with the Ottoman government in their efforts to dominate it, they found themselves at cross purposes with those provincial *Ḏimmîs* who were provoked either by its incapacity or tyranny, or by the incitement of foreign agents, or by both, to rebellion. The *Ḏimmîs* most susceptible to such foreign incitement were the northern Serbs and some of the Bulgarians. And these at first favoured the Austrians, despite their Catholicism. But when the Treaty of Belgrade deprived the Austrians of their conquests they turned their eyes to Russia, recently reanimated by Peter the Great.[1] The propaganda of the Tsars was in any case rendered much more attractive than that of Austria by the fact that Russia was Orthodox; and during the period of our survey it made great headway in many parts of the peninsula, particularly in the last years of peace. Its success, however, was fatal to the Phanariots' aim of increasing their influence in the Empire so far as virtually to control it. For this they could hope to do only by making themselves indispensable to the Moslems in the face of an already vigorous anti-Christian prejudice. And the oftener members of the *millet* were convicted of disloyalty, the more this prejudice was justified and nourished. The two policies, of controlling the Empire, and of escaping from or overthrowing it, were incompatible, and the first was already doomed to failure because it was not exclusively pursued.

The age during which the Ottoman Empire declined as a whole

pression of this see necessitated the application henceforward by the Vladikas of Montenegro to the Patriarchate of Carlovitz—later they were to apply to St. Petersburg and finally Belgrade, ibid. 181. The patriarchs of Alexandria also now habitually resided at Istanbul and were appointed by the Oecumenical Patriarch without reference to the wishes of their (nominal) flocks—ibid. 130. Those of Antioch were also appointed from among the Constantinopolitan clergy between 1728 and 1850—ibid. 134. The patriarchs of Jerusalem, on the other hand, usually nominated their successors—ibid. 137.

[1] *Encyc. Brit.*, art. 'Bulgaria'.

witnessed also the decline of the Jewish *millet* within it. The millenary of the Hegira was a turning-point for both; both attained their greatest prosperity directly before it. Symbolical of this prosperity was the career of a Marano immigrant from Portugal, by name Joseph Nasi. This personage succeeded, during the later years of Süleymân the Magnificent, in winning such favour with that Sultan as to secure his intervention with the Pope on behalf of his co-religionists,[1] and with Henri II of France and his sons on behalf of Nasi himself, to whom they were in debt.[2] Under Süleymân's successor, Selîm II, Nasi grew more powerful still. When as a prince Selîm's succession to the throne had been in doubt, Nasi had supported it; and Selîm rewarded him with unbounded confidence. He became the Sultan's favourite, was approached by the most powerful monarchs of Europe to intercede with his master, was made Duke of Naxos and twelve islands of the Cyclades, brought about a declaration of war on Venice, and even had hopes, as a result of this campaign, which added Cyprus to the Empire, of being created king of that island. In this latter aim he was disappointed owing to the hostility of the Grand *Vezîr* Ṣoḳollu.[3] Ṣoḳollu was not animated by anti-Jewish prejudice, however, since he had a Jewish favourite of his own, Solomon ben Nathan, who also exercised great influence in the state even after his patron's death.[4] Jewish ladies, again, were much patronized by the Imperial *Ḥarem* at this time, chiefly for their knowledge of medicine.[5] Under cover of these powerful advocates at Court the *millet* flourished. By the reign of Süleymân the Italian-Levant trade was already as much in Jewish hands as in Venetian;[6] and by that of Selîm II Jews had come largely to control both the wholesale commerce of the Empire and the collection of customs.[7]

The Jewish heyday came to an end, however, with the death of Selîm and the accession of Murâd III. Although Murâd allowed Nasi to retain his offices and rank, he excluded him from any participation in affairs,[8] and when he died in 1579, confiscated his fortune, as if he were a *Ḳapî Ḳulu*.[9] The Sultan also insisted on the observance of the sumptuary laws as laid down in the *Şerîʿa*, whereby Jews and other *Dimmîs* were obliged to wear distinctive clothes.[10]

[1] Galanté, *Turcs et Juifs*, 13; Graetz, iv. 614–15, 633; Franco, 57.
[2] Franco, 60, 62–65; Galanté, loc. cit.
[3] Graetz, iv. 632 sq., 650; Franco, 55, 61, 62, 65–66. Cf. *Encyc. of Islam*, art. 'Selim II'.
[4] Graetz, iv. 641 sq.
[5] Ibid. 647, 669; Franco, 72–73.
[6] Graetz, iv. 616.
[7] Ibid. 646–7.
[8] Ibid. 665, 668; Franco, 66.
[9] *Jew. Encyc.*, art. 'Turkey'; Franco, 72.
[10] *Jew. Encyc.*, art. 'Turkey'. The decree was due, it is said, to Murâd's resentment at the inordinate luxury of the Jews, whom he had at first wished to massacre.

This was a sign that henceforward the Jews were to be relegated to the inferior status that in strict Moslem eyes was proper to non-believers. In fact, with the turn of the century the prosperity of the *millet* rapidly declined, having endured just 200 years.

This development was due no doubt partly to loss of influence in the state—more necessary than ever in these times of increasing corruption. But it was due also, it appears, to a change of spirit among the Jews themselves. The unaccustomed liberty and favour they had enjoyed under the Sultans' rule for over a century induced a revival of national sentiment, or perhaps we should say an intensification of the solidarity characteristic of Jewry. This was variously exemplified during the sixteenth century: in a movement set on foot for the regular ordination of Rabbis by a central body such as had not existed for centuries;[1] in the reduction to some order by a Palestinian doctor of Rabbinic and Talmudic traditions;[2] and above all in a revival of Messianic hopes, greatly fostered by the spread of Kabbalistic teaching.[3] The theosophical-mystical system of the Kabbalah, which had been elaborated in a reaction against the rationalist legalism of orthodox Judaism from the eleventh century onwards, answered more or less the same religious needs among Jews as did Ṣûfism among Moslems. It also had the same defects: it led to a similar growth of superstition.[4] In the latter part of the sixteenth century two personages made their appearance, announcing themselves as 'precursor' Messiahs of the House of Joseph. They impressed the people with wonder-working, very much in the manner of *dervîş* saints; and the teaching of one of them, Isaac Lurya Levi, gave immense impetus to the theosophical Messianic movement, which made great headway particularly in the Levant during the last quarter of the sixteenth century and the first half of the seventeenth, not only among the Jewish masses but also among the educated. Lurya proclaimed that he and his companion were to be followed by a Messiah of the House of David; and those versed in Kabbalistic lore fixed on the year 1648 as that in which the manifestation should take place.[5] Meanwhile, in 1626, there had been born at Smyrna a Jew of Spanish descent by name Sabbatai, who as a youth, after studying the teaching of Lurya and adopting an ascetic discipline, became convinced that he was the Messiah predicted. Oddly enough Sabbatai was encouraged in his belief by a knowledge of the Millennarianism prevalent in England at the time owing to the circumstance that his father was employed in an English trading house

[1] Graetz, iv. 563–71.
[2] Ibid. 651 sq.
[3] Ibid. 656 sq.
[4] The chief centres of Kabbalistic study at this period were Salonika and Ṣafad—Graetz, iv. 433.
[5] Ibid. 661 sq.; Franco, 82 sq., 88.

established at Smyrna.[1] In 1648 he duly declared himself. He at once acquired a following, but also encountered much opposition; and it was not until, after many wanderings, he visited Palestine and Egypt that his fame became widespread. The Rabbis of the Holy Land excommunicated him, it is true; but when in 1665 he returned to Smyrna he was greeted with frenzied enthusiasm, the following year having been predicted as that in which the apocalyptic kingdom should be established. By now his fame had spread from the Levant to some of the great commercial centres of the west—Venice, Amsterdam, Hamburg, and London. Sabbatai was acquiring world fame. He was reputed to perform miracles, and attracted a following among the Moslems. Hence, early in the fatal year he was arrested on arrival at Istanbul, where the authorities kept him in confinement, later removing him to Çanaḳ-ḳalʿe;[2] and finally, since public excitement failed to abate, he was brought before the Sultan, Meḥmed IV, at Adrianople.

Unhappily for the hopes of his followers, Sabbatai was no hero. He was frightened by the Moslem authorities into accepting Islâm. The disappointment in the Jewish world was cruel. The whole belief in an imminent apocalypse that had now dominated it for a century collapsed. Nevertheless, many of Sabbatai's adherents continued to hope against hope, and after his death, which occurred in 1676, transferred their allegiance to his young brother-in-law, Jacob by name, whom his widow passed off as his son. The centre of the revival was Salonika, where Jacob lived. He, too, preached the mystical theosophy of Lurya, and was revered as the Messiah and even as an incarnation of God. Scandals brought about by his doctrine of divorce, however, led to investigations by the Ottoman authorities; and Jacob, like his predecessor, turned Moslem to escape punishment. Yet, unlike Sabbatai, he made a virtue of his conversion; and dominated his followers enough to carry them with him. There thus came into being a new sect, half-Jewish half-Moslem, that was destined to endure. It is known in Turkish as *Dönme* (Convert). Its doctrine is Kabbalistic; but its ritual has Moslem as well as Jewish features; and the sectaries both frequent mosques as well as their own places of worship and observe Moslem as well as Jewish holidays. Adherents of the new doctrine organized themselves more or less as a *millet*, though it remained unrecognized, their chief religious functionary, for instance, dis-

[1] The English was the most influential of the foreign colonies established at Smyrna. Its members did much to improve the intellectual and economic condition of the region—see *Encyc. of Islam*, art. 'Izmīr'. Cf. Jorga, iv. 26, 265.

[2] This is what is meant by the Abydos of the accounts cited. Abydos had long been a ruin by the seventeenth century and had been replaced by Çanaḳ-ḳalʿe as the chief town on the Asiatic coast of the Dardanelles—see *Islâm Ansiklopedisi*, art. 'Çanakkale'.

pensing justice among them. Down to the period of our survey there were two chief communities, one at Salonika and one at Smyrna. Their numbers, however, were never large.[1]

The revival among the Jews of hopes in the immediate manifestation of a Messiah thus culminated in the formation of a new, and ultimately insignificant, sect. But this was not its most important consequence. Until these hopes were disappointed, the cultivation of the Kabbalistic mysticism on which they were based seems to have thrown the *millet* at large off its balance. No doubt it was to the growing bigotry of the Moslems and the corruption of their institutions that was due the loss by the Jews of the influence and the concomitant prosperity that they had enjoyed in the sixteenth century. But Messianism seems to have contributed to it by concentrating their attention on illusory hopes, and by encouraging the growth of superstition at the expense of culture. In any case they no longer flourished as they had.[2] Nor, owing to the general decline of prosperity in the Empire, and the simultaneous improvement of the conditions under which their coreligionists were able to live in parts of Europe, might they now congratulate themselves on inhabiting the Sultan's dominions.[3] Nevertheless, down to the time of our survey individual Jews sometimes exercised great influence at Istanbul,[4] and the community as a whole seems to have retained in its hands a proportionate share in industry and commerce[5] and to have suffered little more than the humiliation, pointed by the intermittent enforcement of the sumptuary laws, attaching to their status of *dimmî* inferiority. In Egypt, indeed, they were in a peculiarly strong position as brokers of the

[1] Franco, 94–114; *Encyc. Brit.*, art. 'Sabbatai Sebi'; *Encyc. of Islam*, art. 'Dönme'.

[2] Franco, 118; Graetz, iv. 670. Rycaut in his account of the Ottoman Jews (late seventeenth century) states that they were then 'esteemed by the Turks to be the scum of the world' and were so much despised that even Jews converted to Islâm were excluded from burial in Moslem cemeteries. But it is likely that he took his views from the local Christians, between whom and the Jews there was no love lost. For some Christian intrigues against the Jews see Gallanté, 16 sq.

[3] There was even some emigration to Austria, particularly after the Treaty of Passarovitz in 1715, though the emigrants sometimes retained Ottoman nationality—Franco, 119.

[4] e.g. Fonseca, the physician of Aḥmed III (1703–30)—see Franco, 117—and Juda Baruch, the chief *ṣarrâf* (for *ṣarrâfs* see above, p. 23) under Muṣṭafâ III (1757–73)—ibid. 120.

[5] Franco, 115, reports a French Franciscan, Michel Febvre, who lived for eighteen years in the Ottoman Empire in the latter half of the seventeenth century, as stating that in his day the Jews were found in all large centres as bankers, money-changers, coin-clippers, money-lenders, gold-thread-spinners, dealers in second-hand goods, customs officials, market-brokers, doctors, druggists, and interpreters. They had made themselves indispensable to traders of all kinds, including their rivals the Greeks and Armenians, and acted with such solidarity that no one dared attempt retaliation for any dishonesty lest he should be boycotted by the rest.

precious metals, and during the first half of the eighteenth century they monopolized the farming of the customs. But the *avanias* of ʿAlî Bey hit them severely; and the crowning blow was given by the capture of the customs administration by the Syrian Christians in 1769.[1]

Of the Armenian *millet* and all the other Christian communities (whether or not they were still held to form part of it) there is little to relate during the period of decline, except to note the progress made by one of the communities, the Catholic, at the expense of most of, if not all, the others. This progress was due to two causes: first the influence in Ottoman affairs secured by France from the date of the conclusion of the first Capitulations between François Ier and Süleymân;[2] and, secondly, the foundation in 1622 of the Congregatio de Propaganda Fide by Pope Gregory XV as a body of control for Catholic missions. But for the support of France the Catholics would have been too weak in the face of the hostility that proselytization evoked to pursue it with success; and it was not until the foundation of Propaganda that their missionary enterprise was regulated and intensified. The Orders by which it was chiefly carried on were the Jesuits and the Franciscans, particularly the Capuchins.[3] The Jesuits appear to have been especially active at the capital, where, despite a momentary expulsion decreed at the instance of the ambassadors of the Protestant powers,[4] they worked vigorously among the ever-growing population of Galata and Péra.[5] In Bosnia, in Albania (where they even provoked a rising in 1638),[6] and along the Danube, where they were favoured by the still native Hospodars of the Principalities, it was the Franciscans that took the lead.[7] The Franciscans also devoted their attention to the Bogomils of southern Bulgaria, large numbers of whom renounced their errors in 1650;[8] while the Capuchins achieved considerable

[1] See below, p. 260.

[2] The protection of the Latin Christians in the Ottoman Empire by the King of France was first definitely stipulated, however, in the Capitulations of 1673, followed by similar 'protectorates' over Christians in general granted to England in 1675, and over Catholic Christians to Austria in the Peace of Carlovitz in 1699: G. Graf, iii. 22. The Austrians were particularly active in protecting the 'Syrian Catholics' (ibid. 57) and the Uniate Copts (ibid. 75), as well as in the Balkans.

[3] The Capuchin branch of the Franciscans, formed early in the sixteenth century, was recognized as a distinct organization in 1619. For their missionary propaganda see Graf, iv. 191 sqq., and for that of the Jesuits, ibid. 206 sqq.

[4] In 1628: Jorga, iv. 27.

[5] The Genoese colony was reinforced soon after the conquest by an influx of Greeks, Jews, and Armenians. Early in the sixteenth century Moslems began to settle there as well, and to convert both Catholic and Orthodox churches into mosques: *Encyc. of Islam*, art. 'Constantinople'; cf. Jorga, iv. 21.

[6] Jorga, loc. cit.

[7] Ibid. A Uniate Greek was appointed as bishop by the Hospodar of Moldavia in 1647.

[8] Jorga, iv. 20–21.

success in the islands of the Archipelago.[1] Down to this time most of these missionaries were Italians, drawn chiefly from the states of central and southern Italy. But Louis XIV exerted himself to give the leadership to French members of the two Orders. Hitherto French policy, as far as it was concerned with religious matters, had been directed principally to securing the recognition of the protectorate of France over all Catholics of whatever nationality in the Empire. But *le Grand Monarque*, to whom, especially in his later days, the Jesuit cause was dear, desired to take a hand in the conversion of the schismatics. The reconciliation of this policy with that of especial friendliness with the Porte—on which depended the recognition of France's right to protect all Europeans not otherwise represented diplomatically—was no simple matter. The Catholic had always been regarded as *par excellence* the 'foreign' religion. Care, however, was taken to avoid the most obvious cause of provocation: the missionaries were explicitly instructed not to attempt the conversion of Moslems. They were also to aim, discreetly, at converting individuals rather than at effecting the reconciliation of whole communities. These principles were laid down in consultation between the French government, the heads of the orders in France, and a representative of the Holy See.

Catholicism was held to be peculiarly 'foreign' partly because, when the *millets* were formed, almost its only adherents to be found in the Empire were foreigners such as the Genoese of Galata, and partly because it was then the religion of all the 'Franks', the hereditary enemies in chief of Islâm. An especial prejudice against it continued to animate the Sultans, which was exemplified by the policy they pursued in those parts of the Empire that they conquered from 'Latin' rulers, such as the Morea, the islands, and Cyprus, where they championed Orthodoxy at its expense, and by the encouragement they gave to the Coptic Church to break its connexion with Rome. When, near the end of the sixteenth century, the Porte entered into relations with Protestant powers, the influence of these powers was naturally exerted to intensify this prejudice, and did much to neutralize the advantage gained by France as the first European power to ally itself with the Porte.[2] It was not until very much later—after the period of our survey indeed—that the various Protestant churches themselves undertook missionary work in the Ottoman Empire. The relations of Protestant powers with the Porte were not, therefore, complicated in this respect, as were those of France, during the time when the

[1] Ibid. 19. The conversion to Islâm of the Orthodox Metropolitan of Rhodes provided a fine opportunity for Catholic propaganda.

[2] See Jorga, iv. 25, for the support afforded by the Dutch and English ambassadors to Lucaris.

Sultans were still absolute masters in their own house. French diplomacy was, however, conducted with sufficient skill to give the Catholic missionaries wide opportunities for pursuing their aims; and the number of their converts gradually increased. How far they made individual conversions it is difficult to judge. No doubt in many cases converts were brought into the regular 'Latin' Church. But where Uniate churches with other rites existed, conversions were frequently made from the corresponding 'schismatic' community. Moreover, although the policy generally favoured by the Catholic missionaries was to avoid awkward publicity by the conversion of communities, new Uniate churches were formed by secessions from the Orthodox, the Nestorian, and the Jacobite churches. The method most frequently adopted was to encourage the formation of a pro-Roman party among the clergy, to secure the election of one of these to a vacant patriarchate (although the election was not confirmed by the civil authorities), and thereafter to consolidate the new Uniate community around the new (and still irregular) Catholic Patriarchate.[1]

The resentment aroused by this policy in the churches thus attacked, and the resulting conflicts between the clergy and adherents of the rival factions, need not be described here in detail. The reactions of the Gregorian Patriarch were, as might be expected, especially vigorous in the case of conversions to the Uniate Armenian Church. His position as *Millet-başi* enabled him to use various forms of pressure against the converts,[2] and his influence at the Porte secured him a considerable measure of official support in the conflict with the Catholic missionaries.[3] In 1702, in fact, the Gregorian Patriarch Avedik secured not only the expulsion of Uniate converts from Armenia to Persia, but also the closing of the Jesuit schools in Constantinople. In retaliation he was kidnapped by the French minister, put on a French vessel, and taken to France, where he died five years later.[4]

The Uniate Armenians in Constantinople, Anatolia, and Rumelia remained during the whole of our period under the spiritual government of the Latin Vicar Apostolic of Constantinople.

[1] 'La plupart des adhésions épiscopales restaient secrètes et aucune rupture n'existait entre le patriarche et ses suffragants unionistes. C'était l'effet de la méthode adoptée par les jésuites d'obtenir le plus grand nombre possible d'adhésions secrètes pour créer un mouvement sérieux au moment opportun.' *Dict. de Théologie Catholique*, vol. x, col. 519 (with reference to the Uniate Greeks).

[2] Since Uniate converts remained, both in Asia and in Europe, under the civil jurisdiction of the Gregorian Patriarchate.

[3] See Cevdet, ii. 93, for the attitude of the Ottoman government to Armenian conversions in 1630 and 1734.

[4] *Dict. Th. Cath.*, vol. i, col. 1909. On a later occasion, during the reign of Maḥmûd I (1730–54), the fury of the Gregorians was more tactfully placated by the French ambassador: De Rausas, i. 83.

In 1740 a Uniate bishop was elected to the Patriarchate of Sîs and Cilicia; and though he was extruded by the regular Gregorian Patriarch and compelled to exercise his functions from a residence in Lebanon, he was recognized by the Papacy as possessing jurisdiction over all Catholic Armenians in the Arab provinces and Egypt.[1] The Uniate Armenian Church was from this time formally organized, though it was not recognized as a separate *millet* until 1830.[2]

In the same way, the Uniate Greek Church grew but slowly out of the controversies arising from the Council of Florence and the labours of the Catholic orders in Syria. Its first congregation[3] seems to have been formed only at the end of the seventeenth century. Its official patriarchate began with an attempt to occupy the vacant see of Antioch in 1724, quickly countered by the synod at Constantinople, and for the next hundred years it was involved in a bitter struggle with the Orthodox, who had again the advantage of the support of the *Paşas*.[4] The rivalry, sustained by a vigorous polemical literature as well as by open violence and street brawls, had, however, at least one salutary effect, in stimulating a measure of intellectual activity among both parties,[5] each of which set up Arabic printing-presses in Syria during the eighteenth century.[6]

The Uniate secession from the Nestorian Church began in the reign of Süleymân, as the result of a dispute over the succession to the Catholicate in 1551.[7] The dissident Patriarch was recognized by Pope Julius II in 1553 as 'Patriarch of the Chaldeans', but on his return to Diyârbekir he was arrested and died in prison. After a relapse, the Chaldean Patriarchate was reconstituted at Diyârbekir in 1672 and recognized by the Porte, but in spite of the efforts of the missionaries the Chaldean Catholic Church remained a small body, with scattered congregations in Bağdâd, Moṣul, Si'irt, and Aleppo.[8]

[1] *Dict. Th. Cath.*, vol. i, coll. 1911–12. [2] G. Graf, iii. 60.

[3] The term 'congregation' is used here and in what follows in the English sense of 'group of persons meeting together for worship', not in the Roman sense of religious community or monastic order.

[4] See *Dict. Th. Cath.*, artt. 'Melchite' (vol. x, coll. 516–20) and 'Antioche, patr. Grec-Melkite' (vol. i, coll. 1417–20); and cf. Graf, iii. 31–33, and below, p. 256, n. 2.

[5] See for the Orthodox Melkites Graf, iii. 79–159, and for the Catholic Melkites, ibid. 172–248.

[6] The first Arabic printing-press in the East was set up by the Orthodox Patriarch Athanasius Debbâs in Aleppo between 1706 and 1721, and a second Orthodox press was founded at Beyrut in 1751 (Graf, iii. 27). The Uniate 'Abdallâh Zâḫir (for whom see ibid. 191–201) operated a press built by himself at the convent of el-Ṣuweir in Lebanon from 1734. But as early as 1610 the Maronites had printed a Psalter in Syriac and Karşûnî (Arabic in Syriac script): ibid. 51–52.

[7] See *Dict. Th. Cath.*, vol. xi, col. 228. An earlier 'Chaldean' community had been formed in Cyprus in the fifteenth century: ibid. col. 226.

[8] Ibid., also Graf, iii. 64–69; iv. 95–110.

Even less success attended the Uniate secession from the Syrian Jacobite Church, whose adherents were known as 'Syrian Catholics'. The movement was confined mainly to Aleppo, where a patriarchate was established in 1662 with the consent of the Porte. Owing to the vigorous and generally successful opposition of the Jacobites, however, the new Church languished, and remained dependent largely on the support of the Maronites.[1]

Despite the labours of the Franciscans in Cairo and Upper Egypt,[2] the formation of a Uniate branch of the Coptic Church made little progress during this period. In the sixteenth and seventeenth centuries negotiations were repeatedly opened between the Papacy and the Coptic patriarchs, several of whom (possibly influenced in part by hostility to the enhanced position acquired by the Greek patriarchate of Alexandria after the Ottoman conquest) expressed a personal willingness for reunion,[3] but were not supported by the body of their clergy and people. In the eighteenth century some small and secret Uniate congregations were already in existence, though their clergy, owing to local opposition, were often forced to take refuge in Rome, and it was not until the nineteenth that a regular Uniate hierarchy began to be formed.[4]

On the other hand, the labours of the Catholic missionaries among the Maronites of Lebanon were crowned with success. For some two centuries, indeed, although the Maronite patriarchs (who exercised, with or without the authority of the Sultans, all *millet* rights of jurisdiction) regularly received the *pallium* from Rome, there was still a certain degree of ambiguity in the position of the Maronite Church as a whole.[5] But this was finally regularized by the new constitution propounded and accepted at a national Synod in 1736 and still in force.[6]

This success (which was destined to have important political and cultural consequences) was due largely to the favour shown by the Druze chief Faḫr ul-Dîn Maʿn to the Catholic missionaries, when at the beginning of the seventeenth century he made a bid to

[1] The second patriarch died in prison in Adana in 1702; the third died at Rome in 1721, and thereafter the titular 'Patriarchate of Aleppo' lapsed. In 1783 an attempt was made by the converted Jacobite bishop Miḫâʾîl Carwâ to seize the Patriarchate of Antioch, but the Sultan's *fermân* went to the rival 'Orthodox' Jacobite candidate, and the seat of the irregular Patriarchate had to be removed to Lebanon: see *Dict. Th. Cath.*, vol. i, coll. 1430 sqq.; Graf, iii. 56–58; iv. 41–64.

[2] See above, p. 231.

[3] Graf, iii. 70; Butcher, *Church in Egypt*, ii. 254–5.

[4] Graf, iii. 75–76; iv. 159–66.

[5] Cf. ibid. iii. 366–8.

[6] The leading part at this Synod was taken by the famous Maronite scholar, Joseph Simonius Assemani (el-Simʿânî), as Papal Legate. It was to his insistence that was due the acceptance, despite strong opposition, of the papal draft of the constitution: *Dict. Th. Cath.*, vol. x, coll. 79–85; Graf, iii. 445.

achieve the autonomy of the Lebanon. The protection subsequently given by Louis XIV to the Maronites, which went to the lengths of correspondence with their bishops and active intervention at the Porte in their favour, enabled the missionaries to maintain and extend their influence.[1] A certain number of schools were established in the Lebanon and inner Syria by the Capuchins, Jesuits, and Lazarists, at which Maronite children were taught to read and write, and several young men were sent to Rome from time to time for a higher theological education at the Maronite college which had been opened there in 1584. These influences must not, however, be over-estimated during our present period. Volney remarked that the Maronite youths brought back from Rome 'none of the arts and ideas of Europe but a knowledge of Italian',[2] and the European missionaries were faced with a considerable mass of jealousy and opposition among the local clergy and their flocks.[3]

In Aleppo, however, their missionary labours contributed to a remarkable revival of learning amongst the Syrian Christians in the eighteenth century. In the preceding centuries there had been a steady immigration of Maronites to Aleppo, where they engaged mainly in industry and petty trade, and in some cases acquired a certain wealth.[4] This community produced, at the end of the seventeenth century, one outstanding figure in Cermânûs Farḥât, who not only played a prominent part in the religious movements of the time but also, through his contacts with Moslem literary circles in Aleppo, brought about an Arabic literary revival amongst the Maronites.[5] But these activities subsequently aroused the hostility of the Orthodox, who appealed to Istanbul, with the result that the Ottoman authorities, while issuing *fermâns* in favour of both parties, seized the opportunity to bring pressure to bear upon them both.[6] We shall have occasion shortly to consider the consequences of this pressure upon the fortunes of the Syrian Christians, and more especially of the Catholic communities, in the latter half of the century.

The hostility of the Orthodox to Catholicism, which had so much facilitated the Ottoman conquest of the Balkans, thus scarcely diminished as time went on.[7] In one instance, of the late fifteenth

[1] Carali, i. 1, 82; Jouplain, 154–6.

[2] Volney, i. 427.

[3] This is expressed even in the writings of the Patriarch Stephan el-Duwaihi (d. 1704); see Graf, iii. 367.

[4] Ġazzî, iii. 483; Olivier, ii. 307. Waḳfs created by Maronites at Aleppo for religious edifices in Aleppo and northern Lebanon: Ġazzî, ii. 540, 541, 564, &c.

[5] See *Encyc. of Islam* (Suppl.), art. 'Farḥāt' (Kratchkowsky); Graf, iii. 406–28.

[6] Carali, i. 1, 83; Ḥaydar, i. 57.

[7] The Patriarch Parthenios in 1640 declared himself willing for union with

century, the Catholic ruler of an Orthodox population, the Duke of the Ionian islands, took warning from events on the mainland to revive the Orthodox bishopric of Cephalonia, in order that his subjects should have less cause to prefer the sovereignty of the Sultans to his own.[1] But his example was seldom followed. The Venetians, for example, during their tenure of the Morea in the early eighteenth century, did much to alienate the people's loyalty by installing a Catholic hierarchy and forbidding the Orthodox clergy to communicate with Istanbul. The Ottoman Government, as we have remarked, was inclined to favour the Orthodox,[2] and it saw how sectarian feeling might be turned to its own advantage. Thus Köprülü Meḥmed Paşa played with skill on the anti-Catholic sentiments of the Cretans, as also on those of the Protestants in Hungary.[3] The Porte's known inclination to defend its 'native' *Ḏimmîs* from Catholic encroachment, again, provided it with a counter for bargaining: the Catholics must pay for concessions. Perhaps the most notable occasion was when they, literally, bought the keys of the Holy Sepulchre.[4] Its guardianship had until then been a privilege of the Orthodox, who thus suffered a setback that was very bitterly resented.[5] This was a diplomatic success, achieved only because of the support lent to Catholic pretensions by France. But in 1757 a fresh *Ḫaṭṭî Şerîf* deprived the Latins of their possession of the Church of the Nativity at Bethlehem and of the Tomb of the Virgin at Jerusalem, as well as of the custody of the Holy Sepulchre, with only toleration to worship at each. The jubilation of the Orthodox was increased by the fresh persecution of the Catholics during the French Revolution, when most of the hospices and some of the churches of the Franciscans in Palestine were demolished. Thus, at the beginning of the nineteenth century, the Orthodox held the upper hand in Syria, and when the Church of the Holy Sepulchre was destroyed by fire in 1808, it was the

Rome and asked the Emperor's protection for himself and his church. But this is probably evidence of his fear of the Porte rather than of his love of the Pope: Jorga, iv. 30.

[1] Miller, *Latins in the Levant*, 484.

[2] As against Catholicism, that is to say. It did not hesitate to exact ever larger sums from aspirants to the Oecumenical Patriarchate, or to dismiss, banish, and even hang patriarchs when such courses suited its books: see Jorga, iv. 22–23.

[3] Ibid. iv. 138. He also stimulated Catholic-Orthodox hostility in Chios and Jerusalem, ibid. 169.

[4] The rivalry between the Catholics and Orthodox for the guardianship of the Holy Places had begun as early as the twelfth century, when, in 1188, the Emperor Isaac Angelus allied himself with Saladin to obtain it: see *Encyc. Brit.*, art. 'Crusades'.

[5] Jorga, iv. 19. Part of the Holy Sepulchre and the chamber of the Last Supper had been purchased by Robert of Sicily in 1305 for the Catholic Church; but the sanctuary had remained in the hands of the Orthodox. *Encyc. of Islam*, art. 'al-Ḳuds'. But see Jorga, iv. 235, where the French are reported to have been unable to obtain possession in 1693.

Greeks who were authorized to rebuild it.[1] On the whole, the Catholics, despite the efforts they expended, achieved no more than a meagre success in their missionary enterprise. This relative failure was perhaps due chiefly to the corporate character of Ottoman society. Politically, from the Catholic standpoint, individual conversions were advisable; but to convert individuals was to uproot them, and often to be unable to replant them in a native community. Conversion by the formation of Uniate churches was a less brutal operation; but it was likely to meet with greater governmental opposition. In either case, opposition was naturally offered by the community that stood to lose adherents. And the government itself was opposed in principle to the transference of his allegiance by a *Ḏimmî* from one community to another, since this interfered with the assessment and collection of the special taxation to which all *Ḏimmîs* alike were subject, but in which each community collaborated separately with the government officials concerned.

According to the Sacred Law, as we have indicated, *Ḏimmîs* were to be subjected to two special taxes: the *cizya*, a tribute or poll-tax, and the *ḫarâc*, a land-tax, differing from that imposed on Moslems. Both were held by the Ottoman *'Ulemâ* to be still in force; but owing to the fact that all agricultural land in the Empire was declared to appertain to the state, the *ḫarâc* was actually rendered inapplicable, since it might properly be levied only on private holdings. We have already described the various taxes and dues to which, under this ruling, peasants were subjected. It is enough, therefore, to note here that no distinction was made between Moslems and *Ḏimmîs* in the matter of the so-called *'uṣr* (properly the *ḫarâc muḳâsama*), though the proportion taken varied from province to province; and that though the yearly fixed contribution, properly called *ḫarâc muwaẓẓaf*, was popularly referred to by names such as *Çift Akçesi* in the case of Moslems, and by the term *Ispence* in that of *Ḏimmîs*, it seems generally to have been more or less equal for both. Many of the dues levied both on peasants and on the traders were, on the other hand, heavier for *Ḏimmîs* than for Moslems: for instance, the dues payable by landless peasants, both married and bachelor, and the transit and customs duties. But what remained the most striking, if not necessarily the most onerous, disability of the *Ḏimmîs* was their continued subjection to the payment of the *cizya*.[2]

The payment of the canonical *ḫarâc* had ceased very early in the

[1] Finn, *Stirring Times*, i. 7, 38.

[2] Jews and Christians were also made liable by *ḳanun* to a special tax, officially fixed at ten and five *aḳçes* respectively, on the accession of a new Sultan (Hammer, *Staatsverfassung*, i. 224).

history of Islâm to distinguish the *Dimmîs* from true-believers. The return made, or the price paid, by the *Dimmî* communities, under their contract with the Moslem ruler, for his clemency and protection, came therefore to be represented exclusively by the *cizya*. During the nineteenth century, when Ottoman statesmen desired to represent the institutions of the Empire as conforming to the European political principles of the period, in order to minimize the distinctions made between *Dimmîs* and Moslems, they emphasized the fact that the *Dimmîs* were not employed as soldiers, whereas every Moslem was obliged by his religion to fight for it; making the *cizya* appear as a contribution in lieu of military service.[1] This interpretation, however, had no historical foundation, and it was only partially true. The obligation of Moslems to fight was sanctioned only by conscience, whereas the obligation of *Dimmîs* to pay was sanctioned by law. On the other hand, it was supported by the fact that such *Dimmîs* as under the 'old régime' were reckoned as 'soldiery', the Bulgarian *voynuks*, for instance, were excused the payment of *cizya*.[2] The essence of the *Dimmî* status, as appraised by traditional Moslem philosophy, was that it was inferior; and except in so far as the Moslems might be regarded as protecting the *Dimmîs* when they engaged in war, the payment of *cizya* had nothing to do with the exemption of *Dimmîs* from military service.

It may here be noted that by the nineteenth century at least, when the question of the *cizya* loomed large in Ottoman politics for a time, the term itself seems to have fallen popularly into disuse. Confusingly enough it had been generally replaced by that of *harâc*.[3] This improper usage seems to have been adopted earlier, though not in either annals or official documents. The term *Dimmî*, likewise, was popularly replaced by *Ra'îya* (*Raiyet*), though the latter

[1] Thus when in 1847 a law was drafted to require the conscription of Ottoman Christians for naval and military service, it was proposed that those called up should be excused payment of *cizya*—see Enver Ziya Karal, *Osmanlî Tarihi*, v. 184–5 (Ankara, 1947)—and when, eight years later, the *cizya* was finally abolished, the *Dimmîs* had instead to pay a special tax in lieu of military service—*Encyc. of Islam*, art. 'Tanzîmât'.

[2] *Encyc. Brit.*, art. 'Bulgaria'.

[3] The word *harâc* (of Greek origin—*Encyc. of Islam*, s.v.) has undergone several changes of meaning. It began by being synonymous with *cizya*. Then as early as the first century of the Hegira it was used to denote the land-tax payable by *Dimmî* landowners left in possession. Next, when it was decided that all but two provinces of the Caliphate consisted of land subject, regardless of the religion of its owners, to the payment of *harâc*, it naturally came to denote the land-tax in general (losing for the time being all connexion with religious distinctions). Then by the Ottoman *kânûn*-makers it was used for the two types of land-tax, really unsanctioned by but not in conflict with the *Şerî'a*, imposed on the peasant tenants of all the agricultural land in the Empire—see Part I, pp. 240–1. And finally, owing presumably to the fact that these taxes were popularly given other names, it was, quite accidentally, restored to its primitive significance and distinguished by the addition of the term *şer'î*.

was properly applicable to Moslems as well. Consequently we hear much, in European writings, of the payment by *Re'âyâ* of the *harâc* (both spelt in a number of ways) when what is meant is the payment by *Dimmîs* of the *cizya*.[1]

The Sacred Law required the imposition of the *cizya* only on free men capable of earning a living. Hence in the *dimmî* communities not only were women of all ages and conditions exempt from its incidence, but also such males as were slaves, children, infirm or aged. Nor was payment exacted either from those who though capable of earning a living did so with such little success as to be unable to contribute without hardship, or from such monks as inhabited ill-endowed monasteries.[2] Under the Ottoman régime the last provision was extended to include all ministers of religion; and in later times at any rate many of the *Dimmîs* employed in the government service obtained exemption both for themselves and their families.[3] The *cizya* was payable, accordingly, in respect of considerably less than half, perhaps no more than a third, of the *dimmî* population.

The means of the persons upon whom the tax fell was considered, in the Law, not only as regards their ability to pay at all, but as regards the amount that each might be called on to contribute. They were to be divided into three classes—rich, middling, and poor, determined in practice by the individual person's calling: landowners, money-changers, certain merchants, were classed as rich; artisans, such as cobblers, as poor.[4] Even a scale of payments was laid down: the rich were to pay yearly 48 *dirhems* (silver), the middling 24, and the poor 12. The Law in this as in many matters embodied the practice, or perhaps no more than the theory, of early 'Abbâsid times; and even if this scale was observed at the epoch at which it was framed, subsequent changes in the value of money resulted in a frequent neglect on the part of Moslem potentates to observe it. In the earlier days of Ottoman rule the scale upon which the *cizya* was exacted differed, it appears, from province to province. It was reduced to uniformity only in the seventeenth century by Köprülü Muṣṭafâ Paṣa, who regarded the canonical scale as still binding. He decreed that the three classes of *Dimmîs* should

[1] The term *re'âyâ*, applied to *Dimmîs* as distinct from Moslems, is, however, to be found in *fermâns* of the late eighteenth century; cf. e.g. a *fermân* of 1795 regulating the rights of the Syrian Christians at Damietta in Carali, i. 2, 43.

[2] D'Ohsson, vii. 236, 'ministres du culte'; Seyyid Muṣṭafâ, iii. 100, '*memûrîni rûḥânîye*' (spiritual officials). Presumably this includes secular, as opposed to regular, clergy.

[3] D'Ohsson, loc. cit. These exemptions were strongly resented by the *millets*, whose members complained of the abuse of their privileges by the *barâ'atlîs*, and their avoidance of sharing in the communal expenses; cf. *al-Machrik*, xiv. 267–9, and Part I, pp. 310–11.

[4] *Encyc. of Islam*, art. 'Djizya'.

pay respectively 4, 2, and 1 gold coin of the type called *Şerîfî*, which was then equivalent to 12 *dirhems* (in weight) of silver.[1] In the fifteenth century, the *cizya* in Egypt and Syria had been assessed at the uniform rate of 1 gold piece (plus a fraction for collection costs) on each *dimmî* household. This practice appears to have been continued under the Ottomans, at least into the sixteenth century in Syria.[2] The Egyptian rates were apparently reformed only in 1733, when the general scale was introduced there as well.[3] When the revised rates were introduced into Syria has not yet been determined.[4]

The reference to the canonical *dirhem* seems to have been maintained down to our terminal date, since the Chevalier D'Ohsson states that in his time the yearly contributions of the three classes were fixed at 10 *kuruş*, 5½ *kuruş*, and 2¾ *kuruş*.[5] But during the eighteenth century, when in many provinces the control of the central government was relaxed, local governors took advantage of the liberty thus acquired to supplement their revenues by collecting more than was properly due from the *Dimmîs* by way of *cizya*. They did so in the Morea, for instance, where the government, in attempting to restore order in this matter, was obliged to recognize the *Vâlîs'* right to one *kuruş* for every certificate of payment.[6] The careful justice with which the rules for the incidence of the *cizya* had originally been framed was thus neglected; but what was even more inequitable was that the principle by which the *cizya* contributions from each community were assessed according to the number of persons in each liable for its payment was abandoned. Each

[1] Seyyid Muṣṭafâ, ii. 100; see Ch. VI, p. 33 and n. 3 above. Jorga (iv. 168) states that Köprülü Fâḍil Aḥmed Paşa (Grand *Vezîr* from 1656 to 1676) had earlier raised the scale of the *cizya*. On the other hand, Köprülü Ḥüseyin Paşa (Grand *Vezîr* from 1697 to 1702) is said to have reduced it and even to have remitted its payment altogether (*Encyc. of Islam*, art. 'Köprülü').

[2] B. Lewis, *Notes and Documents from the Turkish Archives* (Jerusalem, 1952), 10–11.

[3] They were fixed by a *fermân* of 1733–4 at 420, 270, and 100 *paras* respectively, corresponding fairly closely to the canonical rates *plus* collection charges (Cabartî, i. 146/ii. 10)—the current rate of exchange being 148 *paras* to the *fîndîklî* 'sequin' and 110 to the *zer-i maḥbûb* (see p. 55 above); but additional sums were often exacted (Cabartî, ii. 120/iv 221). In 1798 the rates were 553, 283, and 143 *paras*, due from 9,000, 18,000, and 63,000 persons respectively, giving a total of 14,850,000 *paras* from 90,000 heads. The *Ağa* who farmed the *cizya* of Egypt paid *mîrî* amounting to 2,509,081 *paras* on his office (Estève, 365–7).

[4] By the eighteenth century the official rates in Syria were 11, 5, and 3 piastres per head, but according to Volney (ii. 225, 264) they were often raised abusively to 35 or 40 piastres.

[5] The text has 'trois et trois-quarts', but since in all other cases the poorest is shown as paying half of whatever was paid by the middling, we take this to be an error for 'deux et trois-quarts'. Most of the gold pieces of the period were worth round about 3 *kuruş* apiece; and in 1788, for example, 1 *dirhem* of silver was worth 10 *paras*, so that 12 would equal 3 *kuruş*, 40 *paras* going to the *kuruş*: see Belin, 'Histoire économique', in *J.A.*, 1864, tom. iii, p. 452.

[6] Cevdet, vi. 60.

community in each district was called upon to pay a fixed sum yearly, even though, as was the case in the empire generally and in most regions severally, the *Dimmî* population declined. Moreover, the collection of the *cizya*, like other Ottoman taxes, was in later times confided to tax-farmers,[1] with the result that the ecclesiastical authorities of each *millet* lost the partial control of it that they had originally possessed. This, at least, is to be inferred from the account supplied by D'Ohsson. In his time the method of collection was the following. The eighth department of the Treasury, the *Cizye Muḥasebesi*[2] or Accountancy of the *cizya*, issued towards the end of every (Moslem lunar) year 1,600,000 blank certificates, packed in 180 bundles. The bundles were then sent to all the provincial *Ḳaḍâs*, and were opened on the new year's day, 1st of *al-Muḥarrem*, in a *maḥkama*, a *Ḳâḍî*'s court.[3] The employees of the 'farmers' then began collection, furnishing each *Dimmî*, on payment, with a certificate, marked with the year-date, his 'class', and the names of the *Defterdâr*, the head of the eighth department of the Treasury and the 'farmer' concerned. Their main purpose was to be left with no certificates unplaced. Hence for several weeks before the beginning of a new year they did their best to prevent persons liable for payment from leaving their homes and so possibly escaping it, and for several months after they would stop any *Dimmîs* that they met with and demand the production of their certificates in evidence of payment. Sometimes they even made use of what was now apparently no more than a theory, that the *millet* authorities controlled the incidence of the *cizya* on their members, by requiring these authorities to pay on the certificates that they had been unable to place, on the understanding that they would reimburse themselves by a levy on their communities. Presumably it was only because of the hazards of the whole procedure that the collection had come to provide an attractive opening for speculative 'farmers'. A vestige of the concern for justice that had inspired the original regulations remained in the rule that the certificate bundles should not be opened before 1st of *al-Muḥarram*, designed as it was to prevent the molestation of *Dhimmîs* for payment at any but this time of the year. Its strict observance in the midst of the abuses in which the collection of the *cizya* had become involved was typical of Ottoman administrative methods in their decay.

The method of collection that we have described was not, either as originally planned or as corrupted in later times, current in the

[1] This practice seems to have been introduced under Süleymân I, who gave some of the so-called '*Mulâzim*' officers whom he formed into a special corps, the right of collecting *cizya* in certain districts—see Seyyid Muṣṭafâ, ii. 92.

[2] See Part I, p. 132.

[3] See above, p. 115.

Principalities, nor in the sub-farmed districts of the Lebanon, which paid an annual tribute to the *Paşas* of Ṣaydâ and Tripoli. The Principalities, as we have mentioned earlier, paid a yearly tribute to the Porte, as did likewise the republic of Ragusa. Technically, however, this tribute was also a form of *cizya*. A 'Scriptural' people of the Domain of War might, according to the *Şerîʿa*, contract with the conqueror in certain circumstances for the payment of a fixed sum in perpetuity, instead of submitting to the imposition of the normal *cizya per capita*; and the tributes in question were paid under this head.

The classification in Islâm of *Dimmîs* by their religion, which resulted naturally from the fact that they were similarly distinguished from Moslems themselves, harmonized with their own outlook. But it militated against the solidarity of Ottoman society as a whole: it discouraged among the members of that society the sentiment, which it would have been to the Sultan's interests to encourage, of their being primarily his subjects: it subordinated this sentiment to communal attachments. In some country districts, where *Dimmîs* and Moslems lived side by side, they were comparatively free from sectarian prejudice, partly because they were bound by common interests and like ways of life, partly because countrymen of both faiths tended to be latitudinarian in matters of religion.[1] In the towns, however, and where religious differences were reinforced by racial, the divisions both between Moslems and *Dimmîs*, and between the various *dimmî* communities themselves, were all too marked. For their common status of inferiority was far from inducing a spirit of brotherly love among the Christians of the many persuasions that we have enumerated, or among any of them and the Jews; any one of their communities, indeed, was ready to enlist Moslem help, when necessary, against another.[2] They were not, on the other hand, really willing subjects

[1] The *Dimmîs* of Bosnia, for instance, were on especially good terms with their Moslem compatriots, and (soon after our terminal date) co-operated with them in withstanding Austrian attacks. They were subject only to the payment of one gold piece each by way of *cizya*. Does this mean that they were all reckoned as of the poorest class, or was it a privilege? It is interesting to note that the proportion of Moslems in the population was much higher in Bosnia than elsewhere in Europe. No doubt this circumstance accounts largely for the fact that despite their 'frontier' situation they were less frightened and so better disposed towards their *dimmî* neighbours—see Cevdet, iv. 115.

[2] See, for instance, the graphic description given by Michael of Damascus (p. 3) of the dispute between the Orthodox and the Melkites (i.e. Uniate Greeks) at Damascus in 1786. Three Melkite deacons accused of the murder of a Greek deacon were brought to Damascus and beaten daily. The *Paşa*'s *Kâhya* at length interceded with the Greeks to spare them; and to his question 'Is it lawful in your religion to torture these men who are Christians like yourselves?' received the astonishing answer: 'These men have nothing to do with us. We do not know them, and according to our doctrine their wealth and their blood are lawful spoil.'

of the Sultan. Some of the Christians had submitted with relief to Ottoman rule in the beginning, because they preferred it to rule by the adherents of other churches. But the *ḏimmî* status was not one to which any community could be permanently reconciled. It was at most to be endured, because it was imposed by *force majeure*. In earlier Islamic societies it had been endured by slowly diminishing numbers: the problem had been more or less solved by the gradual absorption of non-believers into the Moslem community till only unimportant residues remained. But in the Ottoman Empire this absorption, though rapid at first, soon all but ceased, and left it with an ominously large minority of these, so to speak, natural malcontents. The early period during which conversions were commonest was that of relative heterodoxy and broad-mindedness among the bulk of the Ottoman Moslems. Islâm was presented in a pleasantly lax and as it were familiar guise; the gulf to be crossed seemed narrow; above all the *ḏimmî* communities were not yet organized under the auspices of the state. But as the governing class turned more and more to orthodoxy and gave the *'Ulemâ* ever greater consideration, Islâm was endued with a more forbidding colour, while the official establishment of the *millets* strengthened the hold of the *ḏimmî* ecclesiastics on their flocks. The tightness of the *millet* organization in the Ottoman system of administration would seem, indeed, to account largely for the failure of Islâm gradually to attract the bulk of the *ḏimmî* populations of Anatolia and Rumelia, as in earlier days it had attracted those of Syria and the 'Irâḳ.[1] The *millet* leaders were reluctant to lose adherents not only on grounds of belief, but for an economic reason. For though *cizya* was originally exacted only from the members of each community liable under the rules of the *Şerî'a* to its payment, the principle of such yearly assessment was later ignored, each community being called upon to furnish a fixed sum, regardless of any increase or diminution in its membership. If the members of a community were reduced by conversion, therefore, the burden falling upon those that remained faithful to it was aggravated.[2]

The Sacred Law does not, as we have seen, offer 'Scriptural' infidels Islâm or the Sword, though it has more often than not been represented as so doing. It offers them a third alternative : the assumption of *ḏimmî* status. It does this grudgingly, however. It

The *Kâḫya*, with righteous indignation, retorted 'You are accursed infidels with no religion at all', and released the Melkites forthwith. Cf. also Mich. Dam. 39–41, 46, and Ḥaydar, i. 57. The disputes between rival sects in Palestine are too notorious to need illustration.

[1] Cf. Jorga, iv. 24, as regards the prevention of conversions by the Orthodox *archontes*.

[2] But there is little to suggest that, down to the eighteenth century, the Ottoman authorities played off one community against another for its own purposes, except possibly in minor provincial matters.

regards them as perverse, and insists that they shall be reminded of the fact. The *Ḳur'ân* itself enjoins humility on the *Ḏimmîs* when they pay the *cizya*;[1] and the 'fathers' of the *Şerî'a* insisted variously on methods of inculcating this spirit, such as the sumptuary regulations. These as we have seen were intermittently enforced by the Sultans; and the more fanatical or brutal collectors of the *cizya* no doubt followed the recommendation of the Law that they should seize by the throat the *Ḏimmîs* that came before them with their annual dues, and adjure them to 'pay, O enemy of God!'[2]

Such treatment, and the disabilities to which the *Ḏimmîs* were subjected in general, were intended partly also to act as inducements to conversion. But when in Ottoman society they were insisted on, while obstacles such as had not existed in earlier Moslem societies were placed in the way of conversion, they merely tended to exacerbate the mutual antagonism of Moslems and non-believers. The position of the Ottoman *Ḏimmîs* was distinguished, moreover, in another way from that of their predecessors: considerable numbers of them in all the commercial centres of the Empire were in far closer touch with foreigners than were their Moslem compatriots: the Christians because the diplomats and merchants of Europe naturally tended to deal with their co-religionists (the Moslems, on their side, being reluctant to enter into close relations with them), the Jews because of the large share they had acquired in the commerce, and particularly the foreign commerce, of the Empire. But the expansion of European trade in the Levant that gave rise to this contact between *Ḏimmîs* and Western merchants went hand in hand with the rise to power of the states that sponsored it, and coincided with the corruption of Ottoman institutions. And as the Empire declined in consequence of this corruption, the Ottoman Moslems, instead of merely despising Europeans as heretofore, came to fear and so to hate them. In so far as the *Ḏimmîs* cultivated especially close relations with the foreigners, therefore, the small esteem that they enjoyed in Moslem eyes was still further diminished. In places less accessible both to European and *Sunnî* influences, the fairly cordial relations subsisting between Moslems and *Ḏimmîs* no doubt remained untroubled. It may be said, nevertheless, that the mutual dislike that animated sections of both parties, smaller perhaps but more important politically, had by now rendered insoluble for the Ottoman government the problem set to Moslem rulers by the injunction of the Sacred Law—to tolerate the scriptural infidels, but insist on their inferiority.

In Egypt, and to a lesser extent in Syria, a fresh complication

[1] Sura ix. 29: '*Ḥattâ yu'ṭū 'l-cizyata 'an yadin wahum ṣâghirûn*', 'Until they give the *cizya* with their hand, humbly'.

[2] See Belin, 'La Propriété Foncière', in *J.A.*, Séri V, tome xviii.

was introduced into the *dimmî* problem in the second half of the eighteenth century by the increasing prominence of Christian Syrians, especially those of the Maronite and (Catholic) Melkite persuasions, in commerce and administration. The indigenous Coptic and Jewish communities of Egypt had long since fitted themselves into the framework of Moslem society, in which they enjoyed certain traditional functions and privileges. The Jews were merchants, financiers, and customs-farmers; and except for a comparatively small number of Coptic cultivators in Upper Egypt and the Fayyûm, the Copts also were largely engaged in industry.[1] But the most remarkable feature was the success with which, through more than a thousand years of Moslem domination, they had succeeded in monopolizing the important function of land registration and revenue collection.[2] Their services were essential to the working of the administration, and in this lay the secret of their preservation and of the vast fortunes which some of them were able to accumulate. Every governor must have a Coptic right-hand man: 'Alî Bey his Mu'allim Rizḳ, Murâd and Ibrâhîm their Ibrâhîm el-Cawharî.[3] Thus, parallel to and in a sense counterbalancing the religious and *millet* organization, under the Patriarch of Alexandria, there existed not only the corporations of minor industries but also the powerful corporation of 'Coptic clerks', which was strongly organized and interlocked from top to bottom.[4] The head of this corporation was one of the wealthiest and most influential men in the country, and it was probably only through the charities and endowments of such high officials that the Coptic Church was enabled to maintain its establishments.[5]

In addition to the Copts and Jews there was a small community of resident Greeks, composed mainly of sailors, petty tradesmen, and artisans, under the spiritual and secular jurisdiction of the Orthodox Patriarch of Alexandria. They were to be found almost exclusively in the northern ports and in Cairo, where they had one *ḥâra* or quarter in the city and another at Old Cairo.[6] They were Arabophone, and are regarded by most writers as the survivors of

[1] Cf. Cabartî, iii. 186/vii. 30.

[2] See Part I, p. 210.

[3] See on the latter Tawfîḳ Iskarôs, *Nawâbiğ el-Aḳbâṭ* (Cairo, 1910), i. 206–368; Graf, iv. 136.

[4] Cf. Cabartî, ii. 262/v. 217–18, and Lancret, 242.

[5] The jealous watch kept upon the activities of these Copts is illustrated by the consequences of the attempt made by Nawrûz, head of the corporation, in 1752 or 1753 to organize a Coptic Pilgrimage to Jerusalem. Although he had taken the precaution of obtaining a *fetwâ* authorizing it, the Moslem mob was turned loose on the caravan just as it was about to start (Cabartî, i. 187/ii. 115–16). For the charities, &c., of the Coptic officials see Tawfîḳ Iskarôs, op. cit.

[6] A. G. Politis, *L'Hellénisme et l'Égypte moderne*, 99–101. Politis concludes that a few Greeks were also to be found in the smaller towns and villages of the interior, but his conclusion is not well supported by eighteenth-century sources.

the Greek colony which inhabited Egypt before the Arab conquest in the seventh century, but this view is somewhat doubtfully supported.[1] The low estimate of their numbers, placed by the best-informed authorities at little more than 500, and the extreme impoverishment of the patriarchate in the eighteenth century, show that they played no prominent part in the life of the country. A more influential section was formed by the fluctuating group of Greek merchants and importers, who had their own *wekâlas* or depots at Cairo.[2] These were engaged mainly in the trade with Istanbul, the Aegean, and Crete (then an important centre of the oil and soap industries), as well as with Syria, where the Orthodox community, mainly Arabophone, played some part in commerce and industry.[3]

One of the results of the Maronite revival and of the measures of repression adopted by the Ottoman authorities in Syria was to induce a gradual emigration of Syrian Christians (especially from Damascus and Aleppo) to Egypt in the second half of the eighteenth century. The Catholic *millet* in Egypt had hitherto been represented only by the small group of Franciscan monks and Uniate Copts,[4] with a few Maronites, chiefly from Aleppo, to whom the new-comers attached themselves. Two circumstances, however, conspired to favour them. It will be recalled that ʿAlî Bey, in pursuance of his attempt to render himself independent, had sought to encourage European trade with Egypt, and that the European business houses usually found it convenient to carry on their transactions through Syrian protégés. In the second place, his close relations with Ẓâhir al-ʿOmar served their interests, since the latter employed them extensively in his administration. At all events, during the government of ʿAlî Bey, Syrian Christians evicted the Jews from the former monopoly of the customs administration[5] and utilized their capture of these key positions to engage extensively in commerce and to fill the administrative posts under their jurisdiction with their fellow countrymen.[6] By intermarriage with the European consuls and merchants they strengthened their position,[7] and their numbers steadily increased in consequence.

[1] Cf. Politis, 77–79.

[2] Ibid. 112.

[3] Greek *waḳfs* at Aleppo: Ğazzî, ii. 540 sqq.

[4] See above, p. 248.

[5] Ḥannâ Faḫr in the Mediterranean ports: Estève, 350; Miḫâ'îl Farhâṭ at Old Cairo (replacing the Jew Yûsuf b. Lâwî): Carali, i, 1, 85; and cf. also Volney, i. 190–1. For later Syrian farmers of the customs, see Carali, i. 1, 86, 110; i. 2, 12; one of these, Yûsuf el-Beyṭâr, a Greek Catholic of Aleppo, was restored to his post at the instance of Ibrâhîm Ṣabbâg, the finance minister of Ẓâhir al-ʿOmar (see p. 67 above), and after his death (in 1774) his widow was married by Carlo Rossetti.

[6] Carali, i. 1, 85.

[7] Ibid. 99, 107.

From the figures carefully computed by the Abbé Carali from the Franciscan registers, it appears that by 1760 there were already about 200 Syrian families in Cairo, and by the end of the century about 400,[1] as well as a considerable community at Damietta and a smaller one at Rosetta.[2] Already by 1772 we hear of a Christian 'Şeyḫ of all the Syrians' at Cairo,[3] a fact which seems to show that they formed an established corporation. How far this intervention of the Syrian Christians played a part in the disruption of the old economic structure in Egypt is a question to which the evidence cannot yet supply a definite answer. But it is clear that they too suffered severely from the violence and disorder of the government of Murâd and Ibrâhîm,[4] until the arrival of the French opened up for them a still wider field of opportunity.

[1] Ibid. 115, 133, but on p. 85 he puts the number of Syrians in Cairo at the end of 'Alî Bey's government at about 3,000—as obvious an overstatement as Volney's reckoning of about 500 in Cairo in 1785 is an underestimate (i. 190).

[2] The latter is put by Olivier (ii. 51) at thirty families. There were very few Syrian Christians in Alexandria at this time (Carali, i. 1, 119).

[3] Carali, i. 1, 106; cf. also i. 2, 48. It appears that at some period during the following decade the Greek Catholics broke away from the Franciscans and the Maronites to form a separate community (Carali, i. 2, 3 and 26).

[4] Ibid. 19, 44, 57, 60, 63; Olivier, i. 51.

BIBLIOGRAPHY OF WORKS CITED[1]

Abdülbâki: *Melâmîlik ve Melâmîler*. Istanbul, 1931.
ʿAbd el-Ǧanî el-Nâbulusî: *ʿIlm el-filâḥa*. Damascus, 1299 A.H.
ʿAbdu'r-Raḥmân Şeref: *Ta'rîḫi Devleti ʿOsmanîye*. 2nd ed. Istanbul, 1315 A.H.
ʿAbdu'r-Raḥmân Vefîḳ: *Tekâlîf Ḳavâʿidi*. 2 vols. Istanbul, 1328–30 A.H.
Abû Yûsuf: *Kitâb al-Ḫarâc*. Cairo, 1346 A.H. (French trans. by E. Fagnan, *Le Livre de l'Impôt foncier*. Paris, 1921.)
Adnan [Adivar], Abdülhak: *La Science chez les Turcs ottomans*. Paris, 1939.
Affifi, A. E.: *The Mystical Philosophy of Muḥyid Dîn ibnul ʿArabî*. Cambridge, 1929.
Aghnides, N. P.: *An Introduction to Mohammedan Law and a Bibliography*. New York, 1916.
Aḥmed Râsim: *ʿOsmanlî Ta'rîḫi*, 4 vols. Istanbul, 1326–8 A.H.
Aḥmed Refîk: *Anadolu'da Türk Aşîretleri* (966–1200). Istanbul, 1930.
—— *Türk Idaresinde Bulğaristan*, Istanbul, 1933.
Akdağ, Mustafa: 'Osmanlî imparatorluğunun kuruluş ve inkişaf devrinde Türkiye'nin iktisadî vaziyeti', in *Belleten* of the Türk Tarih Kurumu, vol. xiii, pt. 51 (Ankara, 1949), 497–571.
ʿAlî Paşa Mubârak: *El-Ḫiṭaṭ el-Tawfîḳîya el-Cadîda*. 20 vols. Bûlâḳ, 1306 A.H.
el-Alûsî, Maḥmûd Şukrî: *el-Misk el-Adfar*. Bağdâd, 1930.
Ammoun, F.: *La Syrie criminelle*. Paris, 1929.
Arberry, A. J.: *Sufism*. London, 1951.
Arnold, Sir T. W.: *The Caliphate*. Oxford, 1924.
ʿÂşiḳpaşazâde: *Die altosmanische Chronik des ʿĀšiḳpašazāde*, ed. F. Giese. Leipzig, 1929.
ʿAtâ, Ṭayyâr-Zâde Aḥmed: *Ta'rîḫi ʿAṭâ*. 5 vols. [Istanbul], 1293 A.H.
Auriant, L. (pseud.): *Aventuriers et Originaux*. Paris, 1933.
—— 'Catherine II et l'Orient, 1770–1774', in *L'Acropole*, vol. v (Paris, 1930).
Ayrout, H. Habib: *Fellahs d'Égypte*. Cairo, 1942.
el-Bağdâdî, ʿAbd el-Ḳâhir: *ʿUṣûl el-Dîn*. Istanbul, 1928.
Baldwin, George: *Political Recollections relative to Egypt*. London, 1801.
Barkan, Ö. L.: *XV ve XVI inci asîrlarda Osmanlî Imparatorluğunda Zirai Ekonominin Hukukî ve Malî Esaslarî*. I: *Kanunlar*. Istanbul, 1943. Cited as *Z.E.E.*
—— 'Istilâ devrinin Kolonizatör Türk Dervişleri', in *Vakîflar Dergisi*, vol. ii (Ankara, 1942).
Baron, S. W.: *The Jewish Community*. Philadelphia, Pa., 1945.
Barthold, W.: *Turkestan down to the Mongol Invasion*. 2nd ed. London, 1928.
Becker, Carl H.: 'Steuerpacht und Lehnswesen', in *Der Islam*, vol. v (Berlin, 1914; reprinted in *Islamstudien*, vol. i, Leipzig, 1924).

[1] A number of books and articles not directly pertinent to the period and cited once only in notes have been omitted from this list.

el-Bekrî, Muhammad Tawfîḳ: *Beyt el-Ṣiddîḳ*. Cairo, 1323 A.H.

Belin, M.: 'Essais sur l'histoire économique de la Turquie', in *Journal Asiatique*, 1864.

—— 'Étude sur la propriété foncière en pays musulmans', &c., in ibid., 1861.

—— 'Du Régime des fiefs militaires', &c., in ibid., 1870.

Blumeneau, F. W.: *Statistisch-geographisch-topographische Beschreibung von Ägypten*. 1793.

Boppe, A.: *Le Colonel Nicolas Papas Oglou et le bataillon des Chasseurs d'Orient*. Paris, 1900.

Birge, J. K.: *The Bektashi Order of Dervishes*. London, 1937.

Björkmann, W.: *Beiträge zur Geschichte des Staatskanzlei im islamischen Ägypten*. Hamburg, 1928.

Blackman, W. S.: *The Fellahin of Upper Egypt*. London, 1927.

Boucheman, A. de: 'Note sur la Rivalité de deux tribus moutonnières de Syrie: Les "Mawali" et les "Hadidiyn" ', in *Revue des Études Islamiques*, 1934, pt. 1 (Paris, 1934), 11–58.

Bowen, H.: *The Life and Times of ʿAlí ibn ʿÍsà*. Cambridge, 1928.

Bowring, John: *Report on Egypt and Candia*. London, 1840.

Braudel, F.: *La Méditerranée et le Monde méditerranéen à l'époque de Philippe II*. Paris, 1949.

Brockelmann, C.: *Geschichte der arabischen Litteratur*. 2 vols. Weimar, 1898; Berlin, 1902; with 3 Supplements, Leiden, 1937–42.

Brown, J. P.: *The Dervishes*. Ed. by H. A. Rose. London, 1927.

Browne, E. G.: *A Literary History of Persia*. Vols. i–ii: London, 1908, 1906; vols. iii–iv: Cambridge, 1920–4 (also reprints).

Browne, W. C.: *Travels in Africa, Egypt, and Syria*. London, 1799.

el-Bundârî, el-Fatḥ b. ʿAlī: *Zubdat el-Nuṣra*. Ed. by M. Th. Houtsma. Leiden, 1889.

Butcher, E. L.: *The Story of the Church in Egypt*. 2 vols. London, 1897.

el-Cabartî, ʿAbd al-Raḥmân: *ʿAcâʾib el-Âṯâr*. 4 vols. Cairo, 1297 A.H. (French trans.: *Merveilles biographiques et historiques du Cheikh Abd el Rahman el Djabarti*, trad. par Chefik Mansour Bey, &c. 9 vols. Cairo, 1888–94.)

Carali, l'Abbé Paul: *Les Syriens en Égypte*. Vol. i: *Au temps des Mamlouks*, 1, Cairo, n.d.; Vol. ii: *Beit Chebab* (Lebanon), 1933.

Carra de Vaux: *Les Penseurs de l'Islam*. 5 vols. Paris, [1926].

Cevdet, Aḥmed: *Taʾrîḫi Cevdet*. (Final edition.) 12 vols. Istanbul, 1309 A.H.

Chabrol de Volvic, M. de: 'Essai sur les mœurs des habitans modernes de l'Égypte', in *Description de l'Égypte, État moderne*, vol. ii, pt. 2, particularly 361 sqq.

Charles-Roux, F.: *Autour d'une Route: l'Angleterre, l'Isthme de Suez et l'Égypte au XVIIIe siècle*. Paris, 1922.

—— *Les Échelles de Syrie et de Palestine au XVIIIe siècle*. Paris, 1928.

Christensen, A.: *L'Empire des Sassanides*. Copenhagen, 1907.

Clerget, Marcel: *Le Caire, étude de géographie urbaine*. 2 vols. Cairo [Paris], n.d.

Clot-Bey, A. B.: *Aperçu général sur l'Égypte*. 2 vols. Paris, 1840.

Combe, Étienne: 'L'Égypte ottomane', in *Précis de l'Histoire d'Égypte par divers historiens et archéologues*. Vol. iii. Cairo, 1933.

Couvidou, H.: *Étude sur l'Égypte contemporaine*. Cairo [*c.* 1873].

Daniëls, C. E.: 'La Version orientale, arabe et turque, des deux premiers livres de Herman Boerhaave', in *Janus* (Leiden, 1912), 295–312.

el-Dawwânî, Celâl ul-Dîn: *Aḫlâḳ-i Celâlî*. (Trans. by W. F. Thompson, *Practical Philosophy of the Muhammedan People*. London, 1839.)

Denon, D. Vivant: *Voyage dans la Basse et la Haute Égypte*. 3 vols. and atlas. Paris, 1802. (English trans. by A. Aikin, *Travels in Upper and Lower Egypt*. 3 vols. London, 1803.)

Deny, J.: *Sommaire des archives turques du Caire*. Société royale de Géographie d'Égypte. Cairo, 1930.

Depont, O., and Coppolani, X.: *Les Confréries religieuses musulmanes*. Algiers, 1897.

Description de l'Égypte: État moderne. 4 vols. Paris, 1809–12.

Digeon, M.: 'Canoun-Namé ou Édits de Sultan Soliman', in *Nouveaux contes turcs et arabes*. Vol. ii (Paris, 1781), 195–278.

Djevad, A.: *État militaire ottoman*, &c. Constantinople, 1882.

Dodwell, H. H.: *The Founder of Modern Egypt*. London, 1931.

Elia Qoudsi: *Notice sur les Corporations de Damas, publié par Carlo Landberg in Actes du VIe Congrès des Orientalistes*, pt. 2. Leiden, 1885.

Encyclopaedia of Islam. Ed. by A. J. Wensinck *et al.* 4 vols. and Supplement. Leiden, 1913–38.

—— New edition, ed. by H. A. R. Gibb *et al.* Leiden, 1954 (proceeding).

Erdoğan, Abdülkadir: 'Hadim Ibrahim Paşa Camii', in *Vakı̊flar Dergisi*, i.

Ergin, ʿOs̱mân Nûrî: *Mecellei Umûru Beledîye*. Vol. i. Istanbul, 1922.

—— *Türkiye Maarif Tarihi*. Istanbul, 1939.

Estève, le Comte: 'Mémoire sur les Finances de l'Égypte', in *Description de l'Égypte, État moderne*, vol. i, bk. 1 (Paris, 1809), 299–398.

Eton, W.: *Survey of the Turkish Empire*. 2 vols. London, 1799.

Evliyâ Çelebi: *Siyâḥet-nâme*. (English trans. of vols. i–ii by J. von Hammer, *Travels of Evliya Efendi*. London, 1834–46–50.)

Finn, James: *Stirring Times, or Records from Jerusalem*. London, 1878.

Forbes, D., Toynbee, A. J., Mitrany, D., and Hogarth, D.: *The Balkans*. London, 1915.

Franco, M.: *Essai sur l'histoire des Israélites de l'Empire Ottoman*. Paris, 1897.

Galanté, A.: *Turcs et Juifs*. Istanbul, 1932.

Gaudefroy-Demombynes, M.: *La Syrie à l'époque des Mamelouks*. Paris, 1923.

el-Ğazâlî, Abû Ḥâmid: *Iḥyâʾ ʿulûm el-Dîn*. 4 vols. Cairo, 1306 A.H.

—— *el-Iḳtiṣâd fi 'l-Iʿtiḳâd*. Cairo, 1320 A.H.

el-Ğazzî, Kâmil b. Ḥusayn b. Muṣṭafâ Pâlî: *Nahr el-Ḏahab fî taʾrîḫ Ḥalab*. 3 vols. Cairo, 1340–5 A.H.

Gibb, H. A. R.: 'Some Considerations on the Sunni Theory of the Caliphate', in *Archives d'histoire du droit oriental*, vol. iii (Wetteren–Paris, 1948).

Gibbons, H.: *The Foundation of the Ottoman Empire*. Oxford, 1916.

Giese, F.: 'Die geschichtlichen Grundlagen für die Stellung der christlichen Untertanen in osmanischen Reich', in *Der Islam*, vol. xix (Berlin–Leipzig, 1931), 264–77.

—— 'Das Problem der Entstehung des osmanischen Reiches', in *Zeitschrift für Semitistik*, 1924.

Girard, P. S.: 'Mémoire sur l'Agriculture, l'Industrie, et le Commerce de l'Égypte' in *Description de l'Égypte, État moderne*, vol. ii, pt. 1 (Paris, 1812), 491–714.

Graetz, H. H.: *History of the Jews*. 5 vols. London, 1891–2.

Graf, Georg: *Geschichte der christlichen arabischen Litteratur*. 4 vols. and index. Vatican City, 1944–53.

Grant, Christina Phelps: *The Syrian Desert*. London, 1937.

Ḥâccî Ḫalîfe (Kâtib Çelebi): *Destûrü 'l-ʿAmel*. Exerpts in Aḥmed Râsim (q.v.), ii. 177 sqq. (Trans. by A. Behrnauer in *Zeitschrift der Deutschen Morgenländischen Gesellschaft*, vol. xi. Leipzig, 1857.)

Ḥaidar Aḥmad Şihâb: *Le Liban à l'époque des Amirs Chihab*. Arabic text ed. by A. Rustum and F. E. Boustany. 3 vols. Beirut, 1933.

Hammer-Purgstall, Joseph von: *Constantinopolis und der Bosporus*. Budapest, 1822.

—— *Geschichte der osmanischen Reiches*. 10 vols. Budapest, 1827–35. (French trans. by B. Hellert, *Histoire de l'empire ottoman*. 18 vols. Paris, 1835–46.)

—— *Des osmanischen Reichs Staatsverfassung und Staatsverwaltung*. 2 vols. Vienna, 1815.

Hamont, P. N.: *L'Égypte sous Méhémet-Ali*. 2 vols. Paris, 1843.

Hasluck, F. W.: *Christianity and Islam under the Sultans*. 2 vols. Oxford, 1929.

Heffening, W.: *Das islamische Fremdenrecht*. Hanover, 1925.

Heyworth-Dunne, J.: *Introduction to the History of Education in Modern Egypt*. London, 1939.

Hughes, T. P.: *A Dictionary of Islam*. London, 1885.

Ḥuseyn Efendi: 'Report', ed. by Šafîḳ Ğurbâl as 'Miṣr ʿinda mafraḳ al-ṭuruḳ', in *Bulletin of the Faculty of Arts*, Fu'ad I University, vol. iv, pt. 1 (Cairo, 1936), 1–70.

Ibn ʿÂbidîn, Muḥammad Amîn: *Minḥet el-Ḫâliḳ*, on margin of Ibn Nuceym, *el-Baḥr el-Râ'iḳ*. Cairo, 1311 A.H.

Ibn Cemâʿa: 'Taḥrîr el-Aḥkâm fî tadbîr ahl al-Islâm', ed. by H. Kofler in *Islamica*, vol. vi, pt. 4. Leipzig, 1934.

Ibn Ğalbûn: *La Cronaca di Ibn Ğalbûn*. Ed. by E. Rossi. Bologna, 1936.

Ibn Ḫaldûn, ʿAbd el-Raḥmân: *Kitâb al-ʿIbar wa'l-Iʿtibâr*. Vol. i: *Muḳaddima*. Bûlâḳ, 1284 A.H. (and other editions).

Ibn Nuceym, Zeynu 'l-ʿÂbidîn: *el-Aşbâh wa'l-Naẓâ'ir*. Istanbul, 1290 A.H. (also Cairo, 1298 A.H.).

—— *el-Baḥr el-Râ'iḳ*. Cairo, 1311 A.H.

Islam Ansiklopedisi. Istanbul, 1940 (proceeding).

Ismâʿîl Ğâlib: *Taḳvîmi Meskûkâti ʿOsmânîye*. Constantinople, 1307 A.H.

Ismâʿîl Ḫüsrev: *Türkiye köy iktisadiyatı̂*. Istanbul, 1934.

Jollois, M.: 'Notice sur la ville de Rosette', in *Description de l'Égypte, État moderne*, vol. ii (Paris, 1812), 333–60.

Jomard, M.: 'Description abrégée de la Ville et de la Citadelle du Kaire', ibid., vol. ii, pt 2, 579–778.

Jorga, N.: *Geschichte des osmanischen Reichs*. 5 vols. Gotha, 1908–13.

Jouplain, N. (pseud.): *La Question du Liban*. Paris, 1908.

Juchereau de Saint-Denys, A. de: *Histoire de l'Empire ottoman depuis 1792 jusqu'en 1844*. 4 vols. Paris, 1844.

'Ḳânûnnâme of ʿAbdu'r-Raḥmân Tevkîʿî', in *Millî Tetebbüler Mecmûʿasî* (*M.T.M.*), i. 497–544.

'Ḳânûnnâmei Âli ʿOs̱mân' (Ḳânûnnâmes of Meḥmed II and Süleymân the Magnificent), in *T.O.E.M.* i (Supplements to pts. 13–19. Istanbul, 1912–13).

Karal, Enver Ziya: *Osmanlî Tarihi*. Ankara.

Kat Angelino, A. D. A. de: *Colonial Policy*, abr. trans. by G. H. Renier, 2 vols. The Hague, 1931.

Khadduri, M.: *War and Peace in the Law of Islam*. Baltimore, Md., 1955.

Kissling, H. J.: 'The Role of the Dervish Orders in the Ottoman Empire', in *Studies in Islamic Cultural History*, ed. by G. E. von Grunebaum. American Anthropologist Memoir no. 76. 1954.

Ḳoçu Bey: *Risâle*. Istanbul, 1303 A.H. (Trans. by A. Behrnauer, in *Zeitschrift der Deutschen Morgenländischen Gesellschaft*, vol. xv (Leipzig, 1861), 290 sqq.)

Köprülüzade (Koprülü) Meḥmed Fu'âd: 'Anadoluda Islâmiyet', in *Darü'l-Fünun Edebiyat Fakültesi Mecmuasî*, Istanbul, 1922.

—— 'Bizans Müesseselerin Os̱manlî Müesseselerine Te's̱iri', in *Türk Hukuk ve Iktisat Mecmuasî*, vol. i. Istanbul, 1931.

—— *Les Origines du Bektachisme*. [Paris], 1926.

—— 'Selcuḳlular Zamanînda Anadoluda Türk Medeniyeti', in *Millî Tetebbüler Mecmüasî* (*M.T.M.*) ii. Istanbul, 1331 A.H.

—— *Türk Edebîyâtînda ilk Mutaṣavvîflar*. Istanbul, 1918.

—— 'Vakf'a ait tarihî istilahlar meselesi', in *Vakîflar Dergisi*, i. Ankara, 1938.

Kremer, Alfred Freiherr von: *Die Kulturgeschichte des Orients unter den Chalifen*. 2 vols. Vienna, 1875–7.

Kunter, Halim Baki: 'Türk Vakîflarî ve Vakfiyeleri', in *Vakîflar Dergisi*, i (Ankara, 1938).

Kurd ʿAlî, Muḥammad: *Ḫiṭaṭ el-Şâm*. 6 vols. Damascus, 1343–8 A.H.

Lammens, Henri: *La Syrie*. 2 vols. Beirut, 1921.

Lancret, M.-A.: 'Mémoire sur le système d'imposition territoriale et sur l'administration des Provinces de l'Égypte dans les dernières années du Gouvernement des Mamlouks', in *Description de l'Égypte, État moderne*, vol. i, bk. 1 (Paris, 1809), 233–60.

Lane, Edward William: *Manners and Customs of the Modern Egyptians*. Many editions.

Lane-Poole, Stanley: *The Coins of the Turks in the British Museum*. B.M. Catalogue of Oriental Coins, vol. viii. London, 1883.

—— *Social Life in Egypt*. London, n.d.

—— *The Story of Cairo*. London, 1906.

Laoust, H.: *Les Gouverneurs de Damas*. Damascus, 1952.

Le Strange, Guy: *Don Juan of Persia*. London, 1926.

Levy, R.: *The Sociology of Islam*. 2 vols. Herbert Spencer's Trustees, London, n.d.

Lewis, Bernard: 'The Islamic Guilds', in *Economic History Review*, vol. viii, no. 1 (London, Nov. 1937), 20–37.

—— *Notes and Documents from the Turkish Archives*. Jerusalem, 1952.

—— 'The Privilege granted by Meḥmed II to his Physician', in *Bulletin of the School of Oriental and African Studies*, vol. xiv (London, 1952), 550–63.

Ligne, Charles Joseph, Prince de: 'Mémoire sur le Comte de Bonneval', in *Mémoires et Mélanges historiques et littéraires*, vol. v (Paris, 1829), 229–488.

Lockhart, L.: *Nadir Shah*. London, 1938.

Lockroy, E.: *Ahmed le Boucher*. Paris, 1888.

Longrigg, S. H.: *Four Centuries of Modern Iraq*. Oxford, 1925.

Luṭfî Paşa: *Âṣafnâma*, ed. & trans. by R. Tschudi. Berlin, 1910. (Türkische Bibliothek, vol. xii.)

Lybyer, A. H.: *The Government of the Ottoman Empire in the Time of Suleiman the Magnificent*. Cambridge, 1913.

Macdonald, D. B.: *Development of Muslim Theology, Jurisprudence, and Constitutional Theory*. London, 1915; 1st ed. 1903.

el-Maʿlûf, I.: 'Industries of Damascus', in *Journal of the Damascus Chamber of Commerce* (Arabic), Damascus, 1922.

Malus de Mitry: *Agenda de Malus, publié par le Général Thoumas*. Paris, 1892.

Marcel, J. J.: 'L'Égypte, depuis la conquête des Arabes jusqu'à la domination française', in series *L'Univers, Histoire et Description de tous les Peuples: Égypte*. Paris, 1848.

Masqueray, E.: *La Formation des cités chez les sédentaires de l'Algérie*. Paris, 1886.

Massignon, L.: 'La Légende de Hallâcé Mansur en pays turcs', in *Revue des Études Islamiques* (Paris, 1941–6), 67–73.

—— 'L'Œuvre hallajienne d'Attar', *Revue des Études Islamiques* (Paris, 1941–6), 117–44.

—— *La Passion d'al-Hallaj*. 2 vols. Paris, 1922.

Masson, P.: *Histoire du Commerce français dans le Levant au XVIIIe siècle*. Paris, 1911.

Maundrell, Henry: 'A Journey from Aleppo to Jerusalem at Easter, A.D. 1697', in *Early Travels in Palestine*, ed. by Thomas Wright. London (Bohn), 1848.

el-Mâwardî, Abu'l-Ḥasan ʿAlî: *Constitutiones Politicae*. Arabic text ed. by M. Enger. Bonn, 1853. (French trans. by E. Fagnan: *Les Statuts gouvernementaux*. Algiers, 1915.)

Meḥmed ʿÂrif Bey: 'Ḫumbaraci Başi Aḥmed Paşa', in *T.O.E.M.* iii and iv.

Mémoires sur l'Égypte, publiés pendant les campagnes du général Bonaparte dans les années VI et VII, VIII et IX. 4 vols. Paris, ans VIII–XI. (Partial English trans.: *Memoirs relative to Egypt*. London, 1800.)

Michael of Damascus: *La Syrie et le Liban de 1782 à 1841 d'après Michel de Damas*. Arabic text ed. by L. Malouf, S.J. Beirut, 1912.

Miḫâ'îl Muşâḳa: *Maşhad el-Iʿyân bi-ḥawâdiṯ Sûriya wa-Lubnân*. Ed. by M. Ḫalîl ʿAbdu. Cairo, 1908.

Miller, W.: *The Latins in the Levant*. London, 1908.

—— *The Ottoman Empire and its Successors*. Cambridge, 1927.

Montagne, R. *Les Berbères et le Makhzen*. Paris, 1930.

el-Mouelhy, Ibrâhîm: 'Le Qirmeh en Égypte', in *Bulletin de l'Institut d'Égypte*, vol. xxix (Cairo, 1946–7), 51–82.

M.T.M.—*see* 'Ḳânûnnâme of 'Abdu'r-Raḥmân Tevkîʿî' *and* Köprülüzade.

el-Murâdî, Muḥammad Ḫalîl: *Silk el-Durar fî aʿyân el ḳarn el-ṯânî ʿaşar*. 4 vols. Cairo, 1874–83.

Muṣṭafâ Nûri—*see* Seyyid Mustafa.

Nallino, C. A.: *Raccolta di scritti editi e inediti, a cura di Maria Nallino*. 6 vols. Rome, 1939–48.

Nicholson, R. A.: *The Mystics of Islam*. London, 1914.

Niebuhr, C. *Description de l'Arabie*. Amsterdam–Utrecht, 1774.

Niẓâm ul-Mulk, Ḥasan b. ʿAlî: *Siyâset-nâme*. Persian text ed. and trans. by Ch. Schefer. Paris, 1891–93.

D'Ohsson, Mouradgea: *Tableau général de l'Empire ottoman*. Paris, 1788–1824.

Olivier, C.: *Voyage dans l'Empire othoman, l'Égypte et la Perse*. 6 vols. Paris, 1807.

Oppenheim, Max Freiherr von: *Die Beduinen*. 3 vols. Leipzig (–Wiesbaden), 1939–52.

ʿOs̱mân Nûrî—*see* Ergin.

O.T.E.M.—*see T.O.E.M.* (for which this is shown in error in Part I *passim*).

Pélissié du Rausas, G.: *Le Régime des Capitulations dans l'Empire ottoman*. 2 vols. Paris, 1902–5.

Pococke, R.: *A Description of the East and some Other Countries*. 2 vols. London, 1743–5.

Poliak, A. N.: 'Le Caractère colonial de l'État mamelouk', in *Revue des Études Islamiques*, 1935, pt. 3 (Paris, 1935).

—— *Feudalism in Egypt, Syria, &c., 1250–1900*. London, 1939.

—— 'Les Révoltes populaires en Égypte à l'époque des Mameloukes', in *Revue des Études Islamiques*, 1934, pt. 3 (Paris, 1934), 251–73.

Politis, Athanase G.: *L'Hellénisme et l'Égypte moderne*. 2 vols. Paris, 1928.

Râşid, Meḥmed: *Ta'rîḫ*. Istanbul, 1740.

Recueil de Firmans Impériaux Ottomans adressés aux Valis et aux Khédives d'Égypte: Sommaires. Cairo, 1934.

Redhouse, Sir James W.: *A Turkish and English Lexicon*. London, 1890 (reprint: Constantinople, 1921).

Richter, G.: *Studien zur arabischen Fürstenspiegel*. Leipzig, 1932.

Rifâʿa Bey Râfiʿ: *Anwâr Tawfîḳ el-Calîl*. Bûlâḳ, 1285 A.H.

Rinn, Louis: *Marabouts et Khouan*. Algiers, 1884.

[Rousseau, J.-B. J. J.]: *Description du pachalik de Baghdad*. Paris, 1809.

Rouyer: 'Notice sur les Médicamens usuels des Égyptiens', in *Description de l'Égypte, État moderne*, vol. i, bk. 1 (Paris, 1809), 217–32.

Russell, Alex., M.D.: *The Natural History of Aleppo*. London, 1756. (2nd ed. London, 1794.)

Sacy, Silvestre de: *Recherches sur la nature et les révolutions du droit de propriété territoriale en Égypte*. 2 vols. Paris, 1818–23.

Samuel-Bernard: 'Mémoires sur les Monnoies d'Égypte', in *Description de l'Égypte, État moderne*, vol. ii, pt. 1 (Paris, 1812), 321–468.

Santillana, David: *Istituzioni di diritto musulmano malichita.* vol. i. Rome, 1926.

Ṣarî Meḥmed Paşa: *Nasâ'iḥü'l-vüzerâ ve'l-ümerâ*, ed. and trans., with introduction and notes, as *Ottoman Statecraft*, by W. L. Wright. Princeton Oriental Texts, ii, 1935.

Sauvaget, J.: *Alep.* 2 vols. Paris 1941.

—— 'Esquisse d'une histoire de la ville de Damas', in *Revue des Études Islamiques*, 1934, pt. iv (Paris).

Savary, C. de: *Lettres sur l'Égypte.* 3 vols. Paris, 1785–6. (English trans.: *Letters on Egypt.* 2nd ed. 2 vols. London, 1787.)

Schacht, J.: 'Die arabische *ḥiyal*-Litteratur', in *Der Islam*, vol. xv (Berlin–Leipzig, 1926), 211–32.

—— *G. Bergsträßer's Grundzüge des islamischen Rechts.* Berlin, 1935.

—— *The Origins of Islamic Jurisprudence.* Oxford, 1950. 'Šarīʿa und Qānūn im modernen Ägypten', in *Der Islam*, vol. xx (Berlin–Leipzig, 1932), 206–36.

Schmidt, A. E.: 'Zur Geschichte der sunnitisch-schiitischen Beziehung' in *ʿIḳd al-Gumân* (Barthold-Festchrift). Tashkent, 1927.

Seton-Watson, R. W. *History of the Roumanians*, &c. London, 1934.

Seyyid Muṣṭafâ Nûrî: *Netâ'icü'l-Vuḳûʿât.* 2nd ed. 4 vols. Istanbul, 1327 A.H.

Snouck Hurgronje, C.: *Verspreide Geschriften.* vol. ii. Leiden, 1923.

Sonnini de Manoncour, C.: *Voyage dans la Haute et la Basse Égypte.* 3 vols. Paris, an VII.

Steen de Jehay: *De la Situation légale des sujets ottomans non-musulmans.* Brussels, 1906.

Süleymân Sûdî: *Defteri Muḳteṣid.* 3 vols. Istanbul, 1306 A.H.

Taeschner, F. 'Das Futuwwa-Rittertum des islamischen Mittelalters', in *Beiträge zur Arabistik, Semitistik und Islamwissenschaft.* Leipzig, 1944.

el-Ṭawîl, Tawfîḳ: *el-Taṣawwuf fî Miṣr ibbân el-ʿaṣr el-ʿuṯmânî.* Cairo, n.d. [1946].

Thomas, Bertram: *Arabia Felix.* London, 1932.

Thorning, Hermann: *Beiträge zur Kenntnis des islamischen Vereinswesen auf Grund von Bast Madad et-Taufîq.* Berlin, 1913. (Türkische Bibliothek, vol xvi.)

Thornton, Thos.: *The Present State of Turkey.* 2nd ed. 2 vols. London, 1807.

Tischendorf, Paul Andreas von: *Das Lehnswesen in den moslemischen Staaten insbesondere im Osmanischen Reiche mit dem Gesetzbuche der Lehen unter Sultan Ahmed I.* Leipzig, 1872.

T.O.E.M. Ta'rîḫi ʿOsmânî Encümeni Mecmûʿasî. Istanbul, 1911.

Tott, Baron F. de: *Mémoires sur les Turcs et les Tatares.* 4 vols. Amsterdam, 1784. (2nd ed. 2 vols. Amsterdam, 1785.)

Tritton, A. S.: *The Caliphs and their Non-Moslem Subjects.* Oxford, 1930.

Turan, O.: 'Les Souverains seldjoukides et leurs sujets non-musulmans', in *Studia Islamica*, i (Paris, 1953), 65–100.

Tyan, E.: *Histoire de l'organisation judiciaire en pays d'Islam.* vol. i: Paris, 1938; vol. ii: Beirut, 1943.

— *Le Notariat et le Régime de la preuve par écrit dans la pratique du droit musulman.* Harissa, 1945.

Ünver, A. Süheyl: 'Büyük Selçuklu Imparatorluğun zamanînda vakîf hastanelerin bir kîsmîna dair', in *Vakîflar Dergisi*, i. Ankara, 1938.

Vandal, A.: *Le Pacha Bonneval.* Paris, 1885.

Vicdânî, Şâdiḳ: 'Ḫalvetîye', in *Ṭûmâru Ṭuruḳu 'Alîye*, vol. iii. Istanbul, 1338–41 A.H.

Volney, Chassebœuf *dit* Comte de: *Voyage en Égypte et en Syrie, 1783–5.* 3rd ed. 2 vols. Paris, an VII.

Wiet, Gaston: 'L'Égypte arabe', in *Précis de l'histoire d'Égypte*, vol. ii. Cairo, 1932.

—— 'Les Inscriptions du Mausolée de Shāfiʿī', in *Bulletin de l'Institut d'Égypte*, vol. xv, pt. 2 (Cairo, 1933), 167–85.

Wittek, Paul: 'Notes sur la Tughra ottomane', in *Byzantion*, vols. xviii and xx (Brussels, 1948, 1950).

—— *The Rise of the Ottoman Empire.* London, 1938.

Wood, A. C.: *The Levant Company.* London, 1935.

Wüstenfeld, F.: 'Fachred-Din der Drusenfürst', in *Abhandlungen der Königl. Gesellschaft der Wissenschaften zu Göttingen*, vol. xxiii (Göttingen, 1886).

Young, G.: *Corps de droit ottoman.* 7 vols. Oxford, 1905–6.

Zinkeisen, J. W.: *Geschichte des osmanischen Reiches in Europa.* 7 vols. Hamburg, 1840–63.

Z.D.M.G.—see Ḥâccî Ḫalîfe *and* Ḳoçu Bey.

Z.E.E.—see Barkan.

INDEX OF ARABIC AND TURKISH TERMS

Abdâlân, 190 f., 195.
Abû midfa' (coin), 50 n., 57 n.
'Acemî Oğlan, 152.
'Âda, 118.
'Adedi ağnâm, 5 n., 34.
'Âdeti ağnâm, 34 n.
Ahlu'l-Ġayb, 187 n.
Aḫi, 183, 189, 191, 194.
Aḳçe, 3 n., 11, 40 n., *49*, *51–56*, 58.
Aḳçe başi, 24 n.
Altmişli (teaching grade), 146 n.
Amân, 213.
Âmedîye, 13, 15 n.
Amîn el-futyâ, 137.
Angarya, 19 n.
Ardi memleket, 166.
Arpa Emîni, 36 n.
Arpa paha, 33 n.
Arpaliḳ, 109, 124, 126, 137.
Arslânî (coin), 50.
'Aṣavîyet (for '*asabîyet*), 28 n.
'Askerî, 4, 16, 35, 87, 88.
'Assâsîye, 8 n.
Aşrâf, *see* Şerîf.
'Aşûrâ, 193 n.
Avania, 49, 60 n., 62 f., 125 n., 244.
'Avâriḍ, 2, 3, 4, 19, 20, 21, 24, 30 n., 31, 36 n.
Awḳâf, *see* Waḳf.
Awliyâ, *see* Evliyâ.
'Awn (Ḳâḍî's usher), 130 n.
A'yân, 22 n.
'Azeb (ocaḳ), 41 n.

Bâb Nâ'ibi, 124.
Baba, 183, 186, 189, 191, 194.
Bâc, 7, 8, 9 n., 12, 15, 20, 34.
Barâ'atli (Ḏimmî exempt from *cizye*), 253 n.
Barrânî (supplementary tax), 60.
Bâṭinî, 181, 182 n., 188, 190 ff., 201, 209 f.
Bayram, 147.
Bedel, pl. Bedelât, 4, 5 n., 16; bedeli cebeli, 32 n.; — cizye, 4, 12 n., 17; — mu'âvenet, 34 n.; — nüzül, 30 n., 31 n., 40 n.; — orduyu hümâyûn, 31 n.; — şâyi', 34 n.; — timar, 32 n.; — ṭopu hümâyûn, 34 n.
Beduin, 62 n., 63, 69, 128, 181 n., 182.
Berât (barâ'a), 23 n., 98 n., 173, 174 n.
Bey-molla, 107.
Bey'at, 147 n.
Beyt el-Ḳâḍî (in Cairo), 130 n.
Beytü 'l-Mâl, 28 n., 29.
Bezistan, 8 n.
Bid'at, 8 n., 33 n., 34.
Boğça (Bohça), Behâ, **107 n.**
Bölük (cavalry), 200.

Câmi', 95 ff.
Cawâlî, *see* Cizye.
Cebeli, 32 n.
Celeb-keşan, **34 n.**, 35 **n.**
Cerîd (lance **or** dart), 152 n.
Ceybḫarcliği, 10 n.
Cizye (cizya), 11, 16, 17, 43, 167 n., 195, **208**, *251–8*.
Cülûs Baḫşişi, 25 n.

Çardaḳ, 8 n.
Ça'uşîya (ocaḳ), 40.
Çeltik, çeltikçi, 19.
Çift Aḳçesi, 251.
Çingene (Gypsy), 16, 167 n.
Çizme paha, 33 n., 171 n.
Çorbaci, 193.

Dâḫil (medreses), 94 n.
Damgâ resmi, 8 n.
Dânişmend, 146, 151.
Dâr ul-'Adl, 134.
Dârü'l-Hadîs, 144 n., 145, 146 n., 147, 151 n.
Dârü'l-Ḳurrâ, 144 n.
Dâr-e Manşûr, 192 n.
Dârü'l-Şubyân, 144 n.
Dârü'l-Tedrîs, 144 n.
Dârü'l-Ṭibb, 145, 149.
Defterdâr, 5 n., 6 n., 11, 17, 21 n., 24, 26, 29, 46 ff., 58 f., 94, 147, 171, 255.
Der âmed, âmedîye, 13.
Derbent resmi, 6 n.
Dervîş, 42 n., 76, 87 n., 152, 174, *179–206*, 241.
Devşirme, 18, 104, 168, 195, *210*, 211, 223, 224, 233 f.
Deymûs, or dîmûs, 43.
Direkli, 50 n.
Dirhem, 40 n.
Dirlik, 21.
Dîvân, 2, 6 n., 36 n., 86 ff., 91, 129, 147.
Dolab, 175.
Dönme, 242.
Dôsa (dawsa), 197.

Ḍâbiṭ (tax-farmer), 44 n.

Ḏimmî, 4, 13, 15 n., 16, 24, 27, 33 n., 165, 192, 195, *207–61*.

Efendi (Egyptian finance official), 46 f., 65 f.
Emîn, 6 n., 12, 21 n.
Emîn el-Buhâr, 41 n.
Emîn ḍarbḫâna (Ḍarbḫâne Emîni), 56 n.
Enderûn, 10 n., 152.
Ekyâl (kile, kayl), 8 n.
Esedî (coin), 50, 53 n., 54.
Eṣnâf, 143 n.
Eşrâf, *see* Şerîf.
Evḳâf, *see* Waḳf.
Evliyâ (Awliyâ, saints), 187, 205.
Evzân (vezin, wazn), 8 n.
Eyâlet, 4, 18, 37, 44 f., 66, 68.

Fâ'iḍ, 40.
Faḳîh, 81, 100, 134, 140 n.
Faḳîr, 179, 186.
Fanâ (absorption in God), 201.
Farḍat el-Taḥrîr (tax), 60 n.
Fatâ, 181 n., 182 n.
Fellâḥ, 38, 41, 43 n., 102 n.
Fetva (fetwa), 85 f., 98 n., 112, 117 n., 130, 134 f., 137, 153, 160 n., 216 n., 259 n.
Fetvâ-emîni, 86, 137, 151 n.
Fetvâ-hâne, 86.
Fiḳh, 81.
Fiki, 140 f.
Fîlûrî (coin), 50, 58.
Fityân, 181 f.
Fîndiḳ altînî, fîndiḳlî (funduḳî, funduḳlî) (coin), 54 n., 55, 57 n., 254.
Futûwa, 181 ff.

Gönül bekleme, 179 n.
Gümrük, 12 ff., 15 n., 16 n.
Güẓeşte, 24 n.

Ğâzî, 181, 183 f., 210.

Ḥabs, *see* Waḳf.
Ḥâcib, 121 n.
Ḥaḍarîya, 31 n.
Ḥadîṯ, 201.
Ḥâfiẓ (one who has the *Ḳur'ân* by heart), 170.
Ḥaḫam Başî, 217, 219, 221, 226.
Ḥaḳḳ el-ṭarîḳ, 40 n.
Ḥaḳḳî imḍâ, 6 n.
Ḥaḳḳî kitâbet, 6 n.
Ḥallâcî (type of Ṣûfism), 181, 191 n., 201.
Ḥamla (due exacted in Egypt), 62 n.
Ḥâra, 259.
Ḥarameyn, 65 n.; — Dîvânî, 171; — Dolabî, 176; — Müfettişi, 92 n., 171; — Muhâsebesi, 97 n., 175 n.; — Muḳâṭa'asi, 97 n., 175 n.
Ḥarbî, 13, 15.
Ḥareketi Altmişlî, Ḥareketi Dâḫil, Ḥareketi Ḫâric (teaching grades), 146 n.
Ḥarem, the Imperial, 10, 240.
Ḥaşîş, 203.
Ḥekîm Başî, 90, 149.
Ḥiyal, 119.
Ḥulwân (advance payment for an *iltizâm*), 41 n.

Ḫamr emîni, 27 n.
Ḫân (caravanserai), 174.
Ḫânḳâh, 186, 202.
Ḫarâc, 16 n., 43, 166, 208, 216, 251, 252 f.
Ḫarcî reddîye, 24 n.
Ḫâric (medreses), 94 n.
Ḫâricî, 71.
Ḫâṣṣ, 6 n., 19, 21 n., 43, 45 n.
Ḫaṭîb, 95–97, 98 n., 99 n., 100 n., 103, 109, 170, 178.
Ḫaṭṭî hümâyûn, 106 n.
Ḫattî şerîf, 98, 174 n., 250.
Ḫavâmisi Süleymânîye (*medreses*), 145 n., 146 n.
Ḫazînei 'Âmire, Ḫazînei Enderûn, Ḫazînei Ḫâṣṣa, 9 n.
Ḫazne (tribute), 65 n.
Ḫidmet, 22.
Ḫirḳa, 186.
Ḫurda, 41 n.
Ḫuṭba, 96.
Ḫoca (ḫwâcâ), 84 n., 90, 94, 109 n., 142 f., 150, 170.

Ibtidâi Altmişlî, Ibtidâi Dâḫil, Ibtidâi Ḫâric (teaching grades), 146 n.
Icârateyn, 177 n.
Icâre, Icâre mu'accele, Icâre mu'eccele, 166 n.
Icâze, 146, 158, 159 n.
Icmâ', 74, 114, 134.
Iç Oğlan, 152.
Iḥtisâb, *see* Muḥtasib.
Ikrâh (in legal theory), 119 n.
Iḳṭâ', 116.
'Ilm, 81.
Iltizâm, 21 n., 41 n., 109, 173.
I'mâlîye (due), 15 n.
Imâm (Moslem ruler), 82, 233; (şî'î), 187, 189; (mosque minister), 90, 95–97, 103, 158, 170, 178 n.
Imânet, 21 n.
'Imâret, 143.
Imdâdîyei ḥaḍarîye, Imdâdîyei seferîye, 31 n.
Irsâliyât, 17, 18.
Ispence, 251.
Istibdâl, 178.
Iẓn-nâme, 98 n.

Janissaries, 1, 35, 63, 78, 88, 101, 104, 108, 190 f., 193, 195, 200, 206, 216 n.

Kâhya, 86, 102, 226, 256 n.
Kâhya Bey, 6 n.
Karâmât, 186.
Karşûnî, 247 n.
Kâşif, 38, 40 n., 61, 129.
Kâtib, 130 n.
Kesri mîzân, 6 n.
Kîs, kîse, 45 n., 58 n.
Kücük Evkâf Muhâsebesi, 175 n.
Kulâh, 189.
Kürekçi, 4 n., 40 n., 66.
Kuşûfîya, 40, 42 n., 60, 64.
Kuttâb (school), 139 n., 141.

Ḳabbânî, 140.
Ḳaḍâ, 3, 9, 12, 108, 124, 135, 150, 255.
Ḳaḍâ Nâ'ibi, 124.
Ḳâḍî, 3, 5, 9 n., 24, 27, 37, 39, 48, 77, 80, 82 ff., 91 ff., 98, 99 n., 100, 105 n., 106, 107 n., 112 n., 115 f., 119, *121–33*, 134 f., 137 f., 140, 146, 151, 156, 162, 173, 175, 177 f., 189, 208, 255.
Ḳâḍî-'asker, Ḳâḍî'l-'asker, 11, *83–89*, 91–93, 97 f., 105–8, 116, 121, 123 f., 132, 135, 151, 155 n., 174 n.
Ḳadin, 143.
Ḳâ'im-maḳâm (Egyptian official), 61.
Ḳalamîya, 48 n.
Ḳalba Baḳici, 179 n.
Ḳalem resmi, 13 n., 58.
Ḳam Ozan, 182 f.
Ḳânûn, 1, 3 n., 8 n., 15 n., 22, 28, 32 n., 38, 40, 43, 44 n., 48 n., 56, 59, 85, 87, 106 n., 116, 119, 120 n., 121, 129, 173, 178, 213, 251, 252 n.
Ḳânûn-nâme, 5 n., 6 n., 38, 48 n., 56, 85, 119, 129.
Ḳanṭar, Kanṭar ücreti, 8 n.
Ḳapan, Kabbân, 8.
Ḳapi Ağasi, 170 n.
Ḳapi Kahyalari, 5 n.
Ḳapi Ḳullari, 1, 12, 18, 28 f., 88, 93, 105, 127, 147, 168, 223, 240.
Ḳapici, 91.
Ḳaptan, 148.
Ḳaptan Paşa, Ḳapudan-Paşa, 60, 92, 132.
Ḳara Ḳuruş, 50–53.
Ḳassâm, 88, 124, 130 n.
Ḳayyim, 96, 97, 170.
Ḳism, ḳasm, 43 n.
Ḳirma, 47, 58 n.
Ḳismet, ḳisma, 206.
Ḳizilbaş, 189, 196.
Ḳizlar Ağasi, 92 n., 170 f., 177.
Ḳoca başi, 237.
Ḳur'ân, Ḳur'ânic, 27, 114, 117 f., 139–43, 144 n., 158, 168, 181, 201, 205, 207, 258.
Ḳuruş, 50, 53, 54, 58 n., 254 n.
Ḳuṭb, 187 n.
Ḳuyruḳlu berât, 23.

Lâle devri, 153.

Macar altini, 50, 56.
Madrasa (medrese), 76, 80, 82 f., 89 91, 94, 96, 100, 104 ff., 109, 125, 135, 140, *143–59*, 161, 165 ff., 170, 174 f., 202.
Mahâkim şer'îya, 115.
Mahbûs, *see* Mawḳûf.
Mâhî'n-nuḳûş, 170.
Mahkeme, Mahkama, 91, 130, 174, 255.
Mahmal, 92 n.
Mahmal Ḳâḍîsi, 92.
Mahmali şerîf, 92 n.
Mahmûdîye, 55 n.
Mahrec, 89, 126, 151 n.
Ma'îşet, 109, 126.
Maḳṭû', 17 n.
Mâl el-hurr, 40.
Malâma, 180 n.
Mâlikâne, 22, 23, 43, 46, 48 n., 109, 137.
Mâlîye ḳalemi, 97 n.
Ma'lûm, 99 n.
Mamlûk, 61, 68, 103, 124 n., 127.
Mangane, 8 n.
Mangir, 56 n.
Mâr Şim'ûn, 228.
Mâristân, 163.
Mascid, 95, 96.
Massâh, 140.
Maşderîye, 13 ff.
Maṭlabci, 87 n.
Mawḳûf, mevḳûf, 166, 175.
Mawlâ, 86 n.
Maẓâlim, 116, 130.
Ma'zûl, 106, 126.
Medin, *see* Mu'ayyidî.
Mekteb, 139, 141–4, 166 f.
Mektupçu, 87 n.
Menâşibi Devrîye, 91.
Menşab Kâğidi, 98 n.
Menşab ve ciheti olanlar, 28 n.
Mesnevî, 152.
Metâwila, 68.
Mevlevîyet (Mollâ's post), 87 n., 89, 91 n., 105 n., 108 n., 110 n., 124, 146 f., 150 f.
Millet, milla, 79, *212*, 214, 216 f., 219–26, 231 f., 234, 236 ff., 245, 248, 253 n., 255, 257, 259, 260.
Millet-başi, 212, 246.
Mîr, 93 n.
Mîrî, 9, *10–12*, 40, 41, 43 f., 46 f., 56 n., 61 f., 65 n., 122, 172 f., 254.
Mîrî Dellâl Başi, 23 n.
Mîrî Kâtibi, 88.
Mîzân, 8 n., 15 n., 33.
Mollâ, 85 n., 86 n., *87–94*, 98, 105 n., 106 ff., 121, 124, 126, 135, 147.

Mollâ Beyi, 107 n.
Mollâ Ḫünkâr, 195.
Mollâ Vekîli, 124 n., 126.
Mu'allim, 90, 170.
Mu'arrif, 170.
Mu'âyada, 91.
Mu'ayyidî (mîdi, medin) (coin), 39 n., 51, 53 n., 56 f.
Mubâşir, 24 n.
Mubâya'aci, 36 n.
Muctahid, 133 f.
Muḍâf, 60.
Müderris, 105 n., 146, 147 n., 150 f., 170.
Mü'ezzin (Mu'aḏḏin), 96 f., 170, 178 n.
Müfettiş, 92, 98.
Muftî, 84 f., 86 n., 94, 98 ff., 101 n., 105 n., 106, 112 n., 117 n., 120, 123 n., 127, 130 n., 131 n., 132, *133–8*, 146, 158, 166, 175.
Muḥâsabet el-ḥarameyn (Ḥarameyn muḥasebesi), 174 n.
Muḥaṣṣil, 44 n., 48 n.
Muḥḍir, 90.
Muḥtesib, 7, 8, 9, 12 n., 15, 34, 80, 116, 129.
Muḫallefât, 28 n.
Mu'îd, 146, 158.
Muḳâṭa'a, 21 n., 22, 24 n.
Muḳâṭa'aci, 46 n.
Muḳâṭa'ayi ağnâm ḳalemi, 35 n.
Muḳallid, 134.
Muḳâyese ḏaḫâiri, 36 n.
Mulâzim (in learned profession), 147 n., (officer), 255 n.
Mulâzemet, 105 n., 150.
Mulk, 167.
Mültezim, multazim, 6 n., 21 n., 24 n., 38–40, 43, 47, 59–62, 66, 172 f.
Müneccim Başi, 90.
Murâsele, 98 n.
Murîd, 186.
Murûrîye, 9 n.
Müsellem (ocaḳ), 16.
Müskirat resmi, 27 n.
Musta'min, 213.
Muṣâdara, 28 f.
Mûṣile (grade in judicial service), 122.
Mûṣilei Ṣaḥn and Mûṣilei Süleymânîye (medreses), 145 n., 146 n.
Mutawâlî, 68.
Mutawallî, mütevellî, 170 ff., 176.

Nagîd, 226.
Nâḥiye, 124.
Nâ'ib, 88 n., 92, 98 n., 105 n., 106, 107 n., 121, 123, *124*, 126, 130–2, 135, 137, 146.
Naḳîbu'l-Aşrâf, 93 f., 98, 99 n., 100 ff.
Nargile, 33.
Nâẓir, 93 n., 170–2, 176, 178.
Nerḫ, 8.
Niḳâba, 93 n., 100–2.
Nîşânci, 94, 147.
Niyâba, Niyâbet, 105 n., 124.
Nüzûl ve avâriḍ-ḫânesi, 30 n.

Ocaḳ, 35, 40 n., 41, 46 n., 47, 61, 63, 198.
Ocaḳliḳ (fief), 2 n., 16.
Ordu Ḳâḍîsi, 92.
Orta, 88.
'Os̱mânî (aḳçe), 49, 51.

Para, 39 n., 40 n., 42 n., 51 f., 53 n., 54, 56 n., 60, 254 n.
Paşa, 30, 38 f., 41 n., 42–47, 56, 64 f., 67, 69, 86, 101–3, 107, 109, 111, 123, 125, 128 f., 136, 143, 159, 160 n., 166, 172 f., 177, 216, 237, 247.
Paşaliḳ, 41 n., 45 f., 48.
Pâye Menâşib, 89.
Pîr, 186.

Raf' el-maẓâlim, 60.
Ra'îs (head of learned corporation), 82, 100, 137.
Ra'îyet, ra'îya, re'âyâ, 16, 20, 28 f., 87, 166, 176 f., 252, *253*.
Rasm, resim, 7 n.
Re'âyâ, *see* Ra'îyet.
Reddiyei temessük, 24 n.
Reftîye, 13, 14.
Ribâṭ, 186.
Riwâḳ, 155, 157, 158 n.
Riyal, iryâl, 50.
Rizḳa, pl. rizâḳ, 173, 177.
Ruḫṣatîye, 15 n.
Rûm, 144, 216, 234.
Rûm milleti, 216, 234.
Rusûl (Ḳâḍî's usher), 1?0.
Ru'ûs, 97 n., 98 n.
Rûznâmecî, 46, 47, 66, 172 n.

Sâliyâne, 40 n.
Sancaḳ, 20, 45, 227.
Sancaḳ Beyi, 17, 19, 30 n., 44.
Sayyâḥ (wandering derviş), 190 n.
Sebîl (public fountain), 140.
Seferîye, 31 n.
Senelik nemâ, 24 n.
Seyyid, 93, 101.
Silsila, 186.
Sipâhî, 21, 30 n., 167, 171, 200.
Sitte-i Rumeli, 122.
Siyâsa (penal law), 119.
Softâ, 146, 151, 153, 202.
Subaşi, 19, 238.
Süleymânîye (teaching grade), 145 n. 146.
Sulṭân (civil authority), 115.

Sulṭânî (gold coin), 42 n., 50 n., 55.
Sunna, 27, 120.
Sunnî, 71 ff., 76 f., 85, 115, 133, 156, 179, 181, 192 f., 197, 210, 217, 224, 232, 258.

Ṣadr, 100 n.
Ṣaḥn (medreses), 94 n., 145, 146 n.
Ṣarrâf, 23 n., 24 n., 47 n., 68, 243 n.
Ṣarrâfîye, 24 n.
Ṣu yolcu maṣrefi, 6 n.
Ṣubaşi, 129.
Ṣûfî, Sûfism, taṣawwuf, 27, 71, 73–79, 111, 161, *179–88*, 190–2, 194, 198–206, 209, 241.
Ṣurra, Ṣurra emîni, 58 n.

Şâgird, 6 n.
Şâhid, 38, 130, 175.
Şerî'a, Şer'î, 2, 7, 11, 12, 16, 18, 28 n., 70, 77, 79, 80, 82 f., 85, 102, 104 n., 106 n., *114–21*, 128 f., 132 ff., 166, 168 f., 174, 179, 180, 185, 201, 203 n., 204 f., 213, 223, 240, 252, 256 f.
Şerî'atî (judge), 88 n.
Şerîf, 58 n., 93, 101, 112 n., 156, 197 n.
Şerîfî (coin), 33 n., 42 n., *50*, 51 f., 54 f., 254.
Şeyḫ (dervîş), 183 n., 184, 186, 188, 196 ff., 201; (head of corporation), 100, 127, 261; (head of Arab tribe), 38, 129; (headman of village), 127; (learned man), 30, 64 f., 76, 99, 102 ff., 121 n., 126 n., 132, 136 f., 139, 155 ff., 164, 174 n., 175; (wâ'iẓ), 96 f.
Şeyḫ el-Azhar, 99, 100, 103, 111, 158, 199.
Şeyḫ el-Beled, 38 n., 57, 65, 130.
Şeyḫü'l-Islâm, *84–87*, 89–92, 94, 97 f., 105 n., 106 n., 107–9, 117, 121, 123, 135 f., 147 f., 151, 170, 193, 200, 216 n.
Şeyḫü'l-Islâm Müfettişi, 92 n.
Şeyḫ el-Meşâyiḫ, 199.
Şeyḫ el-Sâdât, 101.
Şî'a, Şî'î, Şî'ism, 71–73, 75 f., 79, 123, 156, 181, 187, 189, 190 n., 193.
Şikäste, 47 n.
Şûna, 39.
Şurṭa, 116.
Şurût, 119.

Ta'ahhud temessükâti, 24 n.
Tâc, 186.
Tadârîs, 156 n.
Taḫt Ḳâḍîsi, 88 n.
Taḫta Başi, 109, 122.
Taḫtaci, 196.
Taḳdîr, 206.
Taṣawwuf, *see* Ṣûfî.
Taṭbîḳçi, 87 n.
Tawliya, tevliyet, 100, 156 n., 170 f., 174 n.
Tedrîs, 146 n.
Tekke (takîya), 152, 165, 167, 174, 186, 190, 196 n., 197 n., 199, 201 f.
Telḫîşci, 86, 151 n.
Tersâne, 152.
Tetimme (medreses), 145.
Tevcîh Fermânî, 98 n.
Teẕkere, 15 n., 98 n.
Teẕkereci, 87 n.
Timar, 32 n., 43, 45, 46 n.
Tuzcu, 19, 20.

Ṭapu, 166.
Ṭarîḳa, 75 f., 78, 102, 185, 187, 193, 195 ff., 199, 200.
Ṭavuḳ paha, 33.
el-Ṭibb el-nabawî, 162 n.
Ṭopḫâne, 148, 152.
Ṭuğ, 91, 216.
Ṭuğra, 54 n., 55.
Ṭuğrali ḳuruş, 54–56.

Ücret, 166.
'Ulemâ, 2 n., 5 n., 33, 35, 42, 71 f., 74 f., 76, 78 f., 80, *81–113*, 121, 122 n., 124 f., 127, 131 ff., 140, 142, 145, 147 ff., 151 ff., 156, 158, 159 n., 160 f., 164, 179 f., 184 f., 197 f., 201, 203 ff., 217, 233, 251, 257.
'Urf, 'Urfî, 2, 3, 5, 6 f., 19, 24, 31 n., 41 n., 106 n., 167.
'Uşr, 19, 166, 251.

Vaḳâ'i' Kâtibi, 88 n.
Vaḳif, *see* Waḳf.
Vâlî, 254.
Vekîl, 126.
Vezîr, 5 n., 6, 11, 20 n., 30 f., 33, 48 n., 52, 59, 84 ff., 90 ff., 98, 147, 170, 200, 202, 236 n.
Vezîri A'ẓam Mufettişi, 92 n.
Vilâyet, 19 n.
Voynuḳ, 234, 252.

Wafâ'î (corporation of Şerîfs), 101, 197 n.
Waḥdat ul-wucûd, 201.
Wâ'iẓ, 96 f.
Wakîl, vekîl, 137.
Waḳf, 1 f., 11, 29 n., 32, 65 n., 105 n., 109 n., 125, 143, 157 n., *165–78*, 202, 249 n., 260 n.
Waḳfîya, Vaḳfîye, 141 n., 143, 149 n., 167 f., 170, 174 n., 175 f., 177 n.
Wâḳif, 171.

Waşîya, 173 n.
Wazîr, *see* Vezîr.
Wekâla, 41, 44 n., 260.

Yaldîz altînî, 50, 56.
Yevmîyei dükâkîn, 7.
Yük, 21 n., *25 n.*, 58 n.

Zâwiya, 186.
Zer-i maḥbûb, 55, 56, 57 n., 254 n.
Zi'âmet, 32 n., 43.
Zolota, 54.

INDEX OF PERSONAL NAMES

'Abbâs (Şâh), 227.
'Abdallâh b. Huşayn el-Suwaydî, 155 n., 156 n.
'Abdallâh Paşa, 68 n.
'Abdallâh Zâḫir, 247 n.
'Abd el-Ğânî el-Nâbulusî, 164, 198.
'Abd el-Wahhâb el-Şa'rânî, 197 n.
'Abdü'l-Ḥamîd I (Sultan), 141 n., 142 n.
'Abdu'l-Ḳâdir el-Gîlânî, 74 n.
Abû Bakr (Caliph), 186 n., 192.
Abû Ḥanîfa, 82, 123, 218.
Abû'l-Su'ûd (Şeyḫü'l-islâm), 216 n.
Aḥmed I (Sultan), 13 n., 15, 25, 170, 200.
Aḥmed III (Sultan), 32 n., 53 ff., 89, 106 n., 149, 153, 200 n.
Aḥmed el-Badawî, 184 n.
Aḥmed Paşa Cezzâr, *see* Cezzâr Paşa.
Aḥmed Paşa, Küçük, 173.
Aḥmed Paşa, Ṭarḫuncu, 3 n.
Aḥmed Yesevî, 181, 197 n.
'Alâ el-Dawla (of Dhu'l-Ḳadr. dynasty), 172 n.
'Alî (Imâm), 73, 93 n., 182 n., 186, 191.
'Alî Bey (Mamlûk), 56, 60, 62 f., 65, 66 n., 244, 259, 260, 261 n.
'Alî Ḳuşçu, 148.
Assemani, Joseph Simonius (el-Sim'ânî), 248 n.
el-Aş'arî, 73 n.
Athenasius Debbâs (Patriarch), 247 n.
Avedik (Gregorian Armenian Patriarch), 246.
Awrangzêb (Emperor), 112 n.
'Aẓm family, 103.

Baba Isḥâḳ, 183 n., 190.
Baradeus, Jacob, 228 n.
Baruch, Juda, 243 n.
Başîr (Druse amîr), 68 n.
Bâyezîd I (Sultan), 93 n., 125 n., 189.
Bâyezîd II (Sultan), 3 n., 20, 58, 93, 143 ff., 147 n., 148, 170, 219.
Bayrâm, Ḥâccî, 199.
Bekrî family, 101 n., 109, 199 n.
Bektâş, Ḥâccî, 190 f., 194 f.
Boris (Bulgarian Tsar), 214.
Brahe, Tycho, 154.

Cabartî family, 103, 109 n., 164.
Ca'fer Çelebi, 147 n.
Calvin, 235.
Celâlü'd-Dîn Rûmî, 87 n., 152, 194, 201.
Cezzâr Paşa, 57, 61, 62, 66 ff., 69 n., 125 n.
Constantine IX (Emperor), 209 n.
Cyril, Saint, 214.

Damad Nevşehirli Ibrâhîm Paşa (Grand Vezîr), 55, 153.
Dushan, Stephan, 215.
el-Duwaihi, Stephan, 249 n.

Elizabeth I of England, 15.
Evliyâ Çelebi, 152, 197, 202.

Faḫr el-Dîn ibn Ma'n, 173, 248.
Fâṭima, 93 n.
Farḥât, Cermânûs, 249.
Farḥât, Miḫâ'îl, 260 n.
Febvre, Michel, 243 n.
Feyḍu'llah Efendi (Şeyḫü'l-islâm), 90 n., 109 n.
Fonseca, 243 n.
François Ier of France, 244.

Galileo, 154.
Gennadius (Patriarch), 216 n.
Germanos (Patriarch), 225.
el-Gîlânî (Keylânî) family, 93 n., 101 n., 102, 174 n.
Gregory the Illuminator, 220.
Gregory XV (Pope), 244.

Ğâlib b. Masâ'id, Şerîf, 112 n.
el-Ğazâlî, 117, 132.

Henri II of France, 240.
Horaghim (Armenian bishop of Bursa), 221.

Ḥâccî Bayrâm, 199.
Ḥâccî Bektâş, 190 f., 194 f.
Ḥacci Ḫalîfe, 25 n., 26 n., 151 f., 154.
Ḥâfiẓ (Persian poet), 204.
el-Ḥallâc, 180.
Ḥamza family of Damascus, 101 n.
Ḥamza of Bursa (Şeyh), 199 n.
Ḥannâ Faḫr, 62, 260 n.
Ḥasan (Imâm), 93 n.

Ḥasan Paşa (Ḳaptan), 60, 132.
Ḥasan el-Ḥijâzî (poet), 160 n.
Ḥâyîm Farhî, 68.
Ḥuseyn (Imâm), 93 n.
Ḥuseyn al-Maḥallî (mathematician), 157 n.

Ḫâdim Ibrâhîm Paşa, 166, 170, 171 n.

Ibnu'l-'Arabî, 75, 184, 194, 201.
Ibn Nuceym, 125 n.
Ibrâhîm (Sultan), 25, 26 n., 195.
Ibrâhîm Bey (Mamlûk), 61 n., 65 n., 100 n., 259, 261.
Ibrahîm el Cawharî, 259.
Ibrâhîm Gulşenî, 198 n.
Ibrâhîm Ḫân (*waḳf* of), 173.
Ibrâhîm the Muteferriḳa, 153 f.
Ibrâhîm Paşa, *see* Damad Nevşehirli.
'Imâd Nesîmî (Ḥurûfî poet), 191 n.
'Imâdî family of Damascus, 136.
Isaac Angelus (Emperor), 250 n.
Ismâ'îl Ḥaḳḳi of Bursa, 199 n.
Ismâ'îl (Ṣafavid Şâh), 73, 189, 226, 227.
Ivan III (Tsar), 209 n.

Jacob Bar 'Addai, 228 n.
Julius II (Pope), 247.
Justinian (Emperor), 217.

Kapali, Moses, 217 n.
Kâtib Çelebi, *see* Ḥacci Ḫalîfe.
Kemânkeş Ḳara Muṣṭafâ Paşa (Grand Vezîr), 25, 26 n., 52 n.
Keylanî, *see* Gîlânî.
Köprülü Fâḍil Aḥmed Paşa (Grand Vezîr), 33 n., 105 n., 200 n., 204 n., 254 n.
Köprülü Fâḍil Muṣṭafâ Paşa (Grand Vezîr), 33, 52, 253.
Köprülü Ḥuseyin Paşa (Grand Vezîr), 254 n.
Köprülü Meḥmed Paşa (Grand Vezîr), 25, 26 n., 32, 33 n., 105 n., 147 n., 250.

Ḳâḍî-zâdei Rûmî, 148 n.
Ḳa'it Bey (Mamlûk Sultan), 43.
Ḳaramanî Meḥmed Paşa (Grand Vezîr), 84 n., 147 n.
Ḳoçu Bey, 107 n., 126.

Louis XIV, 245, 249.
Lucaris, Cyril, 235, 236 n., 245 n.
Lurya Levi, Isaac, 241 f.

Maḥmûd I (Sultan), 55 n., 56, 142, 174, 246 n.
Maḥmûd II (Sultan), 178.
Maḥmûd Ṣukrî el-Alûsî, 156 n.
Manṣûr el-Ḥallâc, 180.
el-Mâturîdî, 73 n.
Mavrocordato, Alexander, 236 n.
al-Mâwardî, 93 n.
Meḥmed I (Sultan), 189, 210.
Meḥmed II, the Conqueror, 5 n., 6 n., 21, 50, 84 f., 87, 94, 105 n., 143 ff., 147 ff., 167, 170, 215 ff., 219, 221, 231.
Meḥmed III (Sultan), 15, 25, 52, 53 n.
Meḥmed IV (Sultan), 3 n., 26, 52 f., 149, 200 n., 242.
Meḥmed (Muḥammad) 'Alî, 69, 130 n., 178.
Melek Aḥmed Paşa (Grand Vezîr), 6 n.
Methodius, Saint, 215.
Michael, Mihâ'îl, of Damascus, 256 n.
Miḫâ'îl Carwâ (bishop), 248 n.
Miḫâ'îl Farḥât, 260 n.
Mîrim Bey, 148 n.
Mollâ Ḫusrev, 84 n.
Moses Kapali, 217 n.
Movila, Peter, 235 n.
Mu'allim Rizḳ, 259.
Muḥammad the Prophet, 117, 187, 191.
Muḥammad, son of Sinân Paşa, 173.
Muḥammad b. 'Abd el-Raḥmân, 199.
Muḥammad b. 'Abd al-Wahhâb, 112 n., 160 n.
Muḥammad el-'Abdalî, 162.
Muḥammad 'Arabî el-Bannânî, 112 n.
Muḥammad Bey Abû Ḏahab, 111, 157 n.
Muḥammad Demirdaş (Şeyh), 198 n.
Muḥammad Kureym (Seyyid), 63 n.
Muḥammad el-Ḥifnî, 199.
Muḥammad Ṣanan (Şeyh), 103 n.
Muḥammad b. Yaḥyâ (Ḥanbalî Muftî), 112 n.
el-Muḥibbî, 124 n., 164.
Murâd I (Sultan), 144.
Murâd II (Sultan), 144, 148, 217.
Murâd III (Sultan), 15, 20 f., 27, 28, 51, 55, 105, 148, 240.
Murâd IV (Sultan), 25, 26 n., 31, 33, 53 n., 173, 195, 200, 235.
Murâd Bey (Mamlûk), 63, 65 n., 66, 100 n., 112 n., 259, 261.
Murâd el-Boḫârî, 197 n.
al-Murâdî, 101 n., 164.
Murâdî family, 136.
Muṣṭafâ I (Sultan), 25, 32, 200.
Muṣṭafâ II (Sultan), 53 n., 54, 109 n.
Muṣṭafâ III (Sultan), 23, 26, 108, 171, 243 n.
Muṣṭafa el-Bekrî, 198.
Muṣṭafâ Efendi Ebu'l-Meyâmîn, 200 n.

el-Nâbulusî, 164.
Nâdir Şâh, 156 n

Napoleon Bonaparte, 63 n.
Nasi, Joseph (Duke of Naxos), 240.
el-Nâṣir (Caliph), 182.
Nawrûz, 259 n.
Nikussios, Panagiotes, 236 n.
Niyâzî Miṣrî, 198.
Nureddin (Zangid), 184.

Orḫan (Sultan), 49, 51, 144, 148.
'Os̱mân I, 7 n.
'Os̱mân II (Sultan), 25 n., 52, 53 n., 200.
'Ot̲mân Bey D̲û'l-Fiḳâr, 130.
'Ot̲mân Paşa el-'Aẓm, 64.

Paracelsus, 149.
Parthenios (Patriarch), 249 n.
Paşmaḳçi-zâde Seyyid 'Alî Efendi (Seyhü'l-islâm), 200 n.
Peter the Great, 239.
Pîr Uftâda, 199 n.
Pîrî Re'îs, 148.
Ptolemy, 148, 154.

Raḍwân Bey, 112 n.
Râğib Paşa (Grand Vezîr), 171.
Râmî Paşa, 236 n.
Robert of Sicily, 250 n.
Rossetti, Carlo, 260 n.
Rûmî, *see* Celâlü'd-Dîn.

Sabbatai, 241, 242.
Sa'd el-dîn el-Cibâwî, 197 n.
Sa'îd Meḥmed Efendi, 153.
Saladin, 184, 231, 250 n.
Sa'ûd b. 'Abd al-'Azîz (Wahhâbî), 112 n.
Selim I the Grim (Sultan), 17, 50 f., 85, 135, 144, 170, 189, 216 n., 218, 224 ff., 233.
Selim II (Sultan), 20, 144, 240.
Selcuḳids, 144, 148, 183, 190, 194, 210 n., 220, 227.
Seyyid family of Üsküdar, 136 n.
el-Sim'âni, Joseph Simonius, Assemani, 248 n.
Sinân Paşa, 144, 145 n.
Solomon ben Nathan, 240.
Stephan Dushan, 215.
Süleymân I, the Magnificent, the Lawgiver, 3 n., 20 f., 25, 27, 33, 35, 44 n., 48, 53, 58, 64 f., 84 ff., 93 n., 105, 123, 129, 131, 135, 143 n., 145, 147 f., 151, 166, 167 n., 170, 216 n., 218, 224 ff., 231, 240, 244, 247, 255 n.
Süleymân II (Sultan), 33, 52 ff.
Süleymân Paşa, 69.
Süleymân Paşa, Balṭaci, of Damascus, 111 n.

el-Ṣabbâğ, Ibrâhîm, 67, 260 n.
Ṣâliḥ b. Ibrâhîm, 136 n.
Ṣoḳollu Meḥmed Paşa, Dâmâd (Grand Vezîr), 20, 240.

el-Ṣa'rânî, 201.
Ṣarḳâwî, family, 109 n.
Ṣehid 'Alî Paşa (Grand Vezîr), 200 n.
Ṣemsu'l-Dîn Kurânî, 84 n.

Timur, 93 n., 189, 190 n., 221, 227.

Ṭabbâḫ family, 102 n.
Ṭarḫuncu Aḥmed Paşa (Grand Vezîr), 3 n., 10 n., 26 n., 31 f., 34 f., 58 n.

Uftâda, Pîr, 199 n.
'Umar (Caliph), 192.
Umayyad Caliphs, 115.
'Ut̲mân (Caliph), 192.

Yemişçi Ḥasan Paşa (Grand Vezîr), 52 n.
Yirmi-Sekiz Meḥmed Çelebi, 153 n.
Yûsuf, Emir (Druse), 67 n., 68 n.
Yûsuf el-Beyṭâr, 260 n.
Yûsuf b. Lâwî, 260 n.
Yûsuf Paşa (Vâlî of Damascus), 69 n.
Yûnus Emre, 191 n.

Zeyn el-dîn Ḫwâfî, 198 n.
Zeyni Ḫâṭûn, 168.

Ẓâhir al-'Omar, 61 n., 64, 67 f., 260.

INDEX OF PLACE-NAMES

Abyâr, 124.
Abyssinia, 229.
Adana, 248.
Adrianople, 27, 83, 89, 92, 94 n., 110 n., 121, 135 n., 144, 171, 199, 219, 242.
Adriatic Sea, 214.
Aegean Islands, 231, 260.
Aegean Sea, 36 n.
Aghtamin, 227 n.
'Akkâ (Acre), 64, 69, 136 n., 155 n.
Aleppo, 43 n., 44 n., 45, 53 n., 57, 62, 64, 89, 93 n., 98, 100 n., 101, 102 n., 121, 124, 127, 132, 136 n., 155, 163, 174, 196 n., 198 n., 231, 247 ff., 260.
Alexandria, 42 n., 62 n., 63 n., 111 n., 125 n., 136, 224, 226, 229, 231, 235, 239 n., 248, 259, 261 n.
Amasya, 144, 219.
America, 148.
Âmid (Diyarbekir), 53 n.

Anatolia, 37, 73, 75, 84, 87, 88, 106, 121, 122, 144, 149, 155 n., 182 f., 188 f., 190, 196, 198, 203, 210 n., 211, 221, 246, 257.
Anḳara, 29 n., 144, 190.
Antioch, 224, 229, 239 n., 247, 248 n.
Arabia, 41 n., 71, 93, 141 n., 158, 160, 182, 187, 197, 200, 207, 225.
Armenia, Little, 221, 231 n.
Arrân, 220.
Asia Minor, 183, 189, 192, 196, 211, 214, 221, 229.
Austria, 217, 236, 237 n., 239, 243 n., 244 n., 256 n.
Aydin, 19 n.
'Aynṭâb, 91 n.
Âẕerbâycân, 198.

Ba'albek, 46 n., 123 n., 136 n., 155 n.
Bağdâd, 18 n., 44 ff., 53 n., 57, 74 n., 91, 101, 115 f., 121, 123 n., 141 n., 155, 180, 184, 196, 213 n., 228 f., 247.
Balkan Peninsula, 189, 192, 210 f., 214, 222, 232, 237, 244 n., 249.
Baṣra, 46, 156.
Belgrade, 91 n., 144, 236, 239 n.
Bethlehem, 250.
Beyrût, 68, 247 n.
Biğa, 3 n., 20 n., 29 n.
Biḳâ', 68 n.
Black Sea, 36 n., 214.
Boğdân, *see* Moldavia.
Bohemia, 217.
Boḫârâ, 197.
Bolu, 20 n.
Bosna-Sarayi (Sarayevo), 20 n., 91 n., 143 f., 222.
Brusa, *see* Bursa.
Buḥayra, 42 n.
Bûlâḳ, 124.
Bursa, 17 n., 83, 89, 92, 94 n., 121, 135, 144, 171, 199 n., 202, 219, 221.

Cairo, 40 n., 55 n., 57, 65 f., 85, 89, 100 f., 109 n., 110 n., 111, 121, 123 f., 125 n., 130 n., 140, 154, 160 n., 161, 163, 173, 196 n., 213, 226, 229, 231, 248, 259, 260 f.; — Old Cairo, 41, 124, 259, 260 n.
Cappadocia, 221.
Carlovitz, Patriarchate of, 239 n.
Caucasus, 220.
Cephalonia, 250.
China, 228.
Chios, 250.
Cilicia, 221, 230, 247.
Constantinople, 49, 51, 69, 211, 214 f., 216 n., 221 ff., 230, 235, 246, 247. *See also* Istanbul.
Cos, 13 n., 20 n.
Crimea, 122, 219.
Croatia, 231.
Cubeyl, 68 n.
Cyprus, 224 f., 231, 240, 247 n.

Çanaḳ-Ḳal'e, 242.
Çirmen, 17 n., 20 n.

Dalmatia, 236.
Damascus, 14 n., 43 n., 44 n., 45 f., 47 n., 48 n., 57, 64, 67 ff., 76, 89, 92, 98, 99 n., 100 f., 102 n., 103 n., 111, 121, 123, 124 n., 125, 130 n., 131 n., 136 f., 155, 163 f., 173, 196 n., 202 n., 256 n., 260.
Damietta, 66, 155, 253, 261.
Danube, 214, 244.
Desûḳ, 155.
Deyr al-Za'faran, 229 n.
Divriki, 20.
Diyârbekir, 8 n., 20 n., 45, 91 n., 121, 144, 247. *See also* Âmid.
Dubrovnik, 12. *See also* Ragusa.

Echmiadzin, 221, 226 f.
Erḍerûm, 8 n., 93 n.
Erivân, 221, 227.
Eyyûb, 88, 124.

Fayyûm, 41 n., 62 n., 259.
Filibe (Philippopolis), 9 n., 89 n., 91 n., 222.

Galilee, 43 n.
Gallipoli, 14 n.
Gaza, 46, 69 n., 136 n., 162 n. *See also* Ğazza.
Gence, 20 n.
Georgia, 220.
Granada, 218.

Ğalaṭa, 88, 124, 142, 148, 216, 222, 244 f.
Ğarbîya, 61 n.
Ğazza, 155.

Hamadân, 17.
Harput, 20 n.
Herzegovina, 17, 18.
Hungary, 219, 225, 231, 236, 250.

Ḥamâh, 46 n., 101 ff., 155 n.
Ḥijâz, 117 n., 135, 156 n., 192, 211.
Ḥilla, 156 n.
Ḥomṣ, 44 n., 46 n., 103, 136 n., 155 n.

Ḫorâsân, 73 n., 157 n., 180, 183.

Iç Il, 94 n.
Idlib, 155 n.
Indus, 139.
Ionian Islands, 236 n., 250.
Ipek, 215, 234, 238.

Istanbul, 9 n., 14 f., 33, 36 f., 41, 44 n., 45 ff., 53, 54 n., 55 f., 65, 83 f., 88 f., 91, 93, 94 n., 97 ff., 102, 104 n., 108 ff., 125, 135 f., 143 f., 145 n., 147, 149, 151, 155, 156 n., 161, 163, 166 ff., 173 ff., 192 f., 196 n., 197 n., 198 f., 202, 206, 217, 219, 221, 223, 227, 236 f., 239 n., 242 f., 249, 250, 260. *See also* Constantinople.
Izmid, 17 n.
Iznik̦, 144, 148.

Jaffa, 46, 64.
Jerusalem, 43 n., 57, 89, 99 n., 102, 121, 155, 173 f., 224, 226, 229, 231, 235, 239 n., 250, 259 n.
Jezîra, 229.

Kerbelâ, 156.
Kesrawân, 67 n.
Kirkuk, 141 n.
Kotşannes, 228.
Kurdistan, 228.
Kütâhya, 91 n.

K̦astamonu, 144.
K̦ayseri, 92 n., 190.
K̦irşehir, 190.
K̦onya, 8 n., 91 n., 144, 194 f.

Lâḏikîya, 43 n., 44 n.
Lebanon, 67 f., 123, 174, 230, 247 n., 248 n., 249, 256.
Leghorn, 67 n.
Ludd, 46.

Macedonia, 215.
Mağrib, Mağribî, 100 n., 157.
Manṣûra, 155.
Manzikert, 183.
Mardîn, 8 n., 20 n., 46 n., 229 n.
Mecca, 40 n., 42, 46, 58 n., 64 f., 89 n., 92, 112 n., 126, 156, 161, 174, 187.
el-Medîna, 65, 89 n., 112 n., 118, 126, 136 n., 137 n., 156, 174.
Mediterranean, 154.
Mer'aş, 91 n.
Mesopotamia, 79, 183, 209, 218, 229, 231 n., 233 n.
Mitylene, 13 n.
Mokha, 63 n.
Moldavia, 17, 18, 219, 225, 244 n.
Monastir, 215 n.
Montenegro, 215 n., 234, 239 n.
Morea, 13 n., 222, 236 f., 245, 250, 254.
Morocco, 111, 156, 159 n.
Moscow, 235 n.
Moşul, 45 f., 109 n., 141 n., 156, 162, 228.
Muwailiḥ, 103.

Nâblus, 43 n., 44 n., 102 n., 123 n., 136 n., 155.
Naples, 236 n.
Nazareth, 61 n., 68 n.
Nejd, 156 n.
Nejef, 156.
Nicosia, 225.
Niger, 139.
Nikopolis, 219.
Nile, 139.
Novibazar (Yeni Pazar), 215 n.
Nubia, 229.

Ochrida, 215, 238.
Oxus, 183.

Padua, 236 n.
Paris, 153.
Pentapolis, 229.
Péra (Bey Oğlu), 216 n., 244.
Philippopolis, *see* Filibe.
Podolia, 236.
Poland, 217.
Portugal, 219, 226.

Ragusa, 17, 256. *See also* Dubrovnik.
Rak̦k̦a, 45.
Ramleh, 155 n.
Rhineland, 225.
Rhodes, 13 n., 20 n.
Rome, 236, 248, 249.
Rosetta, 63 n., 66, 101 n., 155, 231, 261.
Rûm, 144, 216, 234.
Rumelia (Rumeli), 16, 34, 84, 87 f., 92, 106 n., 121 f., 166, 199, 203, 211, 246, 257.
Russia, 154, 235 f., 238 f.

Saint Petersburg, Patriarchate of, 239 n.
Salamanca, 220.
Salonika (Selânîk), 89, 219, 241 ff.
Samark̦and, 148.
Semendre, 9 n.
Seray (Imperial palace), 41, 90.
Serim, 20 n.
Si'irt, 247.
Sinai, 225.
Sis, 227 n., 247.
Sîvâs, 221.
Smyrna, 89, 121, 241 ff.
Somalis, 157 n.
Styria, 225.
Sudan, 56 n.
Suez, 63 n., 103.
Süleymânîye mosque and medreses, 145 f., 149, 151 n.
Switzerland, 235.

Ṣafed, 43 n., 226, 241.

Ṣaydâ (Sidon), 45, 67, 68 n., 69, 102, 111 n., 155 n., 256.
Ṣofya, 91 n.

Şâm, 13 n., 45, 69.
Şehrizôr, 45, 46 n., 156.
Şîrwân, 198.
el-Şuweir, 247 n.

Takrûrî, 157 n.
Taurus, 221.
Telbîsa, 103.
Thrace, 214, 222.
Tigris, 228.
Toḳat, 13 n., 15 n., 219.
Tiflîs, 17, 18.
Transoxania, 148, 197.
Transylvania, 17, 153, 236.
Trebizond, 9 n., 13 n., 14 n.
Tripoli (of Syria), 13 n., 14 n., 43 n., 44 n., 45, 155 n., 256.
Trnovo, 215.
Tyre, 53 n.

Ṭahṭa, 155.
Ṭor, 103.
Ṭoyran, 3 n.
Ṭûr 'Abdîn, 229 n.

Urfa, 20 n.
Üsküdar (Scutari), 88.

Vân, 228.
Vienna, 26, 236 n.

Wallachia, 17; — Little, 236, 237 n.

Yemen, 73.
Yeni Pazar. *See* Novibazar.
Yeni-şehir, 89.

GENERAL INDEX

'Abbâsids, 82, 85, 93, 115, 253.
Afğâns, 157.
Aḥmedîya (order, also called Bedâwîya), 184 n., 196.
Albania, Albanians, 214 f., 231, 234, 236 f., 244.
Albigenses, 222.
Arab provinces, 17, *37*, 98, 132, 135, 141 ff., 154, 157, 163, 196, 198, 211, 217, 224.
Arabs, 45 f., 61, 65 n., 71 f., 77 f., 115, 129, 196, 209, 229, 260.
Armenia, Armenians, 153, 214, 220 ff., 226 f., 229 f., 232, 243 n., 244, 246; Uniate Armenians, 221, 231 n.
Ashkenazim, 219.
Asia, Asiatic provinces, 91, 97, 100, 102, 122, 128, 197, 218 f., 223, 228, 231, 233 n., 246.
Assyrian (Nestorian) Church, 228.
Aya Ṣofya, 94 n., 97, 144 f., 148.
el-Azhar, 99 f., 140 n., 154 ff., 160 n.

Bâb Zuweyla (in Cairo), 130 n.
Bagratids, 221.
Bâyezîd mosque and medrese, 145 f., 150.
Bayramî (order), 198, 199 n.
Bedâwî (order), 184 n., 196, 197 n.
Bektâşî (order), 78, 152, 183 n., 186 n., 190, 193 ff., 197 n., 200, 209 n.
Belgrade, Treaty of, 239.
Berbers, 75.
Bisṭâmî (order), 186 n.
Black Sheep Türkmens, 198, 221, 227.
Bogomils, 221 f., 244.
Bornuans, 157 n.
Bosnia, Bosnians, 18, 196, 199, 234, 244, 256 n.
Bulgaria, Bulgarians, 214–15, 222, 234, 237, 239, 244.
Byzantium, Byzantines, 84, 209, 213 ff., 217, 220, 222, 238.

Carlovitz, Peace of, 26, 236, 238, 244 n.
Carmathians, 181.
Catholic Christians, 209, 215 n., 222 ff., 229 ff., 235, 239, 244 ff., 259 f., 261 n.
Celwetî (order), 198 n., 199 n.
Christians, 17, 24, 68, 137 n., 163 n., 174 n., 191 f., 195, 203 n., 204 n., 207 f., 210 f., 217, 219 f., 226, 228, 235 f., 243 n., 244, 251 n., 252, 256 ff., 260 f.
Coptic Church, 228, *229–30*, 245, 248; — Uniate, 231, 244, 248, 260.
Copts, 63 n., 163, 230, 248, 259.
Cossacks, 235.
Crete, Cretans, 224, 235, 250, 260.
Crusades, Crusaders, 184 n., 211, 213, 221, 224 f., 229 f., 231 n., 233 n.

Druses, 45 n., 67 f., 123, 173, 181, 248.

Egypt, Egyptians, 9 n., 14 n., 16 n., 17 n., 29 n., 38 n., 41 f., 43 n., 45 ff., 48 n., 50, 54 ff., *59–67*, 69, 77 f., 82 f., 85, 93 n., 98 ff., 109, 111 n., 112, 117 n., 121 ff., 125, 127 n., 128 n., 129 f., 132, 134 f., 140, 142, 154 f., 156 n., 157 n.,

158 f., 160 n., 162 ff., 172 f., 177, 184, 192, 196 ff., 209, 211, 224, 226, 229 ff., 233 n., 242 f., 248, 254, 258 f., 260 f.
England, English, 15, 63, 64 n., 235, 242, 244 n., 245 n.
Europe, Europeans, 15, 16 n., 46 n., 62 n., 63 f., 67, 87, 91, 97, 121, 125 n., 149 ff., 154, 161 ff., 189, 195 f., 203, 218, 220, 223, 225 f., 233, 235 ff., 245 f., 249, 252, 258, 260.
Exilarch of Mesopotamian Jews, 218, 226.

Fâtiḥ mosque (at Istanbul), 145.
Florence, Council of, 230 f., 247.
France, French, 15, 42, 57 n., 63 f., 66 f., 100, 110 n., 132, 154, 163 n., 243 n., 244 ff., 250, 261.
Franciscans, 225, 231, 243 n., 244, 248 ff., 260 f.
Franks, Frankish, 49, 62 n., 64 n., 245.

Genoa, Genoese, 216, 222, 235, 244 n., 245.
Geonim (Hebrew), 218.
Germany, Germans, 217 n., 219.
Greece, Greeks, 63 n., 67, 150, 153, 163, 174, 211, 213 n., 214 f., 222, 225, 229, 233 n., 234 ff., 243 n., 244 n., 248, 251, 259 f., 261 n.; Uniate Greeks, 244, 247.
Gregorian (Armenian) Church, 220 f., 227, 246 f.
Gypsies, 16, 167 n.

Hayduk (Slav brigand), 237 f.
Holland, Dutch, 235, 245 n.
Holy Sepulchre, Church of, 250.
Hospodar, 236, 244.

Ḥamzawî (order), 199.
Ḥanbalîs, 74, 76, 115, 123 n., 155 n.
Ḥanefîs, 40 n., 99, 100, 101 n.
Ḥurûfîya (sect), 191 n.

Ḫalwetî (order), 76, 78, 186 n., 197 ff.
Ḫan (Mongol ruler), 228.

India, Indians, 41 n., 75, 156, 157 n., 197, 198 n., 208, 228.
'Irâḳ, 'Irâḳîs, 14 n., 43 f., 46 n., 57, 73, 77, 79, 118, 123 n., 154 f., 156 n., 157 n., 164, 172, 196, 198 n., 203 n., 218, 228, 257.
Ismâ'îlîs, 181.
Italy, Italians, 64, 213, 231, 235, 240, 245.

Jacobites, 213 n., 220 n., 228 f., 232, 246, 248.
Javanese, 157 n.
Jesuits, 235, 244 ff., 249.
Jews, Judaism, 24, 47, 56 n., 62, 68, 90 n., 153, 182, 207 f., 213 n., 214, 216 n., 217 ff., 223 ff., *240–1*, 242 f., 244 n., 251 n., 256, 258 f., 260.

Kabbalah, 241 ff.
Karaites (Jews), 213, 218 f.
Khazars, 182.
Klephts, 237 f.
Kurds, 46 n., 157 n., 227.
Kutzovlaks, 234 n.

Ḳâdirî (order), 74, 76, 78, 102, 196, 203 n.
Ḳalenderî (order), 180 n., 183 n., 188 f., 190.
Ḳarmatîs, 71.

Lazarists, 249.
Levant, Levantines, 63, 235, 240 ff., 258.

Mâlikîs (madbbab), 114 n., 115, 123 n., 127 n., 136 n., 137 n.
Mandaeans, 207 n.
Manichaeism, 182, 221.
Mardaites, 233 n.
Maronites, 45 n., 67 n., 68 n., 174, *230*, 231, 247 f., 259 f., 261 n.
Marańos, 219 f., 240.
Melâmîs, 179 n., 180, 199, 201.
Melâmetîs, 188, 199.
Melkites, 213 n., 229, 247 n., 256 n., *259*.
Mevlevî (order), 78, 87 n., 152, 165, *193–5*, 196, 203.
Mongols, 155, 172, 183, 227 f., 233.
Monophysite Church, 209, 214, 220, 227, *228*, 229.
Muscovite Orthodox Church, 209.

Naḳşbendî (order), 76, 78, 186 n., 197 f.
Nativity, Church of, 250.
Nestorians, 209, 212, 213 n., *227–8*, 229, 232 f., 246 f.
North African Regencies, 54, 122, 128, 197, 224.

Oecumenical Patriarch, 215, 224, 231, 234, 238, 250.
Oğuz Turks, 182.
Orthodox Christians, 209, 211, 214 ff., 220, 222–5, 227–9, 232–6, 238, 244 n., 245 ff., 249 f., 256 n., 257 n., 259 f.

Palestine, Palestinians, 45 n., 46, 68, 218, 225 f., 241 f., 250, 257 n.
Passarovitz, Treaty of, 153, 236, 243 n.

Patarenes, 222.
Pavleniki, 222.
Persia, Persians, 73, 103 n., 141 n., 152 f., 156, 163, 181, 183, 189, 190 n., 200, 204, 208, 212, 227 f., 246.
Phanar quarter, Phanariots, 216, 236, 238 f.
Principalities (Rumanian), 234, 238, 244, 256. *See also* Moldavia *and* Wallachia.
Propaganda Fide, Congregatio de, 244.
Protestants, 235, 244 f., 250.

Rabbanite Jews, 213, 218 f.
Raḥmânî (order), 199 n.
Rifâ'î (order), 78, 190 n., 196 f., 202 n., 203 n.
Roman Empire, 212, 228.
Rumania, Rumanians, 234, 235 n., 236, 237 n.

Sabians, 207.
Sa'dî (order), 197.
Saint Catherine, Monastery of, 225.
Sasanian kings, 212, 213 n., 228.
Sephardim, 219 f., 226.
Serbia, Serbians, 214 f., 222, 234, 236, 237 n., 239.
Slavs (Balkan), 214 f., 234.
Spain, Jews in, 217 ff., 226, 241. *See also* Sephardim.
Suhrawardî (order), 198, 199 n.
Sunbulî (order), 199 n.
Syria, Syrians, 43 f., 46, 48, 57, 60 ff., 66, 67–69, 73, 79, 83, 92, 100 n., 101, 103, 112 n., 117 n., 121, 123, 126 n., 127 n., 128 n., 135 ff., 140, 154 ff., 162 ff., 172 f., 181, 183 f., 192, 197 ff., 209, 211, 224 ff., 229 ff., 233 n., 244, 247, 249 f., 253 f., 257, 259, 260 f.

Ṣafavids, 183, 189, 190 n., 200.
Ṣafawî (order), 198, 199 n., 200.

Şâḏilî (order), 78, 197.
Şâfi'îs, 40 n., 100, 114 n., 115, 123 n., 127 n., 135, 136 n., 155 n.

Tomb of the Virgin, Church of, 250.
Turkey, Turks, 68, 77 f., 98, 99 n., 102 n., 103, 122, 123 n., 135, 155, 157, 158 n., 160 n., 164 f., 180 ff., 184 n., 188 f., 196 f., 201 n., 204, 218, 221, 225, 233.
Turkî, 181.
Turkish (language), 141 n., 142, 152, 153, 163, 233.
Türkmens, 172, 198, 221, 227.
Türkmençay, Peace of, 220.

Ŭç-şerefeli mosque (at Adrianople), 144.

Venice, Venetians, 13 n., 64, 163 n., 225, 231, 326, 237 n., 240, 242, 250.
Vladikas, 239 n.

Wahhâbîs, 112 n., 160 n., 187.
Waldenses, 222.
White Sheep Türkmens, 221, 227.

Yezîdîs, 79.

Zeynî (order), 198 n.
Zoroastrianism, 18 n., 207 f., 228.

SET IN
GREAT BRITAIN
AT THE
UNIVERSITY PRESS
OXFORD
AND REPRINTED BY
JARROLD AND SONS LTD
NORWICH